T3-BQR-560

Philosophy of Communication Inquiry

An Introduction

Annette M. Holba
Plymouth State University

SAN DIEGO

Bassim Hamadeh, CEO and Publisher
Todd R. Armstrong, Publisher
Michelle Piehl, Senior Project Editor
Abbey Hastings, Production Editor
Abbie Goveia, Graphic Design Assistant
Trey Soto, Licensing Coordinator
Natalie Piccotti, Director of Marketing
Kassie Graves, Senior Vice President of Editorial
Jamie Giganti, Director of Academic Publishing

Copyright © 2022 by Annette M. Holba. All rights reserved. No part of this publication
may be reprinted, reproduced, transmitted, or utilized in any form or by any electronic,
mechanical, or other means, now known or hereafter invented, including photocopying,
microfilming, and recording, or in any information retrieval system without the written
permission of Cognella, Inc. For inquiries regarding permissions, translations, foreign
rights, audio rights, and any other forms of reproduction, please contact the Cognella
Licensing Department at rights@cognella.com.

Trademark Notice: Product or corporate names may be trademarks or registered trademarks and are used only for identification and explanation without intent to infringe.

Cover image: Copyright © 2020 Depositphotos/agsandrew.

Printed in the United States of America.

3970 Sorrento Valley Blvd., Ste. 500, San Diego, CA 92121

BRIEF CONTENTS

ABOUT THE AUTHOR

Dr. Annette M. Holba is professor of rhetoric at Plymouth State University. Her scholarly interests include studying/teaching rhetoric, philosophy of communication, and communication ethics in applied contexts. Having a rigorous scholarly agenda, she has published 10 books, 40 articles, 11 book chapters, and 7 encyclopedic entries and delivered 95 scholarly presentations. Dr. Holba won the Everett Lee Hunt Book Award in 2013 for her coauthored book, *An Overture to Philosophy of Communication: The Carrier of Meaning*, and an ECA Journal Article of the Year award in 2015 for her essay, "In Defense of Leisure," published in *Communication Quarterly*. Dr. Holba is past editor for *Qualitative Research Reports in Communication* and she has served as guest editor for several scholarly journals, including *New Directions for Higher Education; Listening: Journal of Communication, Religion, and Culture;* and the *Pennsylvania Communication Association Annual*. In addition to her scholarly work, Dr. Holba served on various nonprofit boards in her community and continues to partner with local government agencies and businesses developing project-based learning opportunities for her students. Prior to entering higher education as a second career, Dr. Holba worked in law enforcement as a county detective in a New Jersey prosecutor's office where she was assigned to the Sex Crimes Unit and later to Major Crimes. During her time in law enforcement, she also published articles for a county law enforcement publication, *The Centurion*. During both careers, she played violin in the Philharmonic of Southern New Jersey and most recently the Lakes Region Symphony Orchestra. Dr. Holba is an Eastern Communication Association (ECA) Distinguished Research Fellow (2021).

CONTENTS

PART II

Approaches to
Philosophy of Communication Inquiry

PART IV

Emergent Metaphors in Philosophy of Communication Inquiry

PREFACE

have been teaching in higher education now for over 20 years. For a few years I taught college part-time while working full-time in my previous career; for the most part, this is my second career and I love doing it. As a full-time professor who has taught in or currently teaches in the disciplines of communication, criminal justice, education, philosophy, and organizational wellness, I always seek out the best sources possible when planning and preparing my courses. I have taught philosophy of communication in standalone courses with the same name or in special topics courses named differently. In doing so, I noticed how difficult it was to find undergraduate-level texts that lay out the field or provide an overview of it. A number of years ago, Ronald C. Arnett (Duquesne University) and I discussed this problem, and we embarked on changing this and coauthored book entitled *Overture to Philosophy of Communication: The Carrier of Meaning* (Peter Lang, 2012). We oriented the book toward upper-level undergraduate students and graduate students. The *Overture* text worked to provide guidance for those instructors who never took a philosophy of communication course in their own education experience or might have studied philosophy of communication at the graduate level but never taught a philosophy of communication course. Feedback from instructors who used the book was favorable and continues to be. The *Overture* book is not laid out like a typical textbook and it assumes a bit of depth and breadth regarding philosophical constructs. Realizing this, and in discussion with Ronald C. Arnett and other scholars in philosophy of communication, I embarked on this project hoping to fill the gap and provide further introductory context for philosophy of communication students and instructors of philosophy of communication who want more of that introductory overview story of the field. Additionally, this is my story, based on my exposure to philosophical and communicological insights, philosophical and communicological literature, and philosophical and communicological analysis. I clearly admit that there are other stories and parts of stories that can inform this particular approach to philosophy of communication. I offer to those students who are new to philosophy of communication or students who have read philosophy of communication but who are not familiar with it as a field of study to open your understanding by reading this text on your intellectual journey. I also offer this text to instructors who want to orient themselves and their students to philosophy of communication as a field of study—what it is, what it does, and how to do it.

Philosophy of Communication Inquiry: An Introduction, offers a systematic discussion that lays out the study of philosophy of communication, keeping in mind core coordinates, complements, and intersections between communication and philosophy. This text is framed around traditions of philosophical inquiry and the methodologies/approaches that examine communicative experience. This text is written from a Western philosophical perspective, and the guiding themes of the book include tradition, approach, question, and metaphor. Historical periods are identified as key to hermeneutic understanding, and methodologies of philosophy of communication inquiry include hermeneutic, semiotic, phenomenological, psychoanalytical, critical, communicological, narrative, dialogical, and ethical.

A notable feature of this text is its application to public moral argument. Each chapter concludes with a section, "Connections, Currency, Meaning," that ties the chapter content to applications of public moral argument, enriching class discussion by applying the chapter content to public argument and public testing of evidence. The book is divided into four parts, and each part also ends with a "Connections, Currency, Meaning" section, offering the groundwork for having in-class debates applied to current issues and encouragement for the students to identify their own questions and issues for debate. I also include a discussion of Stephen Toulmin's argument model to assist students with learning how to offer effective evidence and arguments for public testing. The ability to identify public evidence, understand what constitutes it, and then having the ability to test it is becoming an underdeveloped skill because of the proliferation of layers of instant information, fake news, and other structures that bombard the human capacity to sift through data. Including a framework for what constitutes as public evidence and how to evaluate and use that evidence is necessary for the praxis of philosophy of communication inquiry.

This is a textbook written in a conversational tone—it is how I tell the story of philosophy of communication inquiry. I provide a glossary of terms for students to use as a support for learning new terms, and I provide a resource list for students who want to read further about philosophy of communication in general or for those who want to read specific applications of philosophy of communication inquiry.

Acknowledgments

Anyone who knows me knows that this project was a massive undertaking for me. I want to thank the reviewers of this manuscript who provided essential feedback for revision, Ronald C. Arnett (Duquesne University), Susan Mancino (St. Mary's College), Christy McDowell (Cornell University), Brent Sleasman (Winebrenner Theological Seminary), and Cem Zeytinoglu (East Stroudsburg University of Pennsylvania). I am indebted to their close read of the manuscript and their very helpful suggestions, corrections, and rhetorical prompts. Through the years my story of philosophy of communication has been shaped by many colleagues and friends through very enriching discussions and scholarly collaborations, with the following: Ronald C. Arnett, Pat Arneson, Deborah Eicher-Catt, Isaac Catt, Janie M. Harden Fritz, Pat Gehrke, Michael J. Hyde, Igor Klyukanov, Richard Lanigan, Susan Mancino, Ramsey Eric Ramsey, Ozum Üçok-Sayrak, Calvin O. Schrag, and Richard Thames.

There is another group of people who provided me incredible support, motivation, and patience; I am referring to my colleagues at Cognella Publishing, without whom I may never have finished this project. My deepest appreciation to Todd Armstrong, publisher for communication, journalism, and media studies for recognizing the need for this book and for the continued encouragement he gave me throughout the writing, revising, and production phases of this process. Additionally, Michelle Piehl, senior project editor, was extremely helpful with preparing my manuscript for the production process. Both Todd and Michelle were professional and supportive, as well as inspiring and fun to work with on this project.

I started this project during a sabbatical, so I thank Plymouth State University for providing me the opportunity to devote time and energy to this project through the sabbatical process. My dear friend at my institution, Nancy Puglisi, provided much support and encouragement throughout the entire writing process, especially when I hit some pretty big road bumps along the way. My dear friend from Duquesne University, Ozum Üçok-Sayrak, shared and maintained a practice of mindfulness and insight dialogue during the course of writing this manuscript—those mindful experiences also supported the work of this manuscript and I am deeply appreciative. Having support from these people in my life was key to the successful completion of this manuscript.

Lastly, thank you to my husband, Dan, who supported me in many ways, from cleaning the house to making dinner, to reminding me to eat or sleep during the writing process. In the backdrop of all of this, I felt the presence of both of my parents, now both gone, but their influence on my life, in particular my work, was ever present throughout this entire process. I also want to thank you, the reader, for listening to my story of philosophy of communication. I hope your curiosity is sparked and you continue exploring philosophy of communication and its essential applications to everyday human experiences.

Part I

Philosophical Traditions to Philosophy of Communication Inquiry

Part I of this book introduces general philosophical traditions and the importance of historical moments to philosophy of communication inquiry. In Chapter 1, the study of philosophy of communication is introduced by situating it within the broader communication discipline and foreshadowing its important features. In Chapter 2, the following philosophical traditions are introduced: the pre-classical and classical traditions, the analytic tradition, the continental tradition, Eastern and Western traditions, and the postmodern movement. In Chapter 3, historical periods and historical moments are introduced through a chronological timeline, including the ancient era, the medieval era, the Renaissance era, the Enlightenment era, and the contemporary era that includes modern and postmodern eras and beyond.

Chapters 1, 2, and 3 end with an applied discussion, "Connections, Currency, Meaning," involving the application of some of the concepts covered in the chapter. This is intended to open a broader conversation in the classroom. This section integrates public moral argument applications.

Chapter 1

The Study of Philosophy of Communication

Learning Objectives

1. Understand the field of philosophy of communication and its relevance to the communication discipline.

2. Understand the significance of traditions and approaches to philosophy of communication.

3. Understand the significance of questions to philosophy of communication.

4. Understand the significance of metaphors to philosophy of communication.

5. Through the application section, "Connections, Currency, and Meaning," explain and analyze how philosophy of communication can inform public argument and debate in contemporary environments.

H ave you ever wondered about why people have different opinions or how people manage to come to different understandings even after seeing the same events or reading the same messages? Have you ever considered why it is important to hold public forum discussions and debates, especially as people try to form opinions about policy, law, and societal governance? Have you ever thought about the importance of public dialogue and the testing of public evidence pertaining to moral issues that have the potential to touch individual lives and shape or reshape how people live? These are some of the questions that are important to the study of philosophy of communication.

As the chapter title suggests, this opening section introduces philosophy of communication as a field of study and its emergence within the broader communication discipline. After a general introduction to philosophy of communication, a discussion of the organizing concepts, including traditions, approaches, questions, and metaphors, provides a framework for those who want to understand how a philosopher of communication engages questions and paints philosophical pictures in order to create, share, and communicate meaning. To open this discussion, I begin with a general definition of philosophy of communication.

Philosophy of Communication and the Broader Communication Discipline

The definition of philosophy of communication, and our understanding of philosophy of communication, is always evolving. There are several broad environments that espouse philosophy of communication; this section pulls those environments together to weave a tapestry that reflects, in a general sense, how philosophy of communication is studied and understood by philosophers of communication and philosophy of communication scholars. First though, a brief distinction between a philosopher of communication and a philosophy of communication scholar is necessary to unfold and frame this discussion.

I refer to a philosopher of communication as someone who systematically explores questions of creating, sharing, and communicating meaning through a philosophically interpretive framework. While my own preference privileges the approach of philosophical hermeneutics, there are also other ways to explore phenomena systematically, as you will see later. A philosophy of communication scholar, in my perspective, is someone who studies and unpacks various perspectives of philosophers of communication but does not necessarily do philosophy of communication independently. This distinction does not mean philosophers of communication do not integrate other philosophical voices into their perspective. Making a distinction like this suggests that to understand philosophy of communication, one does not need to be a philosopher of communication—one might prefer to study how others make meaning through philosophy of communication inquiry.

Definitions of Philosophy of Communication and Their Environments

Philosophy of communication, specifically within the communication discipline, can be found in several explicit environments, and this list is not exhaustive; it is meant only to identify some of the environments where we find communities of philosophy of communication scholars. I have pulled the major environments together and take their definitions and perspectives directly from each website.

Eastern Communication Association

The Philosophy of Communication Interest Group supports scholarship that examines the philosophical presuppositions and implications of communicative praxis. This interest group provides an academic home for ethical, interpretive, qualitative, historical, and dialogic approaches to the study and application of communication. (https://ecasite.org/aws/ECA/pt/sp/interest_groups)

Southern States Communication Association

The Philosophy & Ethics of Communication Interest Group does not offer a public description of the intended focus. However, in the website's interest group public call for paper submissions to the annual convention, there is broad reference indicating "Submissions may be theoretical or applied examinations of philosophy of communication and/or communication ethics." (https://www.ssca.net/interest-groups)

National Communication Association

The Philosophy of Communication Interest Group interrogates the relationship between philosophical frameworks and our understanding of communication. The Interest Group explores the overlaps, intersections, and complements between philosophy and communication. We provide an academic home for work that addresses communication from a philosophical orientation and/or philosophy from a communication perspective, both broadly defined. The Interest Group is open to all traditions of philosophical inquiry (ancient, medieval, modern, contemporary, postmodern, western, eastern, analytic, continental) and is supportive of semiotic, phenomenological, hermeneutic, critical, psychoanalytic, communicological, narrative, dialogical, and other methodologies that examine communicative experience. (https://www.natcom.org/about-nca/membership-and-interest-groups/nca-interest-groups)

International Communication Association

Philosophy, Theory and Critique is broadly concerned with critical thinking that cuts across the various boundaries within the study of communication and its intersections with other modes of studying human interaction. ... Consequently, it provides a forum in which scholars can explore the relations and intersections between the study of media and communication and the range of contemporary theoretical and philosophical concerns, arguments and positions ...

Its members come from many areas and subfields. The philosophical questions they raise vary greatly: from the nature of language, subjectivity or experience, to the epistemology of science and interpretation, to the politics of knowledge and communicative relations. Members bring many different philosophical orientations to bear upon these questions, including phenomenology and hermeneutics, Marxism, feminism, critical theory, media theory, post-structuralism, pragmatism, social theory and cultural critique. The Division seeks exchange, education and conversation, and it encourages tending to the differences produced by these differing orientations. (https://www.icahdq.org/group/philosophy)

Figure/Ground

Figure/Ground was founded by Argentine-Canadian scholar Laureano Ralón in 2010, and was part of the blogosphere explosion that fueled much of the so-called "realist turn" in post-continental philosophy. Since then, it has grown to contain one of the largest collections of scholarly interviews on the web—with a readership in the tens of thousands and numerous volunteer collaborators ranging from senior undergraduates to PhD candidates. Figure/Ground sits on the edges of the academy and the art world; our aim is to bring the voices of academics and artists out of their specialized domains of practice and give them a venue for speaking frankly to the public at large.

Conversation is one of the most basic forms of human communication, yet the interview is a deeply undervalued genre within academic discourse. The majority of peer-reviewed journals in the humanities and social sciences publish mostly articles and book reviews. In an age of digital interactive media, we believe the interview genre can serve as a powerful pedagogic tool and a valuable primary source for the production of new knowledge. Our interviews are being cited in an increasing number of academic articles. We hope you enjoy reading them! (https://figureground.org/about-fg/)

On Being

On Being has its origins in a public radio show called *Speaking of Faith*, which was created by Krista Tippett, piloted in the early 2000s, and launched nationally at American Public Media (APM) in 2003. A journalist and former diplomat who had studied theology, Krista saw a black hole in media where intelligent conversation about religion, meaning, and moral imagination might be. Her show evolved into *On Being* and a pursuit of the ancient and enduring human questions that gave rise to our spiritual traditions and resonate through every institution anew in this century: What does it mean to be human? How do we want to live? And who will we be to each other? (https://onbeing.org/about/)

International Communicology Institute

Communicology is the science of human communication. One of the Human Science disciplines, it uses the logic based research methods of semiotics and phenomenology to explicate human consciousness and behavioral embodiment as discourse within global culture. Cognate subdiscipline applications include: (1) Art Communicology, (2) Clinical Communicology, (3) Media Communicology, and (4) Philosophy of

Communicology. Communicology is the study of human discourse in all of its semiotic and phenomenological manifestations of embodied consciousness and practice in the world of other people and their environment. As a young discipline in Human Science research, Communicology is the critical study of discourse and practice, especially the expressive body as mediated by the perception of cultural signs and codes. Communicology uses the logic based research method of semiotic phenomenology in which the expressive body discloses cultural codes, and cultural codes shape the perceptive body—an ongoing, dialectical, complex helix of twists and turns constituting the reflectivity, reversibility, and reflexivity of consciousness and experience. (http://communicology.org/)

NOUN: Communicology Is the Science of Human Communication

One of the Human Science disciplines, it uses the logic-based research methods of semiotics and phenomenology to explicate human consciousness and behavioral embodiment as discourse within global culture. Cognate subdiscipline applications include:

1. Art Communicology: the study of aesthetic media as cultural transmission and diffusion with particular emphasis on visual arts and performative creativity, e.g., cinematics, dance, folklore narrative, music, iconography, and painting.

2. Clinical Communicology: therapeutic focus on (a) communication disorders within the context of speech pathology and audiology or (b) behavioral mistakes caused by pragmatic and semantic misinterpretations.

3. Media Communicology: the anthropological, psychological, and sociological analysis of human behavior in the context of electronic media, photography, telecommunications and visual communication.

4. Philosophy of Communicology: the study of communication as the larger context for the explication of language and linguistics, cognitive science, and cybernetics within the philosophical subdisciplines of metaphysics, epistemology, logic, and axiology (aesthetics, ethics, rhetoric). (http://communicology.org)

Doing Philosophy of Communication

One of the differences between philosophy and philosophy of communication is the preposition "of." In every sense of the word which, according to Meriam Webster's Dictionary, serves as a function word for, by, or about something else. As noted by Ronald C. Arnett, who while discussing the importance of philosophical hermeneutics to philosophy of communication in a personal communication during the Eastern Communication Association convention in 2019, mentioned the importance of the "of" in making a distinction between philosophy and philosophy of communication. Our discussion centered around Arnett's suggestion that philosophical inquiry without implications to, by, or for something is too abstract. This makes it difficult to understand the abstraction meaningfully. As I reflected on this discussion, it is precisely one of the criticisms about philosophy that arose during the latter part of the 20th century—the idea that abstract ruminations about an abstract concept can not only be tedious but can also be difficult to understand in terms of what the abstraction means to the average person. Philosophy of communication, on the other hand, focuses on the "of" in that it emphasizes the to, by, and for. This means the application and implications of something ruminated on had to mean something to somebody. This is a very pragmatic understanding of philosophy of communication.

Each chapter in this book ends with an application of philosophy of communication in relation to the chapter content and context. This means that after exploring conceptual frameworks in and of philosophy of communication, each chapter provides an opportunity to apply philosophy of communication in the context of public argument. I do this by identifying questions that emerge within the public realm that are stories similar to the case studies offered by Michael J. Hyde (2018), in his book, *The Interruption That We Are: The Health of the Lived Body, Narrative, and Public Moral Argument*. In his book Professor Hyde identifies stories that capture the attention in public discourse by illuminating questions of moral importance to the human experience and identifying the issues that weave public discourse through public argumentation. I chose to demonstrate philosophy of communication inquiry through stories in popular media that engage philosophy of communication inquiry by identifying questions that invite public moral argument as a rhetorical standard to understanding the human condition. To begin our discussion, the next section identifies organizing concepts necessary for approaching a philosophy of communication perspective.

Organizing Concepts for Philosophy of Communication

Understanding from a philosophical perspective emerges as the following organizing concepts come together to shape a story-laden position and perspective. Recognizing there is more than one way of seeing and understanding the world, each concept is plural—acknowledging there is always more. This list of organizing concepts is also not complete as the field of philosophy of communication evolves; it is likely other concepts will emerge, interrupt, and expand the way we think about philosophy of communication inquiry. For now, the organizing concepts I chose to introduce to readers and students of philosophy of communication include **traditions**, **approaches**, **questions**, and **metaphors**.

Traditions

As you will see in Chapter 2, tradition is complex and multidimensional. We sometimes use the word in a derogatory sense as it can imply that if something is traditional, it is old, outdated, or irrelevant; we even see the critique of higher education as an antiquated and irrelevant tradition (Crow & Dabars, 2015). But Hans-George Gadamer (2002) sought to recover the understanding of the term by describing it as the experiences in which we are embedded that inform and undergird our worldviews and that contain our biases and our prejudices. For Gadamer, prejudice is also not a negative word and by this, I mean through our news stories and public discourse, the word *prejudice* has become connotated always as a negative bias that marginalizes certain groups of people or individuals with shared biology or interests. However, that is only one dimension of what prejudice can mean. For example, if one has a prejudice toward something, this means one holds a preconceived understanding or opinion about it, but this opinion can be either favorable or not favorable—it is not always or automatically bad. Gadamer (2002) recognized that the danger associated with prejudice comes from not knowing one's own prejudice. When we are not aware of our prejudice(s), we limit possibilities in our understandings, interpretations, and judgments. An example from my own life experience can explain this more clearly. Growing up, living a rather sheltered life, I never knew any woman with a tattoo. I did see women with tattoos as I got older, but I developed a prejudice against tattoos because of the environments that I saw them in, such as in biker groups and sections of town noted as being lower in socioeconomic status or simply the poor side of town. I simply had no paradigm to be able to relate to these environments or to the experience of having a parent or relative who had a tattoo. Then, after I had my own children, and they grew up, the world changed, and my worldview simply expanded because my entire adult life I intentionally engaged within a variety of environments comprised of a variety of cultures. When my oldest daughter, Michele, asked if she could have a tattoo for her 18th birthday, we talked about it. I remembered that as a younger person, I did not have a positive understanding of tattoos but I set that prejudice aside and, through dialogue, my understanding expanded and supported, participated, and celebrated with her when she got her first tattoo. Through our dialogue and through understanding the world from a more open and diverse framework, my prejudice dissolved very quickly. If I did not realize I had a prejudicial opinion about tattoos, I might not have been able to be open to gain a clearer understanding of what it means to have a tattoo.

We need to recognize that we cannot discard our biases because they are shaped from our experiences within our biographies, histories, and experiences. Though what we need to do is not let them have a negative impact, instead we recognize them and then set intentional practices that disable any possibility of marginalizing someone or something through these biases. Gadamer also stated that when we know our biases and prejudices, we can also change them by changing our engagements within our environments that helped to shape them in the first place.

Tradition is a key component of philosophy of communication because it contributes to our interpretations and understandings of natural phenomena; tradition frames how our sensibilities open to phenomena, which then foreshadows the interpretive or hermeneutical process. Tradition is very important to acknowledge and understand. Gadamer (2002) sees tradition as not limiting the freedom of knowledge but that instead "makes [freedom of knowledge] possible" (p. 361). Gadamer (2002) argues tradition is a "genuine partner in dialogue" (p. 358). If we begin to see tradition as a partner that is open to experience other traditions, knowledge and understanding can be co-constructed. This marks the difference between the use of the word in contemporary settings and Gadamer's use of the term: Gadamer sees tradition as a starting place that is open; in contemporary positions, tradition is seen as closed and limiting. Beginning from Gadamer's position can be a first step in the dialogic and meaning-making process.

Approaches
Approaches refer to how a philosopher of communication engages phenomena. Some people might refer to this as a method, but methodology is

more often generally connected to the scientific method; instead the word *approach* refers to the mind-set, how a philosopher of communication thinks about the phenomena and how the philosopher of communication comes to understand it. Some of these approaches include phenomenological, semiotic, hermeneutical, critical, narratival, communicological, and others. Part II of this book, which includes Chapters 4, 5, 6, and 7, explores these approaches further, but for the purposes of this introduction I provide a general statement about each one so that you might begin to see the differences between them and the shared overlapping aspects among them. This list is also not a final list nor a complete list, as approaches may evolve and transform through the process of engaging them. The philosopher of communication recognizes that how we come to understand our environments always has the potential to evolve and change; therefore, the approaches we take to finding meaning likely evolve and change as well.

Chapter 5 discusses **hermeneutics**, **semiotics**, and **phenomenology**. Hermeneutics refers to the process by which we interpret and make meaning out of our experiences. Semiotics refers to the study of signs and their processes of representation in which we make meaning out of our experiences. Phenomenology is the study of phenomena but, more specifically, refers to structures of consciousness as we experience phenomena—as they appear to us. Phenomenology emphasizes the first-person experience in meaning making.

Chapter 6 discusses the **psychoanalytical**, **critical**, and **communicological** approaches to making meaning. The psychoanalytical approach refers to various psychoanalytical theories that explore the relation of consciousness and unconsciousness in meaning making. The critical approach focuses on understanding and explaining society and culture from various perspectives. It also provides critiques. The communicological approach is the study of human discourse within semiotic and phenomenological implications of embodied consciousness in the world and with others; it is described as a critical study of discourse and of practices.

Chapter 7 discusses **narrative**, **dialogical**, and **ethical** approaches to making meaning. The narrative approach refers to story-centered meaning making that recognizes all human relations are situated within stories and it is the narratives in which we are situated that shape meaning. The dialogical approach recognizes the relationship between self and other as significant to the meaning-making process as meaning is co-constructed. Ethical approaches to meaning making elevate moral and ethical practices in the meaning-making process. Each of these approaches is further developed and discussed in Part II.

Questions

When we ask questions, we are seeking to discover meaning and have an understanding of the particular experiences we have with others. This is not a seeking to explain something; instead, we are seeking to understand something that comes before us. It is also not a seeking toward any universal meaning; instead, we seek temporal and particular understanding (Arnett, 2016). When you think about it, when we think, we might begin with a question that responds to some kind of gap in what we know. Can you recall how often you reach for your computer, iPad, or phone and do a search for some kind of information that you either cannot recall or you do not know? This is an ongoing process that is more circular than linear. We are always engaging in a hermeneutical process as phenomena changes, evolves, and encounters other phenomena; it can be never ending.

Human beings have limits to knowledge and understanding, and the only way to fill in those gaps is to start with a question about what you want to know. In the drama of everyday life, opinions are asserted, evolve, and are shared. These musings with opinions come together and often point to questions unique to the historical moment and the context of which it is made. Paul Ricoeur (1984) refers to this environment in which we are embedded as "emplotment" (p. 31), which is typically described as a sequence of characters and events that come alive through their stories, which are always attentive to that moment through questions that call us out—questions that hail us toward making a response. What breathes life into the bare bones of ideas are opinions that work with the drama of everyday life. This perspective is consistent with the work of Ricoeur (1984) in his exposition about "emplotment," (p. 31) which includes a sequence of activities and characters that must live through a given story, attentive to historicity that gives rise to a question that calls forth human responsiveness.

Questions regularly present themselves publicly within the public domain, creating a home for a rich gathering of differences and opinions. This is where ideas come together in harmony as well as come together and collide. We see these questions as emergent within historical periods that are marked by moments as dwelling places that embody uniqueness and a place where meaning can be created and evolve (Arnett & Holba, 2012). Questions become the explicit catalyst contributing to historical moments and their trajectory of change and sense of urgency. Questions are essential in doing philosophy of communication because if we cannot identify the questions being pursued, we will not be able to respond in alignment with the philosophical picture or with a fitting response to the given situation, thus impacting meaning and the meaning-making process.

Ronald C. Arnett's (2007) argument identifying interpretive inquiry as qualitative research identifies the question and the practice of identifying questions of given historical moments as central to the interpretive process, in particular, philosophical hermeneutics. Arnett (2007) reminds us that the question identifies a demand for responsiveness. The identification of questions and the engagement of investigating and offering a response meets the responsibility of making an offering to public disclosure. This means that tending to questions of a given historical moment is our **public moral duty**.

Specifically related to the importance of the question(s) and questioning, Arnett (2007) points to both Hans-Georg Gadamer (2002) and Paul Ricoeur (1984), both of whom privilege the question. For example, Gadamer (2002), in *Truth and Method*, identifies the qualitative method using coordinates of question, text, and historicity/bias as the principle method of philosophical hermeneutics. This begins with identifying a public question. Gadamer (2002) suggests that if there is no identification of a public question, then an investigation toward understanding cannot occur. When the question is not public, then it is more like a "subjective disclosure" (Arnett, 2007, p. 32) that is not held to the test of public evidence. The value of a public question comes when it is engaged publicly within a public conversation; without the public conversation we cannot make the assumption that everyone will share the same understandings of the text in question. Arnett (2007) suggests that "the importance of public framing of the text responds to historicity/bias" and that meaning of the question and the text must not be assumed (p. 32). As part of finding meaning together, we must illuminate these perspectives and differences as part of the process of inquiry. Left to a private, closed environment, meaning cannot be shared and cocreated—leaving us little to have in common and little chance of moving forward in respect and in dialogue.

Metaphors

In the study of philosophy of communication inquiry, the term *metaphor* expands from a pure literary concept to a broader philosophical concept. The *Cambridge Dictionary of Philosophy* (Audi, 1999) defines metaphor as a rhetorical trope or figure of speech where one thing denotes another thing; it is an implicit comparison between things. Here is an example: In Martin Luther King Jr.'s (1963) book *Why We Can't Wait*, he describes the pace of having equal rights for African Americans in the United States. He refers to the speed that the United States is changing as a "horse and buggy pace" (p. 91). He does not literally mean people are using horse and buggies to gain equality—he denotes the speed on which the country had moved since the end of slavery and the end of the Jim Crow laws. It is simply too slow and there are connotations of comparison between the horse and buggy and automobiles.

Metaphors have been a topic of discussion in relation to public oration and skills in persuasion since the time (and before) of Aristotle. Historically, metaphors were referred to as decorations in speech that do not contribute to cognitive meaning but meaning can be enhanced by using them. Additionally, they are characterized as similes without the use of the comparator word *like*. The *Cambridge Dictionary of Philosophy* (Audi, 1999) refers to metaphors as "elliptical similes" (p. 562). These were the two most common descriptors of metaphors up to the 19th century; however, since then scholars and writers accept that metaphors do contribute to cognitive meaning and are absolutely necessary, especially for religious, secular, and scientific writing because they assist audiences with understanding complex information. Today, there may not be any absolute universally accepted understanding of metaphor. We explore metaphor in Part IV of this book, especially in Chapters 11, 12, 13, and 14. In general, it is important to note that some philosophers of communication define metaphor as "a term whose characteristics exemplify and point us poetically and indirectly to meaningful understanding beyond the symbol itself" (Arnett & Arneson, 1999). It is a way to use linguistic symbols that are responsive to particular historical moments; it is a "dialogic medium" that sits between narrative and the historical situation; and it assists the communicator to navigate the historical moment appropriately as well as is guided by the historical moment (Arnett & Arneson, 1999, p. 299). This means that how we are embedded within our narrative and our histories influences the metaphors we choose to use to guide meaning. Metaphors are double-sided in that they have multiple meanings across multiple persons.

Philosophy of Communication as Carrier of Meaning

Ronald C. Arnett (2007) outlines interpretive inquiry as doing philosophy of communication through the coordinates of responsiveness, public disclosure, and public evidence. Synthesizing ideas from Gadamer, Ricoeur, and Schrag, Arnett (2007) created a framework that guides the application of philosophy of communication. Arnett warns that to do philosophy of communication, one needs a text and that text is interpreted broadly through a tradition and a particular approach. When one engages philosophy of communication outside or above a text, there can be no real consequences and no real impact to human communication and the human condition. Additionally, engaging philosophy of communication without a text engenders an arrogance suggesting one stands above context, which means one stands above the other. Arnett's (2007) framework is a pragmatic application that synthesizes Gadamer's emphasis on the public question, Ricoeur's mapping of a given story through metaphor and **emplotment**, and Schrag's **communicative praxis** forged around the rhetoric of communicative praxis in examining the "by," "about," and "for" in a communicative context. While others might disagree with this perspective requiring a text within which to engage philosophy of communication inquiry, I am intentionally choosing my application using Arnett's framework because consequences do matter. It is within the consequences that meaning emerges, is shared, and is co-constructed.

Philosophy of communication is a story-centered understanding of communication that requires one to acknowledge the bias one brings to a text. There is a danger of bringing philosophy of communication to itself because it does not go anywhere or impact real and lived experience. Philosophy of communication occurs between persons in a story of experiences where consequences actually matter. The aesthetic of philosophy of communication is imbued within an ethical relation to the other. This is why philosophy of communication is tied to the stories within which we live, anchored within the context of history, and responsive to the questions that govern those historical moments.

Arnett (2007) lays out the trajectory of interpretive inquiry as philosophy of communication in the following way:

1. Responsive

    a. Question: *What* is it that is unknown that propels the inquiry?

    b. Text: *How* is the communicative event understood or publicly constructed?

    c. Historicity/bias: *Why* does the bias of question and text construction reveal interests that keep the conversation going in the arena of public inquiry?

2. Public disclosure

    a. Metaphors: *What* is important and why?

    b. Emplotment: *How* does the story frame the metaphors engaged?

    c. Narrative: *Why* is there a public impact from the metaphors emplotted in a given story?

3. Public evidence

    a. By: *What* is the situated position of the person who gathers the evidence?

    b. About: *How* is the evidence significant and how is it gathered?

    c. For: *Why* are others interested?

Doing philosophy of communication is one way to engage public temporal learning (Arnett, 2007). This means that the meaning we find in any given moment is meaning for that particular moment. We cannot hold one meaning for eternity (though we know conflict often occurs when human beings resist change by attempting to hold meaning indefinitely); meaning emerges in moments—moments between a particular time and space within a particular context.

Connections, Currency, and Meaning

There is a danger to just talking about philosophy of communication as an esoteric experience rising above or outside of human engagement because when we stand above or outside of experience, we lose the connection to lived experience and remove ourselves from experiencing the experience. As we stand above experience, we lose our edge—we no longer need to understand. We can be at risk of making judgments or interpretations that are no longer relevant or that do not carry meaning. Each part of this book ends with a section entitled "Connections, Currency, and Meaning." I chose to ground these sections consistently through this book by discussing **public moral argument**. Let me define how I am using the phrase *public moral argument*. Public moral argument is not simply an individual opinion; it must include three distinct components: the argument, a public setting where the argument touches others, and an issue that is explicitly a moral issue or where the case is made for the issue as a moral concern.

First, as an argument, it needs to include a claim and a stated reason. Stephen Toulmin (1958) stated arguments are claims with stated reasons. A simple argument might be, "You should send your child for piano lessons because studying music builds discipline in their character." The claim is that your child should study piano. The stated reason is because studying music builds discipline; of course, the better argument or more persuasive argument would provide the grounds, or evidence to support the reason. Of course, there are unstated reasons/assumptions along with this argument, which Toulmin referred to as the warrant. Much like Aristotle's enthymeme, the warrant does not have to be explicitly stated, though even with it not being stated, the better argument should provide evidence to support that warrant or unstated assumption; this kind of evidence is what Toulmin referred to as backing. Some warrants in the example argument include discipline is good for children to learn and experience. Another is that your child needs discipline because discipline is structure and accountability. Yet another is that studying music does more for character than just learning the technical aspects of a musical instrument. So, an argument is more than making an assertion; it requires stated reasons and evidence to support the explicit and implicit messages in your statement. There are other complicated facets of developing valid and strong arguments, but for the purpose of this book I do not go further into argument development and the system that Toulmin developed to analyze arguments of others or guide the creation of your own valid argument. There are other books that focus on writing arguments based within the framework of Stephen Toulmin's system.

Second, a public moral argument should contribute to public discourse. It is a rhetorical structure that ought to be available in a public context. This is where it is important to be meaningful within some kind of context. Engaging a moral argument privately does not meet the test of providing public evidence. To engage in argumentation and remain in a private domain cannot lead to consequences within the context of a public setting. This does not mean that everything must be public. In fact, one should ruminate and reflect on arguments and issues and evidences before contributing to public discussions because the consequences are high since communication has the power to effect, either negatively or positively, other human beings. The key is to not keep the argument in the private domain—there has to be a public testing of the argument, its reasons, and its evidences in order to make a difference to human discourse. The argument I made about studying the piano, or more broadly, the arts, is part of the public moral argument about education at a national level; it has also been part of the debate involving juvenile justice and other philanthropic approaches to human services.

Third, the argument needs to be or have a moral claim of some kind in its conclusion. Since everyone has different opinions and perspectives about what is moral, this can be a little more difficult to establish. Generally speaking, an easily identifiable moral issue can be related to those religious rules or deontological systems that include claims like, "Thou shalt not kill." They could also be a well-established moral issue that has been debated within public contexts for some time. An example of a well-established moral issue is acknowledging animal rights; animals should be free from abuse and exploitation or the universal declaration of human rights, or the issues surrounding end-of-life decisions. Some moral issues have universal appeals, but there are other moral issues that seem to run across party lines. These partisan issues could include issues related to abortion or certain LGBTQ+ rights. Moral issues can also be contentious, especially when one person believes in something as a moral issue and the next person does not. All of these examples have relevance in public discourse.

Hyde (2018) describes public moral argument as a "form of controversy that inherently crosses professional fields" (p. 16). Hyde (2018) explains that storytelling is a form of public moral argument because it is made public for consumption to a larger arena of people and is intended to persuade the larger polity. Hyde's uses of case studies that involve stories about people's experiences, especially within the "body politic of democracy" and "the health of the lived body" must transcend institutional boundaries of the medical field and the overall institutional establishment (p. 15). Hyde argues that transcending these environments is a civic responsibility to involve the entire citizenry about these issues. He says that when people tell their stories about their illness and their experience, or when a family member tells the story and the extended family experience, it promotes and develops a civic-minded practice of public moral argument. I should note that I am intentionally choosing the phrase *public moral argument*, in particular, the word *moral* instead of *ethic* or *ethics*. The reason for this choice is to align the application sections in each chapter to the stories of people situated in challenging positions that illuminate questions of moral conduct and moral engagement. Hyde's (2018) work does a similar thing in that the stories that guide his case studies form the basis for public moral arguments and cultivate a practice of civic-mindedness through a call of one's moral conscience.

Typically, these kinds of debates are very contentious, but it is through this contentiousness, respectful communication practices, and willingness to meet other perspectives in a public forum setting that all voices and stories have the opportunity to participate and engage each other. This provides a pathway toward developing common ground, interrogating questions through civic mindedness, and evolving policy in an ever-changing world. Without the practice of public testing of public evidence, public moral argument risks collapsing into a singular mindedness that fails to recognize and acknowledge the other in a way that is morally accepted.

Situating the study of philosophy of communication inquiry through public moral argument demonstrates a pragmatic approach to human understanding;

it underscores the value of seeing the "why" of human action and it allows meaning to be shown as it is, not as you want it to be. The application of philosophy of communication can be a revelatory action equipped with opening new perspectives providing enhancement to meaningfulness by/about/for the human condition.

One of the most important things about public moral argument is the way it provides public evidence and a testing of that public evidence in and with a public. Nothing is fully understood in a vacuum; philosophy of communication ensures that more than one voice enters and participates in the conversation. These voices hold each other accountable and respect differences that emerge. Doing philosophy of communication provides an opportunity to engage authentically and cocreates meaningfulness of the matters at hand.

Conclusion

This introduction provides a picture of the path through this book. Introducing philosophy of communication to the reader and the story within which it is embedded opens the possibility for understanding one way of thinking about philosophy of communication inquiry. By providing an explanation of how others think about philosophy of communication and how it is situated within the broader communication discipline, as well as in broader philosophical environments, the reader has a contextual reference. Additionally, defining key organizing concepts and situating its relevance to making meaning through practical applications to public moral argument and discourse provides a helpful backdrop preparing you, the reader, for a more detailed journey into understanding what is philosophy of communication inquiry and how its pragmatic resourcefulness aids in understanding the world around us in a deeper way.

Chapter 2

Philosophical Traditions

Learning Objectives

1. Understand various philosophical traditions that represent movements in philosophical thought.

2. Identify key philosophers from each tradition that contribute to the body of literature in philosophy of communication inquiry.

3. Demonstrate the philosophy of communication praxis by exploring how philosophical traditions impact public discourse involving public moral argument.

This chapter begins with a framing of philosophical traditions in the context of philosophy of communication inquiry. Some of this information might be familiar to you while other information will be new to you. Welcome to exploring philosophical traditions.

What Are Philosophical Traditions?
Traditions in Unity of Contraries

Consider why you think about things the way you do. What has influenced your perspective? What orientation to the world or your particular environment influenced your perspective? What informs the decisions you make? Thinking about these questions can strengthen your awareness and convictions—or change them.

Human understanding requires at least three things to make sense and meaning out of human experience: (a) an orientation, (b) a practice or method, and (c) a dialectical community within which to engage in a process that brings about meaning and understanding so that human beings continue to engage their worlds. Coming from a particular tradition of thought orients the human capacity to observe, learn, and interpret experiences. The Oxford dictionary defines tradition from several angles, including the transmission of customs or beliefs handed down from generation to generation or an artistic or a literary method or style established by some kind of creative artist resulting in attaining followers or starting a movement that shares common attributes. These definitions of tradition suggest tradition is grounded in a shared understanding of the human experience and it is not a singular or individual notion. Philosophical understandings of tradition expand this perspective and warn against potential pitfalls that can occur if tradition is not questioned, checked, and understood. Some philosophers suggest tradition involves a critical examination of what we do and why we do things as human agents; this broader understanding then acts as a starting point or catalyst for some kind of change (Arendt, 2005). This means that by interrogating traditions we find we have prejudices; this opens pathways to resistance to the status quo and to change what we believe is wrong. If we never interrogate our traditions and see they are situated in context, that is when they become invisible, ideological, and dogmatic. This chapter identifies traditions that are important to the philosophy of communication today. These traditions are presented through the lens of what Martin Buber (1878–1965) referred to as **"unity of contraries"** (1966, p. 111). The unity of contraries, having its origins in religious philosophy of Judaism, points to the dangers of extremes, especially in human interaction and human dialogue. Arnett and Arneson (1999) suggest that the unity of contraries plays a role in dialogue in that "dialogue brings us face to face with life as it is, not as we hope it would be" (p. 144). Presenting the traditions here in the structure of contraries reveals tensions between traditions and implies that any extreme for one side of the tradition or another can be dangerous, limit understanding, and close down interpretive possibilities. We need to understand these traditions within the horizons of contraries to understand traditions hold no absolute knowledge. After introducing these traditions, I provide some examples related to connecting the traditions to contemporary human experiences and public moral argument.

The philosopher Hans-Georg Gadamer (2002) wrote in his treatise on human understanding and interpretation, *Truth and Method*, that tradition, comprised of those prejudices and preferences of the individual, "constitute the historical reality of being" (p. 277). This means that we need tradition to make sense of our world and we do this in tandem within communities of others. One of Gadamer's goals was to rehabilitate the notion of tradition because he did not see it as a negative aspect of the human condition. Often, especially in popular media and public discourse, we are told that tradition and prejudices are a bad thing. In some cases, they could be, especially if those prejudices are grounded in hate. However, Gadamer (2002) suggested that prejudices can also be grounded in love and care—prejudices are not always negative, and in fact he says that "there are legitimate prejudices" (p. 277). Gadamer rehabilitates our understanding of tradition by asking the question "What is the ground of the legitimacy of prejudices?" (p. 277). He also asks what distinguishes these legitimate prejudices from other prejudices that are not legitimate. This, Gadamer argues, is the task of critical thinking. We must use our morally grounded discernment to meet this task.

To engage this kind of moral discernment that helps us to identify those prejudices that are legitimate, Gadamer makes a distinction between prejudices that come from "authority" and those that come from "overhastiness" (p. 277). He stresses that prejudices coming from overhastiness are not legitimate prejudices because they are derived from using one's own reason and nothing else. An example would be making a decision only accounting for self-interest and nothing else; no other kind of authority is weighed alongside of one's self-interest. Gadamer suggests that this is the source of human errors. Of course, we must also use our critical thinking and reasoning when determining the legitimacy of the authority we choose to accept as legitimate. For example, many people are familiar with the murders that took place in 1969 by the Manson family (as modern media have described them). The Manson murders have an infamous reputation in American popular culture. Let us reflect on this story and consider it through a critical lens.

In July and August of 1969, nine people were murdered by members of a group of individuals who followed what has come to be known as the Manson cult. Charles Manson (1934–2017) became a form of authority for young individuals for a variety of reasons. During the time that the Manson "family" gathered and lived together in a communal environment, Charles Manson became the moral authority for these young adults who were then questioning the moral authority of society and the traditions in which they were raised. At a time when the grand narrative of religion was being questioned and compromised in the United States, Manson provided security and a sense of belonging to other individuals who were seeking belonging from outside the traditions in which they were raised. Manson himself became their moral authority, the Christ figure, for many of the young adults, and they chose to leave their homes to stay with what was becoming known as the Manson family.

The murders of Sharon Tate, and Leno and his wife, Rosemary, LaBianca in August of 1969 brought Charles Manson and the family into public popular discourse even though these are not the only murders the Manson family are responsible for committing (Mullins, 2008). Charles Manson was convicted of conspiracy to commit murder, though he did not participate in the actual murders. Manson was a form of authority over his followers, most of whom did not use critical thinking or reasoning to determine the legitimacy of his authority. This is where Gadamer might say that members of the Manson family erred. They did not test the authority of Manson's words to determine if they should adopt or believe Manson's arguments, positions, or traditions that formed his opinions and actions. Complicated by the use of psychedelic drugs and what some researchers refer to as the brainwashing of the family members by Manson himself (Bugliosi & Gentry, 1974), the individuals who participated in the gruesome murders failed to understand the value of having a tradition from which to make moral discernments—in fact, several of the Manson family members rejected their own traditions, leaving them to use their own individual reasoning abilities outside of any other kind of authority, and this left them vulnerable. Left to their own singular reasoning, these young individuals did not have the capacity to determine whether Manson was a legitimate authority. Consequently, each member of the family, serving a life prison sentence, who has chosen to share their own stories since the murders recognizes how they erred in judgment—not having the critical thinking skills to judge Manson's authority left them vulnerable to his influence and to be easily deceived.

When we think about learning through experience and evolving as our thinking and actions mature, becoming mature does not mean that a person becomes their own master or source of authority freeing oneself from all tradition (Gadamer, 2002). What it means is that the real source of all morals comes from tradition (and not from individual reason(s)), which Gadamer defines as "the ground of their [reasons] validity" (p. 281). According to

Gadamer, the idea of tradition that is found to be legitimate comes through a hermeneutical process involving the self and others/other authorities with knowledge and reason. Before continuing with unfolding the concept of tradition within a philosophy of communication perspective, let's introduce what is meant by the hermeneutical process.

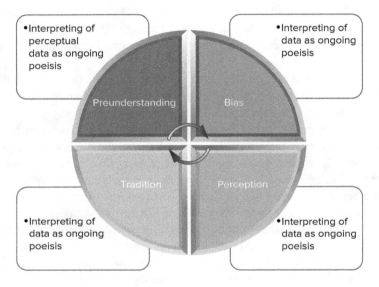

FIGURE 2.1   The hermeneutical process.

The hermeneutical process has been discussed and conceptualized by philosophers across time. Since we are discussing Hans-Georg Gadamer's understanding of tradition, and since the hermeneutical process is key to understanding tradition, Gadamer's conceptual framework on the hermeneutical process, philosophical hermeneutics, provides key descriptions and insights into how tradition is conceptualized and applied within the context of the human experience. Later, in Chapter 5, there is a fuller discussion on hermeneutics and in particular philosophical hermeneutics as differentiated from other approaches to hermeneutics. That discussion will show the natural evolution of hermeneutical thought. However, for the purpose of this chapter, I provide a basic definition or description of philosophical hermeneutics and suggest its importance to philosophy of communication.

Gadamer's philosophical hermeneutics originated from multiple perspectives of origin, including biblical hermeneutics, psychological hermeneutics, and method-focused hermeneutics, leading to Gadamer's position that centered on how one is situated in the world within a given historical moment, moving away from a hermeneutic that focuses on the individual out of a context and focusing on a psychological reading or explanation of the human and history (Warnke, 1987). To the contrary, Gadamer started from a position relying on human situatedness where he acknowledged bias is a natural part of the historical question before us. Gadamer did not rely on a strict unreflective methodological process; rather he envisioned a hermeneutical process that begins with what is directly before us, which he suggested is phenomena that might not be so clear or concrete.

Gadamer believed you cannot come to a historically situated understanding of something if you do not step within the historical contexts precisely where tradition, prejudice, and bias exists. If you do this, then you can be aware of your experience that can close down understanding. When we consider what Gadamer was going after with his emphasis on philosophical hermeneutics, he was more interested in meaning rather than certainty of truth.

Philosophical hermeneutics from Gadamer's perspective emphasizes historicity and the historical moment, situatedness within a context, and the embeddedness of perception that leans one toward some kind of prejudice, bias, preference in the act of interpretation. The hermeneutical circle for Gadamer would include an always ongoing dynamic action as ever evolving since the human experience is an ongoing phenomenon.

To understand Gadamer's philosophical hermeneutics, having a focus or emphasis on methodical considerations is less helpful and the antithesis of human experience and human reflection. Gadamer (2002) suggested that we can only understand by noticing our experience. He also suggested that our understanding of our experiences is always open to change and that it is not fixed understanding. This means that as we experience phenomena around us, our understandings of past experiences can change and be interpreted and reinterpreted through continued experience. Gadamer also accepted the idea that prejudices and our biases, which are predetermined judgments, are part of the hermeneutical process—a cyclical encounter between experiences, perceptions, and our historical situatedness.

Here is one example of how our understandings evolve based on our situatedness and our continued experiences. In 1975, Travis Walton, a member of a logging expedition in the mountains of northwestern Arizona, claimed he was abducted by aliens while on the job in the forest. There were five other witnesses to this event, each a member of the logging crew. After the witnesses reported the abduction, they became suspects in Walton's disappearance, as the police suspected someone actually murdered Walton and the five crew members were covering up the murder. Several days later, Walton was found and, over time, his story of abduction and the experiences that followed unfolded.

Originally, when Walton told his story and wrote a book, *The Walton Experience* (1978), about his experience, he made assumptions based on his bias that extraterrestrial beings would be threats if they existed at all. Later, in 1993, a movie was made based on his experience, *Fire in the Sky*. Fast forward to a new documentary released in 2018, *Travis: The True Story of Travis Walton*, Walton now believes that the experiences he had during his time in captivity were not threatening; rather, he now believes that they were helping him because he was injured, which was the reason they took him in the first place. Over time, as Walton experienced new things during the course of his life, his perception of his experience changed. Walton exemplifies the practice of standing within a context to find meaning. When he based his first understandings on his prejudices, without contemplating his experience as he experienced it, he developed a misunderstanding of his experience. It wasn't until he stepped into his situatedness and his experience that he was able to understand his experience differently.

Philosophical hermeneutics is important in the experience of philosophy of communication. Along with considering how we come to understand the world around us, traditions are also important to the hermeneutical process. The next section explores the importance of traditions and provides brief descriptions of them.

Traditions

We know that traditions are very important hermeneutical processes and contexts because they provide an orientation to how one approaches phenomena toward understanding. Traditions can be the vessel by which meaning is carried. Recognizing meaning is always contingent and temporal; traditions provide a temporal opening and dwelling place from which meaning can emerge. Before considering some of the traditions that those who study philosophy of communication come from, let me make a distinction between traditions and perspectives. For the purpose of this section, a perspective is a framework that I might use to explain, evaluate, or predict something that I am contemplating. However, perspectives are slightly different from traditions in that traditions require me to situate myself within an orientation that has an established history or authority so that I can come to an understanding about a phenomenon. Even though I might still have a different perspective about a particular phenomenon, understanding the tradition from which the phenomenon has been examined will assist me with the hermeneutical process of interpreting and understanding the particular thing in a particular way. For example, the modern and postmodern traditions are clearly very different. In one regard, the assumptions that emerge and are shared within those traditions carry the hermeneutical process in a particular way. So, if I want to learn more about the role of religion in people's lives, perhaps in a particular geographical location such as the United States, if I begin with the assumptions inherent in the modern tradition, I begin with an understanding that religion is a guiding narrative that organizes the lives of people even though the U.S. Constitution also shares the sentiment that there should be a separation between Church and State. That initial assumption may guide my understanding and the process that I use to learn more about this. If I instead start from a postmodern tradition, the assumption that I begin from will be very different since the postmodern tradition announces the fall of the Church as a guiding narrative. Beginning from that assumption will take me down a different hermeneutical path, since religion no longer holds narrative authority in the postmodern tradition as it did in the modern tradition. Regardless of which tradition I situate my inquiry, I can still have my own, and a very different, perspective.

The following are some traditions that emerge within the context of philosophy of communication: pre-classical and classical philosophical traditions, analytical and continental philosophical traditions, humanist and scientific traditions, Eastern and Western traditions, and modern and postmodern traditions. I have chosen these traditions since my own orientation to philosophy of communication is situated within a Western philosophical framework. This is an intentional choice since this text is an introduction to philosophy of communication inquiry and it is conceptualized from my own orientation to philosophy in general. These selected traditions, as they are paired together, reflect a balance between differences, sometimes complementary and other times in stark contradiction. I selected these traditions not only from my own orientation to philosophy of communication but also because these traditions are more often found in the literature and scholarship that is presented at conferences, conventions, workshops, and other public presentations that are designed to share, test, and enlarge our thinking about philosophy of communication inquiry. I anticipate that in 5 to 10 years from now this list of traditions will likely evolve from what it is here and now.

Pre-Classical and Classical Philosophical Traditions

Pierre Hadot (2002), historian of the domain of philosophy, makes a distinction between philosophy and philosophies as well as the history of philosophy and the history of philosophies. By philosophies, Hadot (2002) means "theoretical discourses and philosophers' systems" (p. 1). In other words, how a philosopher or someone engaging in philosophical thinking approaches a particular idea, experience, or action. However, his perspective on philosophy is that it is too difficult to define, though Hadot (2002) acknowledges that philosophy students are introduced to philosophies of people we refer to as philosophers. In his book, *What is Ancient Philosophy?*, Hadot attempts to describe the historical and spiritual features that are represented within the historical time period of ancient philosophy. He also notes that it is important to study the origin of phenomena because that provides context from which our understanding can evolve. Not only is the origin of an event important but so is understanding how the thing itself evolves. For example, the Greeks used the word *philosophia*, which means "love of wisdom." The linguistic origin provides a starting place from which our understanding can evolve. When historians and philosophers refer to pre-classical and classical philosophy, they are referring to moments in Greek history denoting a time when there was no systematic study of philosophical inquiry (pre-classical) and when there is a more obvious and systematic study and discourse of philosophical inquiry (classical). You should also note that this tradition only looks at ancient Greek philosophy and does not represent all of pre-classical and classical philosophies around the entire world. See Table 2.1 indicating the philosophers associated within the timeline.

TABLE 2.1   Western Philosophical Moments and Movements

Historical periods	People (some familiar names)	Movements and traditions (a sampling)
Ancient: 800 BCE–300 CE	Plato, Socrates, Aristotle, Marcus Aurelius, Cicero, St. Augustine	Virtue ethics Rhetoric Epistemology
Medieval: 600 CE–1350 CE	Thomas Aquinas, St. Anselm, John Duns Scotus	Deontology Biblical hermeneutics Scholasticism Natural philosophy

(Continued)

Historical periods	People (some familiar names)	Movements and traditions (a sampling)
Renaissance: 1350 CE–1600 CE	Niccolo Machiavelli, Michel de Montaigne, Desiderius Erasmus	Natural philosophy Humanism Epistemology
Enlightenment: 1700s CE	John Locke, Immanuel Kant, Voltaire, Friedrich Schleiermacher	Human rights Reason Romantic hermeneutics
Modern (includes Enlightenment in some literature): Up to mid-1900s	Jeremy Bentham, Adam Smith, Friedrich Nietzsche, Martin Heidegger, Hans-Georg Gadamer, Wilhelm Dilthey	Utilitarianism Existentialism Analytic philosophy Continental philosophy Critical theory Critical hermeneutics Phenomenology Semiotics
Postmodern: Began sometime in the mid-1900s Scholars are divided on our current historical period—are we will in a postmodern period or have we moved beyond?	Jacques Derrida, Umberto Eco, Martha Nussbaum, Judith Butler, Hans-George Gadamer, Peter Singer	Applied ethics Dialogic ethics Philosophical hermeneutics Deconstruction Semiotic phenomenology

Adapted from Audi, R. (Ed.). (1999). *The Cambridge dictionary of philosophy.* Cambridge University Press.

Hadot (2002) suggests that most histories of philosophy begin from a pre-Socratic time period that is still identified as the classical period in philosophy. For the purpose of this chapter, I will not elaborate on the pre-classical tradition and instead I use the philosophy historian, Pierre Hadot, to frame the classical period since it demonstrates historical evidence of a tradition. I identify key attributes from each philosophical moment in the classical tradition. I also use the *Cambridge Dictionary of Philosophy* (Audi, 1999) to supplement this discussion. This is not meant to be an exhaustive list of philosophical moments in the entire history of philosophy or in the entire classical philosophy tradition. Instead, this is designed to offer a snapshot of the classical philosophy tradition that has consistent importance to the philosophy of communication inquiry.

Classical Tradition

Some histories of philosophy suggest that classical philosophy begins from about the 6th century BCE. For the purpose of this section on traditions, I use this as an approximate starting place to describe the classical philosophy tradition and the movements identified within this tradition. Pierre Hadot (2002) suggests that the discipline and formal study of philosophy began to take shape somewhere during the 5th and 4th centuries BCE. During the beginning of the 6th century, the first Greek philosophers appeared in colonies in Asia Minor in the town of Miletus. Some of these philosophers were Thales (624–546 BCE), Anaximander (610–546 BCE), and Anaximenes (585–526 BCE).

During this time there were intellectual movements that emerged from this formal inquiry focusing on a variety of perennial questions about cos-mogenesis that focused on the origins of the world, of mankind, and of cities. Eventually, these classical thinkers used the Greek word *phusis* to describe these inquiries. *Phusis* originally meant "the beginning, the development, and the result of the process by which a thing constitutes itself" (Hadot, 2002, p. 10). Plato evolved this understanding to be the nature of a human being, the soul (Hadot, 2002). Another movement in the early classical tradition involved the Sophists in the 5th century who continued some of the earlier traditional focus on cosmogenesis and *phusis* through argumentation meth-ods, but they also broke away and from this and offered their critique of this earlier thought, illuminating the conflict between *phusis* (nature) and *nomoi* (human conventions) (Hadot, 2002). The Sophists also tied their teachings to politics and democratic life (democracy to the Greeks is not the same democracy as we see it today). The Sophists were professional teachers, and they covered teachings on science, geometry, astronomy, history, sociology, and legal theories (Hadot, 2002). This foundation of classical philosophies provide insight to exploring issues, questions, and actions in philosophy of communication inquiry. Classical philosophy also opened or established the beginning of documented systematic inquiry about *paidea*, or formal education of virtue and nobility of the soul, ethics, logic, epistemology, and beauty/aesthetics. The classical philosophy tradition laid a foundation for philosophical inquiry through the historical eras or moments and are discussed in Chapter 3.

Analytic Tradition and Continental Tradition

Considering these two philosophical traditions together allows us to see what is different about them and what is similar between them. There is no need to make value judgments about either tradition. To take note of their aims and methods allows for a deeper understanding, as well as, situates them within the larger story of western philosophy.

Analytic Tradition

The philosophical analytic tradition historically referred to ways of philosophizing via realism, logical analysis, logical positivism, and conceptual analysis/elucidation (Weitz, 1966). Other scholars identify the philosophy of language as a major branch of the analytic tradition (Arnett & Holba, 2012). In philosophy of language, a central question involving linguistic meaning centers around the process of logical analysis. This is also true in philosophy of communication because it also explores questions related to language and its function in meaning making.

This definition might sound precise, but the description of the analytic tradition is really not that simple or clear. In the broadest sense, the analytic tradition is an umbrella term that is comprised of a variety of philosophical processes, techniques, and mind-sets (Audi, 1999). I have also heard it be referred to as English philosophy, Oxford philosophy, or solely linguistic philosophy or the philosophy of language. What these labels point to is a focus on the use and function of language (Audi, 1999). These labels are also generalizations and can also be misleading simply because the body of literature in analytical philosophy spans very broadly across issues related to language and meaning.

Analytic philosophers suggest that when human beings attempt to construct meaning, they engage a range of processes that center around the concepts and propositions involved in the linguistic event. Additionally, the central purpose of analytic philosophy is to examine the structure of language as it related to the world. We might see an analytic philosopher cover linguistic aspects of clarity, ambiguity, semantics, and meaning (Arnett & Holba, 2012). Analytic philosophers also study the choices people make in selecting language, how they structure sentences, and how these decisions shape meaning. Some analytic tradition philosophies also presuppose that there are inherent dysfunctions in the human use of language, which causes misrepresentations and misunderstandings.

Some scholars of the analytic tradition suggest that accounts and descriptions about the analytic tradition are sometimes contradictory; they are also sometimes incomplete (Preston, 2007). Other contemporary scholars suggest that there is no clear, accurate, and consistent account that is agreed on by historians of philosophy (Preston, 2007). For the purpose of this section that provides a descriptive account of the different traditions, I must accept that it is unlikely there will be a unifying description of the analytic tradition. I can say that there are numerous versions of this tradition and there are variances in each of the descriptions that one might find. In philosophy of communication, there is an always an ongoing sense of contingency or impermanence since meaning is made only temporally. What I believe is sufficient to know about analytic philosophy is that, like philosophy of communication, analytic philosophers are interested in meaning but in a different way. The analytic tradition assumes there is a lack or a flaw naturally in language, linguistic structures, and the potential processes by which we analyze linguistic structures. In philosophy of communication, that assumption is not part of the hermeneutical process. It is important to be familiar with the tenets of the analytic tradition as well as the challenges those analytical processes face. This tradition informs philosophy of communication to the extent that the questions posed related to how meaning is made share a common element of the uses of language. It is better to understand the analytic tradition as "a tapestry composed of the differing elements that comprise this category of philosophical inquiry" (Arnett & Holba, 2012, p. 121).

Continental Tradition

While both the continental and analytical philosophy traditions emerged for the first time around the turn of the 20th century, they both represent significant departures from the conventions of expressing philosophy (Preston, 2007). Scholars suggest that analytical philosophy is geographically tied to Great Britain and the United Kingdom while the continental perspective emerged from philosophical discourse in France and Germany (Preston, 2007). As we see, analytic philosophy focuses its examination on language, ambiguity, and verification; continental philosophy diverges from that framework by exploring being and being in the world with others, intentionality, perception, temporality, existentialism, historicity, ethics, and otherness (Arnett & Holba, 2012).

Simon Critchley and William Schroeder (1998), who edited the first *Companion to Continental Philosophy*, suggest that the content covered in the continental tradition makes better sense to introduce by name of philosopher rather than by issue or topic discussed because of how it is researched, taught, and talked about in the English-speaking world, which focuses on the thinker rather than the ideas of the thinker. To some extent, this could be also due to the way in which the ideas explored and covered fold into other ideas in ways that make it difficult to separate. Scholars identify Immanuel Kant as the philosopher who is common to both traditions but also the one to separate them (Critchley & Schroeder, 1998).

The term itself, *continental*, refers to something that occurs in a specific place, in this case the European continent (Critchley & Schroeder, 1998). This, of course, can be a limiting perspective and creates other kinds of problems in understanding what exactly the topic areas are when one studies continental philosophy. In Critchley and Schroeder's (1998) *Companion to Continental Philosophy* they provide a textured discussion of these challenges if you want to read further about this specific problem. They also suggest that the geographical distinction fails to identify the methodological distinction that also attributes a separation between the traditions. There are many problems associated with using adjectives to separate these approaches to philosophizing, so the best we can say is that there appear to be differences among the kinds of problems that each tradition explores. We can also say that even if the problems are similar or somehow connected to each other that the method or approach to thinking about these problems differs widely as well.

Critchley and Schroeder (1998) suggest it might be clearer to say that what their companion denotes is a "continental philosophy in the English-speaking world" that includes such subdivisions such as "logic, epistemology, metaphysics, philosophy of mind, philosophy of language, philosophy of law, ethics, philosophy of religion, political philosophy, [and] aesthetics" (pp. 13–14). This list is long and wide; it also contains philosophy of language, which also shows up in the analytic tradition. This means that we must understand continental philosophy as a broad dialogue and dialectic between thinkers about ideas. We also have to accept that what falls under or into the category of the continental tradition is rather arbitrary, temporal, and dynamic. To have any more of a concrete definition or description would probably create arbitrary boundaries that would cause more problems than is necessary. The next tradition pairing to mention is the humanist tradition and the scientific tradition. As you will see, their differences focus on the assumptions centering around subjectivity and objectivity.

Humanist Tradition and Scientific Tradition

Similar to my comment above pertaining to the analytic and continental philosophy section, observing these two traditions side-by-side allows for the observance of similarities and differences. It also illuminates the aim of each tradition and broadens understanding of the role of subjective and objective experiences.

Humanist Tradition

The humanist tradition is a philosophical and ethical positioning that values human agency within all human beings. This tradition has been referred to as coming from a human sciences perspective (Audi, 1999). A significant premise of the humanist tradition is that there is a preference for critical thinking by individuals thinking for themselves instead of blindly accepting dogma or other rigid belief systems. Over time, the meaning of the word *humanism* itself evolved. For example, the term *humanism* was first used by a theologian, Friedrich Niethammer, in 19th century referring to a system of education based around classical literature but has evolved from this narrow understanding to a broader perspective that advocates the ideas of human freedom and human progress (Audi, 1999). The humanistic tradition accepts the tenet that human beings are themselves responsible for their own identity and the development of individual selves in relation to the world around them (Audi, 1999).

There are various deviations of humanism, including but not limited to Renaissance humanism, secular humanism, and religious humanism, and so forth. Scholars suggest that Renaissance humanism is the origin of the humanist tradition and that it reflects a return to the Greek ideal of *paideia*, referring to the education of young children to be focused on raising the ideal citizen of the polis, which some suggest is a continuation or expansion of ancient Greek philosophy (Audi, 1999). For example, tied to scholasticism, which is a closed or limited system of education that focused on Aristotelian philosophy and logic, renaissance humanism focused on a bit broader system of education that prepared students to be doctors, lawyers, or theologians. This system was still very limiting and eventually evolved to become the general humanities disciplines including grammar, rhetoric, history, poetry, and moral philosophy (Kimball, 2010).

Secular humanism rejects supernatural or miraculous claims or foundations. It focuses on human reason and democratic sensibilities of human rights and responsibilities. Its mission is to ensure a free human society imbued with moral and ethical values. We can say with confidence that the humanist tradition emphasizes the human sciences and methods that are often subjective in nature; this is remarkably different from the scientific tradition, which emphasizes the natural sciences and the objectivity of the scientific method.

Scientific Tradition

The scientific tradition emphasizes the natural sciences and the methodological approach of the scientific method, which requires following strict objective standards. This tradition is associated with a natural science perspective; it can also be considered an extension of the analytic tradition and grounding in enlightenment thought. The method of doing the scientific method focuses on evidence that allows us to learn something new. Components of the method include observation, starting with a hypothesis, using induction, conducting some kind of experiment, using some kind of measurement process, testing deductions, refining the experiment, and working with controls in the experimentation.

Researchers tend to use diverse models to incorporate these parts of the process. We can say with more certainty that there is a continuous process—an ongoing inquiry that moves the researcher toward the possibility to understand deeper and to be able to make predictions. This doesn't mean that reason or making arguments is not a part of the scientific method; what it does mean is that a rigorous testing of the hypothesis allows one to use rationality and provide effective reasoning about certain phenomena. This approach allows for iteration, failure, and reengagement. One place where the scientific method connects to the rhetorical tradition is the idea that the hypothesis is a conjecture and conjecture is a prominent part of Cicero's method of stasis, which is a place of opposition in an argument. Conjecture is a disagreement over a fact in a point of stasis. Moving on from the scientific tradition, there are two very easily identifiable geographical traditions that typically have significant characteristics, the Eastern and Western traditions.

Eastern Tradition and Western Tradition

Here there is a similar pattern of observation which will show similarities and differences between these two traditions. Sometimes these are compared through religious or spiritual lenses, as well as social and cultural lenses. However these traditions are observed will reveal differences while acknowledging the value that each tradition can bring to the human condition.

Eastern Tradition

The Eastern tradition in philosophical thought originates from those philosophies that embody Eastern perspectives we see emerged from Eastern thinkers, Eastern literatures, and Eastern histories. Many of these insights call for introspection, prayer, and cultivation of the sacred and the human interiority. This is not unlike the religious domains in the Western tradition, but especially as postmodernity ushered in multiple petite narratives the notion of this kind of inner wisdom was fraught with competing narratives that undermined the expansion of the sacred terrain in the Western world. For the purpose of this section, I specifically connect Eastern traditions to what Tobin Hart (2007) refers to as wisdom traditions that intend to cultivate the human inner landscape. This does not mean that Western traditions do not cultivate the human inner landscape; in fact, Pierre Hadot (1995) does articulate something he refers to as spiritual exercises, Martin Heidegger (1968) does identify meditative thinking as an inner cultivation, and other primarily Western philosophers also reflect similar emphases. However, many of the Western philosophies that align with wisdom traditions are influenced by earlier Eastern traditions. This may not be how all scholars would categorize Eastern traditions, and it is certainly not representative of Eastern traditions, but it is one way for an introduction to make a distinction between the characteristics of one tradition and another.

A wisdom tradition can be considered living words; they give life and they are life—they do not remain static. Words coming from wisdom traditions are meant to be revisited, reinterpreted, and reconsidered for deeper and deeper relevancy and meaning (Hart, 2007). Wisdom traditions excavate meaning by spending time with the words, seeing the words in context, and the words in relation to the self—it calls for introspection (Holba, 2014). Inner cultivation from any wisdom tradition incorporates deep looking, deep listening, and a contemplative practice.

I suppose we know it when we see it; the Eastern tradition emerges when we hear of the Dalai Lama, Gandhi, Thich Nhat Hanh, Muhammad, Abdul-Qadir Gilani, Pema Chodron, and other spiritual leaders who begin from a place of contemplation before any other predisposition. This is a very limiting list as it does not reflect all of Eastern traditions, but in popular culture generally, most people will have heard of most of these names. Eastern traditions are often tied to Eastern geographies and Eastern histories and are grounded in nonjudgment, compassion, and empathy for others. Western traditions that are outside of wisdom traditions, such as religious contexts, have a very different aim or focus.

Western Tradition

The Western perspective in philosophical thought originates from those philosophies that embody Western orientations, Western literatures, and Western histories. While there are wisdom traditions situated within Western perspectives, these are often religious traditions and they focus on aspects of the sacred. The Western tradition outside of wisdom traditions "embody goods that are valued in the Western world context. This is tied to Western culture and Western worldviews. It is difficult to summarize or even lock in one definition of the Western tradition, which would render the definition incorrect and incomplete. It is best to leave it as a diverse sentiment that is tied to Western culture. Though as you begin to read more and think about how Eastern and Western traditions might have influenced each other throughout history, the distinction between these two traditions would likely wane or at least become invisible.

The last two traditions for this section are modernism and postmodernism. This does not mean that these are the only two traditions left. Instead, I use these two as a stopping place. Instead of providing you with a list of absolute traditions that hold some kind of currency to philosophy of communication, take this as a pause in the description of traditions—this list should be dynamic and temporal; it will change.

Modernism and Postmodernism

These two traditions are both a condition and a reference toward a particular, undefined time period. Noting characteristics of one will no doubt lead to contrary characteristics of the other. When exploring these traditions, it is good to keep in mind that the differences between them can point to a radical loss while at the same time, signal a radical liberation.

Modernism

The modern era, also referred to as modernity or modernism, is both a time period and a condition that is described as having a reliance on progress and science—in fact some scholars suggest that progress is privileged over other types of engagement (Arnett & Holba, 2012). During the modern era, which some scholars suggest started during the Enlightenment period through the middle of the 20th century, advancements in science and technology came at rapid speed. At the same time, social and political philosopher Hannah Arendt would say that we lost a commitment to cultivating an "enlarged mentality" (Arendt, 1958) that would give us "individual independence" (Taylor, 1989, p. 192) and the ability to think for ourselves. The modern era also had a dark side that brought periods of colonialism, imperialism, and totalitarianism (Arnett & Holba, 2012). While there was consistency of some things in modernity, there was also building tensions of hegemony, racism, sexism, and other practices that would lead to a fractured spirit across the marginalized. This ushered in a sentiment pushing toward postmodernism. It is difficult to describe or even talk about modernism without referencing postmodernism. In fact, when looking up modernism in the *Cambridge Dictionary of Philosophy*, the entry refers you to the postmodernism entry. The description offered here is not meant for a complete discussion of modernism, but it offers a glimpse or a general sentiment about it. For a more in-depth and clearer discussion and study of modernism, consider reading Stuart Sim's (2011) *The Routledge Companion to Postmodernism* or Stephen Hicks's (2011) *Explaining Postmodernism and Socialism From Rousseau to Foucault*.

Postmodernism

The postmodern period, also referred to as postmodernity or postmodernism, is a condition rather than a specific period, though it began to surface as a sentiment in the early to mid-20th century, occurring across different domains of disciplines unequally. This is to say we did not wake up one day to see ourselves in a postmodern condition. Instead, the sentiment evolved in waves across disciplines during the 20th century. Most certainly, Jean-Francois Lyotard (1984) announced the postmodern condition in his treatise on the human condition, *The Postmodern Condition: A Report on Knowledge*, which was translated into English in 1984.

Postmodernity has been described as an "intertextual cacophony of historical voices coexisting with multiple narratival neighborhoods" (Arnett & Holba, 2012, p. 46). Stuart Sim (1999) suggested postmodernity was actually an announcement that the grand narrative or grand paradigm that organized human life (religion) had fallen and in its place emerged smaller narratives, competing at times, to organize human life. When we hear the descriptor, postmodernity, we think of all kinds of uncertainties in politics, in the workforce, in economic markets, in religious competition, and in the basic tapestry of the human experience. Postmodernity reveals change without assurance; it also reveals the anxiety of competing narratives and traditions.

I am intentionally placing the rhetorical tradition on its own, outside of a unity of contraries framework, because I contend that the rhetorical tradition stands alone and is part of each tradition because it is not possible for any traditions to spread its message and invite engagement without a rhetorical pathway or the rhetorical tradition, which itself is fluid and responsive. This is consistent with the notion that rhetoric is everywhere and it provides us with the opportunity to engage others over ideas, face challenges, and move us to action.

The Rhetorical Tradition

Rhetoric has a long history and a rich tradition comprised of diverse perspectives concerning how people communicate. When we consider a formal history of rhetoric starting with Plato and Aristotle, there is a sense of urgency between the master and his student. Plato sensed the exploitation inherent in the use of certain kinds of rhetoric while Aristotle found that there can be an ethical balance if one studies and understands the relationship between rhetoric and ethics. Today we continue to see and hear an abundance of the exploitive rhetoric where someone takes advantage of another person through language and argument in order to gain something, mislead someone, reorient a particular truth to something it is not, or broaden a perspective. The use of rhetoric in a negative light can be intentionally misleading, and this is the kind of criticism of rhetoric we most often see and hear about, but there is another side of rhetoric that gets less attention. Sonja Foss and Cindy Griffin (1995) introduced us to invitational rhetoric, which points to a very different *telos* from traditional domineering rhetoric. Invitational rhetoric, according to Foss and Griffin (1995), is grounded in feminist principles of "equality, immanent value, and self-determination" (p. 4). Invitational rhetoric aims to understand rather than persuade; its ethos is based in care rather than intimidation; and it is dialogic rather than monologic (Foss & Griffin, 1995). These characteristics of rhetoric are typically presented from a Western framework; rhetoric from an Eastern orientation would likely look quite different.

There is another rhetoric that gets less attention in the rhetorical tradition, listening rhetoric as laid out by Wayne Booth. Wayne Booth (2004) reminds us about "listening rhetoric" (p. 10), where the emphasis is not about dominance or persuasion as much as it is about how we listen to the other. At this juncture, I want to reflect on why rhetoric stands alone here and not presented through a unity of contraries framework like the other traditions. While it is possible to frame this in a unity of contraries framework as Aristotelian rhetoric and invitational rhetoric or rhetoric and philosophy, I believe by doing so this kind of apposition limits the ubiquitous nature of rhetoric in the study of philosophy of communication. At least, keeping rhetoric separate and beyond the limits of a unity of contraries or the limits of a unity of counterparts, rhetoric exists everywhere and for this reason there is no reason to wrap limits around it by situating it with another concept, even though in some cases it might make sense. For the purpose of this introduction to philosophy of communication inquiry, it is more helpful to the beginning thinker to understand the existence and authority of rhetoric on its own as a tradition.

Traditional theories of rhetoric "reflect a patriarchal bias" that seek to dominate others (Foss & Griffin, 1995, p. 2). James Herrick (2001) outlines a survey of the rhetorical tradition highlighting a conceptual framework for evaluating and practicing persuasive writing and speaking—the traditional roots of rhetoric. The rhetorical tradition is rooted in discourses from and between Plato and Aristotle and can also be considered through what rhetoric does. Herrick (2001) suggests rhetoric is planned, it adapts to audiences, it is shaped by human motives, it is responsive to context and situations, and it seeks to persuade. There are also social functions of rhetoric that test ideas, assist our reach in advocacy, distribute power, discover facts, shape knowledge, and build community (Herrick, 2001).

There have been several rhetorical turns or shifts in focus throughout the ages of the rhetorical tradition. Aristotle (1984) began by anchoring the rhetorical tradition in persuasion by defining rhetoric as "the faculty of observing in any given case the available means of persuasion" (p. 19). In the first line of his main treatise on rhetoric, he states, "Rhetoric is the counterpart to dialectic" (Aristotle, 1984, p. 19). This means that rhetoric and dialectic begin with commonly held opinions but diverge since rhetoric employs proofs while dialectic focuses on the engagement in the arena of discourse (Herrick, 2001). So, rhetoric and dialectic are complementary arts of reasoning; rhetoric is aimed at proving an argument and dialectic is aimed at the process of discourse. Aristotle defined rhetoric as an art, a practical and systematic art; he provided a framework and set up an accountability in that he recognized there may be multiple truths to some things and that rhetoric can identify multiple truths and use them in the framework of persuasion.

Aristotle (1984) identified the heart of rhetoric as the enthymeme—a strategic incomplete syllogism designed to allow multiple audiences to complete the meaning themselves so that the rhetorical reach is far and wide. Aristotle (1984) also identified three rhetorical settings, including deliberative (future focused on what should be done), forensic (past focused on has been done), and epideictic (a praise or blame forum blending past, present, and future). It is safe to say rhetoric scholars understand these three domains of rhetoric similarly though might have different ways of explaining them. One thing that most rhetorical scholars have in common involves persuasion and dominance. "Listen to me" and "I have something to say that is important—more important than what others have to say" are common possibilities in rhetorical discourse. When employing rhetoric in a rhetorical setting, the rhetor seeks control over the situation and of others. What is typically not common is listening to the other (Booth, 2004).

One of the first shifts in rhetorical practice occurred during the Middle Ages when rhetoric and the traditional oral style of persuasion changed to writing and various written styles of persuasion. The traditional role of oral delivery was replaced by the written text and the discovery and arrangements of arguments was lost (Herrick, 2001). Written logic took over and the text was often taken out of context when separated from the spoken word. When this occurred, a disembodied text left more to question than when it was connected to a human person through oral delivery (Herrick, 2001).

The next shift occurred during the Belletristic movement when elocution took over and the human action of delivery was again disconnected from the content (Herrick, 2001). What became most important was the delivery of the content and not the actual content itself. Then another shift occurred focusing on the audience and less on the rhetor. Chaim Perelman and Lucie Olbrechts-Tyteca (1969) gave us a new rhetoric where the centrality of audience was key to engaging rhetoric, but it was still focused on persuading an audience. Understanding audience in a deliberative fashion was key to this shift. Additionally, to understand audiences through a lens of multiplicity that included a particular audience, an audience of one, an audience of self, and audience of others allowed for a new understanding of presence. This created the opportunity for emphasizing some information over other information depending on who the audience actually is. In this theoretical framework, the field of audience studies emerged. Another rhetorical turn came in contemporary rhetoric when we focused on the particular situation, drama, and narration, combining rhetorical implications with philosophical positions. All of these shifts remained within a Western framework, but this would soon change as a new rhetoric focusing on the nondominant—the invitation toward the other welcoming the other to enter the conversation—emerged and created a radical shift in how rhetoric is conceptualized and enacted. Now let's take a look at why these traditions are important to philosophy of communication inquiry.

Connections, Currency, and Meaning

It is important to note that these are not the only traditions that are important to philosophy and to the philosophy of communication inquiry—these primarily originate from perspectives in the Western world. Additionally, there are also movements within the traditions I chose to highlight, such as the emergence of existentialism as a form of critical questioning of modernity and experimental philosophy as a way of engaging philosophical inquiry in postmodernity. Movements though, are not traditions in themselves; traditions might encompass multiple and varying kinds of movements. These are the general thematic traditions from which we begin to orient our thinking and make sense of the world.

Connections: We have to remember that the questions we pursue in our inquiry are embedded within a context that connects to a tradition because when we question something, that question has likely already been embedded within a conversation that has been ongoing within tradition(s). Acknowledging this connection to tradition shapes our understanding and provides a starting place from which you can jump off and continue pursuing your inquiry.

Currency: Traditions can provide background and understanding of public moral argument so that one might better participate in dialogue and dialectic over issues that are important to the human community. For example, as I am writing this today, in the news, the state of Missouri has passed legislation that would severely limit *Roe v. Wade* (1973) and ban abortions, making them illegal in most situations. With the changing face of the U.S. Supreme court, leaning toward a more conservative sentiment toward abortion, experts in law and legal theory are suggesting this is a move toward changing, restricting, or overturning *Roe v. Wade*. As some experts suggest, each state in the United States may be on the path to reengage this debate about the illegalization of abortion, which is no doubt one the most obvious hot-button topics concerning morality and the public that we find today. Understanding the tradition(s) from which opponents address perspectives and make their arguments is helpful for people on all sides of this public issue. Without an understanding of tradition and its relationship to the subject or issue that we question, arguments we make on either side of the question risk being less relevant, less clear, less connected to the discourse, less able to make a difference in the moral fabric of public discourse and public life. This does not mean that we cannot move between the different traditions that undergird the issue and the discourse; it means that as we participate in public argument, which is our civic responsibility, we should understand perspectives even down to the tradition or traditions from which they emerged or from which they are still embedded.

Meaning: Traditions are important to acknowledge when we engage in public argument because it is through these traditions that we learn to test the evidence of our arguments and the nature of the issues at hand. Traditions allow us to determine how to test the public evidence and how meaningful that evidence is to the overall argument. For example, in the case of the public argument regarding overturning *Roe v. Wade*, looking for evidence on either side of the issue from the various traditions—classical, analytic, continental, humanist, scientific, Western, Eastern, and rhetorical—shift the focus of the public argument. So, there would be differing kinds of evidence used when listening to or creating an argument from a humanist tradition versus a scientific tradition, one focusing on the virtue of human life or one focusing on the measurable, scientific definition of life—both of which would be fundamentally the extreme of each tradition. In order to have a helpful discussion, finding common ground through a different tradition might be better able to keep dialogue open until more common ground is cultivated. So, perhaps defining life through a continental, a rhetorical, or an Eastern tradition lens would benefit the discourse and lead to a more effective outcome, where there might not be universal agreement (which there likely would not be), but using traditions in order to keep the inquiry ongoing and open to a multiplicity of voices benefit the serendipitous potential of dialogue and dialectic. Traditions are only part of the ingredients of public moral argument—they provide grounding and understanding; they can also shift a perspective when we look at issues through different traditions.

Conclusion

This chapter focused on the importance of traditions and their role in the interpretive process of philosophy of communication inquiry. In particular, it is important to remember how the traditions within which we are situated inform the process of how we make meaning. This chapter offered a discussion of traditions through a unity of contraries that provides a broader view within a rich context because traditions evolve in dialogic fashion, responding to public discourse, human agency, and competing traditions vying for a kind of authority that invites human trust and provides the ground from which we can come to know something. It is, however, important to recognize the limits of traditions and the assumptions they each make as we navigate how we understand the world around us.

Figure Credit
Fig. 2.1: Adapted from Hans-Georg Gadamer, *Truth and Method*. Copyright © 2002 by Continuum International Publishing Group.

Chapter 3

Historical Moments

Learning Objectives

1. Understand and articulate the difference between historical periods and historical moments.

2. Articulate the significance of historical moments to philosophy of communication.

3. Identify general historical periods chronologically and in relation to historical moments.

4. Understand the philosophical concepts of philosophical pictures, narratival neighborhood, conversational horizons, and communicative praxis.

Have you ever wondered how having a general understanding of history can inform how you understand the world today? We are often taught history chronologically, but what if there is another way to conceptualize history? What do you think that would look like? What kinds of information, knowledge, or understanding might be different that you know now? This chapter has the potential to change the way you think about and understand history.

Perceptions and Historical Moments

From a philosophy of communication perspective, the historical moment is framed by perceptions of phenomena that interact, exchange, and evolve. This is why understandings of historical moments have "fuzzy horizons of meaning" (Arnett & Holba, 2012, p. 35). This means our understandings can change moment by moment as our perceptions change. These perceptions come together and form a picture of "a" truth, though perhaps not "the" truth. These pictures inform and shape communicative understandings. Ronald Arnett and I (2012) refer to historical moments as being "communicative dwellings" that bring into a fuzzy focus of a "philosophical picture" (p. 35). This chapter lays out historical periods in general with specific date demarcations, though each historical period is comprised of historical moments, which can be various and differentiating historical moments within historical periods. These historical moments and periods are often linked to temporal cultural and social subjectivity that allow for textures and contours of environments, discourses, and communicative exchanges to reach a level of communicative comprehension.

Similarly, as discussed in the *Overtures* book that frames philosophy of communication as a communicative dance, I want to introduce the concept of "philosophical picture" from Robert Piercey (2009), who identifies the contours necessary for understanding the dynamic engagement embodied in historical periods and historical moments situating how these contours provide the backdrop for our perceptions and what we come to interpret as a truth. This truth though is not fully complete and perfect; rather it is a snapshot of a kind of truth situated within changing perceptions and dynamic shifts in meaning making in general (Arnett & Holba, 2012). Philosophical pictures give perspective and contour to the fuzzy horizon that we find ourselves engaging but we know that philosophical pictures are only frameworks that are not certain, not absolute, and not permanent. In fact, these pictures of the historical moments are always incomplete as is our knowledge in general.

One thing that seeing historical moments and periods as philosophical pictures does is provide the context for seeing the questions that guide those moments and periods. It is through the questions that emerge in historical moments that discourse is opened and meaning is shaped as the questions are publicly asked, vetted, responded to, and addressed. Questions also illuminate other issues that are sometimes not explicit yet. These questions that emerge across historical periods illuminate more than the actual intent of the question. Other philosophers have assisted our understanding of the importance of historical moments. Charles Taylor (1984) suggested that by exploring historical moments, we can better understand our current selves, so we look to the past to understand who we are and why we do what we do in our current historical moment.

I want to discuss in more detail two philosophers who give us a philosophy of communication perspective related to the value of historical moments to how we make meaning and understand ourselves and our own historical moment that we stand within.

Jumping off from Arnett and Holba's (2012) *An Overture to Philosophy of Communication* that introduced Robert Piercey's (2009) "philosophical pictures" to the communication discipline, and weaving Calvin Schrag's (2010) **narratival neighborhoods** and **conversational horizons** that become entangled in the communicative space of communicative praxis, provides a rationale for seeing the value in acknowledging the historical moments in which questions are raised, responded to, and addressed to some extent. These philosophical positions provide the backdrop advocating the significance of historical moments and periods, I then describe, in general terms, the context and contours of the standard historical periods and their relationship to philosophical of communication discourse. Finally, after this, I address how historical periods contribute to connections, currency, and meaning making, using an example of public moral argument in our contemporary moment.

Philosophical Pictures

Understanding of our world, our relationships, our environments, and our existence in general comes to be our individual philosophical perspective. These perspectives are situated within a particular historical moment within particular historical eras. It is these kinds of understandings that open conversations and shape the discourses in which we engage.

Understanding and living within a given historical moment requires one to be perceptive enough to see changes and shifts within content and context (Arnett & Holba, 2012). We can perceive these changes and shifts by illuminating the questions that emerge across, between, and within the historical periods (Krüger, 1984). Philosophy of communication is an applied philosophy. We do not just want to understand things historically; instead, doing philosophy of communication requires one meet, in dialogue, with earlier thinkers and understand their context and content (questions) in the action of trying to understand the questions they identified and tried to answer. Philosophy of communication is an action-oriented philosophical quest for understanding and living, being, and doing of that philosophical perspective.

Robert Piercey (2009) suggests that when we do philosophy historically we follow the development of ideas, which can reveal strengths and weaknesses of the reality of a given moment in time. The philosophical pictures that Piercey (2009) talks about are not static; they do not remain static; they have complexities as they are situated within conversations, actions, interactions, and transactions—these pictures are always already changing and evolve as they encounter phenomena. This is what makes the human experience challenging, unique, and complex. For more on Robert Piercey's "philosophical pictures," please see Chapter 4 on communicative dwellings of Arnett and Holba's (2012) *An Overture to Philosophy of Communication*.

The value of exploring philosophy of communication through historical periods and identifying particular historical moments within and across these periods involves taking a particular approach. Peircey (2009) identifies and elaborates on each approach. For the purpose of this chapter, I will introduce each approach, describe it, and provide its significance to human understanding. The approaches Piercey identifies include narrative, critical, diagnostic, and synthetic. Having various approaches from which one can seek understanding is necessary because individual perceptions are always unique to the individual because of natural flaws in perception, how we punctuate what we perceive, and how we interpret based on what we already know. These descriptions are necessary to introduce here, but a broader discussion of these approaches is articulated in the *Overtures* text if you want to know more about Peircey's perspective.

Narrative: Narratives can be implicit or explicit and they are represented by a common or shared understanding between people. The difference between a story and a narrative, in philosophy of communication, is the agreed-on shared assumptions, practices, and goals (Arnett & Arneson, 1999). Narratives provide the "why" or rationale for our communicative actions. Arnett and Holba (2012) suggest that narratives aid in our negotiation of meaning in and with the world.

Critical: In many first-year college programs, critical thinking is one of the key skills that most colleges advocate students learn, experience, and apply. Piercey (2009) states that if we do not use critical thinking and analyze key arguments that color particular historical moments, it is difficult to identify those emergent questions that guide human thinking, understanding, and action. The key to this critical approach is to recognize that ideas often change over time because of changing contexts in the human landscape of progress and existence. Historical moments shift in focus depending on technological, environmental, political, social, and relational contexts that are always changing. Being critical allows distance that is critical to interpretive possibilities.

Diagnostic: The diagnostic approach, according to Piercey, is a type of critical approach that emphasizes disclosure of intended or unintended deception. A diagnostic approach requires an assumption that without deep diagnostic reflection, the potential to be deceived, especially about things that are widely accepted but not widely studied, is elevated, and for Martin Heidegger (1962, 1966) it is a certainty. Through this diagnostic approach, questions emerge that are often not typically asked due to assumptions (unintentional) and deceit (intentional).

Synthetic: Piercey (2009) describes the synthetic approach as one that brings together ideas and events situated within historical moments related to the human condition. Piercey describes this approach as one that reconciles contrasting positions to aid in understanding perspectives toward finding meaning in their impact upon human meaning making. This means that phenomena, even if they do not appear to be related, have a synthesis in some way—there is always interconnectivity between phenomena. Piercey (2009) suggests that philosopher Paul Ricoeur does this in his work by bringing diverse voices and texts together in ways that offer new insight toward new interpretations. The synthetic approach—the act of synthesis—ensures that phenomena is not reified. Instead, the synthetic assures that phenomena avoids the limits of boundaries in that phenomena, philosophical pictures, are always changing and shifting. Making assumptions about how things are challenged and accepting the idea that nothing is ever always fixed, finished, or rigid maintains the integrity of interpretation and understanding.

From a philosophy of communication perspective, these approaches are key to expressing interpretive possibilities. The approaches themselves are also not mutually exclusive—the approach we take to phenomena can integrate these approaches; the philosopher of communication recognizes that these approaches can coexist together in the process of coming to meaning. Arnett and Holba (2012) state that

> the narrative approach provides stories that illuminate relationships in a
> given historical moment. The critical approach identifies the significance

of taking a critical distance and understanding philosophical differences in competing narratives. The diagnostic approach uncovers historical truths about the possibilities of Being that influence what the human perceives. Finally, the synthetic approach offers an integrated picture of human relationships through co-creating that results in the synthesizing of meaning in everyday life. (pp. 40–41)

Calvin O. Schrag is an American philosopher and emeritus professor (Purdue University) who has significantly contributed to the shaping of philosophy of communication both nationally and internationally. His approach to making meaning is a synthesis of all four approaches, narrative, critical, diagnostic, and synthetic. We see this in his textured discussion on how people make meaning in a decentered world in a space of subjectivity. Schrag (2003) provides the backdrop of communicative praxis and integration in communication and discourse (2010) as the communicative environment conducive of meaning making. Living with others is a basic human need in the human condition. We live with others through communication. Schrag identifies the process of how we communicate with others as communicative praxis. He also explores the communication activities within the sphere of communicative praxis as narratival neighborhoods and conversational horizons. Let's explore each coordinate to understand Schrag's perspective and how these coordinates inform each other and explicate a philosophy of communication.

Communicative Praxis

Calvin O. Schrag (2003) states, "The amalgam of communication and praxis has been designed to orient reflection on discourse and action as being *about* something; as being initiated *by* someone, and as being addressed *to* and *for* someone" (p. ix). Keeping this amalgamation in mind, one sees the importance of understanding communication as a practice that interplays between about, by, to/for, which is an inclusive and open navigation of communication between communicators. Schrag (2003) asserts that communicative praxis between individuals and groups of people are performances that cocreate social and historical meaning. This means that the actions that happen between the about, by, and to/for manifest meaning in and through the action. Schrag (2003) refers to this as "tissues in the display of meaning" (p. 194). This might sound simple, but the reality is that if we do not account for the about, by, and to/for, we risk degrading into monologues that fail to connect with others, which means meaning is not being created between and among others. The potential for making meaning together is ruptured without the recognition of the about, by, and to/for.

Narratival Neighborhoods

Calvin Schrag (2010) identifies narratival neighborhoods as places where we converse with others through remembering, reminiscing, ruminating, and reflecting on communicative transactions, exchanges, encounters, and outcomes. We can do this by reading, thinking, and reflecting on ideas with others. Schrag suggests that these memories, reminisces, and reflections typically emerge through historical moments that are not always chronological or spatially organized. This kind of illumination is dynamic and responsive to the conversations that call us into them. This is more dynamic than thinking within the boundaries of chronology and spatial limits.

An example of how this is dynamic could be a simple as when I was called into conversation with Jacques Derrida, a literary and semiotic philosopher who wrote a good amount on death and coming to terms with the death of others and ourselves. It was when my father died that I read all I could from Derrida's philosophy, which then led me to Martin Heidegger's notions of being-toward-death and the thrownness of existence that I was able to make sense out of the rupture I experienced when he died. It was all I could do—I entered the narratival neighborhood of existential thinkers trying to make sense out of the meaning of death to my particular experience of dying as part of the human condition. I was called into my journey into this existential narrative that informed and restructured my understanding of life and death.

Returning to Schrag's (2003) position, the other, from my remembering, reminiscing, and reflecting, is "inextricably tied to the unfolding of that which is 'my own'" (p. 55). In fact, we cannot unfold as we are without being in conversation with others in our neighborhoods. These neighborhoods shift, change, and evolve as we participate in these emergent conversations.

Conversational Horizons

Conversational horizons are comprised of multiple narratival neighborhoods that are expansive and include varying interests, knowledges, and discourses that are always dynamic and responsive to others in the field of the horizon. This is where we can be exposed to diversity, multiplicity, plurality, and differences—all of which have the capacity to change and shift meanings in an emergent and flexible way. Schrag (2010) reminds us that horizons of meaning are punctuated textualities that can guide how meaning comes together within the narratival neighborhoods. From a philosophy of communication perspective, conversational horizons reveal the interplay of intertextuality that shape how we make meaning of our experiences.

An example of a conversational horizon could be reflected in how I came to terms with my father's death. This involved entering the narrative neighborhood of Derrida and Heidegger's inquiry into the experience of death. After reading much of their published work on the aporia of death, I then reflected on those positions and ideas along with my own knowledge horizon from my previous encounters with death which contained personal reminisces, rememberings, and reflections, including Christian, Buddhist, and Pagan ideals, as well as my experiences in attending churches and temples. Additionally, recalling and reflecting on my experiences with and understandings of the physicality of death from my earlier career as a county detective in New Jersey where, assigned to sex crimes and major crimes, I was tasked with investigating sexual assaults of all kinds and murders, which required me to attend post-mortem exams, composed the texture of my conversational horizon. Along with these experiences and encounters, learning about the ritual practices in the Tibetan Book of the Dead and exposure to other cultural influences pertaining to death have come to directly impact my world view about death. All of these narratival neighborhoods weave together a conversational horizon that informs and shapes the meaning of death to me, thus, allowing me to come to terms with the death of my father.

Summary

The space of communicative praxis is informed by both narratival neighborhoods and conversational horizons. To make sense out of my experiences, integrating the narratives (e.g., Derrida and Heidegger) informs how I understand how others have shared experiences and how they interpret those experiences. Integrating this with the critical approach allows me the reflect and ruminate on the narratival arguments made by Derrida and Heidegger to ensure I understand the relationship between the ontological (Heidegger) and the semiological (Derrida) arguments. Integrating these two approaches and adding the diagnostic approach, I can illuminate what is not said or explicitly present—this is a kind of revelation that is unexpected, which can be pivotal to my own human understanding. Finally, adding the synthetic to these three approaches can be seen when I reflect on the narratives explored in my narratival neighborhood and set them against the conversational horizons that come into my awareness and comprise my existence. From a philosophy of communication perspective, these approaches come together seamlessly, and they coexist in the ongoing quest for human understanding.

Historical Periods and Historical Moments

For clarity, I will make a distinction in how I am referring to historical periods and historical moments. This next section provides descriptions of historical periods that have been generally, though not fully, agreed on by scholars and historians. Historical periods have generally definitive chronological boundaries that might differ somewhat across different scholarly points of view, but in general scholars agree on the general descriptions of these historical periods. Historical moments, on the other hand, are pivotal points of time within historical periods that are marked by questions that emerge from within the dynamic sociocultural contexts that come to define those periods. Historical moments are identified by the public questions that emerge through human interaction and discourses.

Meaning emerges within historical moments through ongoing interpretations and reinterpretations that come to account for a shared perceptual memory. This kind of interpretive engagement occurs within narratival contexts and in relationships between people. When interpretive engagement occurs in this way, we are able to act and react to the actions of others. As an example for philosophy of communication application, looking at Charles Taylor's advocacy for perspective taking through the notion of embedded thinking is helpful. Taylor (1989) examines historical understandings across historical periods to inform his own understanding. He advocates this approach in his text, *A Secular Age* (2007) where he makes qualitative distinctions between historical periods, which demonstrate how and why a society is as it is, and his focus is on how, through history, the secular age has emerged. Taylor advocates for the recognition of the importance of history and historical understandings; he indicates that identifying historical moments through questions that emerge is key to any interpretive understanding humankind seeks. Another key text from Taylor is his 1989 publication, *Sources of the Self: The Making of Modern Identity*.

Taylor (1984) suggests that identifying the parts of historical horizons through the actions of people and the histories associated within the context of people and places provides the conditions for understanding and re-understanding human experience. For Taylor, it is important to identify, analyze, and understand the various narratives, questions, and historical moments to forge together possibilities for interpretations and understanding. Taylor

(1989) models the method of tracing of how one makes the self through identifying historical frameworks—all identities are embedded within a particular historical moment. This means that everyone is born within and attached to some story already in the midst of unfolding. Even though Taylor (1989) suggests that frameworks in general can be problematic by creating or imposing limits, frameworks are necessarily "inescapable" in the task of gaining human understanding (p. 17). Using Taylor and other scholar's descriptions of historical periods, I am setting the stage to show the general agreed-on descriptors of historical periods. Within each historical period, I also identify one or two historical moments that have come to shape each period.

Ancient or Classical Period

The ancient or classical period refers to a chronological time period from the middle of the second millennium BCE through the 6th century CE. Years ago, during a graduate German literature course I took, a professor made a distinction between BCE and BC as well as CE and AD. He told me that in a postmodern era with the decline of the Christian grand narrative and a more diverse American population, it is no longer necessary or appropriate to use a fulcrum point of reference through the Christian narrative. BC is typically interpreted as "before Christ," which assumes a shared acceptance that we should start our calendars from the moment of the birth of Jesus Christ. Instead, we should not assume the Christian narrative is known, understood, and accepted by most people, so scholars changed the reference point to BCE, "before the common era," situating the common era through historically secular reference points. The same thinking was also used to rethink the historical marker of AD, "after the death of Jesus Christ" to CE, the "common era," which also situated the time frame through secular historical markers. For a more thorough discussion of this deliberate shift in demarcating historical chronology, see Joshua Mark's (2017) article in the *Ancient History Encyclopedia* that provides the historical and political context of these demarcations. Though, it is clear that these demarcations are categorized by Christian European influence.

In general, scholars agree the chronology for the ancient/classical historical period is between 800 BCE and 300 CE (Hornblower & Spawforth, 2003). This historical period is marked with historical moments of Homer's classical tales and writings that run through the political rise and fall of Rome (Griffin, 1986). Scholars suggest this is the historical moment that provides the philosophical and cultural foundation of the Western world.

This historical moment within this ancient period also situates human-kind as being dependent on the polis where one's call to civic responsibility was paramount. Of course, this called individuals into service and action. There was also intentional bias within the caste system that included a slave class and women and children as property of men in general (Taylor, 1989; McAllister, 1996).

The end of the ancient/classical period is often situated within the fall of Rome (Kristeller, 1979). Rome did not "fall" in one day. The fall of Rome generally refers to a period of time where things changed through experiences of losing battles, changing allegiances, and other sociocultural changes resulting in the final decay of the Roman Empire through varying leadership changes across the former Roman turf. There are differences across scholarly accounts in setting the end date of the Roman Empire. From a philosophy of communication perspective, the fall of the Roman Empire does not have to represent one date in time; rather, many philosophy of communication scholars allow for various interpretations and rationales for these differences, resulting in accepting that there is no clear and concise deadline demarcating the ancient classical time period.

Middle Ages/Medieval Period

The Middle Ages, also referred to as the medieval period, points to another time range specifically within European history, ranging somewhere between the 5th–15th centuries. Many scholars identify and agree on 600 CE to 1350 CE (Kristeller, 1979). The historical moments in this period are marked by a grand narrative of Christian theology that blended Platonic thought through a perspective that one's self-definition comes from outside the self, or God, instead of from one's own sense of self. Additionally, this historical period was driven by a shifting of importance away from the polis to the Church and its ideology.

In the Western part of the world, the Middle Ages were marked by classical learning in the UK, but there is less evidence of this in Western Europe. We know that scholasticism and Monastic education was the main approach to living and learning (Kristeller, 1979). Historical moments during this period saw advancement of sociocultural transitions marked by conflict between Christians and Pagans. This resulted in a Christian victory and a pushing underground of pagan traditions (Pieper, 2001). The historical period is demarcated as people began to rebel against the church (from within the church as well as from outside of the church). It was during this time that scholars indicate a renaissance of learning, ushering in and identifying the historical period of the Renaissance.

Renaissance Period

The Renaissance historical period saw questions emerge marking the historical moments with inquiry into nature and science; this was a pivotal moment marking a shift toward secularism (Taylor, 2007). Scholars generally date this historical period between 1350 and 1600 (Kristellar, 1979). There was a return to rhetorical education and oral practices similar to the ancient/classical period. By returning to studying and practicing rhetoric a return to classical philosophy emerged that blended into the birth of the Enlightenment historical period. From a philosophy of communication perspective, this birth of Enlightenment does not mean that there was only one enlightenment that occurred in history. In fact, there were at least two enlightenments, a moderate and radical enlightenment. Most of us learn about the moderate enlightenment in our high school history classes, but there is a deeper and darker enlightenment that was pushed underground, allowing the moderate enlightenment to prevail. The difference between moderate and radical enlightenment is centered on the privileging of self over other as literacy evolved (Arnett et al., 2007). For a more detailed account of the radical enlightenment, see "The Rhetorical Turn to Otherness: Otherwise Than Humanism" (Arnett et al., 2007) in *Cosmos and History: The Journal of Natural and Social Philosophy.*

The Renaissance period contained a significant historical moment that reflects a lifting of the constraints put on learning and knowledge by the Church—this was a liberation of the human mind. Within this time period, we see the historical moment of questioning the church, thus sparking the Protestant reformation as well as an increased interest in individuality. This individual creativity then pushed toward the next historical period of the Enlightenment.

Enlightenment Period

Discussions on the Enlightenment have focused on the Western world in the 18th century; some scholars also include the latter part of the Renaissance period (Kristellar, 1979; Taylor, 2007). Descriptions of the Enlightenment period are often philosophically, politically, and socially complex in nature. Scholars also acknowledge two actual enlightenments, the moderate and the radical (Gare, 2006). They argue that the moderate enlightenment, which is what most of us hear about in history overview courses, was unable to bring a full liberation of thought and practice such as what the radical enlightenment pursued (Gare, 2006).

Scholars of the radical enlightenment suggest that the moderate enlightenment advocates pushed the radical enlightenment thinkers underground and were successful at masking the voices in radical pursuit of change. The radical enlightenment was known to have situated people within traditions, as well as acknowledged diversity of people and ideas within a cosmopolitan mind-set (Arnett et al., 2007). The moderate enlightenment did not go that far; instead, it disembodied people from traditions and practices in ways that negated a cosmopolitan lens. The critique is that the moderate enlightenment did not go far enough—it simply fell short of true change and transformation (Gare, 2006).

Contemporary Period
(Modern, Postmodern, and Beyond)

A marker of the modern period lays in the notion of individual freedoms (Taylor, 1989). Taylor (1989) indicated the individual as autonomous and society as human centered are key attributes of the modern period. Emphasis on the individual is a hallmark of the secular age (Taylor, 1989). This individual-centric perspective decentered and replaced any remnants of the connection to the polis, which causes a sense of fracturing in human communities. This shift also removed the ethical and moral burden of watching out for the other.

In the modern period, progress was privileged to the point of fracturing any sense of tradition or honoring of the past. Even though there were many advancements in technology during the period, there was also a loss of what Hannah Arendt (1958) referred to as an enlarged mentality. There was also a keen focus on the independence of the individual at the cost of the other and the polis. This troubling shift led toward the postmodern period, which for some is more of a condition rather than a time period. I suggest that in the contemporary period, modernity and postmodernity are conditions rather than precisely defined historical periods. Within these conditions, we are able to identify questions emerging around people struggling to find meaning in their lives. A question that marks the condition of modernity questions the authority of the Church, the notion of family, and how we come around the mark of difference and live together. These questions pushed and demanded responses, which pushed the condition of postmodernity on humankind, shattering assumptions and celebrating multiplicity. At the same time, certainty about anything became elusive.

Arnett and Holba (2012) describe postmodernity as "an intertextual cacophony of historical voices coexisting with multiple narratival neighborhoods," again with a generalized sense of when we became aware and labeled this sentiment in the latter part of the 20th century. Jean Francois Lyotard (1984) described postmodernity as a condition in which any sense of a grand narrative that we can organize around to make meaning was gone and replaced by petite narratives all around us with no real sense of how to vet them and engage or connect to them.

Stuart Sim (1999) suggests that postmodernity was simply an announcement or public proclamation of human awareness of the loss of any grand narrative—and a recognition of the emergent nature of smaller narratives that pop up and change over the course of time. The postmodern condition can be described as a living within a sense of uncertainty—with certainty being a mark of the past where we did not question whether our jobs would exist over time, we just expected they would, or the idea that everybody went to church and ate dinner together as families on Sundays. These are examples of givens that marked a modern sensibility. Postmodernity carries no such givens; the only constant is that nothing is a given and nothing is dependable. That sense of certainty is no longer a given in postmodernity. The illusion of modernity has been shattered, leaving the human condition to dwell in uncertainty and vulnerability, while liberating human beings toward plurality, difference, and multiplicity.

Connections, Currency, and Meaning

Connections: Historical periods aid in meaning making because they provide a backdrop of the landscape and context for the issues involved in public discourse. For example, the debate over abortion has been ongoing for at least this and the last century, though subtopics within the debate in public moral argument have been different depending on the particular contours of the questions emerging within the historical period and the historical moment. There has been a shifting of questions arising in public discourse at different moments such as questions related to women having a choice about what they can do for their own bodies, or the moment that life actually begins, or the limits pertaining to gestation for having an abortion, or the moral conditions involved in the practice of abortion. These are not the only questions that have arisen during different public moral debates situated within different historical moments. As the participants in these debates shift and change, so will the argument and the questions that precipitate the debate. In the mid to latter part of the 20th century, pro-choice proponents of abortion argued that women's safety and their lives were of paramount importance, which was a fitting response to what was happening time and time again: Women were getting abortions in unsafe places and often ended up with negative health consequences or dying. Today, however, because the historical moment has changed and abortion is legal within parameters, the emphasis has shifted from those dire health consequences to the freedom of choice and protection of a woman's right to decide her own reproductive freedoms. Therefore, the historical moment provides one with a particular understanding that is relevant to the context at hand. This does not mean that the concerns from the previous historical moments are not relevant, but what it does mean is that the rhetor is attuned to the most relevant and urgent issues or exigences related to the current historical moment and the questions or issues that invite the public moral debate in the first place.

Currency: Supporting and participating in public moral argument is central to democracy. When issues are public, and because the issues concern moral values of the human community, they hold currency to the historical moment and the human community. Public moral argument can be tied to rhetorical situations where decisions have to be made in response to an exigency that calls the public moral argument into question (Bitzer, 1968). This is what makes the argument hold currency. Because the rhetor is attuned to the issues and the moral value of the issue to the human community, meaning is made in the context of the historical moment; otherwise, if meaning is pursued outside of the connected context, misunderstandings and missteps can occur, especially in decision making for public policy.

Meaning: Making meaning is only meaningful if meaning emerges from the particulars of the historical moment. From the meaning we gather, we gain perspective and make decisions. If we impose meaning from outside a context of the historical moment, mistakes most definitely can be fruitful and abound. Meaning allows us to test the public evidence that we need to make decisions in and for the public. For example, jumping off from the example about the threat to *Roe v. Wade* that is in the current public moral discourse today, without situating *Roe v. Wade* within the historical moment in which it was adopted, we risk forgetting the institutional memory for why it was essential to address abortion through the courts and through our constitutional laws that govern society. If we fail to remember the reason why legalizing abortion was brought into the public domain discussion, such as women's health risks and deaths due to failing to provide a supportive and healthy infrastructure for women seeking abortions due to a wide range of reasons, as we follow the path toward potentially overturning this law, we will forget to consider the "why" in the first place. If we only say that *Roe v. Wade* can now be overturned because the composition of the U.S. Supreme course is overwhelmingly more conservative now, we fail to recognize and address the inherent risks that exposed the need for a federal law to begin with. The historical moment is an important part of public moral argument and plays a key role when deliberating, determining, and denoting future laws pertaining to abortion. Both recognizing the historical moment in the days, months, and years leading up to 1968 and understanding the challenges facing abortion and its institutional practices today must be a part of the philosophical and pragmatic discussion surrounding our practices related to abortion as a society.

Conclusion

This chapter provided a distinction between historical periods and historical moments, as well as their significance to philosophy of communication inquiry. It also identified the importance of questions that emerge in historical moments that drive how people understand and interpret their environments. This means that in philosophy of communication inquiry, identifying the questions that emerge and drive public discourse are essential as humankind learns how to make meaning together in diverse contexts. Focusing on Robert Piercey's framework of philosophical pictures and Calvin Schrag's conceptual tapestry of narratival neighborhoods, conversational horizons, and communicative praxis help to shape our understanding of how we make meaning together through our engagements with each other and through participating in public discourse embedded within the moral issues that provide the contour of emerging questions that shape human connection and meaning in the world.

PART I

Connections, Currency, Meaning

Recognizing and understanding traditions and movements are important to any kind of philosophical thinking and engagement in public moral debates; it is helpful to have a clear context for understanding issues and for determining what kind of information and evidence will be valuable and additive to the discussion and debate. It is similarly important to recognize the historical moment so that we do not make judgments and claims against people or events out of context. When we stand above history and make judgments from our own history, our arguments may not be relevant to the particularity of the historical moment, including the particular context; it could also involve making incorrect assessments.

Connections

In preparing to engage in public moral argument, one must try to identify the tradition within which arguments are made. The tradition assists with understanding where the issues are coming from and how they are framed and understood by all sides of the argument, and lastly helps shape one's ability to effectively participate in public conversations and debates. The historical period and the historical moment are key factors in understanding the arguments of others and in developing one's own arguments. If we understand the historical context and those key factors driving the historical period, we have a better sense in developing the most prudent and relevant argument or making a general contribution to the issues at hand. Making the connection between the issues and the tradition, as well as the issues and the historical period and moment, is valuable to aid understanding as well as to identify the most fitting evidence. It is also important to remember that it is alright to allow our own perspectives and positions to be altered or to change or adapt in some way.

Currency

As I mentioned earlier, traditions can provide background and understanding of public moral argument so that one might better participate in dialogue and dialectic over issues that are important to the human community. Understanding the tradition(s) from which opponents address perspectives and make their arguments is helpful for people on all sides of this public issue. Without an understanding of tradition and its relationship to the subject or issue that we question, arguments we make on either side of the question risk losing currency to the moment and to the individuals involved in the issue and debate. This means one may be less able to make a difference in the moral fabric of public discourse and public life. This does not mean that we cannot move between the different traditions that undergird the issue and the discourse; it means that as we participate in public argument, which is our civic responsibility, we should understand perspectives even down to the tradition or traditions from which perspectives emerged or from which they are still embedded.

For enriching classroom discussion, brainstorm as one large group or several smaller groups and identify pressing issues relevant to you today. Remember what public moral argument entails; there are three criteria that make an issue appropriate for public moral argument:

1. There must be an argument (remember, an argument is a claim, a stated reason, and evidence to back up the claim; I say more about this in the textbox).

2. The argument must occur in a public setting where it can touch others.

3. The issue has to be an explicitly moral issue.

Use some time during class or for homework to explore information and gather evidence to engage in a public moral debate in the classroom, or make the stakes higher and hold a public moral argument forum in a public setting on campus. Remember, you have to have an argument, you have to touch the public in some way, and the issue must be an explicitly moral issue. Before going further with the discussion, there is a helpful tool that can assist with the development of arguments and assessment of arguments that provides a systematic framework for testing arguments and their evidence. Stephen Toulmin (1922–2009 CE) was a 20th-century British philosopher who focused on rhetoric, ethics, argument, and moral reasoning. His book, *The Uses of Argument* (1958), is most noteworthy because in it he laid out a model for

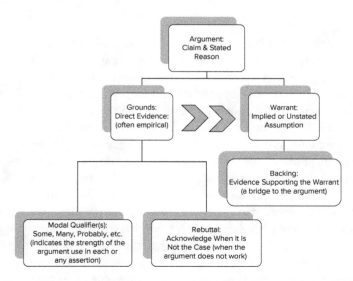

FIGURE I.1   Schematic for Stephen Toulmin's argument model.

developing most effective and practical arguments that can also be used to analyze and evaluate arguments made by other people. The elements of this argument model are claim (the conclusion of your argument), grounds (evidence to support your claim), warrant (an unstated assumption that I not necessary to say), backing (evidence that supports the warrant), rebuttal (acknowledgment of when the argument is not the case), and the use of modal qualifiers (terms that suggest the strength of the argument, such as *some, few, many, maybe, sometimes*, etc.). Following this model when making arguments or analyzing someone else's argument ensures that the argument being made is strong and holds evidentiary value—or can identify when something is either not an argument or has nothing much to support it.

Here are some examples from today, though it is likely these issues may be different examples from what your groups choose:

1. Issue: Police brutality

    Argument: Policing reform is necessary to save black people's lives because too many black men are being unjustifiably killed by police.

2. Issue: Abortion and women's reproductive rights

    Argument: *Roe v. Wade* should be overturned because abortion is committing murder since fetuses are living beings.

CLAIM

The conclusion of a particular argument or a full argument with a claim and a stated reason.
Example:
You should send your child for piano lessons because learning music builds discipline in children.

GROUNDS

The evidence for the claim. These are statements that indicate support of the claim. Often this is the empirical evidence. It can be a precipitating event or it can provide measurable support. It can also be faith based.
Example:
Provide empirical studies that measure the effect of learning music, maybe piano in particular, on children's IQ, success in school, enhanced problem-solving experience, etc. These can also be in the form of qualitative studies or mixed methods studies.

MODAL QUALIFER

The strength of the terms of the claim. It qualifies your evidence or claim and allows for contingencies and probabilities. Use qualifiers across all parts of the argument. Stay clear of absolutes, such as all or none.
Example:
Most children who learn to play an instrument at an early age, tend to do better in school over all than children who are not exposed to music at that early age. (Of course, you would need to provide evidence of studies to back this up—but any claim you make directly or indirectly should consider using modal qualifiers.)

WARRANT

Often this is an unstated assumption. It is the part of the argument that is not stated. Lends to the inductive leap to believe the claim. It is a principle, law, or belief that is commonly accepted. Often it is implied by the arguer and sometimes it is supplied by the listener as an assumption (because of this there can be different warrants based upon the standpoint of the listener).
Examples:
Children need discipline.
Learning requires discipline.
Discipline is good.

BACKING

This provides support for the warrant. Even if the warrant is unstated, the backing should be explicit.
Example:
Find studies that show children need discipline to be successful.
Find in the learning sciences the need for discipline.
Define discipline—Find example from moral sources that discipline is good or a good thing to have.

REBUTTAL

An anticipated condition under which the authority of the warrant would not apply.
Example:
In some cases, children with certain disabilities might not benefit as much from learning music that other children with no or different disabilities.

Rebuttal is not the same as refutation. Refutation is a point by point counter to an opponent's argument. Rebuttal, in Toulmin's model, reveals when the argument is not the case.

FIGURE I.2 Example of Using Toulmin's argument model.

There are multiple sides, a polyphony of perspectives, on both sides of these issues. How could you use a philosophy of communication inquiry framework to explore these issues and engage in public moral argument? You can choose a tradition and you should be aware of your historical period and the particular historical moment. The sample issues are older issues that still have some currency today. What information would you gather? How can you put your own biases aside, be aware of them, but not let them misguide your inquiry? What new things can you learn about these issues? When you read the other arguments, on all sides of the debate, what tradition is the speaker coming from? How does the historical period and historical moment shape your understanding?

Meaning

Traditions are important to acknowledge when we engage in public argument because it is through these traditions that we learn to test the evidence of our arguments and the nature of the issues at hand. Traditions allow us to determine how to test the public evidence and how meaningful that evidence is to the overall argument. Traditions are only part of the ingredients of public moral argument—they provide grounding and understanding; they can also shift a perspective when we look at issues through different traditions.

Making meaning is only meaningful if it emerges from the particulars of the historical moment. From the meaning we gather, we gain perspective and make decisions. If we impose meaning from outside the context of the historical moment, mistakes are likely to abound. So, as you are gathering your information and potential evidence, you need to situate your understanding of it from within its own historical period and moment. Meaning allows us to test the public evidence that we need to make decisions in and for the public. Good luck with thinking through your research by examining the tradition from which it came and understanding the relevance of the historical period and moment.

Figure Credits

Fig. I.1: Adapted from Stephen E. Toulmin, *The Uses of Argument*. Copyright © 1958 by Cambridge University Press.

Fig. I.2: Adapted from Stephen E. Toulmin, *The Uses of Argument*. Copyright © 1958 by Cambridge University Press.

Part II

Approaches to
Philosophy of Communication Inquiry

Part II of this book introduces some approaches to philosophy of communication inquiry. Chapter 4 situates the importance of taking an approach or identifying someone's approach to philosophy of communication inquiry. Knowing the approach or approaches taken to understanding a given experience enables clarity in understanding and guides one's interpretive journey. Chapter 5 introduces the following approaches: hermeneutics, semiotics, and phenomenology; Chapter 6 introduces the following approaches: psychoanalytical, critical, and communicological; and Chapter 7 introduces the following approaches: narrative, dialogical, and ethical.

Each chapter ends with an applied discussion, "Connections, Currency, Meaning," in which a discussion involving the application of some of the concepts covered in the chapter is opened. This section integrates public moral argument applications.

Chapter 4

Significance of Approaches in Examining Communicative Experience

---

Learning Objectives

1. Identify various philosophical approaches to understanding how we come to know things.

2. Articulate the challenges with knowing and understanding phenomena in our environments.

3. Identify key approaches to knowing in philosophy of communication inquiry.

4. Explain the importance of understanding how we know what we know and its relevance to engaging in communicative praxis in moral public argument.

ave you ever wondered what influences things that we come to know? Or maybe, how our perspective, previous experiences, biases, and prejudices affect what we think we know? Have you explored what kinds of lenses you use or approaches you take to interpreting your perceptions or phenomena?

Understanding how we come to know something is a key interest in philosophy of communication inquiry because it opens us to a variety of approaches that inform how we make meaning through a multiplicity of experiences. This opening to a variety of approaches does not limit meaning making to one way or to one approach. When we limit our approach to learning or to understanding what we know, we will more likely obstruct meaning. Philosophy of communication inquiry broadens understanding instead of limiting it. In this chapter, reminding ourselves about the challenges with coming to know something and understanding particular nuances involved in human experience can help us understand the problem of knowing and open our perspective to multiple approaches to making meaning. Some scholars may refer to these as perspectives to do philosophy of communication inquiry; other scholars and organized groups of disciplinary scholars refer the term *approach*. For me, I am choosing the word *approach* to reflect the way in which we either do or engage philosophy of communication inquiry or the way in which we understand doing or engaging philosophy of communication inquiry. After a discussion about these challenges, I introduce ways of knowing within a philosophy of communication inquiry lens. Finally, this chapter ends with an application section foregrounding the importance of communicative praxis, especially in this age of information and dissemination.

The Problem With Knowing

Philosophy of communication inquiry begins with language, its meanings, and its interpretations. Understanding the etymology, or the origins of words, informs understanding about the word and provides a first glimpse into unraveling meaning. Epistemology, the study of how we know, comes from the Greek word ἐπιστήμη, which means *episteme*. The word has been identified with two broad interpretations, knowledge and logos (Arnett & Holba, 2012). Generally, logos is associated with the message and/or evidence of something or some fact. Knowledge is associated with the things that assist us when we apprehend our surroundings and our world; logos is also one of the "modes of persuasion" or modes of proof (the artistic proofs) that Aristotle (1984, p. 19) laid out in his rhetorical theory. The modes of proof that Aristotle (1984) lays out are what constitute his rhetorical triangle, ethos (ethics or credibility of the messenger), pathos (emotions related to the message), and logos (the logic of the message). Philosophy of communication understands the interplay of the rhetorical triangle, and in particular seeks out the meaning of the message, the logos, in the context of ethos and pathos.

In the study of knowledge or how we come to know something, there are generally four different ways of experiencing knowing (Audi, 1999). The first is observing evidence, which is empirical knowledge; this means there is direct observation of phenomena. The second way points to those things we know without seeing them, those things that might already be known without having or needing evidence to back it up. Sometimes this is referred to as tacit knowledge. An example of this is that I know that I must keep gasoline in my vehicle; otherwise, if I do not have gas, my car will not have the fuel, energy, or nutrition it needs to start or move in order to drive me somewhere. I do not need to run out of gas to learn this since I have general knowledge and awareness that cars need some kind of fuel to work. The third way involves gaining knowledge based on word of mouth or what other people tell us; in this case, we have no firsthand knowledge or observations of what we are told. This is considered hearsay evidence in a court of law and it is often not allowed into testimony because it is not a primary source of information. Lastly, we have technical knowledge that might instruct us how to do something. Putting together a new gas grille or making a favorite homemade family recipe are examples of having technical knowledge.

TABLE 4.1 Four General Ways of Experiencing Knowing

1. Direct observation of some kind of phenomena.
2. Pointing to something we already know without seeing it; we refer to this as tacit knowledge.
3. Gaining knowledge based on word of mouth; in the courtroom, this is called "hearsay."
4. Following instructions; this is technical knowledge.

Adapted from Audi, R. (Ed.). (1999). *The Cambridge dictionary of philosophy.* Cambridge University Press.

Each of these ways of knowing or apprehending the environments in which we offer unique and sometimes distinctly different impressions provide varying modes through which we gather what we come to know. To explore the problem of epistemology, this chapter provides a short history of epistemology in philosophical thought, identifying general schools of thought including skepticism, empiricism, rationalism, and traditionalism (Arnett & Holba, 2012). Then, this chapter identifies various ways of knowing within philosophy of communication inquiry. These approaches include **hermeneutics**, semiotics, phenomenology, psychoanalytics, critical theory, communicological theory, narrative theory, the dialogical approach, and the ethical approach. I provide an introductory description of each approach in this chapter and identify the philosopher(s) associated with each approach. Each subsequent chapter in Part II of this text will explore in more depth each approach and identify commonalities and differences between them. The last section of this chapter, "Connections, Currency, and Meaning," explores the significance of various approaches through the philosophy of Calvin Schrag's communicative praxis.

Epistemology: A Short History

Epistemology has been described as a structured way of gathering knowledge about something that assists with debate about ideas, making informed decisions, and taking particular and intentional action (Hendricks, 2007). To situate the philosophical understanding of the study of how we come to know something, epistemology, it may make more sense to begin with the opposite of knowing, which generally refers to being skeptical. Skepticism illuminates the challenges and problems of knowing in general (Arnett & Holba, 2012). Epistemology is concerned with what and how we know; skepticism challenges, questions, and confronts the idea of knowledge, or what we think we know, in what has become a never-ending, ongoing debate in philosophy circles. As you will see in the last section of this chapter, the notion of skepticism is even more important in the contemporary world today as information abounds in both physical and virtual spaces and the concept of fake news has left many people with an ever-present challenge to test what it is they encounter as knowledge. The four main kinds of epistemologies are **skepticism**, **empiricism**, **rationalism**, and **traditionalism**. Let us start with a discussion about skepticism.

TABLE 4.2 Four Epistemological Systems

Skepticism	Empiricism
Suggests that the knowledge we gain should be interrogated, doubted, questioned, and tested.	Knowledge we gain based on direct observation.
Rationalism	**Traditionalism**
A way of knowing that uses reason and construction of rational arguments to come to know something.	A way of knowing that acknowledges the context of people, relationships, and stories are essential for coming to know something.

Adapted from Arnett, R. C., & Holba, A. M. (2012). *An overture to philosophy of communication: The carrier of meaning.* Peter Lang.

Skepticism

Skepticism begins with the assumption that knowledge we gain should be doubted, questioned, and tested. This means we should begin from a natural position of doubt because otherwise there may be errors in understanding or intentional deceit might be overlooked. Having a mind-set of skepticism assumes that there is a possibility of errors in judgment when we take in knowledge; it can also cultivate a hermeneutic of suspicion, which is having a lack of trust or faith in the information and evidence that we encounter from sources outside of ourselves. As a philosophical perspective, skepticism advocates human beings should begin from a position of doubt, which then will allow us to test and form our belief system and structures with a higher degree of certainty. Of course, the question of complete certainty, according to Pyrrho of Elis (360–275 BCE) is impossible to achieve since we can never have enough or adequate levels of evidence to determine whether any knowledge is actually possible. This is what has been known as Pyrrhonian skepticism, which leaves us in a continual state of doubt (Arnett & Holba, 2012). Another perspective from the Greek philosophers is that of academic skepticism, which suggests no certain knowledge is actually ever possible (Hendricks, 2007). The difference between the two perspectives is that academic skepticism is in complete denial of knowledge—we can never know anything. Pyrrhonian skepticism situates the human agent in a perpetual state of doubt where we suspect the evidence for everything. Both of these perspectives can be very daunting if these are the two ways one chooses to see the world.

The skepticism that Plato articulated through his academic partner, Socrates, has an academic perspective that is more hopeful than Pyrrhonian skepticism. In Plato's *Apology*, Socrates accepts his sentence of death for charges against him suggesting that he was corrupting the youth/his students by challenging them to question the status quo and by questioning their elders and leaders in the Greek Polis. Socrates stated, "Well, although I do not suppose that either of us knows anything really beautiful and good, I am better off than he is—for he knows nothing and thinks that he knows. I neither know nor think that I know" (Plato, 2017, pp. 7–8). His statement, "I am better off than he is," referring to the other who thinks he actually knows something when he really knows nothing, takes a perspective of hermeneutic humility, a couplet that Calvin Schrag and Eric Ramsey (1994) develop in their perspective on philosophy of communication, which means it is okay to not know and it is better to wait, listen, observe, and learn before we think we know anything.

Pyrrhonian skepticism suggests we suspend our judgments and attempt to find some kind of absolute truth. This feels defeatist; it simply accepts that we will do the best with the appearances we see before us (Arnett & Holba, 2012). Beyond skepticism as the anti-epistemology, there are other ways of knowing that can be traced across historical periods. In the history of epistemology, there are other perspectives typically identified in introductory philosophy courses. These perspectives are empiricism and rationalism. Traditionalism is another perspective that, while sometimes left out in the histories of epistemology, informs how we come to know and how we make meaning of what we know. Each of these play a role in gathering knowledge and evaluating evidences toward enhancing the human condition in public and private spheres, which is especially relevant to the 21st-century citizen.

Empiricism

Empiricism is based on observation and experience. This involves direct observation and direct experience. There are two main types of empiricism, concept empiricism and belief empiricism. First, concept empiricism focuses on the concept that is connected to an experience; it means that all concepts are derived from experience (and that we cannot know anything without having an experience). An example of this would be the concept of bitterness: One would have to experience bitterness to understand or know what it means or is. Therefore, someone would need to taste something bitter, like a coffee bean or a cup of expresso, two things that typically have a bitter taste.

Belief empiricism suggests that belief about something is situated inherently within the individual. This means belief empiricism does not require one to have direct experience to understand the phenomena—one inherently believes in the concept outside of the experience. For example, belief empiricism accepts that a third-party observation can be enough to connect a belief with an observation. So, in the case of bitterness, if someone observes another individual in a coffee shop drink a cup of expresso and provide both verbal and nonverbal communication indicating that the expresso is bitter, one can have an empirical belief that the expresso is bitter without having to interact with the cup of expresso itself. These empiricisms are countered by those who believe in concept innatism, which is a perspective that some of the concepts we know and believe are innate; they simply do not come from external conditions of an experience but rather they are innate in our being (Arnett & Holba, 2012). Both Plato (427 BCE–347 BCE) and Rene Descartes (1596 CE–1650 CE) supported the idea of innatism, which means that human beings are born already with ideas and knowledge without having to have experiences.

There have been challenges confronting people who believe in the certainty of empiricism. These challenges usually involve a questioning of what makes up evidence, concepts, or beliefs. We certainly see this kind of questioning today in the form of fake news and other kinds of data gatherings and dissemination over social and digital media of all kinds—in both text and image. Sometimes it comes down to language and how we make persuasive arguments. This embodies Aristotle's modes of proof and enthymematic reasoning, with the idea of rationalism and the rational paradigm outlined in Aristotle book, *The Rhetoric*. Rationalism integrates logic, evidence, and rhetoric when weaving together bodies of knowledge.

Rationalism

Rationalism employs reason, rational argumentation, to create the construct of what we know. The employment of reason and rational argumentation offers so much more than direct observation, especially when things are not within the observational horizon or if things are not systematically measurable. The word "rationality" comes from the Latin word *ratio*. In Latin, this means giving an account of something, a reason for something, a reckoning with something, a computation, or a calculation (Simpson, 1968). *Cassell's Latin Dictionary* includes the following statements about ratio: "the faculty of mind which calculates and plans, the reason ... a theory, doctrine, science, knowledge ... philosophical system ... a reason, motive ground" (Simpson, 1968, p. 501). Rationalism assumes that observations and perceptions are fallible and should not be trusted. Rationalism is different from skepticism and empiricism because it is not divided into schools of thought such as academic and Phyrrhonian skepticism and belief empiricism and concept empiricism. Instead, rationalism does not unfold into discrete categories. In general, rationalism appeals to good reasoning by employing logical argument, evidences, and rhetoric (the intentional laying out of Aristotle's modes of proof and enthymematic reasoning).

Before moving further along in this chapter, since I mentioned Aristotle earlier in the chapter and now again, I find it the right time to digress a bit and explain some of Aristotle's rhetorical theory so that it is easier to grasp some of these epistemological perspectives. There are three key components in Aristotle's rhetorical theory that are essential when understanding rationality. The first is Aristotle's (2001) definition of rhetoric, which is, "the faculty of observing in any given case the available means of persuasion" (p. 24). In rationality, a key aspect is the ability to persuade people enough to, at the very least, understand your perspective, and at the most, believe what you say. The second component is what he referred to as the "modes of persuasion," ethos, pathos and logos (Aristotle, 2001, p. 22). Aristotle defined ethos as having to do with the credibility of the speaker and whether the speaker is trained or qualified to deliver the message. The word *ethos* is derived from the Greek word for ethics, situating this mode of persuasion or proof directly tied to the ethics of the message or messenger. Logos is derived from the Greek word *message*, and Aristotle ties logos to rhetoric's counterpart, dialectic, or the engagement of competing evidences (messages with reasons) toward determining a truth or an outcome. Pathos is tied to emotions, and Aristotle indicated pathos is understanding how to put your audience into the right mind-set to receive your message. The modes of persuasion, or modes of proof, are key to engaging in deliberation, framing arguments, and providing intentional communication to various kinds of audiences.

TABLE 4.3   Aristotle's Modes of Proof

Modes of Proof	Meaning	Example
Ethos	Has to do with the credibility of the communicator—ethos comes from the Greek word for *ethics*.	Having credibility involves having expertise to make certain arguments; since I have never changed a tire on a vehicle, you would not want me to teach someone how to change a tire. Likewise, if someone is always telling nontruths, even if they do tell the truth one time, their credibility would not be high and you are less likely to believe them even when they speak the truth.

(Continued)

Modes of Proof	Meaning	Example
Pathos	Has to do with appeals to emotion. In writing arguments, understanding how emotions work helps to make arguments more persuasive. This is a double-edged sword; emotions also deceive and can serve as red herrings.	When Mothers Against Drunk Drivers (MADD) first started their campaigns to change the law in the latter part of the 20th century, they showed pictures of car accidents or severely injured people who drove drunk and had an accident. The images are upsetting and unforgettable. This caught the attention of lawmakers and the general public and led to massive changes across all states. On the other hand, delivering an emotional message with images (such as starving children or abused animals) to raise money is effective but is not always legitimate.
Logos	Has to do with the actual message, argument, statement. This is the rational side of the message.	Making a claim along with a reason and evidence can be most effective. This reflects the logical aspect of the message.

Adapted from Aristotle (1984). *The rhetoric and the poetics of Aristotle* (R. Roberts & I. Bywater, Trans.). Random House.

The third component, though not the last, in Aristotle's rhetorical theory stands at the center of effective reasoning, the enthymeme. In short, an enthymeme is an incomplete syllogism or logical structure—similar to that of Stephen Toulmin's warrant mentioned at the end of Part I. A famous syllogism in popular culture is this familiar argument:

- Major premise: All men are mortal.
- Minor premise: Socrates is a man.
- Conclusion: Therefore, Socrates is mortal.
  - o An example of an enthymeme is an incomplete version of this syllogism:
- Major premise: All men are mortal.
- Conclusion: Socrates is mortal.

Aristotle would say that you sometimes do not need all of the premises in your argument, depending on the nature of your audience. The fact that the minor premise was left out does not change the fact that people generally view Socrates as a man who lived during Plato's life span. Therefore, we do not need to say that Socrates is a man; this is a truth that is assumed. But of course, there are still some people who do not believe that Socrates was actually a man who lived during Plato's time; it is a truth where there is no direct evidence that Socrates lived during Plato's time, though there is much circumstantial evidence that has been derived from numerous historical texts. Putting this into contemporary times, let's try this one:

- All men are mortal.
- Tom Petty is a man.
- Therefore, Tom Petty is mortal.

We know this is true because on October 20, 1950, Tom Petty was born. Most people in the world know him as an American musician and lead singer with the rock band Tom Petty and the Heartbreakers. Most people also know that on October 2, 2017, he died. Now all we have left of his life's work are video and audio recordings and pictures proving that he did exist. Aristotle would ask, do you really need to indicate that Tom Petty was a man? The fact that Tom Petty identified as a man is evident in his work that he did. It is self-evident that Tom Petty is a man; therefore, you do not need that premise in your syllogism. Aristotle indicated that knowing your audience would help you determine how and when to use the enthymeme. This is referred to as enthymematic reasoning. These three aspects of Aristotle's rhetorical theory play a prominent role in any kind of argumentation and the weaving together of rationality.

TABLE 4.4   Three Key Components of Aristotle's Rhetorical Theory

Definition of Rhetoric	Modes of Persuasion/Proof	The enthymeme
"The faculty of observing in any given case the available means of persuasion" (Aristotle, 2001, p. 24)	Ethos Pathos Logos (see Table 4.3)	An incomplete syllogism or logical structure

Adapted from Aristotle (1984). *The rhetoric and the poetics of Aristotle* (R. Roberts & I. Bywater, Trans.). Random House.

Rationalism is based on a reasonable argument. It does not rely on our senses; rather it uses logic, reasoning, and basic modes of argumentation. Rationalism is grounded on the structures of syllogistic reasoning that many students encounter in an introduction to philosophy course or an introduction to logic course. Later in this chapter I will discuss one of the prominent philosophers in the modern era, Immanuel Kant, who wrote a book about pure reason entitled *Critique of Pure Reason*, in 1781. Rational argument is the basis of the U.S. legal system as it weaves together rational argument and empirical evidence, to provide the foundation for the U.S. Rules of Evidence in our court system. Before we move there, we must consider another approach to ways of knowing, traditionalism.

Traditionalism

Traditionalism acknowledges the context of people, relationships, and stories that bring people together in a transactional environment where they make meaning together (Arnett & Holba, 2012). Traditionalism does not receive equal attention in epistemology discourses than the other approaches such as skepticism, empiricism, and rationalism, but René Guénon (1886–1951), a modern French philosopher, identified traditionalism and was considered the main voice of traditionalism for the 20th century (Sedgwick, 2009). Traditionalism emerged as a response to the 19th-century thinkers that began to disconnect from religious and traditional thought, not disagreeing with it but actually ignoring that it was part of the historical landscape, therefore obliterating its existence.

Traditionalism identifies the absence of ground or conventions in postmodern epistemological theories and rejects both empiricism and rationalism (Sedgewick, 2009). This means that traditionalism honors ground, foundations, and conventions in practice or ritual frameworks. René Guénon, the main voice of traditionalism, was critical of having epistemological certainty, pushed back against relying on science for answers to questions, and exposed the loss of foundationalism (Sedgwick, 2009). Traditionalism never rose to the significance as skepticism, empiricism, and rationalism did. Toward the end of the 20th century, contemporary epistemologies emerged as subsets or spinoffs from the three traditional categories of skepticism, empiricism, and rationalism while interest in traditionalism did not grow much at all, especially with the rise of critical theory in postmodernism. A key area in critical theory came from Michel Foucault (1926–1984) and his criticism about foundationalism, which aided the rise of antifoundationalism.

In order to understand major questions pertaining to the problems inherent in epistemology, taking a deeper look at Immanuel Kant (1724–1804) will aid our discussion about the limits of empiricism and the limits of rationalism. Kant was a key figure in the Enlightenment era and the central philosopher to identify what he referred to as transcendental knowledge.

Immanuel Kant, a German philosopher, published widely in history, law, ethics, aesthetics, philosophy, and religion, was a pivotal philosopher of the 18th century, and his work was prolific and had a significant impact on ideas that shaped his particular historical moment as well as all historical periods since his death (Arnett & Holba, 2012). Kant's influence in general philosophical discourse, ethics, and aesthetics in particular is unmatched in depth and breadth (Arnett & Holba, 2012). Immanuel Kant was born in Königsberg, East Prussia, in 1724, which is now Russia. Kant's childhood was marked by poverty. His mother, Frau Kant, was uneducated but very pious and taught him to focus on right action. Kant had five sisters and one brother (Kuehn, 2001). During his school years, he realized the limits of a strict religious system that would not allow him to acquire deeper levels of knowledge or understanding of that knowledge but he did demonstrate a deep desire to learn.

Kant attended the University of Königsberg as a student in theology from 1742 to 1746 but became more interested in math and physics. When Kant's father died, he was left penniless and not able to complete his university education, though he was able to complete it 10 years later (Kuehn, 2001). Kant published works on Isaac Newton (1642–1727), Gottfried Wilhelm Leibniz (1646–1716), and David Hume (1711–1776), but his greatest work came when he published *Critique of Pure Reason* in 1781/1965. Kant continued to publish and work as a professor of logic and philosophy at the University of Königsberg. His interest shifted again to metaphysics and speculative philosophy, which led to other significant publications of *Critique of Practical Reason* (1788/2002) and *Critique of Judgment* (1790/1987). Kant lived until he was 80 years old and died from complications after having a stroke in 1804 (Kuehn, 2001).

Let us look at Kant's thoughts about traditional epistemologies, empiricism, and rationality. Looking at Kant's thoughts about epistemologies does not mean I hold any kind of bias toward his philosophy. I chose Kant to talk about epistemologies because of his major work, *Critique of Pure Reason*, and because other major philosophers often use his work as a starting place for interrogating epistemology in general. He believed that both the empiricists and the rationalists got it wrong—both of them missed the point that by relying only on rationality, which carefully plotted out arguments and evidences in persuasive and rhetorical order, and empiricism, which rested on the assumption that we can observe everything and every truth in existence, that both were simply inadequate. Kant attempted to bridge empiricism and rationality by showing other theorists that their underlying question, "How can we understand the world around us?" was the wrong question to begin their inquiry. Instead, Kant suggested they should be asking the question, "How does the world come to be understood by us?" The world is a priori; it was here first. Changing the question in this fashion allows Kant to suggest we do not try to force an interpretation through our reason or experience because simultaneously there is inclusion and exclusion in both approaches. Instead, to allow the structure of concepts to shape our experiences of objects and things provides for an awareness without occluding or limiting meaning.

Kant stressed the importance of experience though. He stated that "experience is, beyond all doubt, the first product to which our understanding gives rise … . Experience is therefore our first instruction … [but] it is by no means the sole field to which our understanding is confined" (Kant, 1965, p. 41). But because Kant believed that observation, perception, and experience each had inherent flaws in that the structures of each held limits and exclusions, he set out to find a way to bridge them together in a reconciliation of sorts. Up to this point I have not mentioned Kant's revelation about skepticism—which, after reading David Hume's (1711–1776) *An Enquiry Concerning Human Understanding* (first published in 1748/2008), where he laid out his thoughts on skepticism, Kant announced that Hume woke him from his slumber, which encouraged him (Kant) even more to find a way to bring together empiricism and rationalism in a way that counteracts each deficiency. His attempt to do this is in his work, *Prolegomena to Any Future Metaphysics* (first published in 1783/2004), demonstrates this awakening that he famously announced.

Kant laid out a transcendental epistemology that accounted for the limits and problems associated with empiricism and rationality. In *Critique of Pure Reason*, Kant (1781/1965) tried to prove the existence of God, but in the end he could not craft an argument that contained proof of the existence of God. In his attempt to bring together empiricism and rationalism, he found both were insufficient because there are certain phenomena that simply are not observable or arguable. Instead, Kant created a transcendental argument that could counter the weaknesses of both empiricism and rationality. In doing this, he offered a transcendental epistemology. Kant (1781/1965) admitted, "The transcendental object lying at the basis of appearances … is and remains for us inscrutable … [f]or it is of the very essence of reason that we should be able to give an account of all of our concepts, opinions, and assertions, either upon objective or, in the case of mere illusion, upon subjective grounds" (p. 514). Kant indicated that we must be able to account for what we cannot see, and in doing so accept that we must base evidence on transcendental deductions (Kant, 1781/1965).

Kant identified a corrective to empiricism and rationality through a transcendental approach to inquiry that requires the use of synthetic judgments about things that cannot be implied from original experience or observation.

In doing so, he gave birth to a new metaphysics. Kant's (1781/1965) corrective draws these conclusions:

1. Knowledge from "pure intuition," a priori, is "infallible, excluding all illusion and error" (p. 657).

2. Knowledge from empirical and rational approaches is fallible.

3. Kant's new metaphysics allows for both speculative and practical pure reason.

4. A transcendental epistemology "sole preoccupation is wisdom; and it seeks it by the path of science, which ... permits no wandering ... [but can be] discharged[d] only ... aided by a knowledge through reason from pure concepts ... which is nothing but metaphysics" (p. 665).

5. Transcendental knowledge offers ground from which we can communicate (Arnett & Holba, 2012).

Kant's attempt at creating an argument with proof of the existence of God took him to the limits of his own awareness and the problem of epistemology. Recognizing that even he could not manipulate experience and reason to provide an absolute proof of the existence of God led him to discover a new form of argumentation through his own pure intuition and in doing so resurrected a new metaphysics. These problems with epistemology lay the groundwork for inviting and using various other approaches, ways in which we come to a knowing. The next section introduces these approaches common to philosophy of communication inquiry: hermeneutics, semiotics, phenomenology, psychoanalytic, critical, communicological, narrative, dialogical, and ethical.

Introducing Approaches to Knowing

These approaches are not laid out in alphabetical order, but how they are introduced here mirrors how they are laid out in the rest of the chapters in Part II of this book. They are hermeneutics, semiotics, phenomenology, psychoanalytic theory, critical theory, communicology, narrative theory, dialogical theory, and the ethical approach, and they follow in this order:
Chapter 5 – Hermeneutics, Semiotics, Phenomenology
Chapter 6 – Psychoanalytic Theory, Critical Theory, Communicology
Chapter 7 – Narrative Theory, Dialogical Theory, and the Ethical Approach

I chose to group these together in this way because in their chapter discussions I will show intersections and overlaps between the particular approaches. In other words, they somewhat go together while remaining distinctly different in process. I provide the definition for each of these approaches from *The Cambridge Dictionary of Philosophy* (Audi, 1999), with the exception of communicology, which I will define through the ground-breaking and generative work of Richard Lanigan (1992); narrative theory, which I define through Walter Fisher's *Human Communication as Narration* (1989); and dialogical theory, from the integrated works of Martin Buber (1972), Emmanuel Levinas (2000), and Mikhail Bakhtin (1983).

Some approaches or movements within these approaches may be explicitly dealt with in this text. For the most part, this is due to having to make decisions related to scope of an introductory text on philosophy of communication inquiry. While existentialism is certainly a philosophical movement that many students have heard of, it has its influence in a variety of these approaches. If after reading this text you are interested in learning more about existentialism in relation to philosophy of communication inquiry, you can find a discussion of it in the *Overture* book mentioned earlier.

I should also note that as each approach is introduced, I identify particular philosophers and theorists who will be covered in each section. I should note that while a philosopher is selected for and placed in a particular approach, that does not mean their work only speaks to that one approach. For example, In the narrative approach, Paul Ricoeur's narrative theory is discussed. However, more broadly, Ricoeur is considered by some scholars as a hermeneutic phenomenologist. Another example is Emmanuel Levinas, who is a dialogic theorist and ethicist, but he is only discussed in the dialogic approach section. By placing a philosopher in a particular approach, my intention is not to suggest that they are limited to that approach. As mentioned earlier, these are strategic decisions that I am making as part of crafting the story of philosophy of communication. These decisions are also not meant to concretize or totalize any of the philosophers or philosophies. These are merely temporal dwellings for a first look at philosophy of communication inquiry.

Hermeneutics is "the art or theory of interpretation, as well as a type of philosophy that starts with questions of interpretation" (Audi, 1999, p. 377). Of course, there is a rich history of hermeneutics as different philosophers approached questioning a little differently; the practice of hermeneutics evolved from a narrow orientation involving interpretation of sacred texts to a broader vision of expanding "text" to include not only written words but also within the context of human sciences and the "ontological event" between the interpreter and some kind of text (not limited to a book or written word) situated within history/the historical moment (Audi, 1999). Chapter 5 discusses hermeneutics through the lenses of Friedrich Schleiermacher (1768–1834), Wilhelm Dilthy (1833–1911), Hans-Georg Gadamer (1900–2002), and Richard Rorty (1931–2007).

Semiotics is the "theory of signs" (Audi, 1999, p. 833), which is "the philosophical and scientific theory of information-carrying entities, communication, and information transmission" (Audi, 1999, p. 915). Chapter 5 discusses semiotics through the lenses of Charles Sanders Peirce (1839–1914), Ferdinand Saussure (1857–1913), and Umberto Eco (1932–2016).

Phenomenology is generically described as the study of phenomena; however, Robert Audi (1999) explains that it is not quite that simple. Audi (1999) suggests phenomenology is "one of the many contemporary philosophical conceptions" that has become a movement that can go in many different directions, making it difficult to confine to one standard definition (p. 664). In short, for the purpose of this brief introduction, phenomenology studies essences and essentially is interested in "what is 'left behind' after the phenomenological reduction is performed ... . It also considers that the world to be already there before reflection begins" (Audi, 1999, p. 664). Chapter 5 will be an interesting chapter focusing on philosophy of communication inquiry through approaches using interpretation, signs/ representations, and essences; it will also draw from early phenomenologists such as Edmund Husserl (1859–1938), Martin Heidegger (1889–1976), and Maurice Merleau-Ponty (1908–1961).

The **psychoanalytic approach** is often associated with its founder, Sigmund Freud (1856–1939), who developed a process of psychoanalysis, a technique of psychotherapy as well as a mode of inquiry of the "workings of the mind" (Audi, 1999, p. 333). While today the academy understands that Freud might have been wrong often and perhaps sometimes absurd, the fact of the matter is that his inquiries into how the mind works have provided insight into how we live our lives and how we understand ourselves. The psychoanalytical approach seeks to understand the human being and the unconscious, a mind divided against itself, the meaningfulness or meaninglessness, displacement/transference of feelings, sexual motivation, and dream interpretation, and other inner workings of the mind. Chapter 6 explores the psychoanalytic approach beginning with Sigmund Freud's (1856–1939) perspective and expanding through diverse other perspectives, including Jacques Lacan (1901–1981), Julia Kristeva (1941–   ) Michel Foucault (1926–1984), and Jacques Derrida (1930–2004).

Critical theory refers to "any social theory that is at the same time explanatory, normative, practical, and self-reflective" (Audi, 1999, p. 194). Max Horkheimer (1895–1973) is a leading critical theorist from the original Frankfurt School of Critical Theory in the social sciences (Audi, 1999). The Frankfurt School explored and analyzed the developments of state capitalism, family, modern culture, and, most significantly, fascism. In general, critical theories aim toward the emancipation of all human beings instead of engaging in a descriptive process of things as they are—the goal of critical theory is to forge social change. Chapter 6 explores the critical perspective through Jürgen Habermas' (b. 1929) perspective on communicative action.

Richard Lanigan (1992) describes **communicology** as the "discipline which studies human discourse" (p. xv) and situates it as a human science. Lanigan (1992) advocates for a human science platform, which refocuses attention on the "performance and practice of persons communicating at the intrapersonal, interpersonal, group, and cultural levels of context for affective and connotative meaning along with the traditional cognitive meaning orientation" (p. 2). Lanigan (1992) proposes semiotic phenomenology as a "theory and research paradigm for communicology" (p. 3) and admits that communicology as a discipline borrows the phenomenological "method of description and empirical constitution" and borrows from structuralism, the method of "deconstruction and empirical description" (p. 5). In philosophy of communication inquiry, communicology situates itself as a philosophical process of human science. This chapter highlights the work of contemporary philosophers Isaac Catt, Deborah Eicher-Catt, and Igor Klyukanov. Communicology, while borrowing from other approaches, could also serve as the umbrella enfolding all of these approaches to use together as a human science methodology. Chapter 6 will show how the psychoanalytical approach, critical approach, and the communicological approach overlap and intersect, which opens meaningful understanding of human beings in communication together.

The **narrative approach** in philosophy of communication inquiry focuses on Walter Fisher's (1931–2018) narrative paradigm, which we will see overlaps and intersects with dialogical and ethical approaches. The focus in Chapter 7 unpacks Fisher's (1989) understanding of human communication as narration and situates this theory within the human sciences. I will show a distinction between Fisher's narrative theory and other traditional narrative theories from Aristotle (384 –322BCE), Charles Taylor (b. 1931) and Paul Ricoeur (1913–2005). This distinction will blend Fisher's narrative theory to the dialogical and ethical approaches in philosophy of communication inquiry.

The **dialogical approach** in philosophy of communication inquiry is situated within dialogic theories. Chapter 7 focuses on Martin Buber (1878–1965) and Emmanuel Levinas's (1906–1995) dialogic theories. I also include Mikhail Bakhtin's (1895–1975) notion of dialogism and make distinctions between dialogue and dialectic, inviting Aristotle's understanding of them as counterparts. To be clear, in philosophy of communication inquiry, dialogical approaches will also be ethical approaches. Generally, there is no line separating the dialogical and the ethical—they overlap and intersect. They are sometimes discussed as if they are separate, but in human communication they cannot be separated.

Ethical approaches are broad and many. Ethics is generally "the philosophical study of morality" (Audi, 1999, p. 284). To situate ethical approaches within a philosophy of communication inquiry, Chapter 7 focuses on contemporary philosophers, including Judith Butler's (2005) work on identity and interdependence, Sela Benhabib's (1992) communicative ethics, and Hannah Arendt's (1906–1975) political philosophy. Chapter 7 demonstrates how each of these approaches overlap and intersect each other, providing a fuller picture of how narrative, dialogue, and ethics work together in human meaning making.

Part II underscores the value in and opportunities for broadening understanding and cultivating comprehension, which all informs a personal sense of communicative praxis as we communicate to make meaning and we communicate to find meaning. Learning more from Calvin Schrag's communicative praxis can set the stage for how we might use these approaches in our meaning-making processes as human communicative agents.

Connections, Currency, and Meaning

Connections: Communicative praxis can provide signposts for how we navigate what we know, how we know it, and what it means. Calvin Schrag (2003), the George Ade distinguished professor of philosophy emeritus of Purdue University, coined the couplet **communicative praxis** to demonstrate the importance of understanding and explaining the counterparts of interpretation and comprehension in the process of discovery and meaning making. Communicative praxis is strongly tied to public argument, rationality, and ethics in Schrag's philosophy of communication. The word **praxis** is explained by Aristotle who defined it as action that is theory informed. Praxis is intertwined within our communication with and to others (Schrag, 2003). As mentioned previously, Schrag (2003) defines communicative praxis as "an amalgam of discourse and action, interweaving the event of speaking and the history and system of language ... and individual action and history of social practices and institutions" (p. 47). This means theory plays a role in discernment and one's ability to engage in ethical communication practices and behaviors. Communicative praxis opens a reflexive space from which one can respond appropriately to any given situation guided and informed by technical understanding and moral understanding within the particularities of context.

Schrag (2003) states that we express meaning and signify meaning through the experience of communicative praxis. This occurs through a process of **distanciation**, **idealization**, and **recollection**. According to Calvin Schrag (2003), distanciation means to take distance—standing back objectively in order to be prepared to move in subjectively, which births **signative meaning**—the interplay of speech and language within history instead of against history; idealization refers to understanding the idealities of personal ideals, the typification of social action, established institutional goals, and individual and collective ethical norms; and lastly, recollection refers to an accounting for the apprehension of meanings that are not fully known nor completely unknown. Schrag textures recollection within philosophical discourse from other philosophers, including Edmund Husserl's notion of re-presenting, Martin Heidegger's articulation of commemorative thinking and repetition, Paul Ricoeur's understanding of reminiscences, and Hans-Georg Gadamer's interplay with fusion of horizons. Schrag (2003) suggests recollection plays a significant role in the "ongoing dynamics of discourse and action" (p. 64) and our "uses of language and our engagements in social practices invite a comprehension of them through reflection and critique" (p. 72). Schrag suggests we are always entwined and entangled in the work of distanciation, idealization, and recollection.

In the space of communicative praxis, the experience of "critical hermeneutics" involves the workings of distanciation, idealization, and recollection as an ongoing process of discourse and action (Schrag, 2003). This is a dynamic interactive space that engages critical interpretive inquiry where dialogic understanding is cocreated within the interplay of understanding and explanation, leading toward a fuller fruitful comprehension. The space of communicative praxis has a "dialogical consciousness" (Schrag, 2003, p. 158), which Schrag situates as a "holistic and hermeneutical space" that allows for critique, deconstruction, reconstruction, and restoration (p. 158). Schrag resituates rhetoric in the texture of communicative praxis in what he refers to as the "accentuation of discourse and action as for and toward someone" (p. 179); additionally, rhetoric is integral to "the life of communicative praxis" (p. 180) because in the interplay of language there are consequences as discourse and language impact existence from one human being to another.

Schrag notes that discourse and action must be seen as being *about* something (some kind of substance or content), *by* someone, and *for* someone. When you are the speaker, you implicate yourself as speaker, author and actor, and you have rhetorical characteristics. When we enter into a conversation, having some distance from the topic allows new information to emerge. Distanciation invites difference to impact new ideas; idealization allows for possibilities of the ideal to emerge organically from within the conversation; and finally, once idealization occurs, recollection takes up a disposition of an embodied knowing that allows one to make sense out the knowledge that emerges.

For Schrag, communicative praxis always emerges as a recollection with texture. To engage this embodied knowing, one must enter the conversation with distance so that texture and new information can emerge without unproductive bias. Often, it is in the texture that emerges where we truly learn new things and we must remain open to seeing it when it arises. If we are open to learning this embodied knowledge, Schrag (2003) argues we then build on it toward understanding and comprehending, which are two halves that move toward being able to interpret and comprehend something, though Schrag points out that nothing can ever be fully determined.

Calvin Schrag's contribution to philosophy of communication inquiry confronts similar problems with knowing as did earlier philosophers struggling with skepticism, empiricism, rationalism, and traditionalism, as we discussed earlier. But Schrag's (2003) approach is different because he does not presuppose that anything can be known at all, though what he does believe is that embodied knowledge that understands and explains the intertexture between "human action and the fibers of institutional life" (p. 92) open the potential for new ideas to emerge that may be totally unexpected yet relevant for understanding and guiding human interaction toward meaningful outcomes. This becomes important to discourse today, especially with fake news, political upheavals, and rhetorical word play across all kinds of media platforms opening, guiding, and controlling public discourse. Engaging public argument through the lens or space of communicative praxis can provide a constructive pathway to negotiate and test some of these rhetorical challenges.

Currency: For example, the testing of fake news through a communicative praxis lens would require distanciation, idealization, and recollection before coming to judgment about the value of the information or knowledge. Fake news has been defined simply as news that is fake or, more particularly as "false, often sensational, information disseminated under the guise of news reporting" (Burns, 2018), or more complexly referred to as the cousin of yellow journalism, which is a form of journalism that was pervasive in the early days of modern journalism in the 19th century (Burns, 2018).

There are seven types or categories of fake news: satire or parody, non sequiturs or claims that make false connections, misleading content, false content, imposter content, manipulated content, and fabricated content (Burns, 2018). Alison Burns (2018) describes these seven different kinds of fake news in the following way: **Satire** or **parody** content is not intentionally trying to harm any person or situation but it does have the possibility of fooling people who might not understand the dimension of meaning that satire and parody provoke; non sequitur or making false connections usually occurs when the headlines, images, or captions do not support or accurately reflect the content of the piece or article; misleading content is the intentional use of information to frame the report a certain way or to frame an individual with inaccurate, missing, or ambiguous/equivocated information; false content refers to genuine content shared with false contextual information—a mixing of both kinds of information; imposter content refers to content that mixes genuine sources with false or made-up sources, sometimes described as genuine sources being impersonated with made-up sources; manipulated content occurs when genuine information is manipulated to deceive, for example when photographs are manipulated with the intention to deceive; lastly, fabricated content is news content that is 100% false, intentionally designed to deceive. With the proliferation of fake news, engaging in public discourse and argument necessitates the practice of testing public information through the critical hermeneutical space of communicative praxis so that we are able to tell the difference between fake news or news that is not altered, manipulated, or fabricated in some way. This places a burden on the contemporary consumer of information who relies on news and other forms of media to guide decision making.

Consider the news story Alison Burns (2018) highlights in her article, "Dealing With Fake News in the Journalism Classroom" that was published in the journal *Communication: Journalism Education Today*. Burns identifies an article on the internet with the headlines: WHOOPI GOLDBERG: NAVY SEAL WIDOW WAS "LOOKING FOR ATTENTION." Burns indicates that the article began with the comment, "Whoopi Goldberg is in hot water after comments she made Wednesday regarding the Navy SEAL widow who was honored last night during President Donald Trump's historical speech." Burns (2018) continues that the article quoted Goldberg, saying, "She was just looking for attention. These military widows love their 15 minutes in the spotlight," Goldberg said. Burns argued that the problem with the story is that the statement was actually false even though there was a disclaimer at the bottom of the page suggesting, "Anyone who believes this story or any other story on this website needs to read this post." Burns continues that this story had 348 comments and was shared on Facebook over 56,000 time. Burns (2018) reports the instigator of the story was a young person from Florida who created the fake news website called The Underground Report to target "gullible" Trump supporters (p. 16). The creator of the website, which is now down and only slightly searchable in the Internet Archive website (https://archive.org/index.php), stated the website had over 1 million followers within 9 days of creating it (Burns, 2018).

Most people today do not want to be taken advantage of or be found to believe false or misleading information. This means that today, when information is available to anyone, at any time, about anything, media consumers need to be more vigilant in their information consumption and approach everything they read, no matter the source, through a critical hermeneutical perspective. This means engaging the tenets of Calvin Schrag's communicative praxis as an ongoing, regular practice of consuming messages. Additionally, learning to wait before sharing information and only sharing information if the evidence is tested rigorously to be true, real, and actual information that is based within reality and truth to the extent that you can know it is faithful to the **narrative rationality** that Walter Fisher (1989) reminded us is comprised of both **narrative fidelity** (is the information truthful to what you already know or believe?) and **narrative coherence** (does it make sense to the given situation—are there any holes in the story?).

Meaning: Engaging this news story through the lens of communicative praxis could have benefited consumers, pointing them toward the truth and reality of the story. In the space of communicative praxis, taking distanciation, idealization, and recollection would have provided enough insight to not trust the website or the story. Through distanciation, one would take a step back in order to understand the source, read the entire story, not just the headline or any text boxes containing bits and parts of the story, and notice the language used, word by word, to understand the sense of the story (how is the story trying to make you feel?). Through idealization, test the facts of the story; ask yourself, "How do the facts relate to or inform each other? Who is the individual author"; and learn about the credibility or ethos of the author of the website and of the article if it is different. Explore the ethos of the website, institution, or organization that sponsors the site. Through recollection, consider the interplay of language and action and messages in the story, check dates, and notice your own biases as the reader and evaluator of the site and its message. Test the evidence alongside other evidence and or go to other experts for their perspective and comparison with other data already in public discourse.

Through Schrag's (2003) specific critical hermeneutic inquiry, engaging ideas, testing information, and drawing your own conclusions through sound practices within a space of communicative praxis can be your own frontline defense against fake news today. Approaching public discourses where knowledge is assumed and evidence can be produced, manipulated, and augmented without obvious notice through a lens of philosophy of communication inquiry can arm your reading, interpretation, and evaluation practices of consuming information with intellectual humility, caution, and integrity. This ensures the relevancy of philosophy of communication inquiry for public engagement in the 21st century. As our knowledge grows at such a radical rate, we must assume practices that keep us awake, alive, and reflective in an ever-changing mediated environment.

Conclusion

Philosophy of communication inquiry enables meaning making through consideration of what we know and how we come to know it. Problems with epistemology have not changed so much since the time of Plato and Aristotle up through modern philosophical notions of epistemology. However, what is different in contemporary times is the interplay of text, language, culture, image, and sense complicates our hermeneutical prowess. Philosophy of communication inquiry demonstrates the following:

1. Communication begins from an epistemic gathering that is interpreted, understood, and comprehended in some fashion.

2. Knowledge, interpretation, understanding, and comprehension provide the framework from which we test and judge public communication.

3. It is important to understand *how* we come to our judgments, through processes such as distanciation, idealization, and recollection.

4. We should recognize that no knowledge is complete but should not let this limit inquiry.

5. The inherent limits to human knowledge can be addressed through transcendental and hermeneutical approaches that recognize standing within contexts and do not reduce the experience as subjective and less valuable. In fact, this perspective recognizes we are human so we know our limits and how to move beyond them instead of hiding our subjective selves behind the guise of complete objectivity—something that is not possible in human contexts.

6. We remain open to alternatives for knowing what we know and how we come to know it.

Philosophy of communication inquiry relies on knowledge, interpretation, understanding, and comprehension as a mode for making meaning in the world. How we come to know things can vary, but we need to remember that all ways of knowing are incomplete, that there is not one true way of knowing. This is key to realizing there is always more to gain through philosophy of communication inquiry. Epistemology, hermeneutics, and communicative praxis are fundamental possibilities in the process of making meaning that provide interpretive insight to move us beyond impressions and appearances toward seeing a mosaic of meaning guided by experience, interpretation, practical reason, and praxis.

Chapter 5

Hermeneutics, Semiotics, and Phenomenology Approaches

Learning Objectives

1. Identify seminal philosophers and their philosophies pertaining to hermeneutics.

2. Identify seminal philosophers and their philosophies pertaining to semiotics.

3. Identify seminal philosophers and their philosophies pertaining to phenomenology.

4. Apply these approaches to philosophy of communication inquiry through examples.

While we might be aware of how we came to learn something new, do we consider more deeply how the interpretation process informs our knowledge? Even more challenging, how do signs and symbols come to inform our knowledge base and development? In our everyday experience, how often do we see things as they are themselves? How is it that we see everyday phenomena for what it is and not for what we want it to be?

This chapter focuses on different approaches to engaging philosophy of communication inquiry. As mentioned in a previous chapter, there are multiple approaches one can take in philosophy of communication inquiry. Most scholars recognize one approach is not necessarily better than another approach and that they are simply different. Each approach to philosophy of communication inquiry enters through a different lens or entrance, which means that the outcome of the inquiry will likely be either different or will hold differing interpretive texture. The approaches identified in this chapter are hermeneutics, semiotics, and phenomenology. As you will see toward the end of this chapter, I have a particular preference or bias toward one approach over another; however, this is particular to me and my own interests. It is most likely that others will have their own and very different approaches that emerge from their individual preferences.

The important thing to remember when we make an argument for one approach over another is that we provide the basis for that preference—this is where we provide evidence that can be publicly tested. As I mentioned earlier, philosophy of communication inquiry should be about something or some kind of action—that is why certain teachers and philosophers, such as Ronald C. Arnett, advocate the philosophy of communication "of" so that there is some kind of application or implication to the inquiry. This then provides a remedy for the accusations that philosophy is too abstract and not meaningful to living in the world with others; this is the critique we saw attached to philosophical study during the latter part of the 20th century. In no particular order other than my conceptual preference, hermeneutics is the first approach to open this discussion.

Hermeneutics

Epistemology and how we come to know something is not the same mental activity as interpretation. According to Richard Palmer (1969), Friedrich Schleiermacher (1768–1834) established a system of interpretation of sacred texts referred to as biblical exegesis, or biblical hermeneutics. Schleiermacher eventually shifted more toward a psychological approach to hermeneutics, sometimes referred to as romantic hermeneutics. The practice of interpretation evolved and was expanded by Wilhelm Dilthy (1833–1911), who rejected the psychological or romantic focus on hermeneutics and emphasized a method toward a strict systematic approach. Hans-Georg Gadamer (2002) rejected both ways of engaging interpretation, stressed the notion of situatedness, and saw the individual as an "embedded historical actor" (Arnett & Holba, 2012, p. 87). As I understand philosophical hermeneutics, it joins prejudice or bias and respect for the text. Therefore, we acknowledge our bias toward a text; we also respect and honor the text encounter. Respect must guide our engagement with the text.

Gadamer (2002) suggested that bias is present in the questions that come before us because we are embedded within a tradition that has a historical consciousness. It is not possible for one to escape the situated bias that frames our initial understanding. Gadamer suggested that there is no releasement from this kind of situatedness, and he emphasized that what we begin with is what is right before us and is not an abstract truth; it is an embedded truth. So, the certainty of truth is not really what matters because any kind of certainty stands above the situatedness and embeddedness of given contexts, which does not allow shared meaning to emerge if there is any kind of standing above the other. One of Gadamer's main intentions was to rehabilitate the terms *bias* and *prejudice* because by the end of the 20th century both terms became affiliated to their negative connotation instead of remembering the neutral and constructive side to having a bias.

Gadamer lays out philosophical hermeneutics by uniting three essential coordinates: the interpreter, the text, and the historical moment united in dialogic fashion (Arnett & Holba, 2012). Philosophical hermeneutics offers an interpretive alternative to subjective understandings and objective understandings of phenomena. Gadamer situates this alternative in a horizon of significance that allows us to see the embeddedness, giving us information that allows us to interpret with richer understanding.

Philosophical hermeneutics also requires that the interpreter approach a text with respect to the ideas and the positions of others because these ideas and positions shape their interpretive identity. This also guides the engagement with whatever text is under consideration. Recognizing that texts have a life of their own, we cannot bring demand toward the other or toward the text to make the same meaning we already come with (our bias). Gadamer's position on philosophical hermeneutics is squarely centered on the notion of situatedness within a given historical moment because it shifts the focus of attention away from an individual motive toward an embedded historical actor.

Gadamer's description of "historicity of historical understanding" (Warnke, 1987, p. 27) indicates that bias is always present in whatever question comes or emerges before us. The historical situatedness of interpretation actually rejects an emphasis on method and an emphasis on psychological or romantic interpretation because these approaches obscure meaning from the interpretant. Philosophical hermeneutics offers alternative ground for an existential understanding of interpretation—this is where the meaningfulness to human understanding resides. This perspective evolved from Husserl's (1970) "life-world," which insisted on historicity and situatedness in finding understanding and meaning (Warnke, 1987, pp. 36–37). Meaning resides in historically situated tradition, prejudice, and bias that interacts with broader historical understandings and evolving experiences.

Gadamer (2002) started from a position of honor and respect toward the text because he suggested that this kind of position allowed wisdom to emerge from a textured understanding of multiple and competing traditions. This permits the discernment of bias and prejudice to take hold. Gadamer's work provides a pragmatic understanding of how he honored the interpreter and the text within given traditions and within identifying questions and text through a dialogic fusion of multiple horizons. Understanding tradition also means that we gain distance from our biases as we learn about other traditions.

Philosophical hermeneutics offers a dialogical notion of interpretation that acknowledges a pragmatic reality of the fusion of multiple horizons of interpreter and text that is always open to challenge—temporal interpretive realities are what philosophical hermeneutics provides. In human experience, bias or prejudice is inescapable and inevitable. Our bias and prejudice shape our identity; they are also temporal since as we respect all positions and traditions, we make room for altering our biases and prejudices. We accept that there could be many wrong or incorrect interpretations as there could be multiple correct or good interpretations. This means that we need to approach all texts within a framework of respect, which is how we can turn around or away from the impulse to meet the text within our own subjective demand.

Semiotics

The study of semiotics is known colloquially as the study of signs and symbols, focusing on the process of how they work to make meaning. It is recognized that signs and symbols evoke and provoke meaning; they also represent something else that is sometimes obvious and other times subtle. When the study of semiotics is overviewed in general communication courses, often only one or two theories are presented within a narrow framework and students often leave those courses with minimal understanding of the breadth and depth of semiotic influence and studies that have been widely established. For the purpose of this chapter, I will highlight some early origins of semiotic or sign theories taken from ancient, modern, and contemporary philosophers with the understanding that trying to understand signs and symbols and how they work in communication is much older than the early classical texts that provide very early and rugged sign and symbol theories.

Ancient hieroglyphs in both the Eastern and Western world, as well as prewriting cultures that passed on meaning through the oral tradition, both had their own understandings of how signs, symbols, and nonverbal communication made meaning between subjects and passed on meaning to future generations. Those early traditions are incredible in themselves, but for the purpose of this text I want to begin with Aristotle's theory of signs which is contained in his text, *The Rhetoric*. Aristotle (1984) identified two kinds of signs:

1. Natural signs

2. Conventional signs

Natural signs happen in nature, such as the cries of animals, getting a fever, and seeing lightning or hearing thunder. For example, I live in a rural part of New Hampshire and in the summer when we have the windows open all night we often hear the call of the coyotes as the pack surrounds their prey. That call leads to what we hear as screams as they tear apart their prey. Afterward, there is very loud silence as they are finishing eating their prey and moving on through the forest. The first call and then the screaming (as I am describing it) signifies a capture and a victory. In the case of a fever, when my grandchildren had a fever, it indicated they had some kind of infection that required medical attention. This happens naturally when the body is fighting a foreign threat; it also happens during normal bodily processes, for example when a woman ovulates each month. The fever signifies that something is happening in the body and it requires some kind of action even if it just provides awareness to the person. Even lightning and thunder signify the presence of atmospheric disturbance; it could even signify the time of year because often lightning and thunder are not typically associated with winter, though that seems to be changing as we see the consequences of climate change impact atmospheric engagement around the world.

Conventional signs, according to Aristotle, resides in arbitrary associations such as human speech and the alphabet. The linguistic symbols that make up any alphabet were organized in a system for a communicative purpose so that human beings can make meaning together in order to live and create society together. These are not signs from nature; human beings had to arbitrarily make them. St. Augustine's theory of signs, *Theory of Signa Data*, expands Aristotle's earlier thinking. St. Augustine (354–430 CE) was a common man who experienced a lifestyle conversion from living a life away from God to a man who converted toward God; he eventually became a bishop in the Church and a teacher of biblical values and spent the rest of his life as a disciple of the living Word. Augustine (2014) suggested that a sign is a thing that makes an impression on the senses and causes one to think about something else. Augustine explained conventional signs as signs that we exchange for sharing our thoughts. He suggested that spoken words work as correlates of our mental words and that they are things that show themselves to our senses. Augustine would say that a sign is always a sign of something to some mind and having a communicative function is essential; otherwise there is no reason to signify anything. The only reason to signify, according to Augustine, is for human beings to convey what is in their mind (the sign giver) to another human being (sign receiver). These early theories of signs and symbols provided a starting place for more sophisticated theories that tried in minute detail to explain how signs and symbols function within the signification process.

While there are other philosophers who espoused their own perspectives on how signs and symbols work to make meaning, the French linguist Ferdinand de Saussure (1857–1913) laid out a theory of semiotics that would have significant influence on future philosophers and the modern theoretical starting place to talk about how signs and symbols work in human meaning making. Saussure depicted a linguistic sign as a two-sided entity, which he referred to as a dyad. In this dyad there is a signified (mental concept) and a signifier (material aspect of the sign). Since a communication event is a transfer of contents between minds—from one mind to another mind—the signified and signifier are inseparable because there can be no communication without the process of signification. This is a strong absolute statement but until human beings can communicate telepathically from mind to mind, signification is the only way to find meaning in a communication event. For Saussure, signs make up the code of circuits between two or more minds.

The relationship between signified and signifier is also arbitrary, so it is not natural, nor is it found in nature. This is a conventional relationship that emerges, like conventional signs, in agreement between human beings. This means there are agreed-on rules that govern the relationship between the sign and the signifier. Saussure labeled individual speech acts as *parole* and the system of difference between signs as *langue*. In general, Saussure's theory situates significations taking place through linear combinatory relations and paradigmatic relations, which allow for substitutability. For example, this image provides an example for how we might combine different linguistic signs to make different meanings.

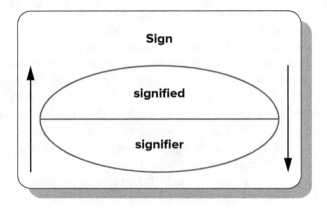

FIGURE 5.1 Saussure's two-sided entity.

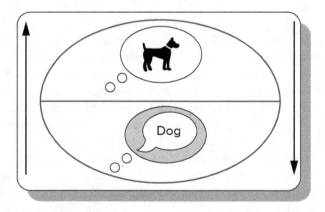

FIGURE 5.2 Saussure's two-sided entity applied (with a dog).

This is just the tip of Saussure's philosophy of linguistics, though it gives us a jumping off place to understand Charles Sanders Peirce's theory of signs. Unlike Saussure's theory, Peirce (sounds like "purse") designed a more complicated theory, one that accounts for the abstractness in Saussure's theory. Instead of a dyadic theory, Peirce posed a triadic theory with more conceptual dimensionality (Hoopes, 1991). Peirce's triad involves three coordinates: representamen, interpretant, and the object.

Peirce

Representamen – this is the sign that has a relation to the object and which needs an interpretant.

Object – this is the actual man who is Peirce.

Interpretant – this involves the sign in the mind as a result of some kind of action or encounter. It involves action, implications, and consequences of interpreting all of these parts of the process.

FIGURE 5.3   Peirce's triadic semiotic model.

The representamen is the sign that stands for something else. In this case, the representamen is the written word, *Peirce*. The object is the man, Peirce, himself; it is the thing that the representamen stands for. The interpretant is the trickiest part of the triad because it refers to the sign that is in the mind, which is the result of some kind of encounter with a sign. In other words, there is more happening that just someone interpreting meaning; it is an embodiment of the sign as it is being experienced. So, the interpretant is more than just me interpreting something. In a broader sense, the interpretant extends beyond me—it includes action, implications, and consequences of interpreting signs. How we interpret signs matters, and my interpretation of something comes in a package of all of these experiences. Additionally, the fact that the interpretant extends beyond a singular interpreter is accounted for by the power that signs have to bring people together or divide them, to initiate war between countries or initiate peace, to liberate countries from oppression and tyranny or to become a totalitarian country. There are also different kinds of interpretant experiences.

According to Peirce, there is an immediate interpretant that is the correct understanding of the sign, a dynamic interpretant that offers a general understanding of the sign, and a final or precise, particular, and specific understanding of the experience (Cobley & Jansz, 2012). For example, when I moved to New Hampshire from New Jersey, I felt like I was seeing the night sky for the first time. Being in a very rural place in northern New England, the night sky and stars are vibrant, bright, and simply amazing. Living in New Jersey near Philadelphia (in the Delaware Valley), it felt more like a city that was always on and always lit up even at nighttime. So, using a starry night as an example, the immediate interpretant, having a correct understanding of the sign, would look at the sky and see precisely the star that the finger points to—this is the correct understanding of the signification. The dynamic interpretant who has a general sense of the sign would look at the sky point in a general sense or general area of the sky, not becoming involved with finding a specific star. The final interpretant points to the sky and looks precisely at the star that the finger points to and realizes that the pointing finger indicates the star is a particular star. There is no general acceptance of the particular star like the immediate interpretant who does not acknowledge their own finger as it is pointing. The final interpretant makes this acknowledgment.

Like Saussure's combinatory sign system, the interpretant has a significant role in the triad for Peirce since it can be placed in a relationship with a further object that then requires another interpretant, which then transforms into another sign/representamen and becomes an unending process. The interpretant can produce more signs because it triggers a chain of associations; this is referred to as unlimited semiosis, which can remove the meaning quite far for an original intent. This can be a good thing or a bad thing; it can be good if you want diverse groups of people to have multiple instances of meaning. It can be bad if your audience instead becomes confused.

This is not the end of Peirce's semiotics, quite to the contrary, it evolves from 10 sign types to almost 60,000 sign types (Cobley & Jansz, 2012). Some of this expansion includes very familiar terms such as the kinds of objects including icons, symbols, and index; the representamen including qualsign, sinsign, and legisign; and the interpretant including rheme, argument, and dicent.

TABLE 5.1   Peirce's Semiotic Theory (in the Context of a Stop Sign)

	Quality Firstness	Brute Facts Secondness	Law Thirdness
Representamen **Firstness** A sign that stands for something else	Qualsign: **This is a representamen made up of a quality** (e.g., a stop sign—the quality of a color, the color red (or redness)	Sinsign: **This is a representamen-existing physical reality** (e.g., a stop sign)	Legisign: **This is a representamen made up of a law** (e.g., the cars that stop at a stop sign or the police officer who conducts a car stop after a vehicle does not stop at the sign)
Object **Secondness** The physical thing itself	Icon: This a sign that **relates to an object through likeness/** resemblance (e.g., in relation to the stop sign example, a red octagon)	Index: This is where the sign **relates to an object in terms of causation** (e.g., a stop sign causes vehicles to stop before proceeding)	Symbol: This is where the sign **relates to an object by means of convention** alone (e.g., human beings in a shared geographical area agree stop signs should be the shape of an octagon and be red/white)
Interpretant **Thirdness** The interpretant is not just the interpreter; it is comprised of other aspects of actions, relationships, consequences, etc.	Rheme: This is when the **sign is represented to the interpretant as a possibility** (e.g., an idea or concept; the interpretant understanding something is needed at the intersection to move traffic in an orderly and safe fashion)	Dicent: This is when the **sign is represented to the interpretant as a fact** (e.g., some kind of descriptive statement, such as seeing that there are four stop signs at this intersection; the interpretant, in the awareness of being there and looking at the intersection, comes to understand the facts about how the intersection looks/appears)	Argument: This is where the **sign is represented as a reason** (e.g., people take turns in order of who gets to stop sign first when there are four stop signs at one intersection; the four stop signs are the argument that people take turns)

Note: These terms designate relationships that occur within experiences as one is experiencing them (Chandler, 2002; Cobley & Jansz, 1993, 2012).

These are not the only philosophers or linguists who have made significant impact to semiotics. Some others include Roland Barthes (1915–1980 CE) and Jacques Derrida (1933–2004 CE). Barthes contributed to semiotics and other kinds of analysis during his career. Notably, he observed and critiqued popular culture by deconstructing cultural practices. He did this by identifying connotations of everyday living and identified how these connotations were carefully constructed (Chandler, 2007). You can find examples of these critiques in his book *Mythologies* (1972).

Derrida, who I discuss in a later chapter, is often referred to as the father of deconstruction, which is one way to express semiotic analysis. In deconstruction, Derrida indicates that a sign always refers to other signs, so there is no final sign that refers to itself (Chandler, 2007). Deconstruction also looks at the relationship between signs as hierarchical, and Derrida critiques this hierarchy. For Derrida, deconstruction means that there is no determinable meaning in any kind of sign system. Derrida identified the concept of *differance* which points to the notion that meaning is endlessly deferred (Chandler, 2007; Derrida, 1978). While I cannot list everyone who has contributed to semiotics in this introduction, and I recognize these two mentions are brief in themselves, I must mention one more, Umberto Eco (1932–2016 CE). Eco, known as a philosopher, literary critic, cultural critique, linguist, and novelist (to name a few), is often credited with introducing "interpretative semiotics" (Bianchi & Vasallo, 2015). By this, Eco emphasizes the role of interpretation (and translation) in the semiotic process. Eco wrote many books on semiotics and interpretation; for a more robust discussion from Eco himself, you might read any of the following texts: *A Theory of Semiotics* (1976), *The Role of the Reader* (1979), *The Limits of Interpretation* (1990), and *Interpretation and Overinterpretation* (1992). In these texts, Eco focuses on the various kinds of limits that the reader imposes on any text (Bianchi & Vasallo, 2015). As you might guess, semiotics involves many considerations, perhaps because the only way human beings can communicate is through some kind of sign or symbol system. Identifying these systems and striving to understand how these systems work is an unending pursuit for those curious enough to think deeply about how human beings come to meaning, which is, for the most part, mediated in some fashion.

We might ask ourselves why semiotics is so important to how we understand meaning making. I believe it is helpful to understand how representation works because when we communicate we want the opportunity for communicating to effectively shape understanding. Realizing how representation works can make our lives easier if pay attention to how signification and representation shape our communicative messages. There are other theories of semiotics not covered here, but this section is designed to provide the reader with a general exposure to the topic so that we can understand how these approaches inform philosophy of communication inquiry. Before moving to that discussion, exploring phenomenology will be helpful to our application section at the end of this chapter.

Phenomenology

Phenomenology is a way to inquire about the human experience by asking questions about what and how things present themselves to us. We typically hear the word *phenomenology* used to describe a philosophical movement that is known to focus on how human beings perceive the world around them. From a strict scientific method perspective, phenomenology is not too scientific since it depends on perception. However, phenomenologists suggest that phenomenology provides an alternative to strict science; they recognize that there are questions that science cannot ask, and I suggest there are questions that science cannot answer (Wiener & Ramsey, 1995).

The systematic inquiry outlining phenomenological perspectives begins with Edmund Husserl (1859–1938), who provided a starting place to describe the experience of how we perceive phenomena that forms before us. A phenomenological perspective explores what we see as phenomena disclose themselves to us. It might initially feel like you are only looking at a part of something, and you might be, but phenomenology allows us to see what we could not before or have not yet (Holba, 2014).

Components or aspects of phenomenology include, in no particular order, appearances, attention, absence/presence, intention/intentionality, and cointending. As we explore things phenomenologically, we engage in some practice of reduction and cointending. Here is an explanation or description of each aspect, which can provide a conceptual frame for understanding what phenomenology can mean or be perceived and how it can work in our own experience.

Appearances

Appearances alone are even more significant to us today because of the fragmented experience of technology in our culture, our social spaces, and in our personal lives. Appearances are disclosed to us through rapidly changing technologies and through our rapidly changing social fabric. I will even suggest that as we become more and more fragmented in our lives due to the advances in technological evolution, phenomenology is even more important than it has been in the past when the world was slightly more predictable than it is today.

Appearances come and go; they are transient—they appear and disappear; change and shift our perceptions and provide perspective outside of the conventions we carry with us every day. They represent the fragmentation of part and whole, they are present and absent, and they interplay together. A deeper phenomenological understanding of appearance suggests it is a phenomenon of consciousness and it is structurally different than illusion (Merleau-Ponty, 1967/2013). In the structure of appearances there are sensory characteristics that are undeniable.

And while they exist through sensory perception, they could also be illusions, an interval between one thing or another, or an illumination of one's consciousness (Merleau-Ponty, 1967/2013). This means appearances can be true or false or they can be neither true nor false. A false appearance can actually cover over a present reality just as likely as the true appearance has the potential to unveil or reveal a present reality (Holba, 2014). Perhaps in all of its questionability, appearances should be taken at face value as we recognize they are transient as well. Maurice Merleau-Ponty (1908–1961), a 20th-century phenomenologist, provided us with a great example of this characteristic of appearance through his example of a cardboard box. He stated that a large cardboard box might seem heavier to one person than a small cardboard box. He stated that if we confine ourselves to these pre-judgments without picking up the box and determining this through our senses, we limit the possibility of our perceptions. He suggests that this kind of intellectualism, privileging our thinking minds over bodily experience, creates illusions that are not based in sensory knowledge (Merleau-Ponty, 1975). In his example, the cardboard box is not measured but we accept the appearance of the box as a sensory experience and draw a conclusion or make a judgment about it. In this case, appearance happens before judgment. It can be true or not true. When we consider appearances, they should be considered against the backdrop of other constants or things that are more reliable or regular or consistent.

Martin Heidegger (1962) reminds us that appearance actually has a double meaning. First, it suggests that "appearing, in the sense of announcing itself, as not-showing-itself; and next, that which does the announcing ... that which in its showing-itself indicates something which does not show itself" (p. 53). This means appearances reveal a referential relation as it can only be fulfilling when it shows itself to the other. Heidegger (1962) tells us that when considering temporality, the "past" either means that something is no longer here, or present, or it means something is present but actually has no effect on the present moment. An example of this could be referring to the remains of some historically relevant location in history. There is extraordinary ambiguity in what it means in the present—while it belonged to an earlier time, the presentness of it cannot really be understood without acknowledging the experiences and realities of the past in which it had a vibrant existence. In phenomenology, we recognize that that parts can only be understood against the backdrop of the appropriate wholes or differing wholes. In order to make sense of these appearances, we must seek and reflect on the relational exchange between part and whole. This is relatable to one's attention, which is another aspect of phenomenology that is central to a phenomenological perspective.

Attention

Attention in our awareness becomes awakened by our perception of appearances. Attention recognizes what we perceive—what is already there; our attention does not create what is there. Attention acts like a search light in total darkness (Holba, 2014); we perceive objects and sensations that are already there—our attention is called to these sensations. There is also a secondary kind of attention that we refer to as a recalling of some kind of sensation or experience that we had already.

Furthermore, "to pay attention is not merely to further clarify pre-existing givens; rather it is to realize in them a new articulation by taking them as *figures*" (Merleau-Ponty, 1967/2013, p. 32). When we attend to things that call out to us, or when we are recalling previous attentions, these perceptions are preformed horizons embedded into our intellect consciousness (Holba, 2014).

When attention meets intellectual consciousness, this is an approximate attention. Approximate attention occurs when our attention is moved toward something else; it is actually moving within an intellectual openness within dialogic conditions that confront and divert us to something else. In other words, our attention is met with otherness and is open to the possibilities of otherness and its effect on our sensory experience. Attention revels to us the interplay and exchange between presence and absence.

Presence and Absence

We cannot see anything without the backdrop and interplay of between presence and absence. Presence puts a burden on our space and time. Absence is not empty but demonstrates an adaptability. They are independent and at the same time they coexist. Simone Weil (1952) suggested that we need self-diminishment (absence of the self) in order to have attention toward ourselves or some kind of attentive presence. This suggests that we cannot have any kind of presence without some kind of absence. Our attention is what intellectually discloses the interplay of absence and presence. Weil (1973) provided an example of the interplay of absence and presence in her description of the image of Jesus Christ on the cross. She stated that its presence pointed to the absence of Christ within an overabundance of presence of love. Our attention is drawn to this interplay, for example, during holy week leading up to Easter in the Christian faith tradition. During this week, the death and resurrection of Christ is remembered, through the iconic crucifixes and statues of Joseph and Mary that frame the altar area and the purple cloth that covers the crucifix and crosses. When one visually perceives the purple cloth, attention is drawn to the absence of Christ while at the same time there is anticipation of Christ's resurrection and return, both figuratively and literally.

People have their attention on the purple cloth with an understanding that on Easter day the purple cloth will be removed, symbolizing the presence of Christ again, even though he is not physically present. The purple cloth points our attention to the interplay between Christ's presence and absence. So, the idea of being present means to be present in participation with something else; this means there is a present involvement in the idea or thing that is being experienced. Beyond appearances, attention, and presence and absence, the aspect of intentionality is central to the phenomenological experience.

Intention/Intentionality

Schrag and Ramsey (1994) work out a pathway toward how to engage phenomenological research or engagement. They suggest that in doing this intellectual work, we do it with a consciousness of something, or an experience with something; it represents what our attention is directed toward or pulled to—whether an object, an imagination, or a memory. Every act we do with some kind of intention has an intending object to it. Now, this kind of intention or intending is different than the kind of intending we have when we act toward a goal. In this case of phenomenological intending or intention, we are concerned with our focus of intention, having a conscious relationship with an object of some kind. In this practice of intention, we engage in a practice of reduction to some extent. This means that one turns away from the thing and turns toward the meaning of the thing—the essence of the thing.

There are six commonalities that can be universally applied to the phenomenological method:

1. There is a difference between the natural world and the philosophical attitude; there is also difference between philosophy and science. This accounts for two perspectives found within the phenomenological movement: first, that phenomenology is concerned with questions of epistemology, and second, the position that phenomenology is concerned with questions of ontology.

2. Even with this first difference, there is a necessary and complex relationship between science and philosophy.

3. Reduction is a necessary part of phenomenology, but each phenomenologist will engage reduction differently, some radically and others lightly.

4. Intentionality is central to a phenomenological approach in philosophy.

5. Phenomenology is focused on exploring the question about meaning and Being of beings and how Being of beings and the Being of the world are constituted.

6. A level of intuitionism is essential and part of phenomenological inquiry that manifests in a primordial form; this is what Husserl refers to as the principle of all principles (Audi, 1999).

Phenomenology leads us to question the reliability of perception—as it should, since perception is always unique to the individual. There are many perspectives on perception, and each perspective focuses on at least one of these three principles: (a) the common factor principle, (b) the phenomenal principle, and (c) the representational principle (Fish, 2010). The common factor principle assumes that different experiences are either more or less correct. This is easily applied to visual experiences we encounter daily. We come into contact with things in our perceptual field every day and we make judgments about the correctness of what we believe we perceive. The phenomenal principle assumes an if-then format such as if this appears before me sense perception, then there is something there that possesses a particular observable quality.

For example, if I perceive a red violin, then I know that there is something, a violin, that exists, that has a quality of redness. The representational principle assumes that all visual experiences are deliberate since something draws our attention to it. So, the thing that appears before us intentionally calls out to our intention as a representational object of something. Even when we think carefully about these principles, they are really incomplete or at least leave us with even more questions about our perception.

Considering intentionality in the phenomenal range of experience, we might say that the world is actually not a place where human experience occurs. Instead, we might see it as a place where one turns toward experience as it comes before us. We self-implicate as a response to stimuli as an intentional perceptual behavior. Sensations or sense perceptions are experiences we have between ourselves and the object of our intention. In this way, the perceptual is always something that comes in the middle or between things—it is embedded in a particularity. Our perceptions are always incomplete though, and they inescapably include, involve, and negotiate presences and absences through the action of cointending.

Cointending

When Merleau-Ponty (1975) clarified his perspective on perception, he suggested that if we cannot see the phenomena in its entirety, we must consider how we describe the nonvisible aspects of the phenomenon. He argues, in this case, we only have the possibility of something since we cannot see it. Merleau-Ponty provides an example of a lamp. He states that part of the lamp is hidden or obscured from our vision and that this makes parts of the lamp unseen. While we cannot see inside the lamp or the bottom or back of the lamp in our perceptual field, we must anticipate those unseen parts. This means we cointend the unseen parts (Sokolowski, 2000). When we cointend the parts against the backdrop of the whole, it is the synthesis of the cointending that constitutes its unity, giving meaning to our perception of the object.

We might say that perceptions are paradoxical since the thing we are perceiving exists only when this possibility is cointended. A helpful example of this reminds me of the story about the mystical place, Brigadoon. In the story, the village of Brigadoon does not exist until it is perceived by a human being—the human being encounters it as it appears (from nowhere) before him. When the village is perceived, at the moment of the cointended perception, it is then that the mythical/mystical village comes into existence. This creates a paradox of the immanence and transcendence in human perception. The experience of perceiving Brigadoon demonstrates immanence because Brigadoon is not alien to the one who perceives it since it is contained in the mind of the perceiver; perceiving Brigadoon acknowledges transcendence because it is comprised of something more than what is present in the perceptual field of the observer. The observer must cointend the village of Brigadoon since much of it does not enter into the observable perceptual field.

Another example I like to use when I talk about cointending is that of my violin. When I see my violin I see only part of it. When I open my case, I see my instrument but only the top of it and part of the sides of it. I also see my scroll, which is cylindrical, and that allows me to see the top and bottom tip at the same time. Though, I cannot see the back of my instrument and I cannot see inside the f-holes where I cointend the sound post, which is what actually makes the wood vibrate and make sound. I know that to fully perceive my violin I need to see all of its parts; without cointending, I only perceive the possibility that is before me. By cointending what is outside of my perceptual vision, I complete my picture and understanding of the object in my incomplete perceptual field. When we think about this, our perception is always incomplete and we are always practicing cointending.

There are those who critique cointending as having a conflict to this reasoning. It is the interplay between presence and absence that cointending engages; some scholars suggest the problem occurs with the idea of absence that cannot co-create a presence (Sokolowski, 2000). However, I prefer to see presence and absence as a unity of contraries, such as Buber identifies in his dialogic philosophy. This kind of critique does not impact the idea that we usually never see the whole—there is usually some kind of absence present within our perceptual field.

Connections, Currency, and Meaning

Connections: These three approaches, hermeneutics, semiotics, and phenomenology, can sometimes become intertwined as the experiences in these approaches can overlap and bleed into one another. This is evidenced when we hear philosophers talk about semiotic phenomenology or philosophical hermeneutics as having an embedded interpreter within a phenomenological experience. So, even though they can sometimes overlap, we identify them specifically based on how they are engaged by the human seeking understanding and meaning.

Currency: These approaches are relevant today because we realize that human experience is not purely scientifically measurable. Each of these approaches acknowledges that there are multiple contours of meaning that unfold to us in different ways. These approaches allow us to experience these differing ways, which can ultimately provide us with new or expanded understanding of the life world around us.

Meaning: When we seek understanding, we begin with a question that discloses itself to us as it comes into our perceptual field through different phenomena. For example, what kind on interpretant am I and what is involved in the process I choose if I want to make sense out of a particular experience I have when I want to go out to the voting booth during election time? To think about my choice, my vote, and how my vote contributes to me as the interpretant with a desired outcome and the byproduct that emerges from my actions is necessary for understanding myself and others. I can apply a hermeneutical, semiotic, or phenomenological approach that might or might not end up with the same outcome if I employ each approach in my attempt at understanding. For example, to make a decision about which local candidate I will vote for to serve on the board of directors for my electric company, I might use a hermeneutical approach, understanding that I am the interpreter of a public text that is situated in a given historical moment. I would want to understand the historical moment and what is important to the environment, the community, and the practices pertaining to how we generate our energy locally. I would also digest any text associated with the candidates running for the board. These texts could be their candidate statements, their record of service and decision making if they are already on the board; or I would seek out other kinds of public texts, such as social media texts, newspaper texts, meeting minutes (which is only good if they are already on the board) from whatever current position they hold at whatever company their work. I would respect these public texts and evaluate them as best to my ability to consume the narratives I encounter. I would also need to understand my motives, my biases, and my interests in participating in the vote.

Approaching my vote through a hermeneutic entrance might look very different from a semiotic lens, especially if I choose to interpret the signs, symbols, indexes, rhemes, arguments, and other uses of language made by all of the candidates. I would need to question what kind of interpretant I am and what is involved in the process I choose. I could also instead choose to enter phenomenologically and consider what is present, what is absent, what appearances emerge from each candidate, and where my phenomenological focus of attention goes when I consider each candidate as well as where are they focusing their attention. It is very likely that the approach taken to my decision will determine how my vote ends up. Being aware of these different approaches enables me to give due diligence to all of my decisions from how I will explore candidates to what my vote ends up being. In this case, the approach taken in this process holds a lot at stake.

Conclusion

This chapter explored three approaches in philosophy of communication inquiry that take into account the text, the subject, and the environment in the process of how we come to know, to understand, and to make meaning of our experiences. As human beings, in most cases, we have autonomy and agency in how we make meaning of our experiences and what we come to know. The next chapter explores three other approaches that have interconnections and similar assumptions: psychoanalytic theory, critical theory, and communicology.

Figure Credits
Fig. 5.1: Source: https://www.cs.princeton.edu/~chazelle/courses/BIB/semio2.htm.
Fig. 5.2a: Adapted from https://www.cs.princeton.edu/~chazelle/courses/BIB/semio2.htm.
Fig. 5.2b: Source: https://commons.wikimedia.org/wiki/File:Dog.svg.
Fig. 5.3: Adapted from Paul Cobley and Litza Jansz, *Introducing Semiotics: A Graphic Guide*, p. 23. Copyright © 2012 by Icon Books LTD.
Fig. 5.3a: Copyright © 2014 Depositphotos/macrovector.

Chapter 6

Psychoanalytic, Critical, and Communicological Approaches

Learning Objectives

1. Identify seminal philosophers and their philosophies pertaining to the psychoanalytical approach to philosophy of communication inquiry.

2. Identify seminal philosophers and their philosophies pertaining to the critical approach to philosophy of communication inquiry.

3. Identify seminal philosophers and their philosophies pertaining to the communicological approach to philosophy of communication inquiry.

4. Apply these approaches to philosophy of communication inquiry through examples.

H ow do you know when there are structures of power and injustice embedded within systems and structures that organize society? Have you ever thought about what kind of privileges or restraints you have experienced within institutions, organizations, or other systems in society? How can we identify, reveal, and eliminate unfair or inhuman structures that seek to limit human engagement and human opportunities? Just because we say we are a democracy, does that mean everything in our society and culture is fair, unbiased, and equitable?

This chapter explores the seminal philosophers and philosophies that have made significant contributions to philosophy of communication inquiry through interrelated approaches, including the psychoanalytic approach, the critical approach, and the communicological approach. These approaches are important to the philosophy of communication inquiry because they are oriented toward examining power structures in language, politics, and power in the meaning-making process. Some commonalities among these three approaches include the influence from the Frankfurt School, which was a sociological and philosophical movement that became part of an institute for social research in Frankfurt Germany at Goethe University, which was forced to close during the Nazi party reign and eventually moved to the United States and attached to Columbia University in New York (Audi, 1999). The school emphasized a critique of modernity and embedded structures in capitalism.

As mentioned in previous chapters, I have selected just a few philosophers and philosophies oriented within each approach based on their currency in philosophy of communication literature today. Of course, in a different historical moment and from a different author, these choices could be different. I chose these particular philosophers and philosophies because contemporary philosophers of communication have been influenced by them and are presently engaged with them. The main philosophers included in this chapter are Jacques Lacan, Julia Kristeva, Michel Foucault, and Jacques Derrida for the psychoanalytic approach (it should be noted that Foucault and Derrida would fit in several other approaches perhaps better than they fit here due to the focus of their work aligning well with several other approaches including hermeneutics, phenomenology, semiotics, and ethical—but they also explicitly recognize the value of the psychoanalytical approach to philosophical inquiry in their own work, so I included them here to provide texture to the discussion on the psychoanalytical approach. I talk about this later in the discussion on Foucault); Jürgen Habermas for the critical approach; and Richard Lanigan, Deborah Eicher-Catt, and Igor Klyukanov for the communicological approach. I begin with the psychoanalytic approach.

Psychoanalytic Approach

The psychoanalytical approach in philosophy of communication focuses on the unconscious mind and how the unconscious drives actions, experiences, and thought. This approach relies on the idea that human behavior and one's response to experience is a consequence of past experiences that have become forced, stuck, or pushed into the unconscious mind. Many sources attribute the origin of the psychoanalytical tradition to Sigmund Freud (1856–1939) and his systematic development of psychoanalysis in the treatment of various kinds of neuroses (Audi, 1995). I introduce Freud here to open our discussion on the psychoanalytical approach to demonstrate a key perspective that did have influence across other psychoanalytical thinkers. This does not mean that Freud's thought is the foundation for this approach. In fact, having any kind of foundation, to some scholars, philosophers, and theorists associated with this tradition, is rejected.

Sigmund Freud was an Austrian psychologist and neurologist known for his study of hysteria, the unconscious mind, the displacement and transference of feelings, psychosexual development, and sexual motivation (Audi, 1999). Freud identified theories of neuroses, repression, and dream interpretation; he also developed a system of psychoanalysis that was ultimately questioned and replaced with another approach to psychoanalysis by Carl Jung (1875–1961), a Swiss psychologist. Jung's system of psychoanalysis diverged form Freud's approach because it was based on the collective character of the unconscious and on archetypes (Audi, 1999). The archetypes Jung identified were generally archaic and universal patterns that underlie human nature and constitute elements of the collective unconscious (Audi, 1999); these archetypes include the great mother, father, child, trickster, hero, and wise old man or woman. Jung also identified archetypal events such as birth, death, separation, marriage, as well as identifying archetypal motifs or themes, such as the apocalypse, the creation story, sacrifice, death, and resurrection.

While Sigmund Freud was a psychoanalyst, he was also sometimes considered a philosopher; however that attribution is not shared by the philosophical community. However, his work in psychoanalysis did influence the philosophies of Jacques Lacan (1901–1981), Julia Kristeva (1941b.), Michel Foucault (1926–1984), and Jacques Derrida (1930–2004). Because Freud's work influenced, to some extent, Lacan, Kristeva, Foucault, and Derrida, each of whom are also associated with structuralism, post-structuralism, semiotics, or phenomenology, this section discusses the implications of their philosophies to the philosophy of communication inquiry.

Jacques Lacan

Noted as a philosopher of French structuralism, Jacques Lacan, influenced by psychoanalytical thought, built off of Freud's understanding of the unconscious mind while shifting away from the idea of being biologically determined by libidinal instincts and drives. Instead, Lacan moved toward a semiological structure concerned with how language has its own "logic of dreams, fantasy, and symptom" (Kearney & Rainwater, 1996, p. 329). This shift represents a combination of Sigmund Freud's psychoanalytic theory and Ferdinand Saussure's (1857–1913) semiological insights. Lacan called for a radical reinterpretation of Freud's psychoanalysis and suggested one cannot assume an authority of conscious ego because of his perspective of the "split subject" (Kearney & Rainwater, 1996, p. 329). A split subject is a divided self—a reflection of desires of others (Kearney & Rainwater, 1996). However, Lacan (1991) suggested that the conscious ego is always trying to keep the illusion of its unity intact. The ego does this by engaging in narcissism so to avoid noticing the fragmentation (Lacan, 1949). Acknowledging the symbolic nature of language allows one to separate from the imaginary ego. Through language, the split subject is forced to acknowledge and confront its own division. Lacan (1949) suggested that trying to conceal this fragmentation and lack was misguided, and he called out Freud for situating himself within ego psychology. Lacan deeply dissected psychoanalysis and critiqued it as being sometimes dangerous because it implies there is a cure for this illusion and also implies the infallibility of the analyst (Kearney & Rainwater, 1996). Having gone to medical school himself, Lacan believed that to understand the unconscious desires in dreams, or the outcomes of symptoms, there needs to be more artful inquiry and less scientific emphasis.

Jacques Lacan's contribution to philosophy of communication is broad. For the purpose of this discussion, focusing on the "mirror stage" offers a good introduction to his psychoanalytic approach to his philosophy of communication. The mirror stage that Lacan (1991) described is based on a relation between experiences that are disconnected, discordant, and "in pieces" while at the same time offering a unity in which it is merged and repaired although keeps the subject alienated (p. 50). Lacan (1991) described the relation between this fragmentation and unity as a dialectic that undergirds "every level of structuration" of the human ego—this means that it forms and shapes human communicative engagement, for better or worse. Understanding this dialectic helps one to better make meaning with and from the subject's communicative behavior.

Understanding the relationship between the subject and the system that the subject uses to represent a communicative idea "is at once divorced from his/her means of representation but at the same time is constituted as a subject by that means of representation" (Cobley & Jansz, 2012). This means, for Lacan, that language is actually outside of the subject, which severely limits what the subject can express, and what the subject expresses is far from what the subject actually intends to express or communicate. This involves challenges in all communicative intentions. Therefore, the subject relies on signification to communicate even though Lacan would see the subject as being dominated by the signifier—the thing that signifies (Cobley & Jansz, 2012). This means that the signified would slip underneath the signifier, giving primacy to the signifier (Chandler, 2002). Lacan spent a lot of time examining these semiological constructs in order to broaden his psychoanalytical practice and theoretical understandings because he believed it is only through language and communication that psychoanalysis occurs. Not only is studying these sign systems important to communicating to others, it is essential to understanding the psychoanalytic process, which helps the subject understand themselves and their relations to others and the world around them.

Julia Kristeva

Julia Kristeva is known for viewing language as a "critical fulcrum in a wider cultural domain" (Kearney & Rainwater, 1996, p. 289). This means that she extended linguistic analysis to cultural systems of signification. As a French linguist, novelist, and social theorist, Kristeva also practiced psychoanalysis; she is presently retired and professor emeritus at the University of Paris Diderot. She is well known in structuralist and post-structuralist thought, feminist theory, critical analysis, semiotics, psychoanalysis, and as a novelist. During the course of her scholarly career, Kristeva won impressive awards including the Hannah Arendt Prize for political thought; she is also the founder of the Simone de Beauvoir Prize (Jardine, 2020). Her contribution to the academy and to social and cultural thought is significant. Like many other philosophers and theorists in this book, I chose to include Kristeva in this chapter for her contribution to the psychoanalytic approach.

Kristeva's integration of the psychoanalytic approach to her social and cultural theorization is not without criticism. In the early 2000s when focusing on male adolescence, she indicated that a male adolescents' need to believe in ideals is central to their development but when those ideals are shattered, they resort to nihilism. Her critics complained about her allegiance to psychoanalysis and its reliance on a heteronormative bourgeoisie and emphasis on the individual psyche, discounting social and political forces

(Jardine, 2020). Kristeva's supporters came to her defense, but others still resisted her work wrongly assuming she thought male adolescents commit terrorist acts for no other reasons. This is simply not the case.

While Kristeva's body of work is prolific, for the purpose of this chapter, I am going to focus on her concern and question that drove her inquiry into the crisis that she observed in western civilization. She described this crisis as a result of the assault from media and technology on human subjectivity (Jardine, 2020). During the 1980s and 1990s, Kristeva wrote theoretical books about the sense of the human condition and its unending state of being in permanent crisis. Her book, *New Maladies of the Soul* (1993) was one of her strongest books emphasizing the need for the psychoanalytical approach to be used to think about these social conditions and understand these maladies better in order to help individuals suffering with this crisis, recognizing media technologies are not going away. Her theoretical books were explicitly focused on the psychoanalytical way of approaching social and cultural criticism, she turned to writing novels as another way of examining these aspects of the human condition.

Her perspective on linguistics is infused with the psychoanalytical approach as her semiotic theory focuses on the subject as "embodying unconscious motivations" and "an articulation of the signifying phenomenon as a dynamic productive process" and not a static sign-system which other linguists and semioticians modeled (Audi, 1999, p. 477). One of Kristeva's most significant contributions to philosophy emerged out of her book, *Revolution in Poetic Language* (1984), where she integrates psychoanalytical, linguistic, semiology, and literacy approaches to examine the symbolic and the semiotic. She distinguished the symbolic from the semiotic in that the symbolic designates the system of rules that govern denotative and propositional speech. The semiotic (which is different from Saussure's semiotics) isolates an "archaic layer of meaning" that is not representational nor based upon any relations between signs (Audi, 1999, p. 478). For Kristeva, the symbolic and semiotic are two dialectical modalities in the process of how one comes to meaning. Augustine Perumalil (2009) suggested Kristeva's notion of semiotic resonates with Freud and other psychoanalytical thinkers' notion of the infantile pre-Oedipal influence and Lacan's pre-mirror stage. This is tied to natural instincts within a field of emotions that exist within language.

As a practicing psychoanalyst, it is clear that psychoanalytic thinking informs Kristeva's philosophical endeavors and theoretical approach to meaning and understanding. This is just a snapshot of her work and influence in the field of philosophy of communication. Her philosophy spans multiple approaches integrated with the psychoanalytic framework. Richard Lanigan

(1992) indicates she is a "summary theorist whose work (following from Lacan) on the symbolic, the semiotic, and the chora spans all categories ... her commentaries on, and analysis of, [e]xistentialism and [s]tructural [l]inguistics, along with phenomenology and semiology (including the practice of discourses as rhetoric)" provide insight and texture to her work (p. 77). Kristeva's influence within the psychoanalytic approach is multifaceted and can be integrated across other modalities of meaning exploration. The next two philosophers, while not explicitly part of or described as psychoanalytical philosophers, recognize the value of the psychoanalytic approach and its complementary contribution to other approaches in the search for meaning. Their philosophy also, like Kristeva, spans across multiple approaches toward finding meaning, making it difficult to isolate them as one thing or another. I start with Michel Foucault and then move to Jacques Derrida.

Michel Foucault

Michel Foucault is not a psychoanalytical philosopher but his perspective on this approach is valuable; this is the reason why he appears in this chapter and section. Let me explain. Foucault set out to be a historian, not a philosopher (Strathern, 2000) but by the end of his historical and philosophical inquiry journey, many now consider him to be a hermeneutic phenomenologist due to the influence Fredrich Nietzsche's philosophy made on his thinking about the human subject living in the world with others. However, Nietzsche was not the only thinker who influenced Foucault's thinking. Foucault also has been labeled a structuralist thinker, which does align with certain periods of his work, though he "does not fit unproblematically with such pursuits of structural analysis as Levi-Strauss or Saussure" (Kearney & Rainwater, 1996, p. 336). Foucault could also be included in the next discussion on the critical approach since he emphasizes critique of social structures, however, I decided to include him here, no matter how unorthodox it might be, because he explicitly discusses, along with Derrida who we discuss next, the value of the psychoanalytical approach to meaning and understanding. Now, much of his thought focused on the relationship between power and knowledge, hidden or latent power structures, and how these structures organize and control human social structures. The themes of power and knowledge and hidden or latent power structures that govern human experience necessarily impact all human experience. Foucault recognized the tensions that influence human interactions may also force or push experiences into the unconscious mind. Foucault's work then, as a historian, provides an archaeology of sorts to unearth these hidden power structures that liberate those less able to see the truths in their own existence. Foucault acknowledged how psychoanalysis informs and aids in the process of philosophical analysis (Spector, 1973). In *The Order of Things: An Archaeology of Human Sciences* (1994), Foucault stated that psychoanalysis offers a critical function in the process of understanding the human (and human sciences) in that its task is to bring out the discourse of the unconscious to consciousness. In fact, he stated that "psychoanalysis advances and leaps over representation ... and thus reveals ... that it is possible for there to be system (therefore signification), rule (therefore conflict), norm (therefore rule)" (p. 374). Foucault (1994) stated that this approach had been dismissed as Freudian mythology, but the reality is that it is very useful in the process of philosophical analysis and taps into what other approaches might miss. In short, Foucault is not a psychoanalytical philosopher, rather, he acknowledges quite strongly that a psychoanalytic approach informs other approaches and provides additional meaning that is complementary to other approaches in philosophical analysis. Foucault's work provides significant importance to communication and the philosophy of communication inquiry no matter what label is attached to his work because of the "trenchant critique of universal truth" (McKerrow, 2018). This means that his critique of the existence of universal truth was vigorous and acutely sharp. This perspective provides the background for his analysis of the relationship between power and knowledge (McKerrow, 2018). According to philosopher and scholar Raymie McKerrow (2018), there are four key terms that emerge from Foucault's philosophy central to communication: power/knowledge, relations of power, freedom, and **problematization**. For example, McKerrow (2018) synthesizes Foucault's concern about the nature of relationship between power and knowledge and suggests that it is not really the relationship that matters as much as understanding what happens to create one or the other as a condition of change. While power creates knowledge and knowledge creates power, what really matters in this dynamic is how one becomes a condition of change over the other. Understanding this in the relationship is paramount to how human beings engage with one another, which is tied to his philosophy of communication ethics.

McKerrow (2018) explains how Foucault's understanding of the relation of power is embedded in our relationship with others through power shifts. Foucault also suggests that power is something that exists between self and other though it is not a possessional relationship (McKerrow, 2018). Instead, it is a phenomenon that can be either destructive or constructive—destructive in the sense that one controls the other and constructive in the sense that good intention might produce something previously not possible (McKerrow, 2018). Foucault criticized power structures between people when it involves abusive action or behavior and he celebrated power between people when the power is used supportively and constructively.

Another key term for Foucault is *freedom*, which is often constrained in varying degrees across varying environments. He argued that when there is no freedom and no possibility for freedom, there is no power. He suggested that power can only exist and operate when there are conditions of the possibility of freedom—without the possibility of freedom, to have absolute control and authority over another person is entirely something other than power that is worse than power. It is a totalization of subjugation of the other (McKerrow, 2018).

The last key term that McKerrow (2018) identifies as central to Foucault's philosophy of communication is *problematization*. Foucault (1982, 1999) believed that questioning the taken-for-granted structures in society could open possibilities for change that are necessary for moral and ethical engagement with others. He believed that we should question, reexamine, and reconsider assumptions, practices, policies, and other forms of rules and laws to determine currency and relevancy in given historical moments or time periods. Without questioning our practices through time, errors in judgment or irrelevant practices occur and harm people. This key aspect in particular is tied to an ethics of existence for Foucault that manifests in communicative practices and communicative behaviors.

The question that guided Foucault's philosophy of communication inquiry, presented by McKerrow (2018), is, "What ... constitutes the human subject—what makes a person this particular subject rather than another?" (p. 168). Another question that also arises in Foucault's work is "What is the nature and purpose behind truth-telling and why is it an important feature of how one acts in the world?" (McKerrow, 2018, p. 169). Foucault's questions are deeply ontological as he focused on understanding human behaviors—both physical action and communicative action. Interrogating perspectives, practices, and prerogatives was the first step for Foucault, never taking for granted underlying motives and relational ties between people. Building on this semiotic aspect in the psychoanalytical approach is the work of Jacques Derrida.

Jacques Derrida

Like Foucault above, some may argue that Jacque Derrida (1930–2004) does not belong in this section. Though, Derrida, like Foucault, did acknowledge the importance of the psychoanalytical approach to philosophical inquiry. The decision to include Derrida here in this chapter and section is due to his outspokenness about the value of psychoanalysis to interpretation and understanding. In Derrida's (1998) book, *Resistances of Psychoanalysis*, he argues that psychoanalysis as a practice and approach to understanding has not been fully examined and that by resisting it, we might miss its value and lose opportunity for some kind of meaning. Admittingly, I already mentioned Derrida in the previous chapter in the semiotic approach; his early work can be characterized as post-structuralist and postmodern philosophy. His work uncovers relations between words and structures that hide a latent hierarchy making certain terms subservient to other terms—most people are unaware of this relationship. If we consider the power hidden in language so subtlety, we see how it subordinates people to those structures of power and authority. Derrida spent a lot of time addressing resistances to the psychoanalytical approach in an effort to re-enliven attention to it as a way of philosophical inquiry, and while not necessarily a psychoanalytical philosopher himself, he devoted much of his philosophy to discussions with Lacan and Freud. For this reason, I decided to include Derrida here in this chapter and this section. Jacques Derrida is one of the most widely known controversial philosophers to have emerged from the 21st century, being criticized as either a charlatan or a supreme thinker (Kearney & Rainwater, 1996). He broadly rejected logocentrism, referring to words and language as the authority for reality, and devised strategies that we have come to call deconstructionism, which gave him the label father of deconstruction, to reveal the weaknesses of logocentrism (Kearney & Rainwater, 1996). Of course, the label itself had no meaning for Derrida. Derrida studied phenomenology through and with the great works of Edmund Husserl, Martin Heidegger, Emmanuel Levinas, and Paul Ricoeur. Prolific himself as a writer, philosopher, and literary critic, he attacked the **metaphysics of presence** (using presence to determine truth and reality and not acknowledging what is absent or hidden), **logocentrism** (privileging words and language to reflect reality), **phonocrentrism** (privileging speech over writing), and **signification** (representation or conveying meaning of language) (Kearney & Rainwater, 1996). He is known for developing the construct of *différance*, which is a neologism that reveals what is different and what is deferred (Kearney & Rainwater, 1996). Additionally, Derrida challenged loaded oppositions that have an already dominant term or part. He challenged the privileging of presence over absence, nature over culture, masculine over feminine, and literal over metaphorical in the process of human meaning making (Chandler, 2002).

Derrida understood communication broadly. He viewed communication as not just the transmission or exchange of linguistic signs but rather communication as an event, an action involving movement, force, and emotions

(Cooren, 2018a). This broader understanding is textured and goes beyond any singular speech act or utterance. While people do communicate by transmitting and exchanges messages, the contextual features of a communication event include human beings as well as spaces and technologies that far exceed communication as an utterance or speech act (Cooren, 2018a). According to François Cooren (2018a), Derrida recognized "the iterable character of what makes communication im/possible, i.e., marks, traces, signs, utterances, texts, gestures, etc." (p. 118), but he also believed that this iterable character can be compared to machines, in that they have some kind of autonomy that allows them to express and unfold what they are supposed to do in a conventional way.

One of the most significant contributions to meaning making in Derrida's philosophy focuses on the notion of *différance*. In his essay *"Différance,"* Derrida (1973) suggested that *différance* is neither a word nor a concept; he suggested that it is a strategic note or connection that indicates a closure of presence. In pursuing the meaning of *différance*, Derrida (1973) turned the question on itself and suggests that before we ask the question, what is *différance*, we question the questions themselves and the form of each question. He suggested that *différance* is derived from the starting point of being present—of what is present. Acknowledging what is present asserts a power that results in differing, thus creating *différance*. Thus, Derrida (1973) stated *différance* is active discord that allows for questioning of authority and recognizing that language is built on power structures. To understand and make meaning within the obstructions inherent in language and speech, we should be questioning these structures and questioning our questions that we bring to them.

Derrida's theory of communication can be considered an invitation to the "spectral or ghostal character of our world" (Cooren, 2018a, p. 118). This means communicative effects and gestures make themselves present in person and in virtual spaces through traces, marks, utterances or signs. We no longer conceive our communicative terrain as a physical terrain where human beings talk with one another—Derrida rejects this logocentrism and asks us to illuminate the traces, marks, and signs that are not captured conventionally through utterance and writing.

Critical Approach

The critical approach to the philosophy of communication inquiry harkens back to critical theories that emerged from social theories seeking to explain, normalize or be practical and self-reflexive (Audi, 1999, p. 195). Critical theory describes the relationship between the ideas undergirding social conditions and social practices and negatively evaluates these conditions and the outcomes of the practices. In short, there are embedded nontruths that provide the framework for particular social conditions and practices that deceive and control populations of people (Audi, 1999). The term *critical theory* was first used by Max Horkheimer in his description of how critical analysis came to be notably known as the Frankfurt School (previously discussed at the beginning of the chapter). The Frankfurt School started as a group of philosophers who focused on critiquing culture and a group of social scientists mostly affiliated with the Institute for Social Research, who centered on engaging in social and political critique (Audi, 1999). Some of the key names associated with the Frankfurt School include Max Horkheimer (1895–1973), Theodor Adorno (1903–1969), Erich Fromm (1900–1980), and Walter Benjamin (1892–1940). The Frankfurt School is known for transforming Marx's critical philosophy into a way of engaging in critical philosophy, integrating traditional philosophical reflection with the explanatory aspects of social science research (Audi, 1999).

Max Horkheimer's thought focused on identifying the relation between philosophy and social science; he also provided a clear definition and outlined the framework for developing a critical social science initiative (Audi, 1999). He emphasized the need to rethink one's epistemologies to the sociology of science (Audi, 1999). The second and third phase of the first generation of the Frankfurt School emerged through Adorno's writings that focused on expanding the critical perspective to aesthetic experiences and their imitative relation to nature (Audi, 1999). In reaction to Adorno's contribution to the latter parts of the first phase, a second generation of critical theorists emerged who spent their careers building on the early critical theorists. One of the most influential philosophers of communication in this generation is Jürgen Habermas, who laid out a theory of communicative action and discourse ethics.

Jürgen Habermas

Jürgen Habermas (b. 1929) argued for a new normative foundation in the social sciences and a return to interdisciplinary research (Audi, 1999). He emphasized a theory of communicative action and positioned a theory of discourse ethics. The emphasis in his theoretical approach was placed on truthfulness and authenticity. This situates Habaermasian discourse ethics in a deontological framework which, according to Pat Gehrke (2018), identifies eight standards that contribute to creating the ideal speech situation.

Gehrke organizes these eight standards into three general principles: (a) the principle of noncontradiction; (b) the principle of giving an honest argument; and (c) the principle of equality.

For Habermas, these principles are intrinsic presuppositions that any person contributing to discourse should have when they engage in speech acts. The act of not subscribing to and embodying these principles is a contradiction and fails to meet the normative claims of public discourse (Gehrke, 2018). The argument might still persuade the public, but the argument would still be invalid if there is a contradiction (Gehrke, 2018). This is an almost insurmountable goal to reach, to have everyone in public discourse adhere always to these principles, and Habermas recognizes this. However, it is helpful to remember that these are for the ideal speech situation, something we should all strive for as we consider how our communicative impact influences others.

Habermas's understanding and analysis of communication focused on developing norms of discourse that are outside of traditional hegemonies. He sought nondominating structures and encouraged a broader understanding of reason, especially so that more people had the opportunity to participate in public discourse. Habermas believed very strongly that emancipatory change in human culture lies in communication and discursive rationalities and practices (Audi, 1999).

Characteristics of a Habermasian public sphere engulf a multiplicity of meaning because of its open public nature and the accessibility to multiple realms of engagement. This setting is not limited to a physical setting. Instead, it is a space where individuals come together to talk about ideas, share information, or complete a task—this could be a physical or virtual space. Jürgen Habermas sought to develop a theory of communicative action situated within a setting that provided for an "ideal speech community" that was devoted to conditions of rational discourse (Herrick, 2005, p. 236). For rational discourse to exist, Habermas noted two characteristics for this to occur. The first characteristic is **communicative competence**, which is acquired through *phronesis* or practical wisdom (Habermas, 1987). The second characteristic is **communicative rationality**, which Habermas suggested is everyday language used by people to defend their opinions (Habermas, 1984). Communicative competence and communicative rationality paint a portrait of an ideal speech community in which public relations can be practiced.

Habermas's ideal public space is constructed on the basis of a rational order that allows individuals the freedom to engage discourse as equals. In this type of communicative sphere, individuals are provided the opportunity to speak to one another, having equal availability of information and an abundance of it, so that the range of information is emancipating for each person (Habermas, 1984; Herrick, 2005). The availability of information, or truthful information, is central to Habermasian rationality (Habermas, 1984). Critics question how one determines the truth of information. Habermas responds logically, suggesting that claims are subject to evaluation of proofs through refutation and the process of communication in general (Habermas, 1984). So, the question of truth is not really a stumbling block to Habermas. The more important aspect of Habermas's argument is the interaction process for critical argumentation that opens critical discourse for individuals to evaluate information on their own. This allows one the opportunity of shaping a common place where there is a shared understanding of a particular topic and a commitment to truth, suitability, relevancy, and good faith. This activity of opportunity is the rhetorical heart of Habermasian theory. Necessary for this rhetorical heart to function is the idea of communicative competence.

Communicative competence is an idea connected to Habermas's (1987) universal pragmatics. The idea behind communicative competence is the underlying condition creating the environment for rational communication to emerge. Generally, there are three elements to Habermas's (1987) idea of communicative competence: (1) a truth claim, (2) hearer understands and accepts the speaker's intention, (3) speaker adapts to hearer's world view. Habermasian communicative competence is based on the following elements: Whatever is spoken or uttered is true, the speaker is trustworthy and authentic, the utterance is worthy or has value, the utterance is considered a fitting response, and the utterance is intelligible and understandable. Any disagreement about the truth of a claim should lead to discourse or argumentation that should lead to a resolution. Habermas's idea of communicative competence is comprised of a partnership between wisdom and eloquence as the ground for a competent citizen, leader, and communicator.

The three elements of communicative competence opens the opportunity for emergences of communicative rationality. If the three elements of communicative competence are present, communicative rationality can be met. Communicative rationality involves these conditions: (1) the discussion is unrestrained, (2) all participants have the right to speak, (3) a set of norms and expectations should be in place to ensure the equal conditions of rational discourse, and (4) participants overcome their individual subjective perspective (Habermas, 1984). This kind of communicative engagement is not oriented toward a competition—it is focused on coming to a successful outcome. This means it is about achieving shared understandings, being open to criticism, and being able to pivot in one's perspective (Habermas,

1984). Communicative rationality has the potential to create a public sphere that is open and worthy of being trusted and useful.

Habermas (1984) argued that utility of reason and discourse should be a primary method for addressing human problems. In application, public relations practice often deals in human problems (Dezenhall, 2003). Reason and discourse could be sound conditions for public relations practice. In application, the practice of public relations can be thoughtful and effective by engaging reason and inviting discourse. No longer should the practice of public relations involve one-sided monologue. Rather, if public relations aims at building reputation, addressing a crisis situation, or providing evidence in support of a particular political candidate, using sound reason and being open to discourse, can offer a respectable and equitable path toward those means. Public relation practices that emphasize an aesthetic experience grounded in truthfulness can help to recuperate criticism of questionable practices because the notion of an aesthetic experience is a social contract bound by responsibility to and mindfulness of the other. Reason and discourse engaged as an aesthetic experience can enhance the reputation of the practice of public relations in general.

Public sphere theory, in general, holds that the best way to conceptualize a public is as a discursive construction (Finnegan & Kang, 2004). For example, Seyla Benhabib (1992) posits a theory in which human beings engage other human beings as "particular" others in a discursive environment. G. Thomas Goodnight (1982) identifies the public sphere as being within discursive discourse itself. Gerard Hauser (1999) illuminates discursive communication within a reticulate public sphere. The idea of a communicative aesthetic experience is a discursive space that invites notions of dialogic scholar and literary theorist Mikhail Bakhtin's (1990), **heteroglossia**, referring to a multiplicity of voices coming together to cultivate a fully negotiable consummated experience. Many of these theories, such as Benhabib and Bakhtin's theory, aligns well with interpersonal communication, and while public sphere theory involves the public political realm, there are aspects that overlap, especially when negotiating outside of the public forum to prepare for engagement in the public forum. These kinds of discussions occur often and regularly, though they are not highlighted or discussed openly. But if one is effective in one's interpersonal capacities, the hope is that one can use those capacities in their public, political engagement.

Thomas Goodnight (2007) describes Habermas's philosophy as a critical philosophy of communication that explores why human beings have a sustained confidence in communication that can explain, explore, repair social exchanges and cultural understandings that occur when communication fails. There are theoretical challenges that impede and inform philosophy of communication—these challenges are engaging multiple ways of communicating (technologies), and this communication occurs within complex, competing, and sometimes unintended conditions of social, institutional, individual and collective environments—ever coming to encounters with rhetorical disruptions and surprises while attempting to feel fully connected and responsive to the every day we must encounter.

Habermas developed a sophisticated, elaborate and worldwide-ranging philosophy of communication that continues to challenge, puzzle, frustrate, provoke, engage, and inspire his public that grapples with his theory of communicative action that paves a way for communication in challenging and diverse conditions (Goodnight, 2007). The Enlightenment period in Western history has been hailed as a time of great awakening of ideas, inventions, and mass literacy. However, Habermas critiques the Enlightenment as being comprised of communication failures that structurally embedded errors in reason and power-driven oppression. Goodnight (2007) argues Habermas's theory of communicative action attempts "overcome" the failures of the Enlightenment, which he refers to as the "dark night" of reason (p. 92).

Today we are challenged by multiple communication technologies and platforms that are situated within technological complexities that fragment and fracture traditional forms and structures of communication. What Habermas does is try to help us communicate more effectively, efficiently, and ethically within our political and technologically contentious environment.

A somewhat narrower perspective on the critical approach suggests it provides an alternative way to think about a particular history or phenomenon. We can use a critical approach to guide human thinking, perception, discourse, and action by seeking those emergent questions within particularities of historical moments. We can learn from looking critically at histories and see how they have changed over time. A critical stance is important to philosophy of communication because we need to interpret and reinterpret our environments and how they are engaged in order to more fully understand. Taking this critical distance broadens awareness and vision, allowing one to see the emerging questions and the horizon within which they are situated. From this position of distance, developing a critical perspective allows one to be attentive to questions and deliberate around those questions and the terrain of responses across perspectives. Critical theorists and critically focused historians understand that critical insights emerge only when we look through other or contrasting perspectives. The communicological approach enfolds both the psychoanalytic and critical perspectives and explicitly expresses a broader approach.

Communicological Approach

A communicological approach to the philosophy of communication inquiry has a broad framework that includes the integration of multiple other approaches. At its broadest conceptual understanding, communicology is considered a human science (Lanigan, 1992). Richard L. Lanigan, the executive director and fellow of the International Communicology Institute and university distinguished scholar and professor of communication, emeritus, at the School of Communication, Southern Illinois University, has held several positions of distinction in various scholarly organizations leading philosophy of communication inquiry and has received numerous honors and awards for his contribution in the study of communication across various subfields from national and international venues. Lanigan (1992) broadly defines communicology as the formal study of all of human discourse. Lanigan argues that communicology represents qualitative research in the communication discipline. This section begins with the scholarship of Richard Lanigan and expands the discussion with the contributions of contemporary philosophy of communication scholars Deborah Eicher-Catt and Igor Klyukanov, both of whom are former students of Richard Lanigan, and each of whom have unique communicological perspectives of human communication and the unfoldment of meaning.

Richard Lanigan

Richard Lanigan (1992) cites communicology as not something new in the field because philosophers have been engaging in philosophical discourse about human communication for centuries; though, Lanigan's project is to bring together the qualitative human science approaches to understanding human communication under the umbrella term of communicology. He makes a specific distinction between communicology as a "qualitative and human signification" as opposed to the quantitative and technological reference of "cybernetics," "communications," and *"informatiques"* that emerges from systematic social science and scientific research in the field (p. 3). Lanigan (1992) offers some familiar starting places to discuss communicology, starting with semiotic phenomenology as a theoretical and research paradigm for communicology, noting that it has its origins in the domain of philosophy. Semiotic phenomenology is often privileged over other approaches to understanding human communication since it is a useful approach for both human sciences and social sciences. Chapter 5 introduced semiotics and phenomenology in a general context; Lanigan provides a deeper and more sophisticated discussion of semiotic phenomenology in his book *The Human Science of Communicology* (1992).

As a discipline, Lanigan (1992) suggests communicology borrows from other approaches. He states that communicology borrows the method of phenomenological description and phenomenological reduction from phenomenology; he also states that he borrows from structuralism the methods of deconstruction and empirical description. I intentionally did not include structuralism as an approach in this book, although Saussure's theory of linguistics is noted as structural linguistics. However, as a larger umbrella term, structuralism is a method that implicates human culture as having structures and systems that undergird all of human action, human thinking, human sensibilities, and human perception. It certainly does have importance to how we understand human communication. Structuralism also overlaps the critical approach to human communication, understanding, and meaning making. This is why I noted earlier in this textbook that I made certain choices about what to include as far as approaches are concerned, and the point that someone else might consider including other approaches. Philosophy of communication inquiry, as an open system of inquiry, affords these intentional choices to be made.

Lanigan (1992) provides particular definitions of phenomenology and semiotics as he highlights semiotic phenomenology. For example, he defines phenomenology as "an examination of the discursive models of being human and ... the examination of normative logics as communicological theory"; he also defines semiotics as "the examination of human models of discourse and ... the examination of normative logics as communicological praxis" (p. 7). These definitions focus specifically on the processes of human communication and theory-informed communicative action.

The International Communicology Institute's website describes communicology as a human science discipline that uses logic-based research from semiotic phenomenology to study human consciousness and behavioral embodiment of discourse across landscapes of human interaction: art communicology, clinical communicology, media communicology, and philosophy of communication. The rest of this section highlights some of the contributions to the communicological perspective through the work of contemporary philosophy of communication scholars Deborah Eicher-Catt and Igor Klyukanov—I chose these scholars because they represent interesting focus of attention to language, from a semiotic phe-nomenological perspective within a communicological framework. They are not the only scholars doing this work, but they are some of the most well known in the discipline.

Deborah Eicher-Catt

Deborah Eicher-Catt is professor of communication arts and sciences at the Pennsylvania State University York campus. One aspect of her philosophy of communication scholarship is that it exemplifies a communicological feminist perspective, adding dimensionality to her philosophy on language, semiotics, and phenomenology. For example, in her essay, "The Myth of Servant-Lead-ership: A Feminist Perspective," she conducts a feminist interpretation and understanding of servant leadership grounded in a semiotic analysis of the gendered language used to describe and constitute the model of servant leadership (Eicher-Catt, 2005). She explores the rhetorical language and connotations that epitomizes paradoxical language that accentuates and normalizes gender bias (Eicher-Catt, 2005).

Deborah Eicher-Catt (2010) also demonstrates communicological sophistication in general semantics through her perspective that the relationship between our experiences and consciousness is not one-di-mensional and if we cannot see this relationship any other way, we limit the potential for understanding that particular relationship as multidi-mensional. Eicher-Catt (2010) suggests speech is not simply speech; she states that speech involves bodily gestures that include expressive and perceptive capabilities. In her examination of E-prime, which is a way of engaging the English language without the usage of any form of the verb "to be" (e.g., be, is, am, are, was, were, been, and doing) to "destabilize any taken-for-grated acceptance of language and discourse ... conceptualiza-tion," she suggests it serves as an extensional device in general semantics (Eicher-Catt, 2010, p. 18). This perspective views writing as an embodied gesture that functions phenomenologically and semiologically, which moves writing toward a postmodern perspective on language and discourse that recognizes the process and product of writing as being reversible and exhibits a reflexive relationship between presentation and representation (Eicher-Catt, 2010). Lanigan (1988) suggests this is a both/and instead of an either/or consideration. Eicher-Catt (2010) holds a multidimensional postmodern perspective on language reflecting an emphasis on the process and product of discourse, which offers a richer appreciation of how human beings communicate within a speech community—it's not just noise. She also suggests this perspective accentuates orality and writing as both embodied events of culture.

Igor Klyukanov

Igor Klyukanov is a contemporary communication scholar and philosopher who teaches at Eastern Washington University and who interrogates the nature of communication. Klyukanov (2012) understands communication has been theorized in many different ways, including but not limited to storytelling, deliberation, making arguments, and translation across cultures. One of the ways he interrogates communication is through an ethical lens of self and Other beyond a simple reciprocal relationship. Klyukanov (2012) penetrates deeper into the meaning between communicators and explores what it means to be "existentially bound" to the Other in the midst of interpretation and signification. Because nothing is ever static, Klyukanov considers the best way to understand this communicative relationship between self and Other is to see it as a process by which meaning is temporal. Therefore, in human conversation there is intersubjectivity and reciprocity that is perpetually reified and abused. He raises the question of the philosophy of communication ethics into the foreground of how we think about our communicative relationships with others.

Klyukanov (2010) has a naturalistic and evolutionary approach to communication through a communicological framework, invoking themes of semiotic, hermeneutic, and phenomenological analysis. He unfolds an integral understanding of communication consciousness that reaches into the essence of communication arriving at the heart of communication, love. Ultimately, he suggests that essence of meaning occurs in the identity between one and the precondition of the possibility of a predicate, which means that the meaning we find occurs in the self-reference—in between the subject and the predicate. Language is the vehicle to identity and meaning.

Connections, Currency, and Meaning

Connections: These approaches to philosophy of communication have a good bit in common in that they question assumptions, authority, preconceived meaning, and established foundations of human communicative interactions in public and private realms of engagement. Often philosophy of communication scholars integrate these approaches in their inquiry and applications to lived experience because each approach opens meaning in different ways, providing a broader perspective as well as remaining open to revelation and discovery of new and renewed understandings. We know that the more open one can be to seeing possibilities and the more we question those fixed understandings that we have, we become empowered to grow and see things in different and new ways.

Currency: If we look at a problem in the public domain, we can find value in understanding the problem from any of these approaches. For example, as the time of this writing, the Coronavirus, COVID-19, is the biggest story on all of the news channels, with regular daily local and national press conferences. The coverage is nonstop and pervades almost every aspect of issues and stories that are made newsworthy. Take for instance, the question of whether President Trump should be tested for the Coronavirus since he had come in contact with someone who had tested positive for the virus. For days, Trump stated numerous times when questioned about being tested that he did not feel he needed to be tested. Reporters and analysts continued to press him about his decision because they could not understand how his decision was appropriate for the situation, especially since it contradicted what experts were saying about who should and should not be tested.

By approaching this issue from either of these positions, psychoanalytical, critical, or communicological, we can see how meaning is shaped and eventually would change the situation. From both a psychoanalytical position and a critical position, the resistance to be tested for the virus at a time for acute pandemic response had the appearance of contradiction, denial, and positional power overreach. From a communicological position, President Trump had no other choice when pushed about his resistance to being tested.

Meaning: For a few days, none of this made sense. The only way for the president to communicate presidentially would be to do exactly what the public health officials and the medical experts were communicating—get tested. For a president to act presidential one must recognize that meaning occurs in the identity between one (the president) and the possibility of a predicate (to act presidential), which means the meaning we find in the question of testing occurs in the self-reference—in between the subject and the predicate. The president had no other choice but to be tested; otherwise, most Americans would not be able to understand his resistance to test and thus creates a contradiction for observers. Meaning emerges through communicative action in response to doing what makes sense logically, critically, and communicologically.

Conclusion

This chapter explored important philosophers and philosophies that are often associated with the psychoanalytical, critical, and communicological approaches to philosophy of communication. These approaches are interrelated because they are oriented toward examining power structures in language, politics, and power in the meaning-making process. These approaches might question assumptions, authority, preconceived meaning, and the notion of foundationalism; they open meaning in new ways by remaining open to revelation and discovery, and they offer the possibility of reinterpretation and identification of renewed meanings. Likewise, the next chapter opens meaning but from a different set of approaches, which are narrative, dialogical, and ethical.

Chapter 7

Narrative, Dialogical, and Ethical Approaches

Learning Objectives

1. Identify seminal philosophers and their philosophies pertaining to the narrative approach to philosophy of communication inquiry.

2. Identify seminal philosophers and their philosophies pertaining to the dialogical approach to philosophy of communication inquiry.

3. Identify seminal philosophers and their philosophies pertaining to the ethical approach to philosophy of communication inquiry.

4. Apply these approaches to philosophy of communication inquiry through examples.

What is it about human communication that makes our connections to others life affirming and life giving? Why is it that we make sense out of our circumstances through our connections to other beings? What is our ethical and moral responsibility to the other? Why is it that we ought to care for the other as we care for ourselves? Or, do we?

In the last chapter, I introduced you to three approaches to the philosophy of communication inquiry involving the psychoanalytical, critical, and communicological perspectives/approaches. We saw that there were interconnections between each of those approaches. In a similar way, this chapter explores the significance of **narrative**, **dialogical**, and **ethical** approaches to philosophy of communication inquiry. Similarly, this chapter identifies philosophers and philosophies that have shaped these approaches and how we study them. It is also the case that I chose particular philosophers to discuss in the same fashion as in previous chapters, and I acknowledge that these are not the only philosophers of substance and I could have chosen many others. But for our purpose, I believe these philosophies and philosophers have made significant contribution to the philosophy of communication inquiry. In this chapter, the three approaches are narrative, dialogical, and ethical. The philosophers and their philosophies selected for this discussion are Charles Taylor (1931–), Paul Ricoeur (1913–2005), and Walter Fisher (1931–2018) (for narrative); Martin Buber (1878–1965), Mikhail Bakhtin (1895-1975), and Seyla Benhabib (b. 1950) (for dialogical); and Emmanuel Levinas (1906–1995), Martha Nussbaum (b. 1947), and Judith Butler (b. 1956) (for ethical). As I mentioned in other chapters, choosing to include these particular philosophers for this chapter reflects my biases toward their work. Some of these philosophers could easily be situated in other approaches but I find them relevant to this chapter and these particular approaches. As I introduce each philosopher, I make my case for why they are in this section. Beginning with the narrative approach, we focus on the significance of stories and how they inform philosophy of communication.

Narrative

A narrative begins from a speech act that is engaged and vetted by multiple and competing perspectives. Through this process the speech act becomes a story that includes players in the story (characters); some kind of background imbued with relationships, environments, and experiences; and a direction of some kind as a result of communicating within the environment and with one another (Arnett & Arneson, 1999). From the initial speech act, a story emerges when it is agreed on and shared among the characters or people.

From the perspective of philosophy of communication, narratives provide the backdrop of stories that illuminate relationships in a given historical moment. A philosophy of communication begins with the assumption that multiple ideas and stories come together to create a narratival picture that suggests some stories are accepted and some are not (Arnett & Holba, 2012). Some stories are overlooked; some stories are hidden. Other stories can be outright rejected. Whether a story is accepted relies on one's beliefs, attitudes, and values, all of which come together and create a moral point of view that guides the individual discernment process in their interactions within the narrative they are situated or in new narratives individuals explore or seek to join. Narratival multiplicity allows one to expand their perspective and see beyond their own narratival limits, thus allowing for seeing beyond the horizon before them and opening to new possibilities for human agency.

A simple narrative is a story; yet it is not so simple. It is put together from common practices that are agreed on by a group of people who accept the synthesis of the stories and practices. There is a collective sense of agreement that emerges and simultaneously separates one particular story from the larger narrative.

A narratival position from within a philosophy of communication framework asks one to rethink and possibly change their understandings whenever limits in the narrative emerge or are disclosed. Accepting that the world is constantly changing, we also must accept that it is not very predictable. Therefore, within this impermanence, we have to reflect and discern often and notice when and how the narrative changes. Without opportunities for reflection and discernment, we cannot fully see what is before us that obstructs our ability to understand our surroundings. In this case, Richard Rorty (1979) suggested we use language to navigate through our narratival neighborhood, but we have to understand that language is inherently ambiguous, which causes challenges with our perceptions of our environment and of people. He believed that narratives assist our negotiation in the world, which requires an understanding of the stories within narratival structures, and that our agency occurs within a narratival embeddedness. Our actions are never really separate from our stories and our narratives. To discern different narratival perspectives, I've identified three philosophers of communication (though I am not sure they would refer to themselves with this label) to explore the significance of narratives in philosophy of communication: Charles Taylor, Paul Ricoeur, and Walter Fisher.

Charles Taylor

Charles Taylor is a Canadian philosopher who taught at McGill University until he retired and focused a good amount of his scholarship on the history of philosophy and intellectual histories. While these are not the only interests he had in philosophy, he emphasized the backdrop or situatedness of human experiences within historical narratives that are demarcated by particular moments in history. Taylor (2007) suggests it is the search for meaning that enables human beings to make sense out of questions situated within a given historical moment—these questions often drive human engagement.

Questions that Taylor asks to find answers for include understanding what it means to be a human agent within the narrative contexts of a sense of self, living with freedom, understanding one's individuality, and recognizing embeddedness with other human agents within narrative structures (Fritz, 2018). Taylor understands that sources of our selves are often hidden and occluded from our own awareness and perspectives. However, in order to make sense of life and the decisions we make traveling through our lives, we need to be able to articulate what is good and what we need to see our way through challenging situations. Once we unearth these moral under-standings, we can better work our way through them, make decisions, and understand our decisions based on what we value (Fritz, 2018). This is an authentic way of being a moral human agent (Taylor, 1991).

Taylor's (1991) understanding of language as it relates to authenticity is important to narrative structures. He holds a moderate understanding of authenticity, which denies the idea that because someone uses self-centered language does not automatically mean they are selfish—in fact they might actually be driven by an internal moral compass (Arnett & Arneson, 1999). A narrative framework allows one to understand the contextual environment of authenticity in a way that does not render the use of language empty or contentious. Taylor would also say that these things we find good that drive our human agency must be articulated because it moves us closer to them—we are drawn to a sense of articulacy and that is part of being human (Fritz, 2018; Taylor, 1989).

The sense of narrative and its connection and constituency role to human agency is also identified by another philosopher, Paul Ricoeur. Whether connected to authenticity or what Ricoeur refers to as emplotment, there is a shared understanding that what is valued or a shared good must be articulated whether verbally or nonverbally. Paul Ricoeur provides another orientation to narrative in the human quest for meaning making.

Paul Ricoeur

Paul Ricoeur was a French philosopher interested in phenomenology, hermeneutics, linguistics, and other theoretical frameworks designed to get at the heart of how human beings make meaning and come to meaning. Ricoeur's (1984) understanding of how human beings make meaning is situated in narratives and the notion of emplotment. Emplotment is basically a sequence of activities and interactions between various characters who are living within a story that is situated within a given a particular historical consciousness where questions arise that require human responsiveness. As human beings navigate this embeddedness, Ricoeur illuminated aspects of drama, emplotment, and character. Emplotment keeps the story and the drama going—it both moves the agency and creates the tensions that keeps the story unfolding.

Ricoeur's philosophy of communication is active because of the emplotment as it unites multiple pieces of the story with an interconnectivity imbued with tension and release. This approach required a marriage of diverse texts in dialogue that is a synthesis toward exploring new interpretive possibilities through a historical consciousness that allows rejection of past and fixed understandings. By bringing together multiple texts and multiple perspectives, new insight, new questions, and new responsiveness can emerge with radical possibilities. Paul Ricoeur relied on human interconnectedness and transactional relationships to undergird interpretation and meaning. The concept of emplotment allows us to understand more deeply and more clearly that events connected to other events and to multiple characters or persons provide much deeper insight into interpretive understanding.

Ricoeur is known for his emphasis on emplotment. His theory is a hermeneutic phenomenology of mimesis; he also emphasized that a multiplicity of referents within emplotment illuminates new insights rather than imitation insights. This descriptor itself points to a possible other approach where Ricoeur would also comfortably fit. But even with the descriptor, hermeneutic phenomenology, Ricoeur could be situated across and within several different approaches that we have discussed so far. This is a good example of the openness of philosophy of communication inquiry that requires the understanding that "this" is not "that" mind-set and that overlap naturally occurs at any given moment in time.

Ricoeur (1984) identified "mimesis" as a process of "creative discloser" within time and within narrative—both of which interact in a transactional engagement (Reagan, 1996). Scholars suggest Ricoeur moved toward the concept of "narrative identity," which emerged from his development of human testimony as a communicative act (Reagan, 1996). In this, narrative identity navigates transactional experiences between identity of sameness and identity of change (Reagan, 1996).

Narrative opens to a telling or a testimony that is governed by limits and that acknowledges identity as being embedded within something. Narrative allows for transactional responsiveness, which allows for opposing viewpoints. Ricoeur situated narrative as necessary embeddedness of the human condition, which demands the human being to act and respond in good times and in times of suffering. It is how we choose to respond to that suffering that shapes responsibility within a given moment in time.

Walter Fisher

Walter Fisher was a communication scholar and teacher specializing in Kenneth Burke's theoretical model of dramatism and the advancement of communication theory through the development of the narrative paradigm. When he died in 2018, he was professor emeritus at the Annenberg School for Communication. His contribution to the communication discipline and to philosophy of communication is significant.

Walter Fisher's (1989) groundbreaking work in human communication theory provided an alternative perspective from the dominant perspective based on the assumption that human communicators are rational beings and used rational methods in their communication. He first countered Aristotle's rational paradigm with his own narrative paradigm. Then, he provided a conceptual framework for narrative rationality. The rational world paradigm presupposes five characteristics. First, human beings are essentially rational. Second, the most common ways of human decision making are based on rational argument. Third, the approach to and conduct of the argument is ruled by the situation within which the argument is presented, such as legal, scientific, legislative, public, or other. Fourth, rationality is determined by what one knows about the subject, one's ability to make an argument and one's skills in advocacy for a given area. Finally, the fifth presupposition is that the world itself is a set of logical puzzles that can be solved through rational analysis and application of an argument construct (Fisher, 1989). These presuppositions guide our understanding of rational thinking, rational argument, and rational human communication. But Fisher (1989) argued that this is not the only way human's engage in communicative agency. He suggested there is an alternative to Aristotle's rational paradigm and that is a narrative paradigm. Fisher laid out presuppositions: (1) Human beings are essentially storytellers; (2) the way in which human beings make decisions is based on what they perceive as good reasons; (3) the production of these good reasons is based on a person's individual history, biography, culture, and character; (4) rationality is based on a person's awareness of narrative probability or coherence and narrative fidelity; and (5) the world is a set of stories that we continue to create and recreate through our choices and interactions.

TABLE 7.1 Aristotle's Rationality and Fisher's Narrative Rationality

Aristotle's Rationality	Fisher's Narrative Rationality
1. People are basically rational thinkers.	1. People are basically storytellers.
2. People make decisions based on logical arguments.	2. People make decisions based on good reasons.
3. The type of speaking situation determines the kind of argument one will make (e.g., legal religious, scientific, etc.).	3. The individual history, biography, culture, and character of a person determine what one thinks is a good reason.
4. Rationality is determined by what a person knows and how well a person argues.	4. Narrative rationality is determined by the coherence and fidelity of stories that a person hears or tells.
5. A person understands the world as a set of logical puzzles that we use rationality to negotiate and solve.	5. A person understands the world as a set of stories from which we chose to engage, and people constantly create and recreate their lives through these choices.

Adapted from: Fisher, W. (1989). *Human communication as narration: Toward a philosophy of reason, value, and action.* University of South Carolina Press.

Unpacking the differences between each of these presuppositions is helpful in determining how these claims differ. First, Aristotle began with the notion that human beings are basically rational beings, which means that they think, deliberate, and communicate through rational means, whether inductive or deductive, it doesn't matter—it is somehow systematic, fair, and just. Walter Fisher began his narrative framework from the position that people are basically storytellers, which is embedded with and employs a more emotional approach to thinking, deliberating, and communicating. If you think about it, the stories that we experience in our lives frame how we think about the world and our place in the world. It is those experiences that we more often go to when we think, decide, and communicate. This does not mean we are never rational in our thinking; what it does mean is that traditional rationality is not the only way human beings engage their surroundings, and perhaps the more frequent way is through emotions and stories or a narrative rationality.

Second, rationality is a way of thinking, deliberating, and communicating that is systematic, provides evidence, and is as clear as possible. When we are rational, we provide some kind of reasoning that is logical and valid. Fisher (1989) believed that people make decisions based on good reasons and what individuals perceive as good reasons is not always rational—in fact it could be emotional and based on past experiences. For an example of this, we know that in most states there is a seatbelt rule that requires every person driving and at least every person sitting in the front seat of the vehicle to wear a seatbelt. I live in New Hampshire, and at the time of writing this textbook, anyone over the age of 18 years does not have to wear a seatbelt.

Most of us believe that seatbelts are good to use and effective at keeping people safe. We have evidence from many scientific studies that say seatbelts can save lives and reduce the kind of injuries one might experience. This is a rational decision, to wear a seatbelt. However, when I met my husband 30 years ago, he never wore a seatbelt, and we were living in a state at the time that required people to wear seatbelts in a moving vehicle. When I asked him why he refused to wear a seatbelt, he told me that as a young police officer, when he was in patrol, he was often a first responder to many vehicle accidents. He stated he saw, more than once, a person who was not able to get out of a vehicle after an accident and consequently the person was burned alive. This experience was an emotional experience for my husband and was the basis for his "good reason" to never wear a seatbelt. While I might not agree with his decision, I also did not have his experience, but I can see where it would make sense to him to not want to wear a seatbelt. So, his decision was based on his experiences, his culture, and his individual emotional biography and biology. As a police officer, his career relied on rationality but in his personal individual experience, he used his own narratival good reasons to make his own decision. When we think about this, I believe all of us have memories of when we used our narratives to make decisions based on good reasons and when we used a logical rational approach to making a decision.

Third, good reasons are governed by our history, biography, culture, and character—this is exactly how my husband came to his good reason for not wearing a seatbelt. He allowed his past experiences, his identification as a first responder, his individual autonomy that undergirds his life in a democracy, and his character that has empathy and compassion for others to frame his reason as good. Fourth, his good reason was governed by a narrative rationality that is comprised of narrative probability or coherence and narrative fidelity; this means that it made sense to him that if he does not wear a seatbelt, then he cannot get stuck in one in the event that he would need to get out of the vehicle—it is also true to what he observed when someone died because of not being able to get out of the seatbelt. Lastly, the world is made of stories, so my husband knows that his perspective can change as his story changes. I recall after moving to New Hampshire when one of our daughters had a baby, our granddaughter, Lily. Once we started to drive our car with our granddaughter in it, he began to wear a seatbelt, which greatly surprised me. When I asked him about it, he stated that he wanted to be a good role model for her and wanted her to be safe when she was in a vehicle. This reflected the idea that his story changed. Once he knew he would have a baby, our granddaughter, in the car, he focused on safety for her instead of the experience he had when someone burned to death in a car. As our stories change, so do our reasons. Important to narratives and engagement within them is dialogue—the dialogical approach situates the importance of ethics in philosophy of communication.

Dialogical

The dialogical approach is grounded in dialogic ethics, which situates ethics within human communication. Historically, philosophical ethics have been engaged abstractly but dialogic ethics offer more pragmatic application to the communicative relationship between people. While in the philosophy domain we recognize Peter Singer as the "father" of applied ethics, I have often told my own students that dialogic ethics is really the first applied ethics and, historically, Martin Buber and other philosophers have been applying their dialogic ethics long before Peter Singer emerged in the mid-20th century. Though, I would agree that it was not until Peter Singer grabbed our attention with modern application of philosophy that the need to not only philosophize theoretically but also to begin to put their words into action constituted the field of applied ethics in philosophy. This section introduces the dialogic philosophies of Martin Buber, Mikhail Bakhtin, and Seyla Benhabib—each of whom are dialogically focused within the lens of communication ethics.

Martin Buber

To engage in dialogue, one should be skilled in effective and compassionate communication. Dialogic communication can occur within spiritual, moral, and pragmatic moments while encountering the other (Cissna & Anderson, 2018). Buber (1965) differentiates between genuine dialogue, technical dialogue, and monologue. Genuine dialogue is either silent or spoken. Buber (1965) stated that in genuine dialogue communicants have one another in mind, authentically and deeply, turning toward each other with intentional desire for establishing a living and dynamic mutual relation. This can be demanding at the level of authenticity this requires. This is why human beings often use technical dialogue to navigate the communication terrain on a basic level. Technical dialogue is a functional approach to communication—something based on needs and desires of the situation and individual understanding. The level or depth of communicative authenticity is not the same or as deep as it is in genuine dialogue. I see technical dialogue akin to phatic communication, which is communication that is functional, deliberate, objective, or something to pass the time.

We all engage in both of these kinds of communicative expressions. I can recall my own experiences with phatic communication such as passing by colleagues as I cross from building to building as classes change or when I am going to a meeting across campus. That passive and empty hello or "How are you?" as we pass our colleagues or friends without waiting for a response from them are functional forms of acknowledgment without attachment to a response. Another form is when I am waiting in a line at the grocery store and I have small talk that is superficial with other shoppers or the cashiers. This is communication designed to pass the time and demonstrates an awareness of the other, but beyond that it does nothing to cultivate a mutual relation. However, this superficiality can evolve to something more like or toward genuine dialogue. In fact, it would be difficult to have genuine dialogue without initially engaging in technical dialogue. In some cases, technical dialogue can be nurtured and grow to become genuine dialogue and build relational ties at deeper levels, though this happens occasionally more than regularly. Buber's dialogic theory juxtaposes I-it and I-thou moments of dialogic exchange. I-thou is genuine dialogue; it occurs less frequently than I-it exchanges because it takes more time, energy, and thoughtfulness to be fully present with the other in deep connection and dialogue. I-it exchanges are more technical kinds of exchanges and more phatic in nature. However, Buber, Arnett, and I have also argued for repositioning I-it exchanges to be necessary for creating the potential space for I-thou and genuine dialogic exchanges. I-it exchanges, in a positive and constructive light, allow for trust building to occur in relationships. I-it exchanges can be building blocks toward genuine dialogue (Holba, 2008).

Buber (1965) also described monologue as being disguised as dialogue where people meet but do not listen to the other and in some ways deceive themselves into thinking they are listening and responding to others while they really are not—they do not realize they are talking with themselves and not listening to the other. Buber (1965) suggested that real dialogue (genuine and technical) is hidden everywhere in all kinds of places and spaces and emerges in all kinds of ways. However, those who live in monologue are usually not aware of the other and miss opportunities to connect deeply with them.

There is an interesting story that Buber (1965) wrote about that had the most profound impact on his revelation about dialogue. In his book, *Between Man and Man* (1965), Buber tells a story about when he was 11 years old visiting his grandparent's home and had his first dialogic moment. In his story, Buber described a moment with his horse that transcended the physical experience:

> [I would] steal into the stable and gently stroke the neck of my darling, a broad dapple-grey horse. It was not a casual delight but a great, certainly friendly, but also deeply serious happening. ... What I experienced in touch with the animal was the Other, the immense otherness of the Other. ... When I stroked the mighty mane ... [I] felt the life beneath my hand, it was as though the element of vitality itself bordered on my skin ... confided itself to me, placed itself elementally in the relation of *Thou* and *Thou* with me. (p. 23)

Buber continued to describe this experience and stated that when he noticed that his hand was his hand and separate from the horse, that the genuine dialogic moment he shared with his horse ended. It was that quick—for moments he felt he was at one with the Other transcending the separateness between self and other. This is a defining moment for genuine dialogue that suggests it occurs when egos are set aside and deep genuine care for the other enfolds the communicative exchange. Buber's understanding of genuine dialogue has a spiritual or sacred element to it especially in experience of the immense otherness of the Other. Mikhail Bakhtin's dialogism also has a sacred element to it.

Mikhail Bakhtin

Mikhail Bakhtin was a Russian philosopher and literary critic who lived during a contentious time in Russian history when the world saw two world wars in the same century. During this time monologism and a single hegemonic ideology set the backdrop of Bakhtin's life (Klyukanov & Sinekopova, 2018). Within this environment, Bakhtin's dialogic imagination opened and focused on ethical dimensionality of human communication and dialogue. Imbued within his philosophy and literary criticisms is a dialogic ethic that also shares an element of sacredness. Bakhtin's philosophy is vast and multidimensional as he covered topics such as "authoring," "responsibility," "participatory thinking," self and other, just to name a few (Bakhtin, 1993). For the purpose of this discussion, I will focus on his theory of **dialogism** and the ethical implications of **answerability**, and the sacredness of dialogue through the **superaddressee**.

Dialogism is Bakhtin's response to the challenges he saw and lived with during Russia's monologic history. Dialogism recognizes multiplicity in voices and perspectives. Within this framework, Bakhtin (1983) demonstrated his knowledge of musical theory in the adaptation of words like **polyphony**, which is the musical term for many voices, in dialogism. From his linguistic background, Bakhtin also uses the term **heteroglossia** to also reflect multiple voices necessary for dialogism to be effective. Dialogue is something that is meant to be interactive—voices in dialogue or interacting with each other. A simple concept in theory but not so simple in application, especially in an environment more aligned with monological structures imbued in political ideology. Bakhtin recognized the value of hearing multiple voices and perspectives as an ethical dimension of how human beings communicate together. This ethical dimension is developed in his notion of answerability.

Answerability can be approached two particular ways (Klyukanov & Sinekopova, 2018). The first is as one being responsible for one's own actions, recognizing that any action changes the world in some way. This suggests that answerability recognizes the systems connections that dialogue must be responsive to. The second way is that there is an obligation on the part of the one performing an ethical act to make the act intelligible for the other, which sets up the communicative exchange as answerable (Klyukanov & Sinekopova, 2018). Dialogism recognizes that communication is endless and that all we can do is create the environment for answerability, something that monologism cannot and does not do.

There is also a sacred element of Bakhtin's dialogism and that is dialogue is a triadic experience, which creates some kind of contradiction, especially in the contexts of dyadic dialogism. In Bakhtin's (1981) theory, the "superaddressee" is a concept he created that represents the possibilities in dialogism. While there are differing understandings of who or what the superaddressee is, it is in general a theoretical concept that points to the existence of a higher level or transcendent addressee that is present (but not observable) in every dialogic encounter. The superaddressee is another listener who is easily conceptualized as one over, above, and between interlocutors—one who listens actively and compassionately and understands justly.

Bakhtin (1981) is not referencing dialogue as conversation but broadens the dialogic environment as one that is complex and one that exists on different levels or dimensions.

Acknowledging our contemporary technological environment, dialogism occurs spatially and locally in face-to-face conditions as well as through mediated technologies within distance and asynchronous platforms. As a literary theorist, Bakhtin also acknowledged that dialogic expression does not have to be an embodied experience. Rather, he allows for dialogic encounters to happen in writing and the telling of stories.

The superaddressee may work in this way as an "indefinite, unconcretized other" (Bakhtin, 1986, p. 95). It is a radical part of any dialogue because it can influence the outcome of the dialogue as it is described as an ideal listener. Scholars describe the superaddressee as the embodiment of hope; as an expression of an ideological or theological belief—or God (Morson & Emerson, 1990); or a listener who is above and over the listener as a transcendent being or as a metalinguistic aspect of dialogue (Midgley, 2011).

Mikhail Bakhtin's dialogic philosophy is rich with texture and is multidimensional itself, just as dialogue is when it is engaged. His theory provides a reminder that monologism holds dangers of limited possibilities and marginalization of communicants. Bakhtin advocated for ethical engagement of language and relationships within human relations. Approaching philosophy of communication through the lens of dialogism provides not only a textured landscape of perspectives and voices but also points to the ethicality inherent in human communication. It also illuminates the sacredness of dialogue through the unseen aspect of the superaddressee. This can feel abstract at times, but Seyla Benhabib offers a dialogic framework that is pragmatic and just.

Seyla Benhabib

Seyla Benhabib is the Eugene Meyer professor of political science and philosophy at Yale University. Her scholarship pursues questions related to identity and culture and the relationship between the rights of others, identity, and how we maintain civic structures in societies (Fawkes, 2018). Benhabib aligns with Jürgen Habermas's critical stances, especially related to discourse ethics; she shares a similar universalist perspective as Habermas in that she observes the importance of a moral universalism as it relates to civic structures for the process of dialogic engagement.

Benhabib (1992) suggests that the "I" is constituted through a "narrative unity" that acknowledges what I "can" do and what you "expect" of me (p. 6). These understandings of wants and expectations are constituted through language and how language is interpreted by each communicant. There is a moral element of dialogue that points to a particular stage in the development of the socialization of human beings that is politically and socially articulated when there is dialogue that comes to terms with the general rules of governance. This occurs through narratives and people coming to agree on those rules. A moral point of view within dialogue correlates with a particular point of reasoning when there is a division or a disjointedness between actual embodied and practiced norms and hypothetical reasoning. This refers to a disconnection between a moral ought (where we engage in hypothetical reasoning) and what is socially acceptable and practiced. According to Benhabib (1992), disjunctions such as these open opportunity for ethics to be engaged in practical, critical contexts.

Benhabib (1992) uses the term *enlarged thinking* when she discusses the importance of the critical contexts when navigating the disjunction between the "ought" and the "what is" (p. 9). She borrows the term from another social, political philosopher, Hannah Arendt (1906–1975), who actually borrowed the term from Immanuel Kant (1724–1804), the Enlightenment philosopher. Enlarged thinking, for Benhabib, refers to what happens when one enters a conversation where there must be some kind of agreement and we not only dialogue within ourselves but also are always in communication with others. Questioning our own assumptions and presuppositions is necessary as well as being in dialogue with others, allowing that dialogue to broaden or open thinking in order to meet the agreement as it evolves from the dialogue. Through this experience of enlarged thinking, Benehabib (1992) suggests that the identity of the moral self must evolve and be reconceptualized. Enlarged thinking teaches us to be better able to reason and to understand those larger issues that are important to ourselves and others beyond an individual ego.

In the context of enlarged thinking and reconceptualizing the moral self, Benhabib (1992) identifies the generalized other and concrete others. She suggests that the concept of a generalized other means that each individual is considered a moral person who is equipped with the same moral rights as others; the concept of the concrete other suggests that every moral person is a unique individual with their own history, narrative, disposition, needs, and limitations (Benhabib, 1992). These qualities of the concrete and generalized other are bestowed on each person and exist on a continuum that situates a universal respect for all moral persons on one end of the continuum, and situates care and solidarity for the collective and those with whom we share in relationships on the other. Benhabib (1992) thinks about this through the critique of the integrationist who wants to reconstitute communities by reformulating around an **integrationist** vision of fundamental values and principles. However, this is not acceptable to Benhabib because it is incompatible with individual autonomy. Rather, she elevates the notion of **participationist**, which reflects a community centeredness that brings people together through dialogue and debate to engage a democratic process that creates the condition for developing enlarged thinking that can undergird social and political discourses. Benhabib's take on dialogic ethics opens to the next section that considers the ethical approach to philosophy of communication.

Ethical

An ethical perspective in philosophy of communication inquiry is better stated as the philosophy of communication ethics and it is perspective laden (Arnett et al., 2018). This means that there is generally no consensus and no one way to think about and speak out something. It also means that there is always an ongoing interrogation between self, other, community, and historical context. Though, to study or pursue communication ethics, one cannot assume or look for a straight path and a concrete, unchangeable response. However, what one may find is a possibility for guidance through one's navigation in a world of narratives and narrative contentions. These three philosophers guided by a philosophy of communication ethics shape our conceptual understanding of ethics in the context of philosophy of communication inquiry: Emmanuel Levinas, Martha Nussbaum, and Judith Butler.

Emmanuel Levinas

Emmanuel Levinas focused on ethical praxis and strived to develop ethics as first philosophy. Levinas implicated that every single day human beings have an existential burden to each person we meet and each particular moment we find ourselves in to honor the uniqueness of our responsibility for the Other. Key components of Levinas's philosophy include the face of the other, the echo, and the trace. From these philosophical components, Levinas outlined a first philosophy of communication ethics that obliges one to the other through the lens of "I am my brother's keeper" and it becomes a "spiritual awakening" (Arnett, 2017, p. 217).

Levinas situates our ethical responsibility toward the face of the Other—ethics and ethical reasoning resides in the face of the Other (Arnett, 2017).

When we encounter the face of the other, we move from a static observa-tion to an audio attentiveness that obliges us to the other (Arnett, 2017). His notion of the Other points to alterity as not an alter ego of the self but rather recognizes the Other as a separate, different Other to whom one is responsible. Levinas develops the face of the Other as being the forefront of the alterity of the Other (Levinas, 1961; Pinchevski, 2018). The face is not silent; it speaks, though perhaps not orally. The presence of the face opens the possibility for addressing and being addressed. The face of the other is responsible for calling one into responsibility with only a trace or an echo.

The echo and the trace are conceptual fragments that have a significant role in Levinas's ethics as first philosophy. Contemporary scholar, philos-opher, and professor Ronald C. Arnett (2017) describes Levinas's project toward ethics as a "conceptual house for ethics" comprised of the following coordinates: the human face, a voice that is immemorial (something from the past), attentiveness to the historical moment, and an intellectual prac-tice of education that can be formal and informal (p. 8). The echo is that immemorial voice calling us out in responsibility for the Other. The trace represents a call of that responsibility—the face of the Other we can never fully see but that calls us to respond ethically to the Other. Arnett (2017) provides a pragmatic understanding of Levinas that can be situated as a practical ethical guide for human communicative engagement.

Arnett (2017) explains that reflecting on a situation where one feels a responsibility but does not have clarity or direction makes one feel not quite adequate or up to the task because of ambiguity and uncertainty. But people, whether teacher, doctor, or firefighter, take action and move forward in spite of the uncertainty that nags at them. The face of the Other calls to them to act out of respons-ability; they are able to respond but they respond within a frame of uncertainty and without any promise of a certain outcome (Arnett, 2017). This takes continual learning and acknowledgment of the face, the trace, and the echo—there is no turning our backs on these nudges and calls for action and response. This is a human beings' first responsibility.

Levinas's philosophy is significant to philosophy of communication because of the focus on the face-to-face experience that makes the self feel answerable to the Other; one is drawn out of oneself in a way that is unable to avoid the Other (Bergo, 2007). This inability to avoid or elude the face of the Other then calls one to respond to and for the Other. This is where responsibility for the Other begins—in that trace of the face of the Other and that immemorial echo that is unavoidable.

From a Levinasian perspective, ethics originates in person-to-person contact. We should become preoccupied with the Other such that we embrace the maxim, "I am my brother's keeper," though this cannot be demanded on the Other. The emphasis is on the needs of the other. For Levinas, ethical dialogue creates common ground where there is no power imbalance and we have a responsibility to put our own self-interests aside so that we can respond to the other with the Other as a central focus. Martha Nussbaum's ethical approach is grounded in the unique capabilities of each particular other.

Martha Nussbaum

Martha Nussbaum is a professor of law and ethics at the University of Chicago, and much of her philosophy is grounded in and influenced by ancient Greek thought. Her philosophy has been described as *eudaimonic*, a term derived from the Greek word *eudaimonia* that is translated as human flourishing, or more colloquially known as having to do with happiness (Arneson, 2018). This means she begins her philosophical positions from the assumption of privileging human dignity and asks the question, "What do people need to flourish in this life?" (Arneson, 2018). While Nusbaum covers a broad range of philosophies, her understanding of emotion and ethics and her capabilities approach to the social contract is central to her philosophy of communication.

In the interpersonal communication literature, emotions are often key to human connections and human conflict. The literature explores the psychological aspects of emotions and how they shape human interaction. Nussbaum does not see emotions merely as carnal energies or impulses that human beings cannot control. Instead, Nussbaum looks at emotions differently by situating them as necessary for practical reasoning (Arneson, 2018). She defines emotions as a discriminating response about what and how things are and about what is important (Nussbaum, 2010). This means they are also deeply connected to what people value as a good and what is intimately important to them (Arneson, 2018). Nussbaum (2010) states that emotions actually inform our ethical decision making as they inherently make value judgments about what matters to individuals. Emotions are not the only influencer to one's ethical decision making. Nussbaum developed the capabilities approach to ethical decision making, which focuses on what people are actually able to do as each human being is unique and has different capabilities.

There are two dimensions to the capabilities approach: (a) quality of life in a comparative way and (b) being able to theorize about justice (Arneson, 2018). These dimensions share five principles: Take each person as an end; focus on choice and freedom instead of achievements; engage pluralist values;

speak out about social injustices and inequality; and press government to improve quality of life for everyone with the understanding that the good life may mean different things to different people (Arneson, 2018; Nussbaum, 2011). Ethical decision making must recognize that not all human capabilities are equal and that social and political structures should adapt and acknowledge these differing capabilities. A challenge with Nussbaum's capabilities approach is that what she identifies as capabilities can be abstract or open-ended so that this will allow for interpretive leniencies so as not to have concrete understandings that cannot adapt to various physical or nonphysical realities.

Nussbaum's political philosophy is grounded in human relationships in that it offers insight into the relational nature of ethics. Her philosophy of communication provides advocacy for those who are not equal and who have different capabilities from the mainstream or majority of thinkers and doers. Nussbaum expands the social contract to think about how focusing on individual capabilities can broaden the social contract and give voice and advocacy to those who have been left out of the conversation in the past. Like the capabilities approach focuses on individual qualities of what one is capable of, Judith Butler also focuses on a critique of individualism and provides a new feminist understanding of identity.

Judith Butler

Judith Butler is the Maxine Elliot professor of comparative literature in the Departments of Rhetoric and Comparative Literature at the University of California, Berkeley, and also holds various other positions and honors such as a position at the Columbia University Center for the Study of Social Difference and the Andrew Mellon award for Distinguished Academic Achievement in the Humanities, and she is the 2012 recipient of the Adorno Prize in Germany. Butler offers a feminist critique of individualism related to how the category of "woman" is produced. Butler emphasizes the study of individual identification in an embedded context of being with others. Identification is not about being a singular isolated identity, but instead it is situated deep within the context of being embedded with others. Butler has made significant contribution to feminist studies, political philosophy, queer studies, and philosophical and applied ethics. Her philosophy is an active philosophy in that she discusses identification of woman as being a "term-in-process" (Salih, 2002, p. 7). In much of Butler's work, there are strong indications of the influence of some of the most significant thinkers through the ages, such as Foucault and Derrida, who we discussed earlier in Chapter 6. Butler

(2005) attends to the relationship between the individual and the community in the context of difference.

Butler's (2005) understanding of subject formation is related to how we understand identity and subjectivity. She states, "I cannot explain exactly why I have emerged in this way, and my efforts at narrative reconstruction are always undergoing revision" (p. 40). Butler identifies and examines the process by subjects come into existence. She wants to know which structures shape subjects—which structures are helpful and which are not helpful.

Butler (2005) argues that making an account of oneself is always partial. She also reminds her readers that there is no one definitive story of how individuals form—and this story is always being reconsidered, reconstituted, and reorganized. Butler (2005) identifies the ethical violence that lays the groundwork for how we understand moral positions through our individual lenses. Her construct of accounting for oneself helps readers understand how violence emerges from indifference and reflects a worldview of living as individual moral beings. Butler (2005) suggests the indifference can only be erased if we see ourselves as moral beings living with other moral beings. In this reconstitution of how we see ourselves as being within a plural morality, we can get stuck within an abstract universality of individualism that does not acknowledge particularities of others. An example of this is that if socially we do not acknowledge the particularities of others who may be differently abled, how can we make public accommodations for those individuals to navigate the public environments successfully? An abstract universality would ignore the needs of those differently abled; erasing this indifference allows for the awareness and understanding of the needs of others within whom we are socially embedded.

Butler (2005) suggests that all human beings are embedded in a web of existence, a "story of a relation" within a community (p. 8). Butler (2005) understands that there is freedom in the embeddedness of communities and subject formation within communities is a precondition for engaging moral inquiry. One of the most important terms that Butler develops in her dialectical ethical framework is **subject formation** that involves two processes, **performativity** and **interpellation**. It is through these processes that individuals become accountable for their self-accounts. Performativity is the enactment of the self; prior to enactment there is no individual subject—the subject becomes constituted as a result of the performativity between subject and other as well as subject and context.

Butler (2005) states that identity is constituted as an ongoing process of performativity that can be seen as a sequence of acts that presupposes the existence of a subject. She describes a "scene of address" that demonstrates an embeddedness between one's self and the other (p. 50). Butler (2005) suggests that one gives an account of oneself to this other and that the process of accounting is situated within rhetorical conditions whereby there is a responsibility—an ethical charge—that calls one out to attend others through language and linguistic terms. This relationship with the other demands that I make an account of myself for my relation with the other. I make an account of myself through performativity.

Performativity communicates an enactment of the self; this enactment is continuously reconstituting my account of myself. Performativity comes before the narrative of engagement emerges—this means there is no narrative before or without performativity. In performativity, a narrative or narratives emerges. Performativity is not the same thing as a performance. Performativity emerges when the self meets a linguistic social context; it is engaged as an authentic mode of being instead of what we think about when we hear the word *performance*—a staged, practiced, concrete representation of something for a particular purpose. This means that there is no "I" outside or separate from language (Salih, 2002; Arnett & Holba, 2012). An example of this is the idea and practice of gender identity. Butler (2005) suggests that language constitutes gender, which means that there is no subject identity before language—language gives birth to identity.

In Butler's philosophy, the process of interpellation occurs after performativity. Interpellation is a kind of linguistic interaction referring to an action that calls out the other and demands a response. Butler (2005) states that interpellation forces us to give accounts of ourselves because we are rendered accountable by the existence of the other who because of the embeddedness of self and other within a narrative are bound by the relational scene of address. Together one makes an account of one's self through the integration of performativity and interpellation. For Butler, this is a morally constituted action of acknowledgment.

There are social implications to Butler's philosophy. In her work, performative assembly situates how one lives the good life in the midst of precarity. She suggests that the good life emerges when one lives alongside the other where one is able to make the other's life more livable. This is our responsibility through performativity: the ethics of living alongside the other in harmony and observing responsibilities toward the other.

Connections, Currency, and Meaning

Connections: Narrative, dialogic, and ethical approaches to philosophy of communication at times are counterparts and at times offer different hermeneutic entrances from which to view communication that is embedded within context, tied to other human beings, and grounded in moral and ethical domains of engagement. These approaches are all relevant to public moral argument because when goods are in contention and argument arises, usually narratives emerge around the goods in question. Dialogue opens the possibility of argument, and because human beings are involved in staking claim to a particular good, there are always ethical encounters in these discussions and transactions. Public moral argument deals in stories, through dialogue, and within ethical domains of communicative action and behavior. In many ways, these three approaches overlap and integrate at times. Let's look at another current example related to the communication surrounding COVID-19, the coronavirus pandemic.

Currency: As mentioned earlier, at the writing of this manuscript, we are in the midst of a global pandemic involving the coronavirus, COVID-19. There have been many stories in the news, in television commercials, in social and digital media, and any form of communication that currently exists. These stories are moving people to participate in some kind of action, whether engaging in open dialogues or acting and participating in particular events or actions. A few days ago, the state of Michigan became a public example of public moral argument when people protested the state house after the governor imposed a restrictive lockdown of the state. While Michigan is considered late to the game for shutting down government, the stringent details of this lockdown angered many citizens in the state.

People came together in their cars to maintain social distancing, which is a federal requirement during this time, and in person, where they stood next to each other on the grounds of the building with signs and oral sharing of their stories of resistance. Many petite narratives emerged where people were angry at some of the restrictions, such as not being able to go to the store to buy seeds for planting at a time when there is also disruption of the food chain nationally. The competing goods involved ranged from simple liberty and ability to move around the state so people can provide for their families to closing businesses that some citizens believed were essential services, like a hardware store. On the other hand, the governor had to consider the public health threat—the risk to the public if people start coming together in large groups while a contagious invisible virus raging war against the human body is present. Narratives were conflicting, and dialogue was reduced to emotion-laden outbursts instead of calm and rational communication. This was an epic failure on the part of everyone. Like we saw with Levinas, Nussbaum, and Butler, our ethical responsibility should undergird our narratives because we are in narratives with others. Our ethical responsibility, especially as a first philosophy, should weave through our dialogue so that we can truly respond to the other in a way that addresses the issues responsibly. This does not mean everyone gets their way. What it will do is begin to create the space for common ground and shared understandings, whether we agree or not. There must be a way for engaging in public moral argument so that voices are heard and shift from the "What is in it for me" mind-set to "How can we help the situation?"

Meaning: How we come to meaning is very important. The path toward meaning actually shapes meaning. Being responsive to the narrative, recognizing that one is embedded within narratives, is helpful and constructive. Understanding the fundamental aspects of dialogue, such as suspending one's individual need to clearly see the perspectives and needs of the other is key to cultivating ground for meaning to emerge. We also cannot avoid ethics simply because we know human beings have differing value-based needs and perspectives. There will always be goods in contention—narratives and dialogue can help us navigate within our contexts in order to participate effectively in public moral argument.

Conclusion

This chapter explored three approaches to philosophy of communication that are significant and interrelated: narrative, dialogical, and ethical. As in earlier chapters exploring varying approaches to philosophy of communication, this chapter also identified some key philosophers and philosophies associated with these approaches. This is the last chapter to identify particular approaches, and I want to remind you that the choice for inclusion of particular philosophers and philosophies in particular chapters is my own choice and if someone else would have written these chapters, other choices would likely have been made. This is a characteristic of philosophy of communication, in that there is not one absolute answer or interpretation that is the correct one. Because interpretation is ongoing and dynamic, there is always a possibility of something else—a different way of seeing, interpreting, and understanding the world. Especially with these three approaches, narrative, dialogical, and ethical, they can be considered counterparts that offer different hermeneutic entrances from which meaning can emerge.

Ultimately, all of the approaches covered in this chapter and the two previous chapters are relevant to public moral argument because when goods are in contention and arguments arise, narratives emerge around those goods. Navigating public moral argument requires a dialogic process that is imbued within an ethical framework. However, there can be no public moral argument without the interplay of hermeneutics, semiotics, and phenomenology because those processes shape how phenomena come to us and how we find meaning in the disclosure. Additionally, the psychoanalytical, critical, and communicological approaches remind us that there are hidden structures that we either do not see or take for granted that also impact meaning and shape the discourse in public moral argument. All of these approaches have a role of some kind in how human beings come to meaning and, through that, engage public moral argument. They shape how we think and act.

PART II

Connections, Currency, Meaning

P art II explored approaches to philosophy of communication inquiry. This section looked at nine approaches that are not fully separate and distinct from one another; in fact, some of them have some clear connectivity. For example, as an approach, hermeneutics overlaps with phenomenology, semiotics, and narrative; the psychoanalytic approach may have points of overlap with the critical approach; and the dialogical approach has some overlap with the ethical approach. These are just a few points of overlap, and the more we learn and explore about each approach the more junctures of overlap emerge, though, they each still have unique elements specific to themselves. This points to the notion that in philosophy of communication inquiry there is a commitment to remaining open by understanding that there is no one answer to any given question and, if this is so, then there has to be no one approach designed to look at a particular phenomenon. Approaches do overlap and each approach illuminates different phenomena, understandings, and meanings.

Connections

In preparing to engage in public moral argument, one must try to identify the approach taken to the inquiry. Understanding the approach taken to the issue determines the focus of the inquiry and foreshadows the querent's path. The particular approach taken, for example, approaching the question of police brutality, might benefit from a psychoanalytical or critical approach, which allows for engagement in the debate to understand key aspects of the argument in deeper ways related to the self, identity, and experience. It also allows one to consider using other approaches to complement or counter the arguments put forward. One might use narrative or ethical approaches to complement or counter arguments from those psychoanalytical and critical perspectives. By recognizing the interconnections between approaches, one can adapt their own argument or adapt their perspective as a result of these exchanges.

Currency

Currency underscores the importance of being familiar with the different approaches, because in public moral debate, one is required to understand and engage in multiperspective taking when interpreting their environments, experiences, and public knowledge. If we look at a contemporary case of public argument and identify and evaluate evidence from all sides of the debate, we begin to engage in the praxis of philosophy of communication inquiry. For enriching classroom discussion, brainstorm as one large group or several smaller groups and identify pressing issues relevant to you today. You can use the issues you found during your brainstorm from Part I, "Connections, Currency, Meaning," or you might have other or new issues that emerged due to your research and discussions. Remember (again) what public moral argument entails; there are three criteria that make an issue appropriate for public moral argument:

1. There must be an argument (remember, an argument is a claim, a stated reason, and evidence to back up the claim).

2. The argument must occur in a public setting where it can touch others.

3. The issue has to be an explicitly moral issue.

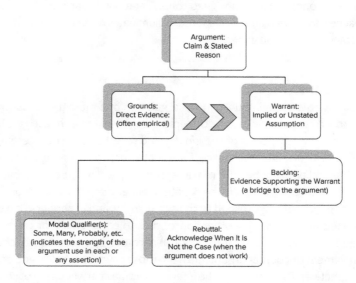

FIGURE II.1   Schematic for Stephen Toulmin's argument model.

Use some time during class or for homework to explore information and gather evidence to engage in a public moral debate in the classroom, or make the stakes higher and hold a public moral argument forum in a public setting on campus. Remember, you have to have an argument, you have to touch the public in some way, and the issue must be an explicitly moral issue. Here are the two initial examples from the last section in Part I, but I encourage you to find your own issues with the most currency.

1. Issue: Police brutality

   Argument: Policing reform is necessary to save Black people's lives because too many Black men and women are being unjustifiably killed by police.

2. Issue: Abortion and women's reproductive rights

   Argument: *Roe v. Wade* should be overturned because abortion is committing murder since fetuses are living beings.

As you begin gathering evidence and perspectives from different voices, try to determine what approach is taken to the argument. It might be that some of the information you gather can be applied across one or two approaches from the chapters in Part II. Identify the nuances of each approach and analysis and evaluate which arguments hold up stronger. You can also identify what is needed to strengthen an argument; maybe evidence from within another approach could be used to strengthen the argument. If you want to counter an argument, which approach would be best utilized for each of your specific arguments? From identifying the approach taken to an argument, what new information emerged to inform the broader discourse? How do you put your own biases aside when selecting your approach to your argument? What new information emerges when you explore arguments from different approaches? How does this new information inform your own understanding?

Meaning

Approaches are important to at least be aware of when we engage in public argument because it is through these approaches that we learn to test the evidence of our own arguments, arguments counter to our own, and the nature of the issues at hand. Approaches allow us to determine how to test the public evidence and how meaningful that evidence is to the overall argument. Approaches are only part of the ingredients of public moral argument—they offer and open perspective taking; they can also shift our own perspectives.

Approaches determine the kinds of evidence we select as relevant and important when we make our arguments. The meaning we gain is shaped through the specific approach taken to the questions and issues involved in the argument. So, as you are gathering your information and selecting potential evidence, you need to recognize the approach taken to those arguments you plan to use. The meaning we make from these approaches allows us to test public evidence and engage in decision making. Good luck with thinking through your research by identifying the approach from which it came and determining how the evidence relates to other approaches.

Figure Credit
Fig. II.1: Adapted from Stephen E. Toulmin, *The Uses of Argument.* Copyright © 1958 by Cambridge University Press.

Part III

Questions That Guide Philosophy of Communication Inquiry

P art III of this book introduces the importance of questions and the act of questioning in philosophy of communication inquiry. Chapter 8 situates the importance of the question and the reason for and process of questioning; Chapter 9 examines the questions that emerged from particular historical periods and from particular traditions and how philosophers have pursued them. Chapter 10 situates the importance of historicity and how meaning is made through the lens of communicative praxis, the hermeneutical theory from Calvin O. Schrag.

Each chapter ends with an applied discussion, "Connections, Currency, Meaning," in which a discussion involving the application of some of the concepts covered in the chapter is opened. This section integrates public moral argument applications.

Chapter 8

The Importance of Questions and Questioning

Learning Objectives

1. Understand the value of questioning structures of meaning in both abstract and pragmatic applications.

2. Identify the importance of discovering questions that philosophers are pursuing when engaging their philosophy of communication inquiry.

3. Articulate the processes of questioning in philosophy of communication inquiry.

4. Apply the process of identifying questions in the contemporary historical moment.

This chapter discusses the importance of questions and the questioning process in the philosophy of communication inquiry. The idea of identifying questions in given historical moments provides insight into those historical moments that undergird how one understands the world and their environments and finds meaning, especially in times of shifting sensibilities, confusion, and uncertainty. When considering the question, the context of the question is just as important as the question itself. The approach to the question is also key in how meaning is made. In order to unfold the importance of illuminating questions and interrogating them, this chapter introduces three philosophers and their philosophies that broaden our understanding of the value found in identifying the questions that frame meaning making. It can be challenging to decide which three philosophers can best inform this chapter, and like in other chapters the choices made here are mine and mine alone. First, this chapter explores the notion of questions and the questioning process in philosophy of communication inquiry. Second, three philosophers who illuminate the importance of the question and the value of questioning are discussed. These philosophers are Martin Heidegger (1889–1976), Hans-Georg Gadamer (1900–2002), Calvin Schrag (b. 1928). Third, this chapter ends with a discussion on identifying questions in the contemporary historical moment and engages the process of questioning.

Questions and Questioning

There are a variety of perspectives pertaining to identifying questions of given historical moments in the practice of doing philosophy. In doing any kind of philosophical inquiry, this requires an awareness of context, especially within times of shifting historical terrains. We recognize these shifts in content and context through the topics and questions that philosophers engage (Krüger, 1984). Pragmatic philosopher, Richard Rorty (1979) suggested that in the practical doing of philosophy, identifying emerging questions that are situated within context and embeddedness within narratives is necessary for practical understanding. Robert Piercey (2009) states we should learn from our histories, pay close attention to how ideas change over time, and recognize how historical moments shift and change, which then alter how we understand those histories. Philosophers like Alasdair MacIntyre (b. 1929) and Calvin Schrag suggest that in order to see the questions of given historical moments, taking critical distance is necessary to see the entire question within its context so that one can see the horizon of the question. Likewise, Charles Taylor (2007) notes that it in the search for meaning questions help human beings make sense out of situations, especially if they are complex and textured—most of which are. Viktor Frankl (1959) acknowledged that any quest for meaning can arouse an inner tension that is only satisfied by seeking answers to questions that emerge in given contexts. Generations of peoples often cannot see those questions—they are obscured by unending minutia that disrupt stories and narratives that usually provide meaningfulness. Frankl (1959) refers to this as the existential vacuum, which is an inner emptiness that does not allow them to have an awareness of meaning for their lives.

Frankl talked about questions in a very different way and offered their importance to the unfolding meaning, though not so much in the answering of those questions but in asking relevant questions can human beings find their way through to see the questions before them within their own historical moment. Frankl (1959) suggests that many times in the past people did not know how to look for those pertinent questions—instead they often asked the wrong question. His example is this instead of asking "What is the meaning of my life?" one ought to allow life to question the individual life, specific to oneself. This means one ought to allow questions about existence to emerge and be able to identify what the questions are through listening to the historical moment and not by attacking head on by controlling what you want the question to be or assuming what you think it should be. When life questions the individual, the individual can respond in a constructive way that is answerable for oneself. Frankl (1959) argues that it is answering for oneself that is the very essence of human existence. This means when we are questioned by life, we respond to the questioning in an open and dynamic way instead of starting with a question that is very specific and perhaps narrow; this approach can eliminate opportunities in seeing the fuller horizon of the interrogation.

In Arnett and Arneson's (1999) project on dialogic civility that brings together both philosophy of communication inquiry and philosophy of communication ethics, they situate the questioning process within praxis, which they state requires a reflective integration of action and theory. The historical moment in which one is situated makes a difference to what one knows, does, and understands. Arnett and Arneson (1999) suggest that the interpretive processes in which we engaged are shaped by the question or questions that guide our inquiry—our asking and our responding. They provide a relevant example of this through a story about a man and his horse:

> In 1865, a man rode his horse into town and asked, "Where is the livery stable? I need to take care of my horse." No one thought his question was even slightly unusual. The existential demand of 1865 at that given moment made his question not only sensible, but necessary. The owner of the livery stable made a good living—until a contraption called the

"horseless carriage" threatened his livelihood. (Arnett & Arneson, 1999, p. 34)

This story shows that questions we ask and the process of responding to questions is governed by our historical moment, which are always in motion, shifting, pivoting, and adjusting to phenomena that nobody can fully control. Another example today is the question, "Where is the gas station?" We might imagine in 50 years that our vehicles are not powered by the gasoline of today—that we might rely on solar, electric, or other energy forms. How we respond to questions changes with the shifting historical moments. This requires listening to the historical moment and being attentive to how questions are asked, perceived, and answered (Arnett & Arneson, 1999).

The main domain or discipline of philosophy, in the broadest sense, is understood as a risky and sometimes responsibility-laden practice of turning toward and asking those perennial questions that have to do with how one lives well (Wiener & Ramsey, 2005). This is an important task and those questions, left uninterrogated, can cause more harm than good. Philosophy of communication inquiry is situated between the questions at the intersection of philosophical inquiry and communication studies that focuses on human communicative engagement and the human condition (Holba, 2010). These questions are typically related to the nature and function of human communication and there are ranges of approaches or different lenses form which one can engage philosophically, as the last three chapters explored (Arneson, 2007). These questions reveal "temporal coordinates" that demonstrate to self, other, and community how communication shapes society and how it shapes social issues that frame, emerge, or guide society in public fashion (Arneson, 2007). To take up the task of philosophy of communication inquiry, we ask "What is the meaning of communication?" (Ramsey & Miller, 2003, p. 11). In philosophy of communication, one seeks to illustrate a logic of questioning, a kind of rhetorical performance, that is situated against the backdrop of conversation or other people engaging and interrogating the same or similar questions (Schrag, 2010). This means there is a systematic approach to the question or questions. The role of the question in philosophy of communication inquiry is to be informed by the call of the other—in conversation (literally, virtually, or intellectually through reading, thinking, and responding by writing). Some might suggest this occurs in the realm of ethics or perhaps points us toward a sense of duty. When we do this, we not only question what we encounter but we are responding to what has already been said (Schrag, 2010). To question is also to respond.

Philosophy of communication begins from questioning; this means its origin is a question that one asks in the pursuit to understand some kind of experience situated within particular communication environments (Arnett, 2016). There is a difference between providing an explanation of some particular phenomenon and the discovery that enables one to understand what that phenomenon means that stands before us. Later in this chapter this aspect is more fully developed through the lens of Hans-Georg Gadamer's inquiry into the question. Philosophy of communication inquiry begins with a question and then engages a variety of practices such as reading, writing, thinking, editing, and interpretation (Arnett, 2016). The process can be quite textured. Each part of the process, which may not go in any particular order, requires the inquirer to listen to what and how one reads, writes, thinks, edits, and interprets this experience of inquiry. Philosophy of communication inquiry begins by exploring the questions of others, which also requires an objective discernment within the awareness of individual constraints of bias or prejudice that automatically emerges within the inquirer. The inquirer also understands that philosophy of communication does not give a final answer to questions; however, it does provide temporal understanding (Arnett, 2016).

Temporal understandings are part of what Richard Rorty (1979) stated would keep the conversation going when he articulated the challenges with epistemology and advocated a move to hermeneutics. Some people are not looking for temporal understanding; instead, they want concrete answers, so philosophy of communication inquiry would not be their preference, even though the concrete answer would likely be insufficient and change over time. Philosophy of communication inquiry elevates and acknowledges difference and temporality—this allows for the broadest understandings. Though it must be understood philosophy of communication inquiry begins with a question in response to some kind of gap in one's knowledge, that opens curiosity into the gap (Arnett, 2016). It is also likely that the inquiry will open more gaps, which requires then further inquiry. This is so because of the temporal nature of understanding and the fact that our understanding is always partial, which requires one to be vigilant in the pursuit of inquiry. It will help to explore three philosophers' perspectives on questions and questioning. The next section explores philosophers introduced earlier in this book, Martin Heidegger, Hans-Georg Gadamer, and Calvin O. Schrag.

Three Philosophers on Questions and Questioning

In this section, I discuss three philosophers who provide insight into why questions and questioning are important in the human quest to find meaning. Philosophy of communication inquiry "investigates philosophical thought about how humans are communicatively situated in the lived world" (Arneson, 2007, p. 7). Arneson indicates this pertains to contemplating ideas that we use to analyze, describe, and interpret communication as lived experience. This means that philosophy of communication inquiry both reveals gaps in philosophizing about ideas and simultaneously tears open gaps in order to see things in new ways, expand understanding, and resituate meaning toward serendipitous possibilities in how we understand and engage in the world. Philosophy of communication inquiry "examines questions related to the nature and function of human communication" (Arneson, 2007, p. 8). Additionally, there are multiple perspectives of philosophy of communication that invite differing perspectives to enter the conversation together and to bounce off of one another in a way that allows perspectives to change and have influence over other perspectives. This is not in a controlling way, but rather in a way that allows all perspectives to be honored, which when done authentically; held perspectives must allow for change and transformation if they are truly open and inviting. This section highlights three philosophers who do just this, Martin Heidegger, Hans-Georg Gadamer, and Calvin O. Schrag.

Martin Heidegger

To begin with, Martin Heidegger is noted by some scholars as *the* premier philosopher in the 20th century who other philosophers go to first before reading other philosophers. Therefore, it is safe to say that this next section is not intended to summarize his whole body of philosophy. Instead, this section uncovers how and what Heidegger thought about questions and questioning. This understanding, for all three of the philosophers included in this chapter, is that questioning is always tied to the hermeneutic circle, which we also discussed in an earlier chapter—we will come back to this connection between question and the hermeneutic circle in the final section of this chapter.

Heidegger's (1996) hermeneutical approach privileged questions and the task of questioning that often were taken for granted by others and literally unasked. In his questioning, he gathered all of his interpretations to inform his judgments and decisions, which led to actions (Arnett & Holba, 2012).

Some philosophers suggest this kind of questioning is based on destruction and restruction—such as a turn or return to something. The question, however, is asked within the conditions of temporality, or I should say temporality creates the condition for the question to emerge (Heidegger, 1996). In his magnum opus, *Being and Time*, Heidegger (1996) would come to say that in his investigation of existence, the question of being, and the question itself, provided a "disclosive understanding" through "a secure horizon for questions and answers" (p. 398). This situates the importance of questions and the action of questioning as providing the substance for philosophical abstraction, which can then illuminate the pathway toward the "fundamental ontological question, and *follow it*" (Heidegger, 1996, p. 398). The task of doing philosophy and philosophy of communication inquiry is always governed by the questions that guide the inquiry.

Heidegger (1996) suggested that every question asked is a seeking and that the task of seeking is directed by what is sought. He explained that questioning then "is a knowing search for beings in their thatness and whatness" (p. 3). The search then becomes an investigation, and it begins to reveal things and this begins the interrogation (Heidegger, 1996). Heidegger (1996) also clarified the importance of the framing of the question. For example, his question of being was not asked "What is being?" Instead, he asked, "What is the meaning of Being?" Heidegger also illuminated the importance of explicitly formulating the question or questions we ask to the point of complete clarity, at least as clear as it can be asked. When we look back at Heidegger's question of being, if framed "What is Being?" We are looking at a question that implies there is a concrete answer: "What is ..." implies this. However, if we look at the way he framed his question, "What is the meaning of Being?" there is an interpretive aspect to Being that will take time to unpack the "innermost meaning of the question of being" (Heidegger, 1996, p. 7). This is not a concrete task of what is; rather, it is an investigation of what discloses itself through the question. Expanding on the centrality of questions and questioning, Hans-Georg Gadamer further elaborates.

Hans-Georg Gadamer

We discussed the philosophy of Hans-Georg Gadamer in an earlier chapter when we explored the importance of tradition to the philosophy of communication inquiry. Expanding on tradition, the practice of questioning and identifying questions that philosophers pursue is central in Gadamer's philosophy of communication inquiry. In Gadamer's (2002) discussion of historical consciousness he states that it is a hermeneutical task. He also states that we cannot stand outside of the situation, because if we did then we can have no objective knowledge of it. When we find ourselves within the situation, we can gain the objective nature of it, but the situation with which we find ourselves can never be completely understood because Gadamer (2002) reminds us that "to be historically means that knowledge of oneself can never be complete" (p. 302). This means part of our understanding of ourselves is important to take to every single question we ask. This reminds us that our knowledge is always contingent and incomplete—it also reminds us that if and when we stand within a situation and our knowledge is still incomplete, then to stand outside of a situation, our knowledge is even more incomplete and, more likely, marred with misunderstanding.

Gadamer (2002) introduces us to the concept of **horizons**, which refers to a range of vision one has when one stands in a particular vantage point. Gadamer distinguishes between people who have a horizon and those who do not. For example, a person who does not have a horizon cannot see far or broad enough to have a well-informed understanding of something. Consequently, this person only values what is closest to what is seen nearby. This is limiting to one's perspective and discernment. On the other hand, a person who has a horizon means that the person can see beyond what is closest to them and therefore understands the relative significance of all that is seen. The aspect of horizon is important in the philosophy of communication inquiry because in order to work out the hermeneutical situation one must have a horizon of inquiry for the question or questions that emerge. Additionally, the horizons situate the inquiry in a way that can claim a historical consciousness that allows one to see the past in its own terms as one stands within history and not above it or outside of it (Gadamer, 2002).

Gadamer (2002) develops the conceptualization of horizons in his discussion of individual prejudices, which we all have whether we realize it or not. Gadamer states that there is a horizon of the present, which is always being formed and reformed because we are always testing our prejudices. Testing happens when we encounter things from the past as we understand the tradition(s) from which we emerged. This means that our horizon from the past is always interacting with our horizon of the present. Gadamer (2002) refers to this as "fusion of horizons" (p. 306). When we ask questions, we recognize these horizons and traditions coming together with natural tensions betwixt and between; this frames the encounter of the hermeneutical task toward understanding. We are always trying to make sense of things through the fusion of horizons.

For Gadamer (2002), to ask a question and the task of questioning itself is tied to opening up the possibilities of meaning. One way to ask a question is to read a book and search for meaning to emerge from the text. Gadamer also discusses speaking with another person as a different kind of experience from reading. In discussing the dialectic of question and answer, Gadamer (2002) suggests it demonstrates an appearance of understanding through a reciprocal relationship that can be considered a kind of conversation. In both contexts, it is important that the question is situated within a horizon so that the experience opens to the possibilities of meaning. Gadamer (2002) describes the back-and-forth nature of questioning. This he ties to play, which allows for creativity and opens to seeing things in new ways. Gadamer (2002) argues that in philosophical hermeneutics, one begins with a responsiveness to a question—the question is primordial and creates the condition for the question. Opening to interpretive possibilities also occurs in what Calvin O. Schrag refers to as communicative praxis and simply having dialogic transactions with others.

Calvin O. Schrag

There are multiple approaches to philosophy and philosophical insight. Some philosophers like Pierre Hadot (2002) focus on the history of philosophy; other philosophers seek to advance further understanding of the philosophical canon or parts, periods, and movements of it (Kant, 1965). Some philosophy proposes a new development or turn from a previously accepted philosophical method, such as logic, epistemology, metaphysics, or ethics (Rorty, 1979); it could also be integrated subject matter with other disciplines like science, technology, or religion (Singer, 2017), some of which Calvin O. Schrag has done during the course of his lifetime. However, for this section, we look at Schrag's work in which he uses dialogue and conversation as the mode for examining philosophical thought. Schrag (2010) states taking a dialogical and conversational approach to doing philosophy "illustrate[s] a logic of questioning and rhetorical performance against the backdrop of conversational interaction ... and in doing so elucidate(s) issues in a rhetorically situated philosophical reflection" (p. 1). In fact, Schrag (2010) argues that forging philosophical understanding through dialogue as it enfolds and emerges through dialogic exchange, where communicants or interlocutors, consent and dissent responsively, is not really new—Plato used this process, through his dialogues, to present his philosophical musings and positions, and later Aristotle came along with his own version of this rhetorical undertaking. What Schrag does is different from Plato and Aristotle though. Schrag (2010) uses the features in storytelling of "conversational transactions and epistolary exchanges, historical observations, autobiographical musings, meditations, testimonials, and thought experiments" to navigate questions of importance.

Questions emerge and unfold in radically different ways depending on one's tradition, historical embeddedness, and temporal placement of given ideologies and concerns. This rhetorical enterprise that Schrag (2010) unfolds is a historical and narratival inheritance that seeks questions within a lifeworld that is the backdrop for the rhetorical constructions and emerging possibilities where questions open understanding toward dynamic meaning. Schrag (2010) is careful to say that even through his own conversations, reminiscences, and reflections, it is not only his story that unfolds. He is clear to say that his story can only unfold through the experience of questioning with other voices in the conversations through oral and written modes of engagement. However, it is the shared interest in the questions that create the conditions for this dialogic entrance into hermeneutical expression. It is through reminiscences that questions emerge, as Schrag suggests, rather quickly and to the forefront of one's curiosity.

Schrag (2003) outlines a new humanism, which is a space of public argument grounded in and guided by rationality. This new humanism emerges through the texture of communicative praxis. Communicative praxis is a textured space of dialogical transaction that contains expressive discourse, which is different from referential and narrational discourse. Referential refers to displaying how something proceeds; narrational discourse refers to the telling of a story about something (Schrag, 2003). Expressive discourse is described as a "multifaceted event" that is comprised of speaking, writing, and language (Schrag, 2003, pp. 32–33). In this space, the nonverbal exists with the verbal.

The Process of Doing Philosophy of Communication Inquiry Through Questioning

There is no universal or absolute way of doing philosophy of communication inquiry. There is, however, some commonalities that cross between philosophy of communication modalities that can be identified. Understanding these three coordinates assists with understanding the doing of philosophy of communication inquiry. First is recognizing the difference between history and the conceptual understanding of **historicity**. The second coordinate unfolds around identifying the question(s) that frame and emerge within a given historical moment. The third coordinate of importance is being open to seeing varying hermeneutic entrances from which one can explore a question or questions.

Historicity

Historicity is dynamic and alive and exudes a sense of immediacy. History tells a story about something in/of the past that already occurred and that is not dynamic or changing in facts—however, our understandings of the stories in history change and evolve as time passes and as more distance between the past and the present increases. Historicity is complex and situated within an embeddedness that is always folding and unfolding in meaning. Historicity allows for meaning to emerge and reemerge, which is central to philosophy of communication inquiry because there is no fixed understanding that must be adhered to and accepted unconditionally. Gadamer (2002) suggests historicity should be considered an element of hermeneutical experience. This ties well to a historically effected consciousness: "Historical consciousness is a mode of self-knowledge" (Gadamer, 2002, p. 235). A historical consciousness is not limited to a basic understanding of the tradition in which one stands but it is a consciousness that has a reflective posture integrating itself and the tradition in which it is embedded (Gadamer, 2002).

Emerging Questions

The question is a hermeneutic priority; it creates the condition for inquiry—it also drives the inquiry. By listening to and for the questions that arise, the questions open the possibilities for meanings to emerge given historicity and the historical consciousness. As meaning unfolds and understanding emerges, the horizon of the question shifts and changes. When we anticipate the answers to the questions, this means that, potentially, the questioner is part of the tradition, which can limit the possibilities of meaning and any outcomes from the questioning (Gadamer, 2002). But to truly reach a fuller understanding that acknowledges alterity or the other, one not lonely puts forward their own perspective but also allows for their perspective to be transformed by others, and in doing so one cannot continue to be the who or what that they were (Gadamer, 2002). Questions are truly transformative.

Hannah Arendt (1998) talks about the value of questions when she discusses the differentiation and relationship between the public and private realms of engagement, specifically by identifying and distinguishing between the *vita activa* (the active life) and the *vita contemplativa* (the contemplative life). She states that by raising or putting forth the question of public and private realms of human engagement, she discovered that activities of the *vita activa* had been largely ignored or considered only from the position of the vita contemplativa. Her questioning led to broadening her understanding and her awareness of both of them and their political significance (Arendt, 1998). Arendt's perspective and understanding changed, perhaps strengthened and transformed into a particular advocacy for honoring both the *vita activa* and the *vita contemplativa*.

Hermeneutic Entrances

Richard Palmer (1969) agrees with philosophers such as Aristotle and Heidegger that philosophy should be hermeneutical. In fact, Palmer (1969) suggests that all literary interpretation should be hermeneutical. This does not mean that all interpretation will be the same or even similar. This is because the approach one takes to trying to understand a phenomenon can be different, which will garner different conclusions or outcomes. One thing is for certain: The approach or perspective taken toward finding meaning or understanding something provides a unique lens, or as literary theorist and philosopher of rhetoric Kenneth Burke (1966) might say, a particular "terministic screen" (p. 45) that shapes the outcome of understanding. This is what Gadamer (2002) means when he talks about horizons and fusion of horizons. It is like a kaleidoscope in some ways: How you look at something plays a role in how you understand and interpret the phenomenon.

The language that we use is also part of the way meaning emerges. Palmer (1969) reminds us of this when he states that the "hermeneutical experience is intrinsically linguistic" (p. 242). This means that language is the medium that we use when we stand in the world or come to the world—the world comes to us, standing before us, and entering into us, all in order to find and make meaning. Palmer (1969) also suggests that the hermeneutical experience is an event—a language event (p. 243). This means we make meaning through dynamic engagement with an other or text; it means that how we understand things or make meaning of things is not merely conceptual or a thought experiment. Additionally, the hermeneutical experience is objective but not in the sense that we normally think of as objectivity, which we get from the hard sciences. Palmer (1969) suggests that the hermeneutical experience is objective because it deals with human experience of the linguistic event, and it is validated in the "reflexive operations of the mind"—subjectivity (p. 243). Objective subjectivity is a historical kind of objectivity, which means when one meets resistances of the world, the things one cannot control or shape, one moves within them and conforms to them, becoming the tradition in which one understands and sees the world. This is purely unique to one, but it is also situated within time and history (Palmer, 1969). This quality is difficult to understand, so here is an example. I cannot control where or how I am born into this world. I am born into a particular time period, for me that is 1960, nearing the end of the baby boomer generation. I am also born into a particular history embedded within Pennsylvania Dutch county in central Pennsylvania. Both of these terministic screens shaped my early perspectives and initial worldview about religions, social norms, and engagement in school (other things as well). Growing up Catholic and receiving the sacraments, my understanding of religion was actually very narrow, but to me it was very objective because of linguistic and social experiences. Catholicism was an objective truth to me as my family engaged in lived action and experience in the Church. This is the kind of objectivity that is hermeneutical experience, ever so real and embedded in within an historical objectivity.

Hermeneutic entrances vary, and each of them as valid as the others but in different ways. They provide the backdrop for our embeddedness in historical objectivity. We can look at questions in particular historical moments through different hermeneutic entrances to understand something that comes before us. We must also recognize that if we change the hermeneutic entrance, we may come to a different understanding. That is what hermeneutical experience is about—it is an opening of the text or the experience to see what comes before us and come to new understandings and enriched understandings. I can provide another example here too. Early in my academic experience I began to explore leisure in the context of rhetoric and the human condition. While I thought I knew the meaning of leisure, as I started to read about leisure from different hermeneutic lenses, I quickly realized I really did not understand leisure at all. I read multiple dictionary definitions, I researched its etymology in Latin and Greek languages, I had my own memories of what I thought was leisure, I heard stories from other people about their experiences of what they perceived as leisure, I read about it in magazines and manuals from the leisure industry, and I read about leisure in both ancient and contemporary philosophical discourse and contemporary social science research. Each of these pathways had different objectivities and very different understandings of leisure. I knew the least about the philosophical discourse on leisure, so I decided to learn all that I could from that hermeneutic entrance. This then became a focal point of my scholarly interest. It was a discovery like an avalanche. Noticing the different hermeneutic entrances and then entering them, I discovered a lifetime of knowledge that I never could have conceived of had I not been open to other approaches and understandings. I am sure that with this small example, you can see your own experiences with different hermeneutic entrances. Each question pursued can be sought through differing hermeneutic pathways.

Connections, Currency, and Meaning

For this section, looking at the question of reopening the economies, from local, to regional, to national, is helpful in understanding the importance of recognizing questions and their role in how human beings make meaning. It is also important to remember that meaning is temporal—it changes as the questions evolve naturally. Meaning also changes as human beings insert action and reaction to the questions.

Connections: The connections between questions that emerge and guide public discourse to the hermeneutic entrance one takes to the question or their questioning does shape, in some way, the interpretive outcomes. It is important in the interpretation and meaning-making process that paying attention to and developing some understanding of the connections between questions and the hermeneutic entrance is going to shape the meaning. This provides a clearer temporal picture from which one gains understanding.

Currency: Understanding the value of questions and questioning in the historical moment at this writing is most obviously tied to the COVID-19 environment and each human being's response to it. Right now, today, the question in the United States and even around the world that surfaces in most public discussions about the COVID-19 situation is "When is it time to open back up?"—of course this refers to the question of reopening government. In the democracy that shapes this country, generally, the federal government is supposed to be "hands off" most times. Prior to this time in May 2020, there was a federal recommendation that was supported by the medical experts leading our country's approach to the COVID-19 problem: States, led by their governors, could choose to shut down their economies and their public gathering spaces in order to stay ahead of the curve and to work toward flattening that curve. The reference to the curve refers to the moment in time when the COVID-19 tracking data stops increasing, and the projected numbers of infections and actual deaths would decrease. This means that the numbers would either drop or lower and stay the same or eventually begin toward signifying a downward trend.

At this particular time in the pandemic's trajectory, the federal government provided a set of guidelines for states to use to determine when the time for reopening should occur. According to the White House (2020), these guidelines are as follows:

1. There is a downward trajectory of influenza-like illnesses reported within a 14-day period AND there is a downward trajectory of COVID-like syndromic cases reported within a 14-day period (this has to do with symptoms only);

2. There is a downward trajectory of documented cases within a 14-day period OR there is a downward trajectory of positive tests as a percent of total tests within a 14-day period, which means there is a flat or increasing volume of tests (this has to do with actually confirmed cases);

3. Hospitals can treat all patients without moving into crisis mode/care AND hospitals are able to implement a robust testing program for at-risk healthcare workers, this includes emerging antibody testing.

These criteria for reopening the country and allowing people to return to work have to be accompanied by a rigorous set of preparedness guidelines and the integration of new guidelines that support increased and focused sanitary practices in all work sites and public spaces. As this book is being written, there is a massive gradual and successive limited reopening of the economy in real time. This allows one to observe the overarching question as it evolves and reshapes in response to the consequence of asking the question of reopening the local, state, and national economies. This question points to the moral accountability of leaders, locally, regionally, and nationally. What is valued more, a sustainable or thriving economy or human lives? We know that reopening businesses amid increasing infection numbers will lead to more infections and an increasing death toll. We also know, with a higher national unemployment percentage than the Great Depression in the 1920s and 1930s in the United States, human beings will increasingly suffer in different ways. Seemingly, there is no good answer.

Letting the questions guide public moral argument invites broader understanding of the issues and hopefully a willingness to listen to the other since the consequences of any decision are high and significantly impactful to everyday human experience. In the application of philosophy of communication inquiry, being able to see the contours of the issues is necessary. It is through this kind of openness that dialogue and dialectic can guide the discourse without forcing and controlling outcomes. While philosophy of communication inquiry does not provide or dictate the answers to questions, the process is tied more clearly to the hermeneutic circle we discussed in an earlier chapter. The hermeneutic circle affords one the opportunity to think, rethink, and adjust as meaning emerges.

Meaning: Meaning in this regard is temporal. This means it is responsive to the particularities of the historical moment and the questions that persist and evolve in their persistence. There is no clear answer to these emergent questions, but they do shape and inform how people make meaning within the particularities of their ongoing experiences. The next chapter provides more texture regarding questions and their emergences within particular historical moments. This can help as we try to identify the questions of own current historical moment.

Conclusion

This chapter identified the importance of discovering the questions that philosophers pursue in their search for meaning. The importance of the process of questioning is central to making sense out of human experience. Introducing Martin Heidegger, Hans-Georg Gadamer, and Calvin O. Schrag is also key to understanding the philosophy of communication inquiry since their philosophical pursuits centered around finding meaning of being, understanding temporality, and recognizing language, dialogue, and meaning constitute the human landscape where meaning emerges. The focus on questions and questioning continue in the next chapter for further application.

Chapter 9

A Brief Overview of Questions Guiding Philosophical Inquiry

Time Periods and Traditions

Learning Objectives

1. Identify denotated time periods and articulate their significance in philosophy of communication inquiry.

2. Articulate the relationship between time periods and traditions that arise during those time periods.

3. Describe examples of particular guiding questions within historical time periods.

4. Identify current emergent questions and discuss their particular meanings.

This chapter discusses historical time periods with traditions and offers examples of questions that emerged during those times. This provides a sense of application of philosophical inquiry embedded within context and a fusion of horizons, which wards of any possibility of staying abstract. Philosophy of communication inquiry is always about something in a very pragmatic sense. In order to derive meaning about something, the inquiry must be pragmatically grounded and situated. First, an examination of the periods and traditions is framed to situate guiding questions respectively. Second, a discussion about doing philosophy of communication inquiry about something unfolds the pragmatic value of embedding philosophy into context and application. Third, "Connections, Currency, Meaning" provides examples from what is happening today in public moral argument.

Situated Guiding Questions

People have been asking questions and questioning in general ever since human beings have existed. These questions and forms of questioning have been diverse across traditions and time periods. When we look at the historical horizon that is comprised of people, their actions, and the contexts within which they are situated, meaning emerges (Taylor, 1984). When we can see the whole of the horizon that is fused with other horizons, questions that guide the particularities of the historical moment emerge and begin to shape understandings and interpretations. Philosophy of communication inquiry of something presupposes a historicality within which meaning arises. When questions emerge, we identify them and their role in shaping our understanding. It is helpful to keep in mind that questions and meaning shift and change over time and across time. This section is designed to provide examples but not make an exhaustive list, which in all practicality could not be made anyway. I have organized this by time period, which we already discussed in Chapter 3. This chapter identifies and discusses some of the questions that guided public moral discourse in different historical periods.

Ancient/Classical Era

In order to understand the kinds of questions that fueled public moral discourse and argument, identifying the voices that come into guide this discussion is important. Questions are asked by people, and their questions are usually directed at other people about something in particular or about conceptual thoughts in general. An example of a question that one person asks another person might be "How should we govern our community?" An example of a conceptual question might involve the questions "What is truth?" "What is wisdom?" or "What is justice?" as Plato asked through his Socratic dialogues. For the purpose of this section, I identify particular voices as examples, and I recognize that by picking one or two examples I am also leaving out other voices. This does not mean the voices I select here are more important or better. It just means that these are the voices I chose by convenience on my part or are simply well-known voices I anticipate the reader might already know.

Two questions, one related to the question of truth versus truths and the other question about how to lead the polis capture key public discourse in the ancient world. The first question about truth was widespread in public discussions during the lifetimes of Plato and Aristotle—no doubt it was also a key question in earlier and subsequent times as well. The same or similar questions are engaged today but using different language and conventions like the questions that surface about fake news or competency in the office of the United States president. Plato pursues the question of truth through multiple writings, many of which are through his dialogues. Plato believed that there was one truth and he warned about how the use of rhetoric can present the appearance of multiple truths. In his dialogue, *The Gorgias*, Plato (1987) refers to this kind of truth-saying as cookery and deceit which calls into question the moral possibility of the existence of multiple truths that create contradiction or assert a moral and cultural relativism rendering any argument meaningless. Plato's dialogues were not only historical stories but they were also philosophical ruminations on perennial questions that have preoccupied human beings since the beginning of time. When we read his dialogues, we imagine these gatherings of people and their conversations as events that occurred to some degree.

Plato modeled his dialogues after the way he taught, through a dialectic of question and answer, which allowed for the listener-responder to discover by revelation—or find themselves a hypocrite. In many of his dialogues, however, Plato's interlocuter(s) and himself actually fail to find an absolute answer to his questions. Plato (1997) comes to terms with this when he suggests in his *Apology* that he only realizes that he does not know the answers, a very humbling acknowledgment. Plato's early dialogues rarely come to an absolute answer to a question, which frustrates him to some extent; however, his later dialogues turn a bit and exemplify that the only way to find answers of ethical and metaphysical questions, in an abstract sense, is to engage in these inquiries together in a dialectic fashion (Audi, 1999).

Questions tied to the polis required more particularity in its response. Commitment to life in the Greek polis was a common feature of ancient Greek life, especially during the second half of the 5th century where many of the public leaders concerned themselves with questions pertaining moral, political, and epistemological matters (Johnstone, 2009). This represented a shift away from the pre-Socratic public discourse that focused on naturalistic speculation to a pragmatic intellectual movement focused on the human as individual and practical obligations of civic and personal lives (Johnstone, 2009). One of these practical obligations was the role of language and speech in public civic life; this ushered in discourse related to logos (Johnstone, 2009). Logos, in this sense, is "understood as speech and as reasoned argument" (Johnstone, 2009, p. 87). Logos came to be the instrumental way public judgments were made and therefore questions of right logos were pursued by philosophers, politicians, and orators.

Evidence of this shift toward the dominance of speech and language centered around remaining texts from the time, which include Aristotle's *Rhetoric* (1984) and *Politics* (2001), Isocrates's *Nicocles* (2000), and Marcus Cicero's *de Inventione* (*On Invention*) (1968) and *de Oratore* (*On the Orator*) (1942) (just to name a few). These are only representative texts; there is an entire rhetorical canon that emerged from the ancient, classical period that focused on how one should speak and what one should do in service to the polis and public life (Herrick, 2017). Following a historical timeline, the Middle Ages or medieval era emerged, focusing on a different era of questioning within a theological framework.

Middle Ages/Medieval Era

Most historians describe some kind of allegiance to Christian theology as a guiding framework for the medieval era (Evans, 2001). This kind of allegiance was imbued with Platonic thought, which articulated that self-definition does not come through the individual but rather through an external source, which for the early Church was God. This meant that the center of meaning for the era shifted from the self and engagement in the public polis toward the Church and an affinity for God. During this time, questions of religion and God, especially from St. Thomas Aquinas, were dominant, and questions about access to information thrived. Religious values were situated within the cultural horizons of medieval Europe but toward the end of the era individuals began to rebel against the dominance of religious overreach, which gave rise to a renaissance of learning and focus on the ability to widely access information. Before moving on to the Renaissance era, a discussion pertaining to St. Thomas Aquinas demonstrates the kinds of questions that preoccupied public thought of the era.

Thomas Aquinas (1225–1274) was a Dominican friar, scholar, and preacher who advocated Aristotelian concepts related to ethics and rhetoric and provided commentary on other major works of Aristotle, such as *Metaphysics* and *De Anima* (Maciejewski, 2018). The Church continues to this day to signify the importance of Aquinas's work, both his theology (especially his focus on Christian revelation) and his philosophy (focusing on his commentaries on Aristotle's works). The major work that he is most noted for is his *Summa Theologica*, which is a text that explains Christine doctrine, and it is written for both the faithful student of Christianity as well as those aggressors against Christianity. Aquinas demonstrated the rigor of faith and the system of reason that can support the faith through the *Summa*. In it he addressed many questions that were part of public discourse at the time. Some of those questions include, "What does it mean to be human?" "What are human capacities and what do they mean in our lives?" and "What is the soul?" Interrogating these questions demonstrates how much they overlap but for Aquinas, the important aspect of processing and pursuing these questions is balancing the tensions between faith and reason toward a meaningful understanding of one's life and death. So, one of the significant questions he pursued came in the form of "What is the relationship between faith and reason?"

Because of Aquinas's monotheistic beliefs, he had Platonic tendencies toward faithfulness and truth; because of his respect for reason and argument, he advocated for Aristotle's system of reason, argument, and ethics. The two really are not distinctly separate and discrete capacities. To consider the question, "What is the nature of human beings?" Aquinas thought that human beings needed to understand their essence, and knowing the relationship between faith and reason assists with answering this question. Aquinas believed that for human beings to understand their essence, this is determined by their ends; these ends happen to be moral goods that one attains through their actions. Capacities and actions of human beings demonstrate the moral goods that guide actions—this for Aquinas is a matter of virtue and is how one understands oneself (Maciejewski, 2018). Aquinas asked these questions and answered them in his writings, thus predominantly guiding and shaping public discourse during his lifetime.

Aquinas suggested that in theology one reasons from their predetermined belief in God. However, in philosophy, one reasons through investigation of a human-created reality and argument conventions, thus seeking to arrive at some kind of knowledge. Aquinas had a particular interest in metaphysics, which is "the science of being as being" (Audi, 1999, p. 37). This is different from his theology because God is not the subject of this inquiry (metaphysics) as it is in his theology; there is also no direct vision of God, as is the case in his theology. In his inquiry into metaphysics, he can study "what is the cause of finite beings" as his subject and reason around the existence of God (Audi, 1999). Aquinas used his philosophical reason to demonstrate that God exists through reasoning from effect to cause (Aquinas, 2018; Audi, 1999). Aquinas presented his argument of God's existence in the *Summa* through something referred to as the "five ways" (Aquinas, 2018):

1. First mover

2. Causation

3. Contingency

4. Degree

5. Final ends (or final aim as in *telos*) (Aquinas, 2018)

The first way, God as first mover (but who is unmoved), acknowledges that things are always changing and things change because of something else, but the chain of changing something and being changed cannot be an infinite chain. There must be something that causes change that itself cannot change. Aquinas stated everyone thus knows that this can only be God. Words that Aquinas used are important. He used the word "motion" in his argument, which reflects the transition from having potential to an actuality. He stated that if potential does not yet exist, then it cannot cause itself to exist. It can only be brought into existence by something already in existence. Accepting the apriori existence of God means God is unchangeable and therefore is the first mover or first in existence to move a potential into an actual.

The second way, causation, is quite similar in principle to the first mover. It suggests that one cannot cause oneself and that the chain of causation is not infinite; therefore, there must be a first cause, which is different from being a derivative cause. There has to be a first in existence—which is God. The third way, contingency, is the argument for a necessary being. The idea behind this argument is that things come and go, exist and do not exist, are born and then perish. In this contingency, there can be no existence if everything is contingent—without a first being who does not perish, there can be no existence at all. Therefore, there needs to be a necessary being that is unchangeable. The fourth way, by degree, suggests that in the world there exists varying degrees of good, beauty, truth, honor, and more. This implies there is a judgment and that there is first or highest degree of good, beauty, truth, honor, and so on. If this exists, than in order to judge the degrees, there must be something that provides the highest level of the degree to base the judgment on—this, according to Aquinas, is God, and he suggested that this is universally known and accepted. Finally, the fifth way implies there is no such thing as chance and that if nonintelligent things act in a certain way something of higher intelligence is the author of their actions, because otherwise nonintelligent things would not know how to act on their own. This is a different argument from the mainstream intelligent design theory. What this means is that things that have no obvious intelligence, such as trees or flowers, must be led by an intelligent force or being. For example, when a Black-Eyed Susan daisy drops its seeds, it sows another flower of the same, which gives us fields of golden flowers well into late summer. But it very well could drop its seeds and grow something else, or not cultivate into the ground and blow away only to dry up and die later in the fall. Since there is no obvious intelligence in the flower, there must be something else that leads it and that something else must have intelligence. Aquinas goes through a process of reason and argument to prove the existence of God—this is how he addressed his question about the relationship between faith and reason. As influence from the Church waned, the Renaissance era began to emerge.

Renaissance Era

The Renaissance era emerged after the medieval era or Middle Ages with a focus on nature and science (Taylor, 2007). This is a key feature that subsequently bridged the Western world into a secular age. Unlike the medieval era where the Church held primary authority over education, the Renaissance era focused on expanding education and application in the world, which contributed to a rebirth of how people thought about the world and how they philosophized, which served as a bridge to the Enlightenments (this is covered in the next section). As for the Renaissance era, questions that governed public discourse were again either widely philosophical and abstract as well as focused or subjective regarding human experience.

The Renaissance period was very much a cultural movement that brought back Latin literatures and learning shifted toward the classical sources instead of the Church-sponsored sources for learning. The Renaissance saw widespread educational reform as well as political changes from new political diplomacy to a renewed respect for scientific knowledge based on observations and inductive reasoning (Audi, 1999). This was an age that saw continuing social and political challenges, but it also advanced the birth of art and intellectual advancements. It also gave birth to the colloquial label of the Renaissance man or the universal man, which refers to any individual who has a depth and breadth of knowledge and experience, one who is highly cultured and refined in their social practices, and who can do anything. It was later defined as a person who is neither an expert nor a specialist but someone who knows something about everything and who seemingly can do a wide range of things that are vastly different (Van Doren, 1991). An example of this is Leon Battista Alberti and Leonardo DaVinci just to name two.

The Renaissance era saw of significant development of inventions and movement away from a very closed era of epistemological access. A renaissance of thought opened the constraints on human reason—it also shifted power from the Church toward the autonomy of the individual human being, and this opened up the closed Christian environment toward a new emerging secular environment. The Renaissance emphasized human autonomy and action (Taylor, 1989). This does not mark the time as the fall of the religious paradigm; however, it did open and expand the religious narrative through movements such as the Protestant Reformation in the 16th century. It also ushered in an emphasis on the individual. How individuals made meaning in their lives shifted from an institution, such as the Church, to the individual, through their own imaginations and creativities. This shift evolved even further in the early Enlightenment era.

Enlightenment

Emerging from the Renaissance era, the Enlightenment was multifaceted. Often, when the Enlightenment is discussed, it is presented as a singular, one-dimensional period of time that was either effective or not effective or singularly themed and one-dimensional. The reality is that this is not the case. Aaron Gare, contemporary Australian philosopher, excavates the history of the Enlightenment era and calls for a revival of the **radical Enlightenment** (Gare, 2006). Gare (2006) differentiates between the radical and **moderate Enlightenments**, both of which pursued different but related questions. There is a conventional understanding of the Enlightenment as a failed project having negative consequences for everyday communication (Arnett et al., 2007). These consequences are tied to the victory of the moderate Enlightenment and the covering over or pushing underground of the radical Enlightenment. The distinction between these enlightenments was first articulated by identifying the tensions between defender of tradition and champions of radical reform (Appleby et al., 2011).

Gare (2006) distinguishes between the moderate and radical enlightenment that suggests the moderate enlightenment is responsible for paving the way to a new social order that was a new oligarchy of wealth. Moderate enlightenment advocates believed that freedom had to do with an individual's capacity to control their life by increasing pleasure, and in doing so reducing the unpleasant (Arnett et al., 2007). The radical enlightenment voices were pushed underground until at least the 18th century, which limited their ability to develop the convincing and cohesive conceptual framework for radical change (Arnett et al., 2007). The moderate enlightenment embodied hegemonic tendencies; the radical enlightenment embodied an acknowledgment of diversity of cultures and multiplicity of voices—which did not take hold until postmodernity surfaced in the mid to late 20th century.

Philosopher Johann Gottfried Herder (1744–1803) was an advocate for the radical enlightenment and developed what he referred to as radical difference (Herder, 2001/2002). Radical difference recognizes that people and cultures change over time, so this means that hanging onto embedded traditions without noticing when they should change or evolve in response to changing historical moments limits human experience and potential.

There are also other enlightenments tied to cultures. In the Western world and in traditional educational environments, we immediately think of the English enlightenment, and even though we might recognize some of Scottish thinkers in the enlightenment conversation, like Adam Smith and David Hume, we tend to not focus on the Scottish enlightenment as much, but it happened and it had significant outcomes. Arnett (forthcoming) describes the Scottish enlightenment as "an effort to temper the increase of optimism in modernity's embrace of progress." This definition enfolds Arnett's distinction between, and warning about, optimism and tenacious hope. Optimism is an expectation that an experience will stand up to one's anticipation and needs (Arnett, forthcoming). It is very consumer oriented and, according to Arnett (forthcoming), is bound to a singular direction. On the other hand, tenacious hope is an experience of the unity of contraries that embraces the individual within responsible engagement of a social context—the juxtaposition of the individual and others (Arnett, forthcoming). Arnett (forthcoming) suggests that optimism is tied to a consumeristic demand from the individual to the market; tenacious hope creates the space for a responsibility for the other within a locality and for the locality itself. This exemplifies a contrary perspective against the provincial and utter disregard for difference (Arnett, forthcoming).

The Scottish enlightenment is usually demarcated as occurring across the 18th and 19th centuries. Questions asked during the Scottish enlightenment were focused on the local and the practical—abstract philosophical assurance was rejected (Arnett, forthcoming). Scottish thinkers promoted free thinking and listening to different ideas as well as encouraged practical applications for action. They respected deep philosophical thinking but pushed for bringing them into the lived experience. Questions about the meaning of freedom and liberty were a focal point in public discourse. For example, David Hume (1711–1776) questioned the origins of human nature, reason, and sentiment; he rejected an imposed authority and its implications to real human experience (Arnett, 2018). This meant he resisted controls over human interaction and engagement in social and political public life. Hume's social and political thought was framed in discussions of impressions and sensations that people felt and experienced (Arnett, 2018). He tied everything back to this felt-sense experience, which exemplified his concern for practical and applied discussions instead of abstract pontifications.

There is one philosopher who is key to mention from the age of Enlightenment. Though he will be in a later chapter, I would be remiss if I did not mention him here. Immanuel Kant (1724–1804) was an early Enlightenment philosopher who was prolific and who is someone that most philosophers after him had engaged his work and life project in almost every corner of philosophy in the Western world. As an Enlightenment thinker, Kant's (1999) life work was focused around vindicating the authority of reason, something that the medieval era narrowed in influence and legitimacy (Audi, 1999). As the historical moment began shifting to the modern era, questions shifted too.

Modern Era

The modern era is not the same thing as the modern world (Arendt, 1958). As mentioned in an earlier chapter, the modern era began in the seventeenth century and ended sometime in the early to mid-20th century. In a political sense, the modern world in which we live today really started with the rise of the atomic bomb (Arendt, 1958). Many scholars acknowledge that the guiding narrative of the modern era was progress—the reliance on always moving forward, always some place to go, and the myth that more is better (Arnett & Holba, 2012). Privileging progress goes together with privileging science, which results in great advancements. However, this privileging led to turning away from an **"enlarged mentality"** (Arendt, 1958).

Hannah Arendt (1958), 20th-century social and political philosopher, described the modern era as a time defined by world alienation as she identified a collapse of public and private spheres. Arendt (1993) questioned how the collapse could occur at all and referred to this time as **"dark times"** in the world's history (p. ix). This collapse led to a new and different space for human engagement that she termed the social.

The social realm is defined by the blurred lines between public and private and how one communicatively engages in this new space that leaves recognizing the differentiation between public and private obscured. The emergence of the social realm brought a dark side to the modern era, which was marked by political unrest, imperialism, colonialism, and totalitarianism across Europe and around the world (Arendt, 1958). Arendt talks about these conditions in her political philosophy that was shaped from her experience as a Jewish woman who grew up and was schooled in Germany, was imprisoned briefly by the Gestapo, fled to Czechoslovakia, Switzerland, and finally Paris. After Germany invaded France, she fled to the United States where she taught college, wrote books, and eventually covered the Adolf Eichmann trial in Jerusalem, writing about it for the *New Yorker* magazine.

These experiences caused her to question very deeply, philosophically and pragmatically, what happens when one loses autonomy, fails to think for oneself, and fails to have an enlarged mentality or capacity to think beyond the ego. In her coverage of the Eichmann trial, she received great criticism from the academy and from the public for appearing to reduce his culpability for his actions by describing him simply as a little man who was not able to think for himself and who just followed orders from a higher ranking individual. Years later, the academy and public sentiment changed and came to understand that she was not letting him off the hook for his actions but that she recognized the dark side of not thinking for oneself and the failure to expand one's mentality and capacity to think beyond the self.

While Arendt identified questions of power and control, Fredrich Nietzsche (1844–1900) questioned the legitimacy of religion. Nietzsche (2006) is known for the pronouncement that God is dead, which marked the decline of modernity's grand narrative of religion; this coincided with a foreshadowing of the transition from a modern era to a postmodern era. Nietzsche noticed the decline of adherence to traditional religious and metaphysical ways of thinking and projected the advent of nihilism (Audi, 1999). Nietzsche could be discussed in this section on the modern era since his pronouncements have been considered prophetic, but he also could be discussed in the postmodern era because his questions of authority and truth are hallmarks of postmodern thinking and criticism (Robinson, 2001). I chose to include him here as a bridge between the modern and postmodern eras.

Nietzsche referred to Christianity as a great curse and blamed the belief in a higher transcendence for creating the opportunity for religion to be an opiate for the masses of people. He is known for having a sense of global skepticism, questioning the notion of truth and any kind of foundation—to become known as an anti-foundationalist (Robinson, 2001). The key to his understanding of truth centered on the idea that human beings only ever create truths for themselves that are useful or helpful to their own desires or wants. Truth is therefore invented by human beings and always subjective in nature. This problem of truth, according to Nietzsche (2010), is a problem with language in that he said language is always metaphorical and a key player in self-deception. These are some of the key aspects that surfaced in public discourse during the postmodern era.

Postmodern Era

There is a lot to say about the postmodern era, starting with its temporal borders are blurred and incongruent across disciplines. There are some strong voices that emerged in declaration of a postmodern era or a time and condition of human existence. This declaration refers to a new social and cultural human experience that is defined in opposite terms to human experience in the modern era. Some scholars suggest postmodern is simply a temporal indicator—a time period; others suggest it is more of a convenient description or label for a set of attitudes, values, beliefs, and feelings that explains what it means to be alive in the later part of the 20th century (Robinson, 2001). Others reject this simplistic definition. There is however, from most perspectives, a deeply skeptical sensibility about language and meaning. Discussions pertaining to postmodern sensibilities are often associated with post-structuralist philosophy, some of which we already discussed in earlier chapters when we discussed semiotics. Some scholars suggest postmodern sensibilities are squarely focused on the inherent problems with language that led to skepticism and questions of meaning. For many postmodernists, the focus is on who is asking the questions and the assumptions behind the questions. The postmodern era, while questioning the possibility of meaning, also gives voice to the formerly marginalized and reveals latent structures of power and control and the pervasiveness of hegemonic structures across social, political, and cultural environments.

A seminal text describing the postmodern era or postmodern thinking is attributed to the philosopher Jean-François Lyotard (1928–1998). Lyotard's (1984) major work, *The Postmodern Condition: A Report on Knowledge*, noted that all grand narratives that defined the Western world have been demolished. He describes the concept of petite narratives as the new organizing structures of the Western world and culture that are not organized hierarchically but that are local and parallel. So, instead of assuming there is one Christian narrative, he noted that instead there are a plethora of religious narratives, including the fracturing on the Catholic narrative into a wide variety of Protestant, evangelical, and other Christian-based religions, as well as other non-Christian religions including those that are monotheistic, polytheistic, and pagan. Lyotard also rejected foundationalism and commitment to political certainties (Robinson, 2001). Lyotard advocated for a society that is pluralistic and pragmatic, libertarian and anarchist; one that celebrates difference and avoids certainties (Robinson, 2001). While the postmodern era is quite difficult to describe, the era we are currently living in is even more elusive and most difficult to adequately define. For this reason, I simply refer to it as being in the Now.

Now

There have been a variety of perspectives that describe the era in which we live today. Some of the labels and descriptions attributed to our current historical era include post-postmodern (Holba, 2007), pseudo-modernism (Kirby, 2006), the world rearranging itself (Hutcheon, 2002), hypermodernity (Charles & Lipovesky, 2006), after theory (Eagleton, 2004), and many more attempts at defining a new era. Some scholars suggest that Western civilization is evolving into a post-techno capitalistic society with characteristics of spiritual emptiness and cultural superficiality (Robinson, 2001). There are unending perspectives about the world in which we live, but the reality is that nobody can say with certainty what society is becoming. In fact, the act of describing something that is not fully present creates the possibility of contributing to the change in a way that is unknowable in this moment. The notion of wanting to label something with language that is metaphorical, reaching back into Nietzsche's critique of language, and overwhelmingly obscured is a modern impulse that wants to control and manage the natural order of things.

The best we can do is be ever vigilant in our understanding of our surroundings. We should continue to ask questions and be self-reflexive in our understandings about the world. We must always check our own assumptions and allow ourselves to acknowledge without judgment until a fuller picture of our surroundings arises. This is the task of philosophy of communication inquiry—to listen, to gather, to find the questions, to understand, to consider, to question the questions, and to allow meaning to emerge.

Doing Philosophy of Communication Inquiry

Doing philosophy of communication requires attention to the question. This attention includes seeing the fusion of horizons, recognizing the historical consciousness, and identifying questions of given historical moments.

Philosophy of communication requires a pragmatic sensibility to avoid the arrogance of questioning for the sake of questioning. Philosophy of communication involves a commitment to action that is informed by praxis. Images of past philosophers engaging philosophy reflectively, only concerned with their own thoughts and ruminations, can easily evolve into arrogance and elitism since there is no attempt to take meaningful action. This concern shaped Hannah Arendt's thinking in her critique of Greek philosophers who stayed in their ivory towers to philosophize but who never took the next step to make a difference in their world, unless it benefited them.

This is similar to Plato's advocacy for the philosopher king. Plato believed that the philosopher had the intellectual tools to lead, but these tools are no good unless the intellect could be placed into action. In this regard, kings take action, so the best leaders are those who are both philosophers and kings, who have philosophical prowess and are able to hear and take the call to action into leadership. Of course, there are kings who have no philosophical aptitude and there are philosophers who might have a vision but cannot take something to action. Plato advocated for leadership to have both qualities of the philosopher and the king—the philosopher king. In the last section of this chapter, I explore the importance of questioning to our current historical moment—resisting the urge to label our current historical moment as anything but Now, today.

Connections, Currency, and Meaning

For this section I identify questions that we face amid the COVID-19 pandemic that has overshadowed every aspect of our lives in this moment of time. Identifying questions elevates how important asking questions can be to how we make sense of the world and our place in the world. This is a significant existential aspect in the practice of philosophy of communication inquiry because it keeps the focus on the problem instead of the querent. The reason why the focus must stay on the problem is the risk of morphing the inquiry into a psychological investigation. Philosophy of communication does not advocate psychologism—it refrains from blame and does not embrace psychological judgments. Calvin Schrag (2003) provides a good example of this in his work, *Communicative Praxis and the Space of Subjectivity.* Schrag's approach to philosophy of communication aligns with Gadamer's philosophical hermeneutics that acknowledges subjectivity but is not guided by it. Schrag's philosophy points to what he refers to as new humanism that identifies a place for public argument grounded in and guided by a praxial rationality. We have talked about Schrag's work in earlier chapters and we will read about it again in a later chapter.

Connections: Connections to questions shape human agency. Without noticing questions, our actions risk being meaningless, inappropriate, or worse, cause damage or harm to others or ourselves. Recognizing the importance of questions and questioning is the first step to inform public moral argument. Questions hold society and cultures morally and humanely accountable. Without questions, we risk repeating past mistakes and providing opportunities for new hegemonies and fortification of abusive power structures. Connecting to questions of the time provides avenues for compassion, empathy, and justice.

Currency: In the current historical moment as I write this book, we are still in the midst of the COVID-19 pandemic that we discussed previously. As I look at the current historical moment and being situated within the grips of the moment, the questions I see involve whether to reopen the economy and how to do it, questions of the president's response to the pandemic, and questions of how the political environment is still not able to put aside differences in order to work together to do their jobs. Exploring these questions publicly is important for transparency and trust in our social and political systems. There are other questions that arise that sometimes distract public discourse, such as whether China is responsible for intentionally covering up the virus or if there is another reason for their stockpiling of personal protection equipment (PPE) before they told the world about the virus. But these kinds of questions seem more akin to red herrings in the midst of all of the uncertainty about the virus instead of useful questions that can assist recovery in the current moment. This means that identifying the right questions is not the only necessary thing we need to do as we search for meaning. We must discern the key questions and the questions designed to distract us from understanding our experiences and finding meaning within the chaotic experience of the pandemic. This distinction of questions will aid in the meaning we come to through the process of engaging public moral argument.

Meaning: Questions are important to how we make and find meaning. By identifying questions and asking them ourselves, we are able to shift our focus of attention to places that assist in meaning making. Asking questions and listening to responses as they arise is key to inquiry—it is active and allows one to be fully engaged in their own meaning-making process. This is important in a time when truth and transparency are ever so deluded by technology. We must be vigilant in asking questions and noticing the questions of given historical moments whether we are actively engaged today or seeking to understand the past. The key is the question and the process of questioning. The next chapter explores philosophy of communication inquiry through the interrelationships between historicity, communicative praxis, and meaning making, which informs how we further understand philosophy of communication inquiry.

Conclusion

The intention of this chapter is to provide a rationale for the importance of making connections between time periods, traditions, and questions situated within historical eras in order to find temporal meaning. Temporal meaning shapes understanding of the given moment in history and wards off against a subjectivity that does not recognize the importance of being situated within history. This chapter also identified some of the key questions that were shaping how people made sense of their world at that time. Looking at these key questions emerging across historical time periods demonstrates how the questions shaped the temporality of meaning since the questions were relative to historical happenings and changed over time. The emphasis on questions in both Chapters 8 and 9 should provide incentive to remember that in order to come to meaning, especially in a public context, identifying questions people pursue frames one's understanding and opens understanding and meaningfulness.

Chapter 10

Historicity, Communicative Praxis, and Meaning Making

Learning Objectives

1. Make a distinction between history and historicity.

2. Understand the application of historicity in philosophy of communication inquiry.

3. Articulate key coordinates of communicative praxis.

4. Trace the process of meaning making in philosophy of communication inquiry.

H aving a sense of meaning and purpose provides one with a sense of direction, hope, safety, security, and comfort. These sensibilities help to construct a sense of home and, to some extent, rootedness. How can we be sure that we are not mistaken by the meaning we ascribe to ourselves? How can we know that the meaning we believe we come to know is real? What are the means we ought to follow to protect ourselves from a sense of falsehoods? What can we do to have some level of confidence in our understandings and interpretations about the world around us and about ourselves?

This chapter explores the connections between the components historicity, communicative praxis, and meaning in the practice of philosophy of communication inquiry. Each component has been mentioned earlier in this book, and often. This discussion unfolds each coordinate in order to understand the process of the philosophy of communication inquiry. Meaning making becomes even more important in challenging times. Most eras contain points of crisis that are unique in history. John Herman Randall, Jr. (1976) provides a historical account of the making of the modern mind that outlines historical periods in Western civilization that encountered challenges and crises that demonstrated the tensions between people, societies, and governments.

For example, Randall (1976) identified the settling of Western civilization from the moment of the Christian-centric medieval era through to its disruption that ushered in a new world of the Renaissance and a revolt from the medieval church to a Protestant Reformation that would later mark a unified Christendom when another revolt occurred moving away from feudalism. More crises would occur as the new religion of rationalism took hold while scientific ideals framed this new age of reason (Randall, 1976). Tensions abound around the romantic protest against reason and the public conflict of social ideals emerged heading in the late 1800s into the 20th century where the grand narrative of religion was replaced by the grand narrative of progress—even though we now know faith in progress is just an illusion (Randall, 1976). Throughout history there are always challenges to how meaning emerges across the human landscape. One thing is certain, the importance of cultivating a clear understanding is most helpful to the process of how we make meaning. For this, it is important that these features of meaning making are acknowledged: historicity, historical consciousness (to an extent), and communicative praxis. These features framed within the context of questions, questioning, and traditions provide the best opportunity for making meaning that has currency, is relevant, and makes sense.

Historicity

A basic understanding of historicity involves recognizing that a phenomenon has an historical origin and that this origin provides some kind of historical authority. However, this understanding should not be confused with a historical chronology (Arnett et al., 2008). Historicity frames how a question is understood differently across different historical periods and it is the pronouncement that different questions are foregrounded differently when they are situated in different historical moments (Arnett et al., 2008). When seeking questions or trying to understand questions or a historical era, historicity announces the interpretive space is temporal.

There are varieties of historicity that share common themes and that express subtle differences. It should be noted that the definition here aligns with a German sensibility, coming from the German existential movement, *Geschichtlichkeit,* reflecting a phenomenological and hermeneutical tradition as an essential feature of the human experience and existence in general (Audi, 1999). This means that people are not just *in* history—they are constituted by their past, their social past, their own sense of self, and their future potential. A general sense of historicity found in most general American dictionaries is usually expressed as some kind of "historical actuality" but it does not contain much other description. For me, these short definitions in dictionaries like Merriam-Webster are less than helpful.

Historicity invites what Gadamer (2002) referred to as *sensus communus* (p. 19), which is a commonsense notion intended to mark the humanistic tradition and to cultivate a sense of communication and a collective shared good. Within historicity, meaning is always temporal and while questions might have commonalities, there are always differences among them manifesting in a dialectic of responses as the community negotiates around problems and issues (Arnett et al., 2008). Bringing together an understanding of a historical moment, along with identification of questions relevant to the context, and other interlocutors, dialectic, argument, and meaning are possible; this is how one reads their situation and is able to participate in communicative engagement.

Historicity is a communicative call that announces itself in the emplotment of human life and broader narratives without asking for permission—it just happens (Arnett et al., 2008). The agency within historicity is situated within multiple factors that reside external to the communicative agent; in some way, it hails the agent without approval or consent—there is no choice. Without recognizing the nature of the historical questions that arise lacks the most important element for meaning making (Gadamer, 2002). Attention to historicity asks a communicative agent to listen deeply to a situation so that one is permitted to hear the commonsense question(s) of a particular moment. This means the communicative agent is invited to investigate multiplicity of meaning and emphasize the importance of judgment in one's selection of meaning, or in the pursuit of a particular action. Listening carefully and fully is central to determining the questions and the meaning that arises in the process of seeing things clearly. Additionally, similar questions can emerge at different times across history, and even though they emerge at different times, they can remain linked through their historicity. For example, the Mississippi River floods that occurred in 1927 and in 1993 were both a disaster and raised questions of greed, power, and race (Arnett et al., 2008). Historicity is an emergent announcement of a question, and where one is standing within a historical period shapes the interpretive meaning that arises and dictates the significance and implications of the event.

Historicity is the fore-structure of understanding that harbors prejudices that eliminates tradition of its power and deception (Gadamer, 2002). Meaning begins with these prejudices and then allows them to change in the process of ongoing interpretation (Arnett et al., 2008). Historicity offers a framework for human consciousness situated in limits; the questions reveal these limits within a particular historical moment. The response allows and opens to new possibilities. The response can even change the limits. We can only understand historical events if we reconstruct the questions (not the event) that frame the event. The question and answer places a demand on one to listen and then respond but the response must be situated within the historical horizon that presents the question—the horizon is a unique set of circumstances particular to a particular historical moment (Gadamer, 2002). It is important to remember we do not control the emergent questions before us, not their origin nor how they interrogate the communicative agent.

The historicity of understanding issues, questions, and the historical embeddedness requires a hermeneutically trained mind as well as a historical consciousness. **Historical consciousness** is defined as an understanding of the temporality of historical experiences and of how past, present and future are thought to be connected (Arnett et al., 2008). The voice of a particular historical moment can echo through multiple historical periods and demand attention and response. It calls one to be responsive to the uniqueness of historical particularity and acknowledge that temporality is always part of the embeddedness. Philosophy of communication inquiry attends to the question announced by a given historical moment and invites action within the texture of the question and historical consciousness. Historicity frames the space of subjectivity that Calvin Schrag (2003) described as a space of communicative praxis.

Communicative Praxis

Communicative praxis is a couplet introduced by Calvin O. Schrag (2003) to the philosophy domain and to the discipline of communication with the argument that it is essential to basic philosophical inquiry and to philosophy of communication inquiry. Schrag (2003) pointed back to Aristotle, who used the word *praxis* when he talked about a change of ideas in philosophy. Schrag intended that communicative praxis be added and integrated into the traditional scholarly dialogue in formal philosophy—it is that important. The reason why this couplet is so important to philosophy is due to the nature of communication as being embedded within a human context. Schrag (2003) states that when the terms are used together, communication and praxis, it creates a hermeneutical space where intentionalities of discourse and of action interplay. This is similar to Isocrates's advocacy for *logos* and *ergon* as communicative partners; word and deeds must match, otherwise the human exchange cannot be ethical and has no wisdom.

Schrag (2003) unpacks the linguistic texture in the word *praxis*, situating it in action, performance, or some kind of accomplishment that has knowledge behind the action. This knowledge is the theoretical ground that underlies the action or practice of something. The marriage between action and theory constitutes a kind of practical wisdom, which is what the Greeks called *phronesis*. Praxis is interconnected to phronesis. According to Schrag (2003), practice and praxis are very different. Practice refers to a doing of something, like technique, and praxis is the doing of something that is informed by theory (theory-informed action). It is necessary to start from common understandings of language and sometimes to redefine or clarify concepts in order to make meaning meaningful. This is also a reason why hermeneutics and communication are so important. Schrag (2003) states that communication, "in its variegated postures[,] is a performance with the *topos* of human affairs, and dealings that comprise our social world, making these affairs and dealings an issue by not only questioning, informing, arguing, and persuading but also by planning, working, playing, gesturing, laughing, crying, and our general body mobility" (p. 22). This means the space where human communication dwells is a shared space and has both linguistic and action-oriented dimensions. This as both a space of communicative praxis and a space for praxial communication.

Schrag (2003) understands communicative praxis as expression—an expression of speech and action. Action and speech cannot be separated, and communication is action and words (*ergon* and *logos*). However, these two dimensions are not alone; there is a holistic space that is textured with the interplay of both speech and action. In Schrag's critique of the communication discipline, the discipline relies on social science as a frame to study human communication. He suggests that there is less dimensionality when looking through a social scientific lens—it is too restrictive. However, a humanities approach, often utilizing metaphors, contains texture and allows meaning to emerge as the texture mediates the event and the text involved to unfold meaningfulness. Expressive discourse is really about bringing together and comingling expression and reference. By adding reference, something is always being communicated about—it is narrational that explores a processual of texture between expression, reference, and narration (Schrag, 2003). Expressive action shows human action as dynamic and not flat; it is responsive, full, and complex. It is a patterning of social practices that allows discourse and action to go hand in hand with one another. When this interaction occurs, only then is expression achieved and it is not a mere flat stylistic notion.

In the space of communicative praxis, Schrag (2003) differentiates between distanciation, idealization, and recollection. Having a perspective of distanciation, entering a conversation through distance, allows new information to emerge. It allows the bringing of difference to impact already preconceived ideas. Schrag (2003) recognizes that with distanciation there is no ideal, and from distance comes possibilities, new ideas, and new information. This means that if we begin a relationship with an intention or with framing the way we think it should be, there is no way that the relationship can emerge and unfold organically.

Recollection is an embodied knowing (Schrag, 2003). Communicative praxis is always a recollection because it is imbued with texture. To engage communicative praxis, one always enters the communicative engagement with distance as well as bias. These bring together the ideal situation as an unfolding. A revelation occurs as one synthesizes experience responsively. When new information is brought to the event, the texture is never what one expects and the possibility for the serendipitous to occur emerges.

In the space of communicative praxis the interplay of reading and understanding helps one make sense of things. To have an understanding means to stand under something—this is how one knows it; Schrag (2003) states to stand under something is to be a decentered self, and what one comes to understand is the groundwork for how sense is made of the world. Schrag (2003) also states that there is a hermeneutical demand requiring an interplay of understanding and explanation. These are like twin halves that help us to interpret and comprehend—these are coemergent within praxial space. The term *understanding* is connected to a humanities approach and discourse about the mind; explanation is connected to a scientific approach and discourse about matter (Schrag, 2003). Historically, the perspective on the relationship between understanding and explanation, as we consider human agents (we explain nature but we understand people), causes a split between understanding and explanation. Schrag (2003) states that there should be an interplay between them, not a separation.

When understanding and explanation are split, we disfigure communicative praxis because there is a part left out or not considered. In this space of separate notions of understanding and explanation we find conflict, distress, and empty communication. When intertwined, they become dialogic within a contextualized situation. Dialogic encounters are not perfect by any means; however, even if these kinds of encounters are erratic and messy, the messiness is recognized this is a hallmark of dialogic understanding. Comprehension "is the play between the grasping of the whole in a unitary act of synthesis and an apprehension of the constitutive elements through regressive analysis ... comprehending a discourse thus swings to and fro between the moments of understanding and those of explanation" (Schrag, 2003, p. 79). Without an understanding of both understanding and explanation, comprehension is incomplete. Having only understanding does not provide enough nuts and bolts or the layered reasons for a particular circumstance. For example, I understand my car drives when I turn it on, move my stick into drive, and put pressure on the gas pedal. However, I do not know how or why it drives; I cannot explain the mechanism of how it drives. Therefore, when it doesn't start, I am lost and confused. I have no clue what to look for or what to do. Having explanation of the elements involved with making a car drive would be helpful. I could potentially comprehend why the car doesn't start and fix it. Without explanation, understanding is insufficient.

Having an explanation for how a car drives provides a detailed knowledge of the nuts and bolts of why the car starts or why it does not start when you turn the key, but it doesn't offer you reasons for why you should obey traffic laws or commonsense notions like don't take a coffee cup without a lid into the car and drive it (or you could spill it). An understanding of the dangers of driving without a lid on one's coffee would ensure that coffee is not spilled. Having both understanding and explanation provides a scientific understanding of the car and provides the human-centered context that cultivates practical wisdom based on basic human understanding. Having both will help you be good at driving and maintaining a car. A union of understanding *and* explanation opens to signitive meaning that is a layered comprehension.

Schrag is antifoundational in that he does not privilege any particular foundation because he believes foundations (we know today) are illusions.

Schrag (2003) states that foundation-oriented thinking ensnarls us in our effort to situate the importance of speech and action, language, and social practices, suggesting if we look for a foundation from which we can draw conclusions, we risk the opportunity for hermeneutical exploration. Hermeneutical comprehension nurtures the human experience in the space of communicative praxis where meaning is created and responded to within the context of embeddedness.

In communicative praxis there is no such thing as ahistoricality since there is bias to everything situated in where and what we stand under. Human beings constitute themselves through language and Schrag (2003) suggests that in communicative praxis this language is intertextuality where no one voice is privileged over another. This phenomenon is referred to as "tissues of discourse" (Schrag, 2003, pp. 124–125). In this space, there is a dialectic of dialogue where in response to the other, there is acceptance, rejection, or modification of what is said in a to-and-fro motion—a back-and-forth dialectic of dialogue. Hermeneutical self-implicature avoids epistemological constitution of the other; instead there is an open interpretation of who the other is and a rejection of privileging one over the other. Hermeneutic humility allows one to engage in a negotiated space of intertextuality and subjectivity. It is Schrag's (2003) claim that if we resituate the self as a hermeneutical self-implicature, this is a first step in the recovery of a new horizon of subjectivity that is not driven by the ego or the privileged self. It is a new horizon of dialogic otherness with just and fair intentions—a space of hermeneutic humility. When this happens, a decentered subject emerges.

These new horizons of subjectivity suggest that a decentering and deconstructing of the subject does not displace the subject. Instead, there a replacement and resituation of the subject in the space of communicative praxis. The decentered subject is the consequence of hermeneutical restoration. The question Schrag asks about the decentered subject is whether there is still an ontological sense of the subject once decentered. The short answer is yes. When there is a restorative hermeneutic, there is always an absence of what was present. At the same time, because of the restoration, there is a new presence. Schrag (2003) states that we need both absence and presence as reciprocal partners to understand the nature of coming into being.

In the space of communicative praxis, there are three features of a decentered subject: temporality, multiplicity, and embodiment. **Temporality** refers to a new understanding that time is not fixed. Instead time has to change and be in flux; this allows for the interplay between presence and absence. If interplay does not occur because time stands still, then one, either presence or absence, is lost or occluded. So, to be decentered, one must experience temporality in flux. **Multiplicity** indicates that the subject is always encountering an ensemble of multiplicity such as social memories, experiencing a variety of customs, engaging in habits and ongoing institutional practices. Schrag (2003) suggests there is a lived multiplicity in the world and it is not to be feared or denied. Hermeneutical comprehension cannot occur without recognizing this multiplicity. **Embodiment** refers to embodied thought due to the decentering of the locus of interiority. This means one has a thoughtful thought; it is as if one is thinking of possibilities from a perspective outside of the limits of the ego. This is thinking beyond the self. The features of temporality, multiplicity, and embodiment reclaim the subject in the wake of their decentering or deconstructing.

In the space of communicative praxis, the embedded agent finds meaning situated between the agent and the texture in which the agent is embedded. As an example, looking at a musical note on a piece of paper by itself, there is little one can tell about the note, especially if there are no lines on the page. If the note becomes an embedded agent, situated within the lines of the staff that contains the key signature, time signature, other notes, dynamic markings, and other kinds of musical notation, the note has agency—this is the texture within which the note is embedded. Without the texture, the note is floating and is not able to find meaning and engage in hermeneutic self-implicature. The note has a decentered consciousness that actually enlivens the possibilities for engagement and meaning. Moving back to the communicant, the decentering of consciousness does not mean a banishment from anything. What it really means is a reentering into the space, a holistic hermeneutical space of dialogical consciousness. **Dialogical consciousness** is textured by the interplay of presence and absence, reminiscence and forgetfulness, and disclosure and hiddenness. This occurs within an interplay of temporality, multiplicity, and embodiment. From this, Schrag (2003) identifies a rhetorical turn or a reposturing of rhetoric within the space of subjectivity in communicative praxis. This turn refers to removing rhetoric from an epistemological framework, where it has been historically, and resituating rhetoric into the space of communicative praxis. Resituating rhetoric in this way reunites it with ethics because communication is always for someone, engaged by someone else, and about something. If argumentation is not tempered with nonargumentative forms of persuasion, rhetoric risks degenerating into a coercive technique. This is a problem of only being focused on technique and not on a theory-informed practice. Ultimately, technique can be empty. When we resituate rhetoric into the space of communicative praxis and make possible a grafting of rhetoric and hermeneutics, this allows for learning and discovery rather than a way to adhere to the limits of what one already knows. This situates rhetoric in a hermeneutically informed space of truth. This move also redefines and resituates rationality, which is a discourse that makes manifest something to somebody through a rhetorical situation whereby explanation and understanding are necessary.

Finally, Schrag (2003) advocates for a new hermeneutical space that provides for an organic new humanism to emerge. This new humanism comes with embedded agency. This means that one begins with the idea that communication is about a response to texture that is created by an embedded agent and its purpose is to address something in an embedded historical moment.

Schrag's (2003) new humanism is restorative. Because of the closed way of thinking during the medieval era, humanism received a strong criticism, but Schrag repairs that criticism. For example, the typical and original understanding of humanism involved the following features:

1. A system of thought that centers on humans and their values, capacities, and worth

2. Concern with the interests, needs, and welfare of humans

3. Medicine, the concept that concern for human interests, values, and dignity is of the utmost importance to the care of the sick

4. The study of the humanities; learning in the liberal arts

5. **Humanism,** a cultural and intellectual movement of the Renaissance that emphasized secular concerns as a result of the rediscovery and study of the literature, art, and civilization of ancient Greece and Rome

Schrag (2003) points out that the academy no longer privileges the notion of humanism because scientific inquiry has taken a lead in the human conversation. Schrag repositions a humanism that is workable in a postmodern, or later, world. This is how Schrag (2003) describes a new humanism:

1. New humanism describes a new space of intersubjectivity (a space of intertextuality).

2. In this new space of subjectivity, communication occurs through rhetoric, a hermeneutical rhetoric.

3. Hermeneutical rhetoric directs the discourse and a response is solicited—seeking a dialogical consciousness.

4. It reconnects hermeneutical rhetoric and ethics.

5. It connects ethics to ethos.

6. The decentering and resituating of the subject into a praxial space provides for this connection of ethics and ethos to be at play.

7. Schrag calls this praxial space where agents communicate in the space of subjectivity, communicative praxis.

8. In this space, agents are embedded (*by*); embedded to a historical moment (*for/to*); and embedded within a textured space (*about*).

9. Because of this embeddedness there becomes a descriptive rhetorical situation that requires a fitting response. The notion of fitting response includes a required responsiveness, a critical response, a time for a decision, and a call to action.

Schrag (2003) carefully laid out a new space for communicating in a meaningful way that accounts for the other. Our responsibility for the other is a component of how we find meaning in our lives. Without the other, meaning is always incomplete.

Meaning

There are two considerations for this section. First, what is the importance of meaning in a general sense of why human beings search for meaning? The second is concerned with why the search for meaning in the context of philosophy of communication inquiry is a key feature. The search for and finding meaning provides a sense of purpose in life, which is a very subjective sentiment. It also gives one unique insight into experiences, choices, and decisions that come to shape one's life. To explore these questions, this section starts with words of wisdom from Viktor Frankl, Christopher Lasch (1932–1994), Richard Sennett (b. 1943) and Richard Winter (b. 1943). As mentioned previously in earlier chapters, choosing these thinkers to frame this section is uniquely my choice and informed by my own worldview and impressions from my individual experiences. While I could have chosen other thinkers, these three have deeply informed my own search for meaning. The need to search for meaning is part of the human condition but it is not without its challenges. This section explores this need and unveils some of the challenges in the search.

Viktor Frankl (1984) was an Austrian neurologist and psychiatrist but is known more from his experiences as a Holocaust survivor. Frankl originally published his most well-known book, *Man's Search for Meaning*, in 1946 in his native language, and in 1959 the book was first translated and published in English. Frankl (1984) began his book by qualifying it as not an official historical account of facts and events in various concentration camps during the Nazi invasions and occupations across Europe that sparked World War II, but as an account of personal experiences during the time he suffered in these camps. These experiences led to his discovery of **logotherapy**, which he used in his practice of psychiatry after the war ended. Logotherapy is a process in which the therapist tries to make the patient aware of their responsibleness, leaving it to the patient to understand to what or to whom they are responsible. The logotherapist is responsible for widening or broadening the patient's visual field of potentiality, which allows meaning to arise and the patient becomes aware themselves; responsibility becomes visible in their perceptual field of awareness.

Frankl (1984) lays out reasons for and experiences of the importance of the search for meaning in everyday lives. Frankl suggested that "man's search for meaning may arouse inner tension rather than equilibrium" (p. 126). He also stated that human beings need this inner tension for the sake of their mental health. Frankl (1984) stated that mental health is based on a degree of tension between what has already happened and what one still wants to do. It also comes from the gap between what one is and what one should become (Frankl, 1984). He stated that this tension is central to the mental health well-being of all human beings.

Frankl (1984) warned that it might feel intuitive for human beings to want a balance, equilibrium, or homeostasis, but he suggested what human beings really need is "noö-dynamics," which he described as a "polar field of tension where one pole is represented by a meaning that has to be fulfilled and the other pole by the man who has to fulfill it" (p. 127). Frankl (1984) stated that this is consist for all individuals regardless of their mental wellness or mental illness. Frankl described many of his patients as being in an **existential vacuum** that he described as having a feeling of a total sense of meaninglessness in their lives—that they lack awareness of meaning worth living for and they are haunted by experiences of their inner emptiness.

Frankl (1984) thought the search for meaning could be the big search question "What is the meaning of life?" It can also be the question "What does this thing (person, place, or thing) mean?" Frankl (1984) stated that meaning is different for everyone and that meaning is given or found at particular moments in time, which suggests that meaning is temporal. Temporality is an existential reality and points to the notion that meaning changes, though Frankl stated while it changes it is the persistent question that drives existence. In philosophy of communication inquiry, the search for meaning is temporal in that time periods change and people change, but the search is always ever present and ongoing.

While Frankl was contending with the question of the search for meaning, Richard Sennett, professor, scholar, and philosopher of economics and sociology, identified what he calls the fall of public man, which calls into question the capacity to search for and find meaning. One of the challenges that Sennett (1992) found in his critique of the fall of the public domain was the emergence of narcissism. Sennett (1992) suggested that narcissistic character disorders are the most common sources of psychic distress. According to Sennett (1992), narcissism is not about self-love but it is more particularly a character disorder—self-absorption that gets in the way of one understanding what belongs to the domain of the self and self-satisfaction and what belongs outside of it. So, it is an obsession with what something means to them and a lack of awareness of what something means to others. Sennett (1992) suggests the absorption into the self prevents them from actually achieving what they think they need.

This is very similar to Christopher Lasch's (1991) notion of narcissism in which he described the narcissist as being haunted by anxiety and searching for meaning, all the while being fiercely competitive, demanding approval, and distrusting competition. The narcissist also has no interest in the future because there is no interest or respect for the past (Lasch, 1991). This kind of self-absorption freezes their ability to move forward, reach goals, and be productive. The narcissist is superficial and superficially tolerant, regarding everyone as a rival. Lasch (1991) argued that a narcissistic culture devalues the past and reflects a poverty of ideologies: Narcissists lose grip on realities and demonstrate a poverty of their inner life.

Another critique of postmodern life comes from Richard Winter, professor emeritus of counseling at Covenant Theological Seminary and clinical physician specializing in psychiatry, who studied and published widely on psychology, medicine, and theology. Winter (2002) describes a culture of people who are haunted by hopelessness. He states that many people today believe there are no real answers to the big question about life and meaning. This has led to a culture of tolerance and indifference—apathy and boredom. Winter (2002) suggests that when tolerance becomes the most important virtue there can be no judgment about any action that does not sound prejudiced or bigoted. This is a problem because tolerance means that there is nothing worth standing for or fighting for. Once this occurs, a sense of apathy and disengagement subsumes the individual and all people encountering the same. Winter ties this to boredom, and he refers to a culture of boredom as being dangerous and devoid of meaning. This leads to a search for some kind of foundation, which is rejected by most postmodernists who are those calling for tolerance and acceptance of indifference.

Meaning is essential for one's existential belief system. In philosophy of communication inquiry, meaning making offers openings for seeing the world, finding meaning, and reconstituting meaning already in existence. It is a human question that we do not want to lose. Without meaning, the "why" is no longer relevant or no longer offers purpose. Let's consider the chapter coordinates, historicity, communicative praxis, and meaning making, together to make sense out of the "why" of philosophy of communication inquiry.

Connections, Currency, and Meaning

Philosophy of communication inquiry is about finding meaning by identifying questions emergent in particular historical moments. It is also about acknowledging the historical moment and standing within it instead of above it when learning and judging as one seeks to discover meaning. It is also about understanding the temporal nature of meaning. Connections, currency, and meaning can assist with applying these components to action.

Connections: These three components situate the possibility of meaning within a horizon; the horizon enables discernment and points to possibilities of meaning without eliminating multiple perspectives (Arnett & Holba, 2012). The horizon invites multiple conceptions and orientations to difference. The historical moment provides the textual backdrop for the embeddedness that allows for questions to emerge. Through the backdrop and embeddedness, meaning is sought, negotiated, shared, and interrogated. This is ever so important, especially in public discourse and engagement in public moral argument.

Currency: At this moment in time, we, nearly the entire world, have had an interruption with the penetration of the novel coronavirus, COVID-19. Michael Hyde (2018) reminds us that the interruption that we are makes itself known to us and is marked by a sense of uncertainty for the future. While Hyde (2018) suggests that existence itself is an interruption, our everyday, ongoing existence has itself been interrupted as well. Within the horizon of this historical moment, there is a back-and-forth politicized abduction of public moral argument among not only our local, state, and federal leaders but also everyday people who have some kind of opinion, not necessarily an argument, pertaining to how the United States should or should not reopen and end the basic shut down of our social and economic structures. Most recently, as some states are reopening businesses and social establishments, the public arguments about how to do so have hit a peak.

News reports show that some people have argued it is up to the individual how they should reengage society—to each their own; other people argue that they have been on lockdown long enough and just want to have fun, so if that is what they want to do, it is what they should do (Bonquin, 2020). Additionally, another person argued, if they wanted to go out and get the virus, then it is their decision, not the government's decision (Almasy et al., 2020). These kinds of public moral arguments are simply not informed and fail to acknowledge their connection to the other. These sentiments reflect the pervasiveness of narcissism that both Winter and Lasch warned against.

There is no black-and-white scenario related to the virus, public health, and what should be done. But those making public statements such as these do not acknowledge the historical moment in its wholeness, do not recognize the emergent questions, and do not making much sense either from an argument point of view (which is based in objective science) or a humanistic point of view (based in subjective humanity). It matters that when one engages in some kind of public moral argument, that one should be engaged in the inquiry enough so that they make informed statements. But what media tend to show are those who exemplify with Sennett's fall of public man and narcissism. Self-absorption does not have a place in public moral argument. Philosophy of communication inquiry wards off psychologism and narcissism because the focus emerges from the historical moment and the questions that guide the communicative situation. The self-absorbed perspective has no place in philosophy of communication inquiry because it does not account for the other.

Meaning: The interplay of information and meaning is undeniable. Philosophy of communication inquiry can only be understood by doing it (Arnett & Holba, 2012). Information can and should be gathered, but one must take the next step to do something. One can take that information into action and participate in public moral argument through dialogue and dialectical processes, which would eventually end the emotivistic monologues that obscure meaning and bring people together who are actually interested in finding meaning—not just knowing information. Doing philosophy of communication inquiry changes the communicative texture from two-dimensional (and sometimes one-dimensional) understanding of something, someone, or some event into a three-dimensional meaningful understanding that is not fixed or concrete, which is meaningful in the moment but also open to adapting and reshaping as the context changes around it (Arnett & Holba, 2012). Meaning is pliable, temporal, and conditional. When it becomes fixed, growth is no longer possible. For some, this means that meaning is a nondogmatic search for truth.

Finally, for the student who seeks to not only understand what philosophy of communication inquiry is but who also wants to do philosophy of communication inquiry, there are some recommendations. First, approach your inquiry with an open attitude and a willingness to enlarge your own mentality by seeking multiple positions, inquiries, and arguments in a way that allows your intellect to be broadened, stretched, and tested. Second, be aware of your own subjectivities, biases, and prejudices—then suspend them so that they do not create interpretive limits for your inquiry. Third, be willing to publicly test your perspectives along with other perspectives, so write, present, discuss, and generally share your thinking with others who are also interested in the same, similar, or related things. Fourth, remember to identify the question or questions that you are asking, responding to, or noticing related to your inquiry—this means you will also be informed by the historical period, the historical moment, and the tradition(s) within which these questions emerge and reemerge. Fifth, be aware of the those approaches to inquiry and try to understand the approach you are taking and the approach others take to the question and inquiry. Sixth, look for that public testing of evidences in public arguments—participate in those efforts of public testing. Lastly, remember that meaning is temporal because of all of these features of philosophy of communication inquiry (historical moments, historical periods, traditions, approaches, changing questions, perennial questions, and human agency). This means you allow your position to evolve based on evidence, argument, and public engagement. The philosopher of communication is an embedded agent, a communicative agent, a morally conscious individual who has common sense, *phronesis*, and a praxial mind-set. These skills take time to practice, develop, and engage, always with voices of others and in good faith. These recommendations are at least the beginning of a pathway toward doing philosophy of communication.

Conclusion

This chapter made a distinction between history and historicity. While we have talked about historicity throughout this text, this chapter reached deep into the inner workings of historicity for a close understanding of its relationship to doing philosophy of communication inquiry. Again, while we have talked about Calvin O. Schrag's communicative praxis earlier in the book, this section provided a close reading of communicative praxis to exemplify hermeneutical self-implicature. Finally, this chapter also discussed the human urge to search for meaning and what this means to philosophy of communication inquiry. The next chapter expands on the use of metaphors in philosophy of communication inquiry as they open meaning in ways that cannot happen when metaphors are not used or discovered.

PART III

Connections, Currency, Meaning

Part III explored the importance of asking and identifying questions when engaged in philosophy of communication inquiry. This section looked at the nature of questions and questioning; it also tied question/questioning to philosophical praxis—the doing of philosophy of communication inquiry. In the history of philosophy and philosophical thinking, philosophers entered the conversation through questions and questioning, whether they made their questions explicit or not. Questions imply that one does not know something, so the first thing one must do is to admit that they do not know.

Connections

This section connected the first two parts of this book in the process of doing philosophy of communication inquiry. It connected identifying questions to historical moments and traditions. In fact, philosophy of communication inquiry is an integral approach to making and finding meaning by connecting the question(s) to historicity, and to understanding the tradition within which the question(s) emerged. Even the approach one chooses to inquire through determines how the question is asked and to what extent it goes. In preparing to engage in public moral argument, one must try to identify the question or questions driving the inquiry. Why is it that the inquiry is happening at all? What drives one's interest? What is one curious about? The particular question or questions, for example related to the Black Lives Matter movement or the public moral argument pertaining to George Floyd's life and death, must be illuminated for the specific issues to be understood and so participants in the debates can help shape meaning and call for appropriate and fitting action. It is the question or questions driving the inquiry that shape the body of the discourse; knowing the question(s) is essential to effectively participating in public moral debate.

Currency

Currency underscores the importance of identifying the question or questions. The questions have to be relevant to the human experience and they also must be understood within their particular historical moment. If questions are not understood within their current historical moment, they lose power and can become anachronistic. If we look at a contemporary case of public argument, identify the question(s), and evaluate evidence from all sides of the debate, we begin to engage in the praxis of philosophy of communication inquiry. For enriching classroom discussion, brainstorm as one large group or several smaller groups and identify pressing issues relevant to you today. You can use the issues you found during your brainstorm from Part I or Part II, or you might have other or new issues that emerged from your research and discussions. Remember (again) what public moral argument entails; there are three criteria that make an issue appropriate for public moral argument:

1. There must be an argument (remember, an argument is a claim, a stated reason, and evidence to back up the claim).

2. The argument must occur in a public setting where it can touch others.

3. The issue has to be an explicitly moral issue.

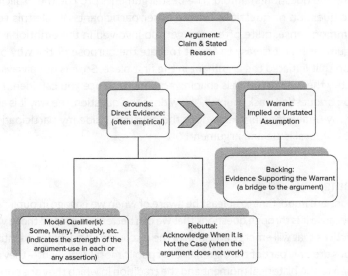

FIGURE III.1   Schematic for Stephen Toulmin's argument model.

Use some time during class or for homework to explore information and gather evidence to engage in a public moral debate in the classroom, or make the stakes higher and hold a public moral argument forum in a public setting on campus. Remember, you have to have an argument, you have to touch the public in some way, and the issue must be an explicitly moral issue. Here are the two initial examples from the previous sections in Part I and Part II, but I encourage you to find your own issues with the most currency.

1. Issue: Police brutality

   Argument: Policing reform is necessary to save Black people's lives because too many Black men are being unjustifiably killed by police.

2. Issue: Abortion and women's reproductive rights

   Argument: *Roe v. Wade* should be overturned because abortion is committing murder since fetuses are living beings.

As you begin gathering evidence and perspectives from different voices, try to determine what question or questions are being pursued in the public discourse or debate. Especially if the discourse or argument does not specifically point out the question(s) shaping the inquiry, illuminating the historical moment, the tradition, and the approach(es) taken to the discussion can provide clues to seeing the question(s) unfold. The best arguments provide the explicit and specific question or questions for the other participants. While this seems like common sense, quite often one gets so involved in the emotionality of the argument that it is easy to forget to state the purpose or the why or the question that initiated the argument in the first place. So, it is not always easy to identify the question that is shaping arguments. Once you can identify the question or questions, ask yourself, "How does this question, the way it is asked, inform my understanding? How does the question guide my participation in the public moral issue and argument?"

Meaning

Questions are important to at least be aware of when we engage in public argument because it is through questions that we can better understand those varied perspectives that will emerge and inform the discourse and debates. Identifying questions are only part of the ingredients of public moral argument—they need to be tied to the historical moment and the tradition in which they are pursued. They may also be framed differently depending on the approach one takes to the question, the subject, and the phenomenon that is being pursued. Questions open our perspective; they give us insight into the varied ways in which people think about their surroundings and the human experience.

Questions and how they are asked shape and guide inquiry. They also assist with the path one takes in conducting an investigation, and they assist with deciding the kinds of evidence we select as relevant and important when we make our arguments—which must tie back to the question itself. Questions help to shape the meaning that unfolds. So, as you are gathering your information and selecting potential evidence, you need recognize there is a question or questions that initiated the inquiry—identifying the question is key to effectively understanding, pursuing responses, and developing one's thoughts about the issue. Good luck with thinking through your research and evidence by identifying the question or questions from which it came and determining how the question is related to the historical moment, tradition, and selected approach to the issue.

Figure Credit

Fig. III.1: Adapted from Stephen E. Toulmin, *The Uses of Argument*. Copyright © 1958 by Cambridge University Press.

Part IV

_____

Emergent Metaphors in
Philosophy of Communication Inquiry

P art IV of this book unpacks the use of metaphor in the philosophy of communication inquiry. Metaphor is defined and described
with various examples. The role of metaphor in meaning making
is explained. Chapter 11 sets up the varying perspectives on metaphor,
differentiating between metaphor as a figure of speech in literature and
metaphor as a philosophical concept. I organize the last three chapters,
where I provide examples of metaphors and their application in philosophy of communication inquiry, beginning with metaphors for self, next
metaphors for other, and lastly metaphors for community. I chose to
order these last three chapters in this way similarly to how Calvin Schrag
approached his book *Self After Post Modernity* (1997). Schrag (1997)
begins by suggesting that one must both know thyself, similar to Socrates's urgent call, and to become attuned to conversations and discourse
already in process. This means the self is a praxis-oriented self, one that
knows oneself first before engaging with the other. The praxis-oriented
self is a new self "defined by its communicative practices, oriented toward
an understanding of itself in its discourse, its action, its being with others,
and its experience of transcendence" (Schrag, 1997, p. 9).Chapter 12 provides four examples of the use of a metaphor of the self in philosophy of
communication inquiry. The metaphors introduced are performativity,
hermeneutic humility, existential rootedness, and philosophical leisure.
Chapter 13 provides four examples of the use of metaphor for the Other
in philosophy of communication inquiry. The metaphors introduced are

empathy, welcome/hospitality, acknowledgment, and the derivative "I." Chapter 14 provides four examples of the use of metaphor for community in philosophy of communication inquiry. The metaphors are witness, dialogic civility, professional civility, and self in community.

Each chapter ends with an applied discussion, "Connections, Currency, Meaning," in which a discussion involving the application of some of the concepts covered in the chapter is opened. This section integrates public moral argument applications.

Chapter 11

Metaphors and Meaning

Learning Objectives

1. Describe the use of metaphor as a figure of speech and rhetorical trope.

2. Explain how metaphors contribute to cognitive meaning.

3. Distinguish between literary uses of metaphor and philosophical uses of metaphor.

4. Articulate Calvin Schrag's implication of metaphor in philosophy of communication inquiry and in his theory of communicative praxis.

M etaphors assist with how we come to meaning in a variety of ways. Can you reflect on how metaphorical meaning weaves through your own life and assists you with everyday decisions? How do you think metaphors enable meaning to emerge, diverge, and converge across people, society, and cultures? In political contexts, what metaphors have emerged in recent political communication that helped to shape meaning for you?

The use of metaphor is used and adapted into all kinds of writing, especially if the intention is to change someone's perspective, make a call to action, reach multiple audiences and publics, or simply make a savvy point in any kind of physical or virtual public space. Metaphor is a tool for making arguments adaptable to any kind of setting, public or private, such as in a news report, in the courtroom, at a school board meeting, in the home, or in a relationship. Metaphors are texture laden. This chapter introduces the concept of metaphor and discusses how it works in language as well as what it means to philosophy of communication inquiry. At some point in time, most people learn about metaphor in middle or high school; this chapter focuses on expanding understanding of metaphor from a basic literary tool to a broader philosophical concept necessary in participating in philosophy of communication inquiry. This chapter begins with looking at metaphor as a figure of speech or a rhetorical trope. The second section explores the understanding of metaphor as a philosophical concept. The third section of this chapter explores metaphor in the context of philosophy of communication inquiry. The final section, "Connections, Currency, and Meaning," will offer an application of metaphor in public discourse.

Metaphor as Figure of Speech

A figure of speech is a word or phrase that is used in a nonliteral sense for the purpose of a kind of vivid effect or to provoke some kind of comparison. This is similar to a rhetorical trope, which is defined as a figure of speech that has an unexpected outcome or twist to it—related to the meaning of the word(s). American Rhetoric is a resource that provides examples of rhetorical tropes, figures of speech, figures of sound, and other rhetorical tools that impact meaning making in public communication. As a figure of speech, the use of metaphor (either a word or a phrase) that usually denotes one thing, denotes another thing (Audi, 1999). Living in rural New Hampshire, many of the mountain and forest areas have ziplines, which are basically heavy-duty cables mounted across a sloped mountainous or forest area designed to use gravity so that one can hang on a pulley and ride the cable from the top of a mountain to the bottom of the mountain (or until gravity no longer works). This is a literal zipline meaning. If I say, "Bretton Woods Canopy Tour is a zipline" anybody can google Bretton Woods Canopy Tour and make reservations for a place on the zipline—this is a literal use of the word *zipline*.

However, if I say, "This relationship is a zipline" the word *zipline* is being used metaphorically to connote a general sense about the relationship. The meaning that unfolds in this sense might be that the relationship is going too fast, or it is dangerous, or it has no controls, or any other application of the zipline experience that is relevant to relationships. In order for this to be an effective use of metaphor, the audience to whom the metaphor is communicated needs to know what a zipline is and, even better, have experienced the zipline physically for optimum meaning to unfold.

The understanding of metaphors has changed over time. Up until the 19th century, there were two themes that emerged from philosophical discourse on metaphor (Audi, 1999). The first theme stated that metaphors are decorations, which is where the phrase "figure of speech" comes from (Audi, 1999, p. 562). The implication of this understanding of metaphor is that metaphors do not contribute to the cognitive meaning of discourse in which the metaphor is used. It also means that public discourse would be just as effective without using metaphor. This, we would not agree with today. The second theme is that it is an elliptical simile. So, instead of saying "the relationship is a zipline," one might say, it is "like" a zipline. So, the word "like" is just left out, making it an elliptical (referring to the use of an ellipsis, which indicates something is left out of an original sentence) simile.

By the mid-19th century into the 20th century, these two perspectives have consistently been questioned and rejected. Today, it is accepted and readily acknowledged that metaphors contribute to cognitive meaning in discourse—in fact, they are indispensable (Audi, 1999). Metaphors are widely used across epistemological domains such as religious discourse, scientific discourse, poetic discourse, and everyday regular discourse. Nietzsche (1999) suggested all language is metaphorical. A famous American literary theorist, poet, essayist, and novelist, known for his extensive theory of rhetorical criticism, Kenneth Burke (1897–1993) provided a framework for understanding metaphor as the first of four "master tropes" (Burke, 1969, p. 503). Burke (1969) identified the four master tropes as metaphor, metonymy, synecdoche, and irony. For the purpose of this chapter, metaphor is the focus in philosophy of communication inquiry, though this does not mean that the other three tropes are not used in doing philosophy of communication inquiry. Understanding metaphor and its nature establishes a framework for the last three chapters of this book.

Burke (1969) suggested that metaphors do not only work in a purely figurative way but that they have an indispensable role in the discovery and description of truth(s). Burke (1969) stated that the application of metaphor is designed to expand perspective. Metaphor is a tool or device used to allow the audience to see something in terms of something else that is easier to understand or that one expects the audience to have already experienced. Going back to the example that a relationship is a zipline, I am considering the particular relationship as having the same or similar qualities as a zipline, rushing downhill, holding on to a pulley while rushing down a cable in the midst of a forest, with all that is part of a forest, bugs, trees, twigs, and branches. All of this requires safety gear because the terrain cannot be fully trusted. The comment that a relationship is a zipline is not a total compliment. Perhaps it suggests that the relationship is a rush, but not so stable. Perhaps it simply means it is not trusted or maybe it indicates there is no controlling the relationship or the other. It might also reflect a fun and spontaneous relationship.

Burke (1984) expanded his discussion on the relationship between metaphor and perspective through his description on how a metaphor functions, especially in scientific literature. Burke (1984) suggested there is a lot to gain by substituting metaphors for standard intellectual methods to convey facts, especially if they are complex or abstract. Burke (1984) also suggested that all abstract general notions are nothing more than analogies between a given fact and other facts of the same class; by using a metaphor, it brings a concrete quality to the ambiguity of the abstract. Therefore, when a concrete metaphor is used, this is only substitution of one fact for another fact, and Burke stated that there is no danger of confusing the concrete fact with the abstract fact. The metaphor functions as a tool to expand perspective for richer understanding and clarity.

There are also different kinds of metaphors, such as perspective metaphors, root metaphors, living metaphors, and action metaphors. This is not an exhaustive list. However, these are some examples representing how philosophers talk about metaphors. Philosophers who elucidate these distinguishing features of metaphors (perspective, root, living, action) intend to show the function of the particular metaphor in its particular context. For example, Van Steenburgh (1965) referenced perspective metaphors as having pictorial meaning while differentiating it from a root metaphor, which has no pictorial meaning though influences an individual's perception. Arnett and Holba (2012) reference metaphor of action and Calvin Schrag (2003) identifies living metaphor as significant to communicative praxis as well as Paul Ricoeur's (1990) notation about metaphors as living and dynamic. What these all have in common seems more important than their subtle differences in that they seek to open meaning, which leads to new understandings and new beginnings.

Giovanni Battista Vico (1668–1744), an Italian humanist philosopher, also had a unique perspective on metaphor since his interests focused on philosophy, rhetoric, ethics, history, and science. He believed that linguistic functions of metaphor and poetry opened one's imagination and possibility for creative decision making (Arnett & Holba, 2012; Herrick, 2001). Interested in metaphor as a figure of speech, Vico also found value in its philosophical and pragmatic potential that it could bring to daily work lives and to the human potential.

There are other perspectives on metaphor that begin to move the discourse into an evolving philosophical theory of metaphor. Paul Ricoeur (1988) expanded Burke's (1969) thoughts on the four master tropes, suggesting that the other three, metonymy, synecdoche, and irony, are variants on metaphor. Ricoeur (1990) also identified living metaphors and root metaphors (just to name a few), which contribute to a taxonomy of metaphor.

Metaphor as Philosophical Concept

Paul Ricoeur (1974) constructed a theory of metaphor situated in the hermeneutical process. Through this, he develops a theory of symbol as he devises a process for analysis of metaphor. In his discussions, he leaned on religious texts and sacred narratives to provide grounding for his theory. Ricoeur (1974) suggested a theory of metaphor should be understood as an existential project—metaphor as a reappropriation of one's effort to exist; it is primordial to being. Metaphor is language that is expressive and constitutive. Ricoeur (1977) stated thought is characterized by symbol and "the symbol gives rise to the thought" (p. 58). For Ricoeur, metaphor is a semantic event that is made possible by tensions (McGaughey, 1988), though the symbol and metaphor function at different levels. Symbols function at the narrative level while metaphor functions at the sentence level. Unlike Jacques Derrida (1982) who suggested with metaphor there is an exploding of referential meaning as the text folds back on itself, endlessly, for Ricoeur, the metaphor announces an explosion of meaning, which breaks open the text to the lifeworld for the first time (McGaughey, 1988).

Ricoeur understood metaphor as a function of discourse (McGaughey, 1988). This function involves three levels of tension in the metaphorical statement:

1. Tension within the statement (between elements such as primary and secondary subject)

2. Tension between two interpretations (literal and metaphoric)

3. Tension in the relational function of the copula (a connecting word in the form of a verb such as be, am, was)

It is the third tension in the relational function that opens up the referential field and announces what Ricoeur (1977) referred to as the implicit ontology that opens the metaphorical utterance to meaning. Ricoeur (1977) suggested this implicit ontology is set up as is or not is or being or not being—the referential announcement he referred to as "ontological vehemence" (p. 299). Ontological vehemence suggests that there is a metaphysical condition of possibility that the metaphor needs to function that is extra-linguistic (McGaughey, 1988). This is where Ricoeur made significant contribution to metaphor and its function; it is also part of the circularity of being that is reflected in the circularity of meaning (McGaughey, 1988).

Ricoeur's foundational project, *The Rule of Metaphor*, situates a path to human understanding as through symbolic expression. Symbolic expression invites reflection and reappropriation of experience. Ricoeur (1977) recognized sacred metaphors function hermeneutically in so much as they become part of self-understanding and of the understanding of human ontology—our own being.

In *The Rule of Metaphor*, Ricoeur (1977) argued metaphor is to be seen as a discursive linguistic act, which is not just a substitution of names, such as Aristotle suggested. Ricoeur (1977), instead, stated that a metaphor works by an extended predication. This suggests that the standardized substitution model does not go far enough and instead he developed a structure of double reference, which tends to connotative values and meaning. Ricoeur (2003) understood metaphorical transfer as a category mistake that then produces an imaginative construction shifting the way the object relates to other objects. This transfer of meaning is at the sentence level and then moves to the text level. Ricoeur (1977) further suggested that metaphor as symbolic language becomes a phenomenological disclosure of being. This is in agreement with contemporary understandings of metaphor as contributing to, shaping, and forging cognitive meaning as well as being.

Ricoeur (1977) introduced what he referred to as his most extreme hypothesis indicating that "the strategy of language at work in a metaphor consists of obliterating the logical and established frontiers of language, in order to bring light new resemblances that previous classification kept us from seeing" (p. 233). Ricoeur (1977) suggested that in time the metaphor could itself become a linguistic convention that serves to drive the need for new understanding and continued for breaking from the conventionality in language. This is what he referred to as circularity of language.

Ricoeur (1974) also provided four characteristics of the metaphor in discourse to aid in the understanding of metaphorical function that offers polarity and paradox:

1. Discourse is an event that has instantaneous existence that appears and disappears—it can also be identified and reidentified.

2. Metaphor is a pair of contrasting traits where the meaning is carried by inner opposition between a singular identification (e.g., this woman, the chair, Mr. Jones) and a general predication (e.g., womankind as a class, heaviness as a quality of the chair, equality with something such as equality with Mr. Jones).

3. Discourse predicates the polarities of the saying of something (locutionary and propositional act) and the doing in the saying of something (illocutionary act).

4. Metaphor is considered as a pair of opposite features that build tensions through sensing and referencing.

Discourse does two main things. First, it reflects a reality reference, such as the extralinguistic reality of the world, and it reflects a self-reference, which is the speaker in discourse. These characteristics combined situate the basic polarities in discourse as "event and meaning, singular identification and general predication, propositional act and illocutionary acts, sense and reference, reference to reality and self-reference" (Ricoeur, 1974, p. 98). Metaphor works within discourse and requires these polarities to bring about the possibility of meaning. Metaphors work within discourse to assist the emergence and arising of meaning. This means the use of metaphor is essential in the philosophy of communication inquiry.

Metaphor in Philosophy of Communication Inquiry

In general, metaphor poetically and indirectly points to meaning beyond the term itself (Arnett & Arneson, 1999). It has been described as a form of linguistic implementation that provides a unique and particular response to a particular historical moment; it is also guided by the communicator's narrative framework (Arnett & Arneson, 1999). Metaphor functions as a "dialogic medium" situated between narrative and historical embeddedness, and it provides interpretive guidance for the communicator (Arnett & Arneson, 1999). For the philosopher of communication, selection and usage of metaphor is personal but not in a psychological sense. This means the historical situatedness and the bias from one's own narrative informs, shapes, and guides one's choice and usage of a metaphor (Arnett & Arneson, 1999). Metaphor is a linguistic event that allows one to construct referential expressions through reliance on abstract terms that allow for broad connotative understanding (Arnett & Arneson, 1999). This means that in using metaphors there is resistance in making concrete assumptions that limit the potential for meaning to emerge. Instead, metaphors open meaning and allow the meaning to unfold by itself in the interpretive space between people and ideas.

Metaphors awaken the individual and their imagination with the power to guide one's actions (Arnett & Arneson, 1999). Metaphors can shape one's value system and guide public discourse toward constructive action. As an example, Arnett and Arneson (1999) identified dialogic civility as a metaphor for interpersonal relationships. They argue that in the narrative of dialogic civility, which they lay out in detail in *Dialogic Civility in a Cynical Age: Community, Hope, and Interpersonal Relationships* (1999), there is not just one metaphor; there is a **"web of metaphorical significance"** (p. 300). This means there are multiple individual metaphors that connect the historical moment and guiding narrative; together they paint a philosophical picture of the narrative of dialogic civility anchored by metaphorical openings of meaning. Arnett and Arneson (1999) state,

> Our web of metaphorical significance connects historical concerns of metanarrative decline and routine cynicism with public background narrative of dialogic civility. Metaphors carry double duty. Individually they connect action, collectively they frame the narrative vision. With such linguistic power, it is clear that metaphors should be chose with care. (p. 300)

As an example, the metaphors that come together to constitute Arnett and Arneson's (1999) web of metaphorical significance in dialogic civility include the following:

1. Listening to the other and the historical moment

2. Being open to additive change (to avoid domination)

3. Between as a reminder of the importance of relationships (it is not about "me")

4. Voice and inclusion

5. Historically appropriate face saving (keep others in the conversation)

6. Seeking meaning in the midst of narrative disruption

7. Abiding by an ethic of care in a life of relational service

8. Cultivating a community memory tied to ideas, people, and institutions

9. Having a willingness to meet broken covenants head on finding new ways to repair, change, and alter a flaw or limitation (p. 301)

Arnett and Arneson (1999) suggest that in their web of metaphorical significance, individually the metaphors can guide one's actions; collectively they form a story about dialogic civility that becomes a value system that has the power to shape and guide interactions with others.

Using Arnett and Arneson's example of web of metaphorical significance, this section provides insight into the use of metaphor to open meaning within the context of philosophy of communication inquiry. First, I introduce Calvin Schrag's (2003) perspective on metaphor, and second I provide an example of communicative praxis and its web of metaphorical significance. Situating Calvin Schrag's perspective on metaphors will aid in understanding more fully his metaphor of communicative praxis, which was discussed in the previous chapter.

Calvin Schrag's Perspective on Metaphor

In laying out the "metaphoricity" of communicative praxis, Schrag (2003) acknowledges a "problem of metaphor" (p. 24). He states that the "omnipresence of metaphoricity" in his theory of communicative praxis is the greatest resource and at the same time it creates the greatest peril (p. 24). The peril has to do with how one translates the metaphors into epistemological claims and metaphysical truths (Schrag, 2003). Schrag admits that the very act of identifying metaphors creates necessary starting points and sets up primacies of certain terms and concepts over others. Schrag (2003) also states when these primacies emerge they assumes an aura of first principle and privilege, both of which are dangerous in both hermeneutical and poststructuralist thought. Schrag (2003) admits there are other dangers in using metaphorical devices such as employing them recklessly so that they solidify into patterns and creating a primacy of perception, which restricts play and boxes in meaning, growth, and development.

To temper these warnings, Schrag provides a historical discussion around the intellectual thought of metaphor leading a hermeneutical pathway for understanding how literature and philosophy domains have navigated understanding of the metaphor and reshaped its usage in public discourse. Schrag (2003) suggests that today the current reflections on metaphor are situated within two interrelated issues—the first is the difference between literal and figurative; the second is the problem of metaphorical reference. Schrag explains these issues through Jacques Derrida and Paul Ricoeur's perspectives on metaphor (something I do not do here, but if you want an in-depth discussion comparing both thinkers, read Chapter 2, "Figures of Discourse," in Schrag's text), which ends with the notion that bifurcation, or division, of the figurative and the literal sets up a metaphysical attachment to the literal and creates displacement that requires a realignment of discourse. This realignment is a reformulation of the existence of the reference (the second issue). The challenge here is that even though the text is transmuted into some kind of discourse, generalizations can be problematic, which in turn become subordinate to textual and linguistic inscriptions.

Schrag (2003) offsets these dangers through his acknowledgment of "textuality" as a key driving metaphor in communicative praxis as he acknowledges that it neither propels in the direction toward a primacy of the text, perception, or action because it gathers a display of meanings within speech and the written word and it encompasses play within perception and human action. Through play, meaning is open, temporal, and ongoing. This yields a holistic space of expressive intentionality that is fluid and dynamic. The next section explores textuality in communicative praxis.

Communicative Praxis Web of Metaphorical Significance

Communicative praxis itself is a metaphor that points to a communicative space of understanding between and among people; it is a space that is temporal and contextual (Arnett & Holba, 2012). Schrag's selection of "praxis" instead of "practice" reflects his concern about practice being unreflective or more like routine or thoughtless actions (Arnett & Holba, 2012). Praxis integrates both action and reflection as an ongoing processual of meaning that yields both making changes and seeing opportunities.

A leading metaphor situated within the web of metaphorical significance of communicative praxis is **textuality**. Texture implies a weightiness, an importance, an ethos, and a spatial importance that goes beyond the sense of practice, which calls us to being attentive to and aware of multiple dimensional contexts and events (Arnett & Holba, 2012). Schrag (2003) frames communicative praxis as **"expression,"** suggesting that meaning unfolds in a space that allows for unfolding, displacing, and refiguring through gesture, discourse, and action (p. 33). Schrag (2003) then lays out a metaphorical map of the terms discussed in the previous chapter, distanciation, idealization, recollection, understanding, explanation, comprehension, self-implicature, decentered subject, dialogical consciousness, and new humanism. While there is no need to restate the conversation from Chapter 10 pertaining to these coordinates, it is important to situate these as a web of metaphorical significance.

There is an integral framework that can be gleaned from these metaphors in that the dialogical consciousness and new humanism that Schrag describes contain each of the other metaphors within them and constitute them as metaphors. If we look at dialogical consciousness, we see a decentered understanding of consciousness that rejects a transcendental rationality and embraces a transversal rationality situating learning and human engagement at the center where one makes meaning. Schrag (2003) turns away from the delusion that one can discern a pristine truth (Arnett & Holba, 2012) and accepts that, instead, one can learn within a complexity of phenomena while accepting that coming to a perfect truth is not possible.

In this space of subjectivity, Schrag does not align with or adhere to universals (Arnett & Holba, 2012). His position actually takes a rhetorical turn that requires one to make a case for why a given position makes sense over another position (Arnett & Holba, 2012). Schrag (2003) turns to rhetoric and hermeneutics that allows him to present a position that requires interpretation, the self, and the other. This is what is required for doing hermeneutics; it must be tied to self and other without resistance. For Schrag, his rhetoric is deeper than the self; it moves beyond a gathering of ideas and information to a hermeneutic that stresses interpretive opportunities that can alter meaning (Arnett & Holba, 2012). This means Schrag's rhetoric is on the move, it is dynamic, and it is fluid. This kind of dialogical consciousness is necessary for a new humanism that requires one to be humbly responsive to the world around us—this moves toward a new alterity, otherness, and learning from all others—appreciating the difference around us instead of trying to conquer it (Arnett & Holba, 2012). What this means is that the communicative agent is required to learn. Appreciating other perspectives can inform and reshape understanding in a reflexive way. This notion is timely, especially in a COVID-19 environment where people around the world are becoming anxious about the uncertain future.

Connections, Currency, and Meaning

In this section, I will make connections between emergent metaphors in the context of COVID-19 and public discourse. Each day holds new and altering meanings. Each day issues crop up and new metaphors emerge or old ones are reconstituted as people try to make sense of their surroundings. It cannot be ignored that transversal rationality is a necessity today in an environment filled with interpersonal tensions and the demand to overhaul public discourse and public moral argument related to the movement Black Lives Matter.

Connections: Making connections between public action and public discourse is necessary if people want to continue to learn and expand their perspective. In public moral argument, metaphor is a necessary counterpart for the process of creating messages and opening meaning, as well as for the distribution across multiple audiences. Metaphors have had widespread usage in all kinds of public discourse and they have also been the crux of major political and social arguments across movements such as the women's movement (in particular the third wave of the women's rights movement) and the civil rights movement—two of the most recent movements in American history. Of course, these are not the only movements since the middle of the 20th century, but they serve as some of the most recognizable examples. Public moral arguments need individual metaphors to open meaning and invite other voices into the discourse.

It is important for the communicative agent to be aware of the historical pictures surrounding particularities in public discourse and to continue learning and expanding their perspective for assurance of bringing an ethos and an ethic into public moral argument. Communicative praxis is an example of a metaphor that can prepare the communicative agent for their public participation while advancing attentiveness to the historical backdrop and their own subjectivity by decentering access of the self, which wards against domination and grasping onto a narrative in decline or one that at least heralds a narrative tension. The communicative agent must meet and respond to existence on its own terms that are no longer part of an anachronistic narrative that makes it easy to be a master of one's own fate without compromise or having providence over another person or peoples.

Currency: In the current COVID-19 crisis, we are in the midst of public discourse about how to reopen economies and balance the continuing fears of a still unknowable virus. Tensions are heightened and each state is advancing at its own pace, despite some evidence suggesting it is too early for some states as they have not met the CDC guidelines of having a decreasing COVID-19 number of new cases daily for 14 days. Each state is deciding for themselves how a reopening will happen; some states are working with their neighboring states since their economies impact one another. Still, some critics believe that the federal government should provide guidance and make a strategic plan incorporating state perspectives. Other people feel the federal government should not be involved with individual state planning. These are typical arguments we hear related to the power of the federal government versus the sovereignty of individual states. In the midst of these public debates, and for many people these are public moral debates because they have to do with individual rights and freedoms. These are significant debates that can impact every single human being and how they navigate around their particular environments. Other public moral debates are focused on the most scared individual right, that is, the right to breathe; the right to exist. On May 25, 2020, an African American man who was being arrested by the police in Minneapolis, Minnesota, died in their custody. George Floyd was being restrained by four police officers, three of whom were kneeling or sitting on him while he was face down in the street immediately next to a police vehicle. One officer stood and watched. The officer who had his knee lodged against Floyd's neck was captured on video. All the while, Floyd was already handcuffed. The officer did not release his knee from Floyd's neck, and Floyd was calling for release, saying he could not breathe multiple times. Onlookers were upset and calling out to police to stop what they were doing and reiterating that Floyd could not breathe. Initial news reports had cell phone video of the event and showed the moment when Floyd stopped breathing. It was clear that he was in distress and it was clear when he died. The officer pushed his knee into Floyd's neck for almost 9 minutes. None of the video footage, up to this point, showed any kind of resistance on Floyd's part; however, not all footage from the police body cameras has been released yet.

This video was outrageous and disgusting. The four police officers were fired almost immediately. On May 29, 2020, the police officer who had his knee on Floyd's neck, Derek Chauvin, was charged with third-degree murder/ manslaughter; it was announced that more charges may be added after the investigation is complete. There are calls for the three other police to be charged as well, but at this time, they have not yet been charged, though the authorities stated that charges would likely be coming.

Since the day Floyd died, there have been riots in the streets, looting, and vicious protests, causing many more arrests in cities across the United States. Celebrities and influencers started speaking out early on in this debacle. Ice Cube, actor and singer, made a public statement via Twitter, "How Long Will We Go For Blue On Black Crime Until We Strike Back?" and Cardi B tweeted about Floyd's death and the riots and looting, "It is what it is" and "Too much peaceful marches, too much trending hashtags and no solutions! The people are left with no choice" (Young, 2020). Metaphorically, rising up invites interpretive possibilities supporting the incivility of protesters, and it is what it is metaphorically suggests that it's time to do what has to be done. Of course, there can be other meanings harboring inside these expressions of discourse as well. The point here is that in public moral argument, metaphorical language opens interpretation, so especially if one is an influencer either through Hollywood or social media, one should be responsible for the selection of metaphors they choose because they can either advance and support public moral argument constructively or advance social contagion and incite and support riotous action.

There is no possible way a prosecutor would not seek charges against the police officers involved. The video is painful to watch, and it is clear that the police officer escalated the situation by his own actions but arresting an individual and applying the appropriate charges is important and should not be done lightly or irresponsibly. If the charges are not adequate, they can be dismissed; if the charges do not meet the facts that will eventually be established, there can be an acquittal. Neither of these situations are acceptable. The police officers were fired almost immediately. This was decisive action and appropriate. But the forthcoming charges have a lot at stake, and getting it right is better than charging without the full evidence to support the appropriate charge. If charging is done irresponsibly, the charges can be dismissed later in motions and appeals.

Everyone has the responsibility to learn if they want to participate in public moral argument and discourse. Learning about the actual statutory laws in the state is a first step. What do the prosecutors have to prove beyond a reasonable doubt for each kind of homicide that could be the potential charge and what does the standard of beyond a reasonable doubt mean? Whether charging with first-degree murder, second-degree murder, third-degree murder, there are differing standards of proof. Each state has different criminal statutes, so we cannot make assumptions about the appropriate charges unless we know more about the criminal statutes. Manslaughter, and other forms of homicide, differ by state; this means that the elements of the definitions of these crimes are also different from state to state. If we learn that there are differences in criminal statutes, we might be more patient with the justice process.

There could also be federal charges applied if there is proof of a hate crime or other conditions representing civil rights violations. All of these possibilities take time to investigate. The firing of the officers signaled that the police are on it and we can assume charges are forthcoming—this is what the authorities stated when they were interviewed. We also want them to get it right because in the past there are many examples of police investigators rushing or jumping to conclusions, which actually made it worse at trial (eg., the O.J. Simpson trial and the investigation of the death of Jon Benet Ramsey—which had no trial, no arrest). In the meantime, metaphorical messaging has the potential to incite riots and invite anarchy. Public moral argument is a more responsible choice than shooting off opinions that can be poorly worded and misinterpreted by a range of audiences and publics. Schrag's space of communicative praxis is an ethical space focusing on learning and honoring the voice of the other. Public moral argument can be effective in the space of communicative praxis because of the responsibility given to all participants to be learners and to honor the other, the otherness of the other. How can we collectively create the space for communicative praxis to house a dialogical consciousness that can lead to effective and real change if we do not learn how to engage in it? The inherent metaphors in these two statements, Black Lives Matter and George Floyd's Life Matters, rests in the implication that lives are meaningful—the word *matter* implies that life is significant, and it implies that life contains substance that means something. François Cooren (2018b) suggests the word *matters* reflects what counts or what is relevant to a particular situation. *Matters* is a key metaphor in Cooren's dialogic ethics. These phrases open the space for dialogue and dialectic that allow for the sharing of new understandings and meaning to emerge. In this space, respectful dialogue is shared as well as solutions and action plans to ensure real change across all possible contexts and communicative agents. But like Schrag warns, it is in the usage of metaphors that we risk meaning if we send the wrong messages or metaphors of action and we are not thoughtful about linguistic choices and how meaning will be opened. These are difficult conversations and people have an entire history of frustrations situated in the historical horizon that can be reengaged and resparked. But there is no other way forward other than creating the space for public moral argument imbued with communication ethics that acknowledge and give voice across participants—but everyone has to show up and be willing to use language to shape constructive meaning for moving forward.

Meaning: Metaphors are powerful. Understanding their history can assist us with how we select metaphorical language in our engagement in public moral argument. Metaphors are constituents of being; they are at the core of existence and should be considered carefully. Understanding Schrag's warnings about metaphor enables one to carefully explore and appropriate metaphors in constructive and meaning-filled ways. Metaphors drive how we come to meaning and are key to doing philosophy of communication inquiry and are applied to action.

Conclusion

Metaphors change as historical moments evolve. Metaphors will also change depending on who the thinker is who is using them. Metaphors are central in philosophy of communication inquiry because they open the text and discourse to meaning that is renewed or fully new. Calvin Schrag's communicative praxis is a metaphor that can be a model for effective philosophizing and for being an active participant in public moral argument.

This chapter explored and described metaphor as a figure of speech as well as a contributor to cognitive meaning. It discussed metaphor in the literary sense and provided an opening to metaphor as a philosophical concept. This chapter also illuminated Calvin Schrag's implication of metaphor to philosophy of communication inquiry through his theory of communicative praxis. The next three chapters identify metaphors as examples of doing philosophy of communication inquiry. The chapters are organized as metaphors for self, metaphors for other, and metaphors for community. In each chapter I note the reason why the particular metaphors are chosen because there are literally hundreds of metaphors that I could have chosen. I mentioned before, the ideas and concepts selected for each chapter in this book are my selections, based on my individual experiences, interests, and studies. If written by someone else, the metaphors would likely be different. This is the nature of philosophy of communication inquiry—it does not presuppose a right from a wrong. What it does is honor voices of others and be open to expanding one's own perspective.

Chapter 12

Metaphors for Self

Learning Objectives

1. Describe key metaphors for the self in philosophy of communication inquiry selected for this chapter.

2. Identify coordinates that constitute each selected metaphor in this chapter.

3. Articulate guiding questions undergirding each metaphor in philosophy of communication inquiry in this chapter.

4. Explain meaning and relevance to philosophy of communication inquiry for each metaphor in this chapter.

Related to the metaphors in this chapter, performativity, hermeneutic humility, existential rootedness, and philosophical leisure, how do you see them relevant to your own lives? What is the role of these metaphors in how you come to meaning in the public or private domain? How do the metaphors in this chapter inform public moral arguments? How do metaphors in terms of literary, aesthetic, and judgment contribute to political, social, and cultural propositions?

In Calvin O. Schrag's groundbreaking work, *The Self After Postmodernity* (1997), he states that the self is curiously diversified. This means that the portrait of the self is not singular, unified, or sharply and perfectly defined. To know the self is a complexity of rendering an account of one's self, the telling of a story, and discernment of perceptual profiles (Schrag, 1997). Schrag (1997) proposes a "metaphorical extension" of the grammar of portraits and profiles by including the "telling and hearing of stories and the performance and reception of action" (p. 1). In the philosophical literature leading up to Schrag's expansion of the self, Nietzsche (2017) declared the death of God, Foucault (1998) declared the death of man, Barthes (1977) declared the death of the author, and Derrida (1997) pared away at the deconstruction of the subject. Schrag (1997) states that the vocabularies used to define and describe the self came under criticism long before postmodern thinking. In fact, he articulated that it was during the modern era and earlier that these constructs had already seen significant criticism. Schrag (1997) points to Gilbert Ryle's (1900–1976) philosophical endeavor to take apart the Cartesian portrait of human subject, which was conceived as an "interiorized mental substance" (p. 4). From these ruminations, Schrag became concerned with alienation or estrangement of the self, wondering how we might overcome it (Ramsey & Miller, 2003). It is in this backdrop and web of metaphorical significance that Schrag changes the question asked about the self. Instead of asking "what is the self?" Schrag (1997) asks, "Who is the self" As such, questions like, "Who is speaking?" "Who is acting?" "Who responds to other selves?" and "Who stands within transcendence?" are questions that shift the vocabularies to identify the "who" of lived communicative practices of speaking, listening, narrating, acting, working, and playing (p. 4).

In this chapter, I have selected four metaphors of the self in philosophy of communication inquiry from which we can explore the "who" in relation to performativity, hermeneutic humility, existential rootedness, and philosophical leisure. Along the way, we will encounter a metaphorical web of significance that includes other metaphorical counterpoints, including emotivism, narcissism, and existential homelessness that assist with unpacking meaning and significance of the selected metaphors.

I should explain how I chose these particular metaphors for this chapter because, as indicated earlier in this book, metaphors are emergent and connected to the historical moment and questions that guide these moments. Additionally, we are each unique individuals with different backgrounds and interests—these metaphors are selected from within these biases on my part.

It is the case that if someone else were to write this chapter, a different set of metaphors relevant to them would have been selected. As I indicated earlier, philosophy of communication inquiry is not about finding *the* answer; it is about exploring phenomena through different hermeneutic entrances, not seeking *the* answer but seeking *an* answer or simply, a response.

I chose **performativity** because of the significance of Judith Butler's (b. 1956) work, specifically the social ontology of the self in a unity of contraries in which she attends to the autonomy of the self in relationality and independence with interdependence (Lipari, 2018). Butler's social ontology is a starting place for her larger project of morality and the social production of the self. She is often referred to as a feminist theorist, but I would broaden that label to a philosopher of the embedded human subject. The reach of her work is expansive and will continue to push and challenge the status quo for a long time, thus giving a voice to those voices that were often left out of the room or those who fail to get a seat at the table of public discourse—these voices are the "who" of Butler's philosophy.

I chose **hermeneutic humility** because the "who" in this metaphor begins with a pause to wait, listen, think, begin, and pause again in moral responsibility and with care to not make assumptions or draw quick and irrelevant conclusions. My interest in hermeneutic humility emerged from discovery of philosophical leisure and contemplative inquiry. I point to the work of Schrag and Ramsey and their development of this couplet through the intersection of philosophy *and* communication. It is also tied to other metaphorical concepts such as wonder and discovery and disclosure in philosophy of communication inquiry. The "who" of hermeneutic humility is tied to an ethical ontology in that the self enters the conversation in a pause and in deep empathy and compassion, giving voice and life to the other, warding against emotivism and narcissism.

I chose **existential rootedness** because our social ontology requires that we are connected to others. We live in narratives that connect us to others within the context of interdependency. The "who" of existential rootedness is tied to ground, the ground where we live and where we engage with others. It is also tied to our ancestors, the past, and the integral horizon that encompasses all of what makes us beings in the world.

I chose **philosophical leisure** because when I discovered that there is a difference between leisure and recreation, this new understanding transformed my life. It is through the engagement of philosophical leisure that the self is contemplatively transformed through a nourishment of the interiority of self. Philosophical leisure is explicated through a unity of contraries including leisure/recreation, participant/spectator, and craftsman/technician.

The "who" of philosophical leisure is tied to Socrates's call to know thyself. The only way to know thyself is to look deeply and broadly—this takes hermeneutic humility, involves performativity, and provides the possibility of belonging and rootedness. The following sections provide an introduction to each metaphor, and I encourage you to select one of them and do more exploring on your own to gain a broader understanding of how these metaphors are engaged in philosophy of communication inquiry.

Performativity

Judith Butler was born in Cleveland, Ohio, in 1956 and currently is the Maxine Elliot professor at the University of California, Berkeley's Department of Comparative Literature and the Program of Critical Theory (Lipari, 2018). She is well known for her philosophical scholarship in the domains of gender studies, queer theory, identity, and ethics of interdependence. For this section, her social ontology of the self is presented through performativity and some related metaphors that frame her key interests and concerns as an applied philosopher.

One of the questions guiding Butler's inquiry is that of the conduct of moral philosophy within a contemporary social lens (Butler, 2005). Butler's question is concerned with how people should engage in public contexts with each other and asks, "How should the individual engage with others within social contexts, especially in the context of social relations?" Butler already admits to or presupposes that moral questions emerge in the context of social relations and that the forms of these questions will change given that social contexts will change. Influenced by critical theorist Theodore Adorno (1903–1969), Butler shares his sentiment that moral questions emerge when moral behavioral norms cease to exist that would normally govern social interactions or cease to be questioned in the public forum and life of the community.

Adorono's influence on Butler's (2005) philosophy suggests a tension that evokes violence between ethos and morality in that having a collective ethos is actually not shared because there is an imposed claim to commonality that occurs only through violent means. This means that anything "collective," such as a collective ethos, instrumentalizes violence to maintain and ensure an appearance of collectivity. The individual "I" is a victim of such violence. Butler agrees with Adorno that there is a divergence between universal interests (interests of the collective) and particular interests (interests of the individual) that creates the problem of morality and that demands attending to this problem.

Butler (2005) suggests that another problem emerges if one tries to understand and respond to the question of morality by situating the individual as being separate from the social context and social relation. Butler advocates that the "I" can never stand apart from social conditions that constitute ethical norms and conflicting moral frameworks; this entails committing violence against the other and causing suffering as we impose the norms within which we are exposed and enculturated. Butler (2005) asks the question, "If the 'I' is never separate from these social conditions, is the 'I' conditioned already by the norms of those conditions?" Then Butler (2005) considers how one makes an account of oneself since it is situated within the context of this social relation. These questions look at whether the self has a causative impact on the suffering of others based on its own, individual actions. Butler (2005) states that the "I" only begins to tell its story, making an account of oneself, "in the face of a you" (p. 11). This is how one narrates the self—we become self-narrating beings to the other. Our stories not only tell our stories; they also begin the process of making an account of the self.

Butler (2005) states that giving an account of oneself depends on being able to relay a sequential set of events drawing on a narrative voice that has some kind of authority and aims at persuading someone about something. It also aims to take responsibility for being the cause or not of another person's suffering. This means that making an account of oneself involves taking responsibility for one's actions. Making an account for oneself is always incomplete or, more so, insufficient (Lipari, 2018). In determining the ethics of the self, self-understanding is limited and insufficient to respond to the question of morality. The use of narrative is also limited and insufficient to constitute the account of oneself, because in narrative there is always predetermined, preexisting, and ideological norms that are really not part of the story of the "I"—they are impositions enacted upon the self that make an authentic narrative nearly impossible because these impositions are not authored by the self though they govern the self. Lisbeth Lipari (2018), communication scholar and philosopher suggests, "We are ethically implicated in the lives of others by virtue of the fact that we encounter others through a life-world of address and response" (p. 89). This is Butler's account of how one makes an account of the self and the challenges of doing so as an embedded self that has some agency within its social conditions.

Beyond Butler's understanding of the challenges in making an account of oneself, in the context of identity, Butler is not so concerned with the particular individual or the experience of the individual. Instead, she is more concerned with the processes by which one becomes a subject, beginning with the assumption that identity is constituted within language and discourse. For Butler, this is a genealogy of identity, which is not a history of events, but it is an inquiry into the conditions of emergence (Salih, 2010). Butler (1990) states that gender is not something that someone *is*; rather it is something that someone *does*. Butler (1990) states that gender is performative, which means gender is constituting the identity it is purported to be. Gender is always *a doing*. This does not mean gender is a performance; rather, it means that unlike in performance a subject is preexisting and in charge of the performance. Performativity contests the idea of the existence of a subject and that gender is announced in its own performative of doing—the subject is constituted in the performativity by the very nature of its doing, which calls it into being. Butler (1990) states it this way: "There is no gender identity behind the expressions of gender; that identity is performatively constituted by the very 'expressions' that are said to be its results" (p. 25).

Philosophy of communication inquiry responds to questions that arise within a historical moment that is comprised on unique social, political, ideological, and ecological conditions. This is just a brief look into Butler's philosophy that is imbued with ethical and moral questions as well as her questions related to gender and identity. Butler situates the verb performativity in the context of identity and social ontology, as well as making an account of oneself that provides a small part of the web of metaphorical significance in her philosophy of communication inquiry that takes one on a journey questioning social and moral responsibilities to the other. For further reading into Butler's perspectives, try these: *Gender Trouble: Feminism and the Subversion of Identity* (1990) and *Giving an Account of Oneself* (2006). She also has penned many essays and you can find her on YouTube.

Hermeneutic Humility

Hermeneutic humility is a metaphor that is grounded in phenomenological humility (Schrag & Ramsey, 1994). Calvin Schrag and Ramsey Eric Ramsey (1994) open their discussion of hermeneutic humility with the argument presented by Hans-Georg Gadamer in *Truth and Method* (2002), which is to say that if there is too much emphasis on method, such as the limits of the scientific method, this creates a methodolatry. **Methodolatry** refers to idolizing one approach while ignoring or discrediting another approach. Schrag and Ramsey suggest that this idolatry of method limits openness and thus limits the possibility of revelation and discovery. They call for a hermeneutic humility to correct the misstep of methodolatry, which only then can allow meaning to unfold. This shift would represent humility in scholarly research and investigation. Schrag and Ramsey (1994) suggest this will "bring our strategies of interpretation 'back to earth'" (p. 132).

The question that Schrag and Ramsey pursued that resulted in this argument and the highlighting of hermeneutic humility can be characterized by asking, "How can we offer a corrective to the glorification of method?" which they noticed was occurring across scholarly domains. Even Gadamer's *Truth and Method* was critiqued by a method-focused academy for having more to do with truth than with method. Schrag and Ramsey (1994) point out that Gadamer intentionally did not privilege method to the point where the obsession with rules and criteriological frames obscures the data from speaking for themselves.

Schrag and Ramsey (1994) proposed two related metaphors that they referred to "methodological directives" that would assist with warding against methodolatry, thus enacting hermeneutic humility. These metaphors are **narratival interpretation** and **transversal comprehension**. Narratival interpretation involves holistic understanding and analytical explanation; transversal comprehension manages any conflicts of interpretations intercalating or inserting something into the interspaces to mitigate and open the interpretational meaning. This recognizes that conflict of interpretations arise when there is a diversity of stances taking a posture of holistic understanding, which can include signification and conceptual constructs that emerge in the analysis, thus also with the possibility of raising conflicts. When this is the case, the historical situatedness and local narratives congeal (Schrag & Ramsey, 1994). When this occurs, there needs to be a strategy to release the impasse, though the strategy may more likely be a "third way" instead of finding middle ground (Schrag & Ramsey, 1994, p. 134). The metaphor of transversality allows for a convergence without coincidence (Schrag & Ramsey, 1994).

Schrag and Ramsey (1994) argue that the hermeneutic circle is not enough as a process for interpretation. They suggest that transversality offers the most possibility for meaning to emerge without constraints and applied limits. Schrag and Ramsey (1994) state that moving from the hermeneutic circle to the "diagonal play of transversality" allows for the emergence of the texture that opens interpretation and meaning (p. 135). They provide an example of the interpretation of the Declaration of Independence in which they show how transversal comprehension opens the text instead of closing it down to hold one-dimensional meaning. They suggest that for the Declaration of Independence to have one universal logos is an error; in fact, they refer to this error as "arrogance" (Schrag & Ramsey, 1994, p. 135). They suggest that we replace the search for a universal logos with the humility of transversal comprehension that fosters understanding in spite of differences—in fact it would welcome difference in the space of communicative praxis (which we discussed earlier). Ramsey (1998) suggests that humility requires that we have the perspective that our world, the one that each individual lives within, is not the only world and that others live within their own worlds and they also should not have the mindset that their world is the only world. One we recognize that there are multiple worlds, perspectives, experiences, and possibilities, we can be open to change of any kind. Ramsey (1998) suggests our understandings are not eternal and that by being open to seeing others as they are, and not as we are, we keep the possibilities open for growth, change, and transformation.

Instead of struggling to find agreement over what a text means universally, transversality forces one to go beyond the prejudices and prejudgments we take to a text. We must acknowledge that there will also be a struggle over what something means, but transversality allows the possibility of meaning to open in a nonthreatening way; transversal rationality and transversal comprehension allow communication to continue in spite of differences, but it is the hermeneutic humility that allows the human to stay in the conversation with an open mind and open awareness and to be open to possibilities of interpretation.

Existential Rootedness

The roots of a tree usually help trees to maintain their place in the ground, and therefore in the environment and in the world. They provide nourishment, stability, and deep connections to the earth and their surroundings. This is true for many plants and vegetation; roots are the foundation from which life emerges and grows strong. For human beings, roots and the sense of rootedness serve as "an interruption of a naïve absorption in a disembedded reality that ignores the larger communicative environment, and of our deep connectedness to a sphere of life beyond individual autonomous being" (Üçok-Sayrak, 2019, p. 1). Communication scholar and philosopher of communication Ozum Üçok-Sayrak describes existential rootedness as an orientation that is immersed in a communication ethic. Üçok-Sayrak (2019) states that this kind of orientation recognizes the embeddedness of human agents together in participating in their surroundings with other human beings. This kind of orientation illuminates an exposedness and struggle in the world that navigates a unity of contraries of disruption/harmony and tension/rest (Üçok-Sayrak, 2019).

Similar to the previously stated notion that philosophy of communication inquiry does not presuppose one answer to a question but instead multiple possibilities for answering emergent questions, existential rootedness is not fixed in one place with one answer. Existential rootedness is an ongoing and dynamic human experience navigating the unity of contraries or dialectical tensions between the sensible/intellectual, closeness/distance/contemplation/action, and silence/speaking (Üçok-Sayrak, 2019). Synthesizing these tensions, Üçok-Sayrak (2019) suggests the distinctive feature of existential rootedness is attentiveness, which may involve the sensibilities of touch, response, and responsibility.

Ozum Üçok-Sayrak (2019) provides the imagery of a lotus flower that emerges from particular ground. No mud, no lotus flower (Hanh, 2014); this reflects the idea that ground matters, even ground that we might not want. Without ground, no matter how messy, harmony and beauty cannot grow. Ground is nourishing and sustains life, but this detail is often forgotten in a fast-paced, immediacy-driven, more is better environment. As Üçok-Sayrak (2019) states eloquently, "Yet in the context of the fast-paced, progress-oriented rhythms of modern life that promote the autonomous individual, the ground and the rootedness of existence gets forgotten or left unattended by many" (p. 2). This sentiment is shared by many other scholars and philosophers, but what is unique to Üçok-Sayrak's perspective is that it is tied to communication ethics and the notion of interdependency—we need one another and we live with those others on land. The idea of land being the ground of our place-based culture, relational ties, and general existence is developed in Glen Scott Coulthard's (2014) exploration of the importance of land to Indigenous populations in Canada. He states that land is a relational field where people live in relation to each other. Üçok-Sayrak (2019) states that Coulthard's notion of land is an ontological understanding connected to an ethics-based interdependency of all human and nonhuman elements. If land provides a place for relational existence and it is this provision that creates rootedness—a place-based home for human and nonhuman agents to exist together ethically, having mutual concern and care for each other.

The questions that guide Üçok-Sayrak's inquiry have to do with how people today can remember their need for roots and sense of rootedness. Üçok-Sayrak (2019) identifies the problem that reveals there is a need for a return to roots and rootedness; in this problem, human beings generally "do not live with a sense of safety, security, and peace but with fear, confusion, and disorientation in the twenty-first century" (p. 3). Üçok-Sayrak bases this description on Jean-Luc Nancy's (1997) description of the world as anxiety-filled, preoccupied, dissatisfied, uneasy, and having a general lack of presence. Üçok-Sayrak (2019) states that this is a description of the "uprootedness of the modern man" (p. 3). Her argument follows that by remembering and being attentive to one's roots and sense of rootedness, these anxieties and generally negative sensibilities can be mitigated by remembering roots and a need for a sense of rootedness.

This is a timely message. The uprootedness of the modern man situates the metaphor of existential rootedness (Üçok-Sayrak, 2019). Existential rootedness is attentiveness to ground; it is a particular orientation that is accompanied by contemplative and communicative practices that are "attentive to self, other, and their dwelling ground" (Üçok-Sayrak's, 2019, p. 3). In order to turn toward this kind of attentiveness, Üçok-Sayrak (2019) argues for "engaging dialogue on the possibility of rootedness that refuses to forget our basic human capacity to turn toward being human and human suffering, beyond individual autonomous existence" (p. 4).

Üçok-Sayrak (2019) warns of the consequences of failing to attend to rootedness, which include developing a sense of **moral blindness** and **modernity's amnesia**. Moral blindness is defined by Zygmunt Bauman and Leonidas Donskis (2013) as the inability for a human being to be insensitive to another human being's suffering. Modernity's amnesia is a metaphor Üçok-Sayrak's borrows from Ronald C. Arnett's (2013a) description characterizing a forgetfulness of the "conditions for the existence" and those dwelling places that nurture the human condition, both of which were given up in the endless cycle of searching for progress. For more discussion on existential rootedness, Üçok-Sayrak's (2019) book, *Aesthetic Ecology of Communication Ethics: Existential Rootedness*, can provide a detailed discussion through a metaphorical web of significance, including the metaphors of poietic meaning, weight of meaning, signlessness, and the breath of the other, just to name a few metaphors significant to developing the metaphor of existential rootedness.

Philosophical Leisure

One might be curious about why I chose to include philosophical leisure in the chapter on metaphors for the self. The justification I provide includes a little bit of background and some clarification between leisure and recreation before laying out the importance of leisure to the self. I should first say that this metaphor is one that I developed in the early part of the 21st century when I asked the questions, "Why is it so difficult to be satisfied with the self?" and "Why do people look for happiness outside of the self?" This announces my bias and preference to include this metaphor, and the metaphor **recuperative praxis**, in this section, though the fact that I pursued this is not selfish by any means. Instead, the rhetoric around philosophical leisure is essential to the human condition and the emergence of the self. In the 2007 publication, *Philosophical Leisure: Recuperative Praxis for Human Communication*, I lay out what I refer to as an eclipse of human communication and a distinction between leisure and recreation. The distinction is a significant one but sometimes difficult to identify.

When referring to an eclipse of human communication, it is described as a moral crisis (Holba, 2007). A moral crisis can be defined as occurring when human communication is imbued with thoughtlessness; when it is unreflective, obscured, deceptive, or false communication (Rorty, 1979). False communication fosters communication imposters (Holba, 2007). This moral crisis is not new to the 21st century. Immanuel Kant (1965) criticized early Enlightenment thinkers of this very kind of communication, such as David Hume's defense of empirical principles in which he claimed Hume's argument created an "illusory semblance of necessity" (p. 55). Today, philosophers from Seyla Benhabib to Michael J. Hyde call for a turn toward the other in an authentic and life-sustaining way, especially regarding how they communicate with the other. In order to do this, one must know oneself. This moral crisis in communication will tie together each other metaphor in this chapter and is discussed in the Connections section.

Before identifying what philosophical leisure means to the self, I provide a distinction between leisure and recreation for clarity. Leisure, philosophically speaking, is a very different activity than recreation, even though we often hear these two terms used synonymously. In recreation, there is a break from work (working for a living) that provides us with a distraction from working or it can be participating in a hobby that is separate from work but often involves constraints that limit the nature of the activity. These constraints might be strict rules (forcing one to conform to given arbitrary structures), a competitive nature (wanting to win), or socially focused (wanting to be part of a certain social group). Some recreation activities are very serious activities and some others are not as serious. For example, one can take an occasional walk during a work break or play in a softball or bowling league after work where social engagement and winning is the focus. Another example is when one plans a family vacation by filling each day and minute with a myriad of activities, which requires one to focus on time and predetermine decisions that are really separate from the experience of the vacation. This makes one feel exhausted during the vacation and upon returning home. Some people might engage in different kinds of activities, such as taking a bus tour, reading a book, or going swimming. These are activities that remain separate from work, or they might occur in between one job and another job. These activities are sought after to relieve tension, and they offer limited respite and are often considered a diversion or a coffee break from regular work-a-day schedules. We do need activities such as these within this context.

Sometimes people engage in recreative activities in a weekly or monthly schedule, but they do not think about the activity in between their playing moments. Some people engage in recreative activities because they are socially encouraged or forced to do so, such as participating in an office bowling league or when a child is encouraged to play a sport, a musical instrument, or try out for the school play (and sometimes all at the same time). Recreation offers one a break from the mundane but one's commitment to the activity is driven by a particular predetermined outcome that creates limits to the range of possible outcomes. For example, if I am on a bowling team for my work or my neighborhood, my participation might be driven by the impending promotion at work or my role and reputation in the community. This means that I am engaging that experience for reasons other than the experience itself. My attention is pulled toward something else (away from the action of bowling itself). If winning is my aim in the action, then I cannot be engaging in the activity for the sake of the activity itself. My phenomenological focus of attention is elsewhere, alienated and estranged from the activity. By focusing on something else and not the actual flow or play of the activity, there is little or no sustained recuperative nature of the engagement.

Philosophical leisure is sustained attention to the thing itself without consideration of time, telos, or predetermined or anticipated outcome. When referring to time, in philosophical leisure experiences, time is experienced as a time outside of time, similar to **kairos**, a timeliness that privileges the experience and its serendipitous creativity. Time in recreation is often governed by a measure of time, **kronos**, or rules governed by *kronos*, that limit possibilities of and for the experience. These limits occur because of the *telos*, or the aim of the activity. In recreation, the aim of an activity is typically outside the experience of the activity (Holba, 2007), for example, to support a social relation or to have a certain amount of time devoted to an activity, in this case such as joining a gym to maintain or to lose weight.

Philosophical leisure is guided by a hermeneutical mind-set; recreation is often guided by an epistemological framework. For example, engaging in an activity for the sake of the activity itself and nothing else, one remains open hermeneutically and therefore anything can happen or be experienced. One is open to seeing what these possibilities are when they emerge. Recreation is governed by rules, time, preconceived outcomes or intentions—these are knowledge based or knowledge inspired. But the constraints or limits imposed by the rules, especially related to time constraints actually limit hermeneutical possibility. The mind is already focused on what one wants, but it does not remain open to see what is there. For more detailed distinction and discussion about the differences between philosophical leisure and recreation, Josef Pieper's (1998) *Leisure: The Basis of Culture*, provides a philosophical and etymological justification for this explanation.

Philosophical leisure is transformative to the human self—it should be considered more of a way of life rather than an interruption in one's daily work-a-day experience (Holba, 2013). Having it as a way of life resonates with what Pierre Hadot (1995) referred to as spiritual exercises that are integral to one's everyday experiences. Philosophical leisure is necessary for the cultivation of the inner self, explicitly the cultivation of one's interiority. This is not a new claim. Plato and Aristotle talked a lot about the inner self and its cultivation, which provides enlarged thinking, a philosophical mindset, and an ethic that connects the self and other. Sustained attention to leisure, as a philosophical act (and not recreation) engages one's aesthetic sensibilities and cultivates the interiority in a way that resists the culture of narcissism or the communicative behavior of emotivism. Philosophical leisure provides ground for ethical engagement with the other. It also connects to the three previous metaphors discussed earlier in this chapter. The next section will connect the four metaphors against the backdrop of narcissism and emotivism.

Connections, Currency, and Meaning

These metaphors allow one to connect with others from a cultivated ground. If you know yourself, you can find yourself; you can also begin your communicative engagement from ground that you already know and have contemplated—the key is to remain hermeneutically open, which resists the impulse to remain fixed and rigid. These metaphors are connected by their opposites of narcissism and emotivism. Christopher Lasch (1979) describes a culture of narcissism that is a sea of human beings who are stuck in their self-absorption and who cannot move forward or backward in their relationships, work, and other aspects of their lives. Lasch (1979) suggests Americans have retreated to "purely personal preoccupations" (p. 4). They have no hope of improving their lives and have an ongoing increase in despair and focus on psychic self-improvement, which involves immersing themselves in all kinds of self-help practices to the point where they want to forget the past and remain tied to the present in a way that negates the other and their responsibility for the other (Lasch, 1979). Being tied to the self in this way creates a culture of consumerism aligned with mass production and mass consumption (Lasch, 1984). These conditions create a false sense of the self, leaving human beings to search for themselves outside of themselves.

This sense of loss and abandonment provokes what Alasdair MacIntyre (2007) referred to as emotivism. MacIntyre asks the questions, "What is the source of ethics and the good for human life?" and "On what grounds may we compare and evaluate the claims of incommensurable moral systems?" (Harden, 2018). MacIntyre (2007) suggests that emotivism is a false doctrine and that what it does is obliterate the distinction between manipulation and nonmanipulation, thus creating an ethical violation toward the other without the ability to see one's actions as they truly are and for what they truly mean. Emotivism reflects that all moral judgments are merely expressions of a preference for an attitude, or a feeling, nothing more. Emotivism projects a narcissism that employs moral judgments to change emotions and attitudes of others in an attempt to change others to think the way you think, thus discounting the moral autonomy of the other. Emotivism is a way to manipulate others and dominate their ability to make up their own minds. Some of the most successful leaders in the world's history were both narcissists and used emotivism as a method to limit individual autonomy and thinking for oneself. Adolf Hitler (1889–1945), leader of the Nazi Party and Germany, Jim Jones (1931–1978) preacher and leader of the Jonestown commune and author of mass murder, and Kim Jong Un (1984b.) leader of north Korea, are just a few that come to mind in recent history.

Social media provides an example of the dangers of emotivism and narcissism, which can be helpful in understanding the value of these metaphors for self. There are features of the dark side of communication that are easy to engage when one uses social media as a platform for negative communication exchanges such as gossiping, bullying, and general deception (or lying). These kinds of negative communicative exchanges occur without face-to-face engagements, which creates a false sense of self when we do not feel accountable to others and we believe our opinion is the only opinion that is correct or necessary. Rendering an account of ourselves, having hermeneutic humility, acknowledging this need for existential rootedness, and cultivating one's interiority through activities such as philosophical leisure can mitigate the development of this false sense of self and remind one that there are multiple meanings, understandings, and perspectives. These metaphors invite transversal rationality and transversal comprehension into our communicative practices because we are open to others and not singularly minded within our own egoic nature. If more people admitted that we are interdependent beings, who have a need for existential rootedness, who should navigate our experiences through hermeneutic humility, and who tend to the cultivation of our interiority through experiences like philosophical leisure, we might very well see a decrease in negative communicative behaviors across social media platforms—and healthier communication face-to-face and online.

Each of the metaphors in this chapter, performativity, hermeneutic humility, existential rootedness, and philosophical leisure, provide a framework for understanding the self as it is or for cultivating the self—knowing how to cultivate one's interiority to expand mentality and to cultivate ethical ground from which the self engages the other. These are metaphors that give perspective, expanding hermeneutical potential for effective and ethical communication with the other.

Connections: A moral crisis in communication ties together these metaphors through narcissism and emotivism. Each metaphor is shown to resist both narcissism and emotivism—to alter the negative effects of these therapeutics and enhance human communicative engagement. Some examples of these connections begin with the notion of performativity and giving an account of oneself. If we recognize that the self is not fixed and that it is a processual of activities, one understands that as human agents we stand in social relations and interdependency with others. Understanding this connection to the other undergirds all communication behavior and action in ways that make one ethically accountable to the other. Judith Butler's metaphors set up the responsibility we have for our individual actions of the self and those implications to the other.

Calvin Schrag and Eric Ramsey's understanding of hermeneutic humility situates the self to be reflective, to wait, to engage in a process of careful, thoughtful self-implicature in a space of possibilities before one assumes an action. Bringing humility to one's interpretative experiences wards away the potential for narcissism and emotivism to emerge. Hermeneutic humility can undergird performativity and the work of giving an account of oneself—it creates a dialogic space imbued with respect and responsibility for the other. Ozum Üçok-Sayrak's call for recognition and remembrance of the human need for existential rootedness offers a way that promoted human connectedness and interdependency. Quietly recognizing that existential rootedness is life sustaining can be coupled with hermeneutic humility and performativity, thus setting up the possibility for negating or diminishing potential narcissistic and emotivistic capacities to develop. This is an ongoing task for human agents—which is why leisure and recreation need to be differentiated. Both activities are needed to sustain human beings, but engaging leisure as a philosophical act and as a way of life provides the optimum possibility for negating narcissism and emotivism and for cultivating the self in a moral and ethical framework that sustains life and opens human potentiality.

Currency: As we look into what is happening today in moral public discourse, a main topic of argument in the news has to do with justice for George Floyd, who I mentioned earlier, and how to move forward making systemic changes as a society that acknowledge our social ontology as well as honoring the human right to exist—to breathe. What we see is a culture of narcissism and emotivism in law enforcement; it has never been more obvious and never more exposed than in the 21st century. Certainly, there is a history of police brutality as well as the history of the entire American correctional system. I am not saying all police officers are corruptly narcissistic and emotivistic. However, I am saying that there are police out there who embody these qualities, and as a system, we need to do better to weed out these individuals and prohibit them from being in law enforcement in the first place.

In public moral argument, there are widespread calls to defund the police across America. This kind of response is an emotional response that is not grounded in an ethical framework or a rational framework. Certainly, some police are bad. Certainly, politicians, priests, bankers, movie stars, and other domains of work have bad apples, but that does not mean the entire domain should be negated. For effective public moral argument, logos is essential; this means having clear, responsible arguments that actually address the issue without creating more significant issues or conflicts. At the writing of this chapter, America has seen weeks of massive protests and riots across many American cities, large and small. What we need to do now is to make a turn and take a next action that involves all voices on all sides to come together and cocreate a response to the situation that acknowledges the challenges, provides multiple solutions, and offers new ways for doing what is right in the backdrop of respecting all of life, all beings.

Having an enlightened, cultivated self assists with bringing together voices that embody hermeneutic humility, recognize the need for existential rootedness for all beings, and understand that making an account of oneself is co-constructed through performativity and interdependency. Philosophical leisure helps to prepare the mind for this kind of expansion discussion. Without a cultivated interiority, there is risk of degenerating into narcissism and emotivism, thus limiting any possibility for finding an appropriate response and action to move forward ethically and responsively.

Meaning: Philosophy of communication inquiry recognizes that there is more than one answer, and it provides a way to come together in dialogue and dialectic to construct and reconstruct understanding, explanation, and comprehension of the ideas that help us live together in a space of subjectivity being guided by shared spaces and voices. The year 2020 has been very difficult with the emergence and expansiveness of the COVID-19 pandemic; it has been an unprecedented time—and then George Floyd died from the reckless, thoughtless, and intentional acts of four Minneapolis police officers. Public moral argument in America has erupted across the country. Contemplating metaphors of the self can enhance how one is able to respond in public moral argument, and philosophy of communication inquiry prepares the self for such an ominous task.

Conclusion

This chapter identified metaphors for self in philosophy of communication literature. For this chapter I selected performativity, hermeneutic humility, existential rootedness, and philosophical leisure. These are different ways in which the self is explored in philosophy of communication inquiry. All of these approaches suggest the self is an ongoing process of being. A commonality of these four metaphors includes their resistance to emotivism and narcissism, a need for understanding the self as it is, and the importance of cultivating the self. This means one must start with the self before being able to engage authentically and ethically with the Other. By starting with the self, one is not preoccupied with the self; instead, one recognizes that one as a self and knowing the self allows one to know the other. Exploring the self through these metaphors allows one to gain perspective and expand hermeneutical potential for effective and ethical communication with others.

Chapter 13

Metaphors for Other

Learning Objectives

1. Describe key metaphors for the Other in philosophy of communication inquiry selected for this chapter.

2. Identify coordinates that constitute each selected metaphor in this chapter.

3. Articulate guiding questions undergirding each metaphor in philosophy of communication inquiry in this chapter.

4. Explain meaning and relevance to philosophy of communication inquiry for each metaphor in this chapter.

Who is the Other? Who is the Other to us? What is the Other? What is our obligation toward the Other? Why should we care about these questions? In philosophy of communication inquiry, we are concerned with how meaning happens. Coming to meaning about something requires an understanding of self and Other explicitly on its own. Once that understanding is unpacked, applications of meaning are deeper and richer. Having a deeper understanding of the Other and the social ontology between self and Other assists with meaning, especially as conditions for existence change.

This chapter focuses on metaphors for the Other in philosophy of communication inquiry and, like the previous chapter, the word *for* in the title needs some explanation. "Metaphors *for* Other" is not intended to be interpreted as a replacement for the Other. Instead, it is intended to reflect metaphors in service to the Other. As articulated in Chapter 12, the metaphors chosen for this chapter reflect philosophical inquiry pertaining to the Other. The selected metaphors for this chapter are tied to Other through a particular ethical lens focusing on **empathy, welcome** and **hospitality, acknowledgment**, and the social ontology of a derivative "I." The selection of these metaphors is situated in my own subjective interest that is grounded in an ethical obligation toward the social relation between the self and the other. The use of the word *social* in this context is not the same as Hannah Arendt's notion of the social realm discussed earlier. Rather, the social referred to here reflects the interconnection between self and Other—that there must be communicative engagement between human beings in order for humanity to survive and thrive. There are bountiful possibilities of metaphors for the self that could have been identified for this chapter; the metaphors in this chapter uniquely emerged for me as some of the most important metaphors that have been driving the philosophy of communication inquiry recently, at least in the last 15 years or so at regional, national, and international environments. Before discussing each metaphor, exploring how the communication discipline unpacks the notion of "other" is important for differentiating the use of the term *Other* from a negative framework we often see in identity politics or in political ideologies. For this chapter, let's consider the Other as a perennial philosophical concept. In identity politics, the other, otherness, othering, or being othered, often has negative connotations that usually reflect a treatment of inferiority and the oppression of individuals who are different than a dominant force. However, in philosophical frameworks, the notion of the other, the Other, or otherness is situated in a phenomenological relational ontology. This chapter is grounded in the phenomenology of the Other/other.

There has been increased attention to the other in the communication discipline since the late 1990s moving well into the 21st century (Murray, 2002). To explain how this chapter understands and works with metaphors for the other, looking toward the philosophy of Emmanuel Levinas (1906–1995) orients the discussion toward a phenomenology of the Other. Turning toward the other calls one to an ethics as first philosophy.

Emmanuel Levinas is perhaps the most significant philosopher to emerge in the 20th century who is known for his phenomenological understanding of and commitment to the Other; this was his life's philosophical project. Levinas's metaphysics of the Other suggest that one's relation with the Other always "exceeds one's ability to know or contain the Other" (Murray, 2002, p. 40). This means that there is more to the Other than what we can perceive and what we can understand and comprehend. Murray (2002) refers to this as an "ethical dimension that cannot be contained within the confines of understanding" (p. 40). Before continuing with the unpacking of the Other/ other, I want to differentiate between the "Other" and the "other"—the difference being one is capitalized and the other is not capitalized. This is intentional. Pat Gehrke (2010) provides a clear and meaningful distinction between the two forms, though it should be noted that not all scholarship or philosophy uses this distinction, but for certain this is a Levinasian dis- tinction. Gehrke (2010) states that the capitalized **Other** "is used for the personal other, the you" (p. 8); he also states that the uncapitalized **other** describes "the common usage of the other, such as another" (p. 8). Gehrke (2010) clarifies that when Levinas uses the capitalized Other, he refers to a singular and unique other that stands before one (or me). Gehrke (2010) states the Other is

> you as an individual, different from all other individuals, in this specific moment, ultimately exceeding every attempt I might make to organize you into a system of meaning or response. (p. 8)

Gehrke (2010) continues that the "I" does not exist prior to the relation to the Other—the "I" comes into being when the Other approaches. In fact, Gehrke (2002) states that that the very possibility of our individual being is owed to the approach of the Other. This understanding is further elaborated on later in the chapter in the explication of the derivative "I."

Levinas's description of the Other portrays the other as a phenomenon that one experiences—a phenomenon of lived experience. Levinas's attention to the Other is his way of revealing the nature of one's relation to the other, and he does this by exploring how the Other presents itself to the world (Murray, 2002). Levinas situates the understanding of the other not as a "knowing" but rather as an ethical obligation to the other. I exist in relation to otherness that is so absolute that it cannot be codified into a dialectic or an opposition (Gehrke, 2010). The relation is an infinite otherness that does not allow for the possibility of containing the relation in thought—the absolute other is the Other that is not a collective "we," nor does it stand on the plurality of the "I" or the same "I." Rather, the Other is that which transcends the self's own subjective consciousness—it is not a representation or reflection of the self (Murray, 2002). It is absolutely Other. This statement comes with a reflection on the contradiction that other philosophers such as Jacques Derrida claim against Levinas's Other, though this contradiction has been corrected as a paradox of the Other (Murray, 2002). According to Murray (2002), Derrida critiqued Levinas's claim that the Other is an absolute Other; the Other that transcends, in absoluteness, the self's own subjective consciousness (Levinas, 1969). Derrida suggested that if this were the case, the subjective self could not recognize the Other as other. Also, if we cannot recognize the Other as other, how would we know if we encountered the other (Murray, 2002)? Derrida claimed this as a contradiction in Levinas's thought; however, Jeffrey Murray (2002) reframed it as a paradox.

According to Murray (2002), the paradox is that the "Other is absolutely other but can be known since the nature of human communication is simultaneously epistemic and ethical." Murray (2002) states this paradox in this way:

> The Other can be known, but despite my knowledge of him or her, even despite my very intimate knowledge of him or her, the Other always calls to me from beyond, from an excess, from infinity. And it is that excess, that which cannot be contained, which is the ground of ethics. (p. 44)

Murray (2002) is stating that the Other is not absolutely Other in the sense that I cannot know the Other—the Other as incomprehensible or as unknowable. Rather, the absolute Other refers to the sense that no matter how much I know the Other, I cannot fully know the Other—there is an excess that which I cannot know. Murray (2002) states that the Other will always surprise me in some way and the experience we have with otherness is not my experience to own—this a reverence for the ethical obligation to the Other. Gehrke (2010) states that the "I" exists for the Other in ethical obligation to the Other; the "I" comes into being because of the Other.

These conceptualizations and discussions lay the ground for understanding otherness situated with the following metaphors. The Other in Edith Stein's understanding of empathy reflects a sensory appearance—an inner perception. The Other in Jacques Derrida's understanding of hospitality reflects a dwelling place of welcome. The Other in Michael J. Hyde's offering of acknowledgment reflects a phenomenological and ontological seeing or observation. The Other in Ronald C. Arnett's illumination of the "derivative I" reflects a birthright. In each of these metaphors, the Other is in relation to the self and the relation is an ethical relation; the ethicality is inherent in the philosophy of communication inquiry. Each metaphor excavates a philosophy of communication ethics.

Empathy

Empathy has deep roots in philosophical literature. The Westernized understanding of empathy emerged from the German word *Einfühlung*, and from the German philosopher, Robert Vischer (1847–1933) in 1873 (Arnett & Holba, 2012). Empathy was integrated into psychology through the work of Theodor Lipps (1851–1914) and Sigmund Freud (1856–1939) (Arnett & Holba, 2012). The term **empathy** is identified as an active metaphor in discussions focusing on human sensibilities and subjective meaning experienced by another—in philosophical circles, Edith Stein is most noted for her attention to empathy and the human condition (Arnett & Holba, 2012). Generally speaking, Edith Stein specifically connects empathy to the development of personhood. The questions that guided Stein's philosophy include, "How does an individual gain true understanding of self and others? How are we, as humans, connected and dependent upon each other for understanding? Can we truly understand another?" (Chastain, 2018, p. 478). Empathy was a part of, and central to, each of these questions.

Stein connected the human person to the necessity of sociality; this situated the primary importance of empathy in human relationships and encounters with others. Stein's interest toward empathy began with the notion of "givenness," which for her involved a primordial experience that opens to the possibility of a phenomenological analyses of person and community (Baseheart, 1997). This meant that empathy was an act of perceiving that does not encapsulate one into the other. Stein was interested in what she referred to as "inner intuition" (Baseheart, 1997, p. 35) and it involved the unity of the "I," which tends to the other cognitively and affectively.

For Stein, empathy rested within the interplay of an intersubjective world between persons (Arnett & Holba, 2012). This interplay involved human sentiment that would shape human rationality. She believed empathy began with "sensory appearance" that makes things known while encountering "foreign experience" (Stein, 1989, p. 6). Empathy is an inner perception of inner intuition (Stein, 1989). Distinguishing between empathy and sympathy, Stein suggested sympathy reflects how we are wired as human beings to each other; it assists us in the sensual engagement of a given environment.

However, empathy requires the same sympathetic attentiveness, as well as a reflective act on the senses. This reflective act affects the body and is an internal response to an external sensation (Arnett & Holba, 2012). It is the reflection from these inner workings that make empathy possible.

Stein suggested empathy included both the psychic and spiritual aspects of being human. She situated the idea of a person as the gestalt that connects a "three-fold oneness" of "body-soul-spirit" (Baseheart, 1997, p. 56). Stein's unique conception of the human person meets the notion of community, which in return calls forth the spirit of the "I." The human community, the spirit, and the "I" require a bridge that connects one person to another; empathy does just this: It functions as a phenomenological bridge between persons (Arnett & Holba, 2012).

Stein (1989) suggested that empathy is a way of feeling oneself into the experience of the other. Stein (1989) described empathy as an experience of another person's experience. These feelings are perceptual and imaginative (Svenaeus, 2017). Stein suggested that empathy is nonoriginal, kind of like a memory is. In a memory, we bring an experience into our present moment but it is not presently happening—though we reexperience the memory. Empathy is similar: We are bringing the experience of the other into our presentness though acknowledging that the content of the experience has never been bodily experienced by us if we are the one experiencing empathy for and with the other (Svenaeus, 2017). This description helps us to understand Stein's description of empathy as a phenomenological bridge to the other.

Stein's understanding of empathy is fourfold because it allows one "(1) to be open to the other; (2) to gain self-knowledge about ourselves from the other; (3) to correct our misperceptions of ourselves and others through the other; and (4) to share in and grasp the past histories of others" (Chastain, 2018). Stein also identifies two types of empathy: reiterated empathy and comprehended empathy. Reiterated empathy emerges when "one realizes that his/her own zero point of orientation is a spatial point among many," and comprehended empathy reflects a "turning or glance toward an earlier historical moment wherein we may meet the spiritual life of the past" (Chastain, 2018, p. 479). This meeting allows new values to emerge from our own unfamiliar values from the past. Understanding empathy as a metaphorical phenomenological bridge between one and the Other offers an opening to the interplay of human encounters. Hospitality offers a similar opening to the Other.

Welcome and Hospitality

Jacques Derrida's essay, "A Word of Welcome" (1999) was written after the death of his good friend, Emmanuel Levinas. What welcome means is what the word insinuates. Derrida (1999) identified six presuppositions of the word, welcome:

1. Saying "welcome" insinuates that one is at home here.

2. This means that one knows what it means to be at home.

3. At home, one receives, invites, or offers hospitality.

4. One appropriates for oneself a place to welcome the Other.

5. Or one welcomes the Other so that one appropriates a place for oneself.

6. When one welcomes the Other, one speaks the language of hospitality.

In laying out these presuppositions, Derrida (1999) also admitted that the world of welcome is one that is not his. In fact, he attributes it to Levinas as Derrida stated, since he [Levinas] "put his mark upon it, having first reinventing it, in those places where he invites us—this is, gives us to think—what is called 'hospitality'" (p. 16). François Cooren (2018) identifies the metaphor of **hospitality** as the key feature of Derrida's ethics of communication. Cooren (2018) suggests that Derrida's principle of hospitality suggested an unconditional welcoming of the Other—a "visitation without invitation" (p. 119). The question Derrida is seeking to answer reflects a curiosity about how we approach the Other in discourse. For Derrida (1999), it is through a welcoming—to welcome the Other in discourse is to have an ethical relation with the Other and to allow oneself to learn from the Other. The welcoming is not the same as an everyday welcome to others. This unconditional welcoming is extended to all beings, human, other animals, and nonliving beings. This is a welcoming that depends on nothing and exposes us to an Other who affects us and who subjects us to their laws or conditions (Cooren, 2018). Hospitality defines who we are as human beings. When we welcome the Other, when we are hospitable, and as the host, we become hostage to the Other.

Derrida situated his understanding of welcome with his understanding of hospitality; both metaphors go hand in hand. When we welcome the Other, it requires one to be able to respond to the Other. In this requirement of response, the capacity for the self or the "I" emerges. The welcoming one offers to the Other creates a hospitable condition requiring a response—one becomes host and hostage to the Other. Ronald C. Arnett (2017) articulates this in his book, *Levinas's Rhetorical Demand: The Unending Obligation of Communication Ethics*, where he states that "hospitality is a communicative act witnessed in the opening of oneself to the visage, the face, of the Other. The face welcomes and bids responsibility for the Other" (p. 225). The welcome originates in the human face and is a catalyst of accountability for the Other that one cannot escape. One is its hostage.

Derrida's (1999) understanding was uniquely his—he suggested that in the welcome, when the host and guest come together, the communicative gesture of welcome moves from a condition of possession of the Other to a condition of obligation to the Other. This movement creates a reversal, the host becomes the guest and the guest becomes the host. Derrida (1999) stated that in hospitality one opens to the infinity of the Other and in this infinity there is already a response; it is "yes" to the Other. This is a responsible response. In citing this act as a communicative gesture, Derrida (1999) stated that it begins with a movement, a right or good movement. But prior to this movement, "[w]e must first think the possibility of the welcome in order to think the face and everything that opens up is displaced with it" (Derrida, 1999, p. 25). When we open to the Other in this way, with forethought of the face and what it means, we receive the Other beyond the capacity of the I. Therefore, the welcome manifests the ethical relation in the receptivity of receiving the face of the Other.

It is the welcoming of the other by the self that calls into question ethics and responsibility for the other. Levinas stated that the notion of the face "opens other perspectives," which brings up meaning prior to the self and is separate from my own initiative and my own power (p. 51). Levinas's project questioned the privileged position of the self in Western culture (Arnett, 2003). The welcome and then hospitality are two metaphors that point to the absurdity of that privilege. The next metaphor, acknowledgment, similarly points to the need to welcome, witness, and acknowledge the Other as a response to the call of conscience.

Acknowledgment

Acknowledgment, as a life-giving gift, is a metaphor that emerged from the scholarship of Professor Michael J. Hyde, the university distinguished professor of communication ethics at Wake Forest University. As a philosopher of communication ethics, Hyde applies his philosophical prowess through case studies in an effort to bring philosophical ideas and ideals into action. The question that Hyde pursues in much of his work, and is the guiding question of this metaphor, is "What would it be like if no one *acknowledged* your existence?" (p. 1). The answer he found in his inquiry is bleak. But first, unpacking acknowledgment is necessary for understanding the fuller implications of the lack of acknowledgment.

According to Hyde (2006), acknowledgment is a communicative behavior; it is something we do that provides attention to others; this attention establishes a space for them in our own lives. Because this is a new living or dwelling space for the other, it opens up new opportunities and new beginnings; it also opens up those much needed "second chances," which have the power to change someone's life in positive ways. Hyde (2006) describes this space as transformative of both space and time. This means that when one acknowledges the other, one goes out of their way, opting in on their own volition, to make others feel welcomed, needed, and wanted. At its very basic nature, acknowledging the other tells the other that there is worthiness of their existence. Hyde (2006) states that acknowledging, offering positive or constructive acknowledgment, is a moral thing to do.

Positive acknowledgment usually makes us feel good, though there may be times when we feel we do not deserve the acknowledgment, especially if our intentions or motivations are not so pure when it comes to the reason for the acknowledgment. However, in general, being acknowledged in a positive manner recognizes something specific about ourselves. Positive acknowledgment can also happen when we are no longer here on earth (Hyde, 2006). We provide positive acknowledgment of others at funerals, through eulogies and basic statements about accomplishments and the nature of their character while alive. Generally, positive acknowledgment provides some kind of meaningfulness of life; it helps us understand our place in the world and the meaningfulness of our existence.

All acknowledgment is not positive (Hyde, 2006). Negative acknowledgment can be hurtful and cause one to question their actions and their life. Negative acknowledgment comes in a range of communicative behaviors such as gossip, sarcasm, misrepresentation of something, lies about other people or their actions, character attacks, and other such negative comments or accusations. While this is still acknowledging the other, it creates a space that makes another person feel bad about themselves or about something they did. Sometimes negative acknowledgment is not our intent; it just comes out that way—sometimes it is just about the language we use. We might use language that makes people defensive just in the language we choose and the tone of our voice; defensive language choices can be mitigated so that we can still provide constructive criticism in ways that are less negative. Sometimes, negative acknowledgment can actually create positive outcomes if it is based in truthfulness. Sometimes, negative acknowledgment comes from nefarious intentions. Regardless of how and where it comes from, it is still a form of communication that acknowledges one's existence. Some negative acknowledgment is institutionalized in government structures, organizational structures, and other industry structures and is exposed through racism, sexism, and ageism. There is a significant amount of negative acknowledgment, sometimes more than there is positive acknowledgment.

Hyde (2006) argues that acknowledgment can be "a life-giving gift and a life-draining force" (p. 2). There is a third possibility of acknowledgment, a state of no acknowledgment. Hyde (2006) argues that no acknowledgment creates a space that cannot support life because the space is barren and lacks nourishment that is derived from the care of others. Both negative acknowledgment (only some forms of it) and no acknowledgment can lead to what Hyde (2006) refers to as "social death" (p. 189). Hyde (2006) describes social death as an occurrence that takes place in any culture where people are "slighted or marginalized because of race, gender, religion, age, sexual orientation, or physical and mental status" (p. 190). Social deaths happen daily around the world; people who experience a social death are imprisoned in negative spaces and their human spirit is defaced, vandalized, crippled, and impaired. Social deaths can also occur to other social beings, such as pets and other undomesticated animals living in nature. This is not limited to a human experience—there are many other abused animals in the world, but usually it is a human who causes the social death of the other. Acknowledgment is an antidote to the phenomenon of social death, but it takes awareness about acknowledgment to reteach people how to treat others; it takes a call of conscience to treat people with dignity and respect.

Acknowledgment that comes from a place of care and conscience, positive, or even if it is constructive negative, acknowledgment brings relief, which gives one a place to dwell within; this is a space of care and support. Without this kind of dwelling space, existence turns to a place of homelessness. The metaphor of "existential homelessness" can be tied to social death since it represents a loss of trust in existence and a negative dwelling space that lacks nourishment and care for the other (Arnett, 1994). Existential homelessness creates a feeling of not being at home—of not being able to trust in your community and of not having a place of rest and refuge. In these kinds of negative spaces, dialogue is absent, the voice is lost or shut down, the social death closes the possibility for engagement—it ends the possibility for life and for living. Acknowledgment as a remedy for social death also recognizes that one's existence depends on the other—the Other in Levinas's Other and in Arnett's (2013b) derivative "I."

Derivative "I"

Responsibility for the Other has no beginning and no ending (Arnett, 2017; Levinas, 1969). Levinas's ethics starts with an "I" that is directed by the face of the Other; this leads to the understanding that "I am my brother's keeper" (Arnett, 2017, p. 129). Arnett (2013b, 2017) distinguishes between the originative "I" and the **derivative "I"** in pursuit of his questioning about the role of agency in ethics. The originative "I" is described as an imperial, sovereign, or hateful self that begins and ends with concern for oneself, disregarding the face of the Other (Arnett, 2017). On the other hand, if one responds to the demands of the face of the Other, which happens when one moves from a visual sense of the Other (seeing the Other) to an "audio ethic" hearing "I am my brother's keeper," this is an obligation to a particular Other (Arnett, 2017, p. 2). The audio ethic frames the communicative agent as a derivative "I" (Arnett, 2017, p. 2). Arnett (2003) states, "The 'I' finds identity in response to the Other" (p. 39). When understanding oneself shifts from originative to derivative, this then occupies a sacred space that honors the Other and puts the Other before the self. The derivative "I" emerges from a place of response, not a place of telling or dictating. The derivative "I" is a byproduct or outcome from the Other, which means it does not dominate or overpower the Other. The Other is in a place of reverence; the derivative "I" is situated in a hermeneutic humility that honors and respects the Other.

Understanding the self as a derivative "I" has the potential to shift the presuppositions that are currently celebrated in Western culture. There are two presuppositions acknowledged in Western culture concerns: individual agency and individual willfulness (Arnett, 2003). Individual agency reflects when an individual acts on their own behalf; the individual has choices and makes decisions that reflect an autonomous being. The notion of willfulness illuminates the fact that the individual has volition and intention when acting. Both of these presuppositions were critiqued by Alexis de Tocqueville (1805–1859), a French political scientist and historian, when he came to America to study the system of education in the United States. De Tocqueville published *Democracy in America* in 1835 in which he critiqued the American system of education. De Tocqueville warned against individualism because of the dangers associated with standing above the community values, mores, and traditions. According to Arnett and Holba (2012), de Tocqueville found that individualism was significantly more dangerous than selfishness because individualism stands above the human condition while selfishness can tend to others around them out of a sense of care even if the reason to do so is selfish.

The idea of understanding the human path as one of caretaking does not come from having a good sense of the "I" but rather from the phenomenological call to attend to the Other (Arnett, 2003). When we start from the self and not the Other, we miss that phenomenological call. When we answer the call of the Other, we develop a relationship with alterity and responsibility. Levinas (2000) explained this unconditionality of being "hostage" (p. 184). There are three presuppositions necessary to ground the perspective of the derivative "I": First, to ignore the Other is to put one's own identity in danger or at risk (Arnett, 2003). Second, we miss the phenomenological reality of life if we ignore the call from the Other. Third, when we start with the Other, when we begin by attending to the face of the Other and that phenomenological call, the path for one's self identity is illuminated. Do nothing, that path can never be seen. The "I" finds its identity by attending to the call of the Other; therefore, individual agency and willfulness can impede the cultivation and development of one's own identity.

Connections, Currency, and Meaning

When human beings forget themselves and acknowledge the call of their conscience—the call of the Other, they selflessly and authentically call themselves into question and submit to their obligation to the Other (Koskinen & Lindström, 2013). This is an unconditional and infinite responsibility, to listen to the vulnerability of the other and to recognize and acknowledge the sacredness and sanctity of the Other, the being of the Other. When human beings do this, their communicative heart opens and allows them to stand in their own vulnerability before the Other.

Connections: The metaphors in this chapter have points of connection to each other and are driven by unique perspectives advocated from a philosophy of communication ethics lens. In each metaphor there is recognition that one needs the Other in existence and that this recognition requires a setting aside of the ego in order to start from the Other and not the self. For example, empathy involves a sociality that is primary to human relationships and encounters with Others. These relationships and encounters do not encapsulate one into the other; instead they breathe life, support, and understanding into the experience of the Other. Likewise, welcome and hospitality enter into this sociality by announcing and revealing the call of ethics and responsibility for the Other situated within care and a giving up of oneself for the Other. Acknowledgment understands the need for this sociality in a positive and constructive way while warning against the dark side of engaging negative and deconstructive structures of acknowledgment that cause the social death of the Other. By understanding that the "I" is derivative from the Other, we acknowledge and honor the sanctity of all human existence—that the Other is the reason for our own existence and is a key to understanding our ethical relation to the Other and to the world.

There are different ways to view and understand the human condition, especially when considering the relationship between self and Other. From a philosophy of communication inquiry perspective, understanding this social ontology can provide guidance for social, professional, relational, and ethical engagement between persons. Each of these metaphors provide a different way to think about how one sets the ego aside to see the Other differently. Each metaphor also demonstrates how the interpersonal connections and influences from our communicative behavior impact how other people live their own lives. While we might be individual bodies, our lives are intertwined and interconnected in life-giving and life-ending ways. This social ontology should open our hearts to living our lives in full regard to and for the Other.

Currency: Contemplation on and for the Other have never been so relevant as they are today. In the news there are daily stories pertaining to COVID-19 and social (physical) distancing, or lack of any kind of wellness-focused distancing. There are also stories of questionable police uses of force and the killing of Black men during the course of policing encounters. This has expanded the Black Lives Matter movement across the country calling for and initiating public moral argument and debate to further illuminate the structural issues in the government and justice systems that continue to be framed by racism and other biases that cause negative effects in the lives of marginalized populations.

It would serve these forums of public moral argument to be exposed to metaphors of the Other so that the dialogue can change. Instead of starting with the self and the reasons why one acts or engages as one does, cultivating the sensibilities of empathy, welcome and hospitality, and life-giving forms of acknowledgment are essential for any kind of system-wide changes to occur. Recognizing that the "I" is derivative from the Other is also a key understanding that provides a kind of primordial disposition for dialogue, argument, and advocacy. Most of the conversations in news media come from the egoic position, but if public discourse can be resituated with new understandings of the Other, healthy and authentic dialogue has more of a chance to make a difference.

Meaning: Some of the most known peaceful resistors who led social change had empathetic sensibilities and embodied the nature of welcome and hospitality. Consider Martin Luther King Jr. (1929–1968) and Mahatma Ghandi (1869–1948), both known for advocating peaceful resistance, but even in the presence of their most outrageous antagonists they demonstrated empathy and hospitality to their foes. Both of them recognized that honoring the Other respectfully is the only way to make real change. This kind of recognition opens possibilities for effective public moral argument and positive outcomes. Both King and Ghandi provided positive acknowledgment even when they had to critique the culture, and they both recognized the social ontology of the "I" and the Other, recognizing that there would be no other way to engage effective public moral argument without acknowledging the social ontology and social relation between self and Other. Meaning emerges when one contemplates on social ontologies that begin with the Other.

Conclusion

This chapter explored metaphors for the Other in philosophy of communication literature. The metaphors selected for this chapter include empathy, welcome/hospitality, acknowledgment, and the derivative "I." Each of these metaphors are tied to each other through an ethicality that is slightly different from one another yet clearly advocate responsibility for the Other. In many ways, this is a discussion on our human social ontology and the idea of a phenomenological relational ontology. Each of the metaphors in this chapter recognize that the "I" or the self needs the Other in existence and that in the relationship between self and Other, there is no dominance—each entity breathes life into each other. In a very applied way, having knowledge of the human social ontology can provide guidance for our social, professional, relational, and ethical engagement in the world.

Chapter 14

Metaphors for Community

Learning Objectives

1. Describe key metaphors for community in philosophy of communication inquiry selected for this chapter.

2. Identify coordinates that constitute each selected metaphor for this chapter.

3. Articulate guiding questions undergirding each metaphor in philosophy of communication inquiry in this chapter.

4. Explain meaning and relevance to philosophy of communication inquiry for each metaphor in this chapter.

Have you ever wondered why human beings create structures to live and move through life together, such as building social structures like housing communities, creating public or private school systems, or building movie theatres? Think back to a neighborhood or environment where you grew up; what about it gave you a sense of comfort, happiness, or belonging? Why do you believe human beings are drawn to these kinds of places? How do you imagine the future community in which you will live? What about that community attracts you to it?

A community requires an invitation. This invitation requires three elements necessary for developing a common language for inviting community. Bellah et al. (1985) suggested that community is not really about feelings or that feelings do not come first in a community. The first aspect for developing community is a commitment to story-centered values. Individual feelings are unique to the self and they are subjective. For community to emerge, feelings are not enough to sustain the collective—there needs to be a commitment to something beyond the self, and while feelings or sentiment might also have a part, feelings cannot come first because they are driven by the ego. Feelings set up a language tied to the self and to the individual but a commitment to something beyond the self sets up a language guided by the stories that cultivate the bond that brings people together (Arnett & Arneson, 1999). Second, Bellah et al. (1985) suggested that the relationship between people cannot drive the community; it is the story-centered values that bring birth to cultivating common ground through "community sensitive language" and that creates a vocabulary of commitment, sacrifice, loyalty, and principle (Arnett & Arneson, 1999, p. 273). This means that relationships emerge from attending to story-centered values. The relationship does not come first; it is byproduct of the coming together around values. Lastly, Bellah et al. (1985) suggested the language that emerges through attending to story-centered values creates a community of memory. This does not happen overnight; it requires attending to the stories in the community and contributing to the language that emerges from engagement (Arnett & Arneson, 1999). This, in particular, is even more important when engaging in and contributing to public moral argument.

What emerges in community is a communicative center that can unite persons of difference and disagreement. This notion of a communicative center differentiates communities from places of association (Arnett, 1986). A communicative center "nourishes the connectedness" of people through storytelling (p. 124). When we meet people in public spaces or from the edges of private spaces (for example, in a neighborhood where one lives), or social or business events in the larger community, meaning is derived from those encounters. While we may not also agree in meaning with every person we meet, our individual meaning expands the more we come in contact with other people. This is how we acknowledge the existence of multiple meanings and how our meaning expands as it is confronted by those multiple meanings. Communities are open and allow for a communicative center to emerge and evolve (Arnett, 1986). This is done through dialogue, dialectic, public moral argument and many forms of communicative experiences. Communities are a part of our stories as human beings; by engaging in communities, stories are shared, and values emerge. When disagreement occurs, communities provide the communitive center for dialogic and dialectic engagement to guide us through that space and come to a constructive response. Community needs difference and disagreement in order to evolve, sustain, and thrive. Ronald C. Arnett (1986) suggests that we are in a time of "multiple meanings for some, meaninglessness for others, and utter confusion for more than a few," and he admits that there are no instant or immediate answers for us (p. 140). But what we need to do is walk between the extremes to discover meaningfulness, and we do this by "taking, giving, and at times, just standing in the face of the absurd and saying, 'I do what I do, because I can do no other'" (Arnett, 1986, p. 140).

The commitment to story-centered values in the emergence of community is key to Seyla Benhabib's (1992) understanding of communitarian thinking that is necessary to reconstitute community under conditions of modernity. Before offering her perspective on community as it is tied to public moral argument, it is helpful to understand communitarianism in relation to the concept of community. **Communitarianism** is a system of social organization that is based on smaller communities that self-govern. It is a social philosophy that privileges individual ties to family and that individual identities are constituted through the individual's relationship to the community. This kind of social composition is essential for any kind of political life.

In the latter part of the 20th century, Amitai Etzioni, a German-born Israeli and American sociologist and philosopher, was one of the premier voices of the communitarian movement. Etzioni stated (2015) that communitarianism is a social philosophy that emphasizes the importance of society over the importance of the individual. In this framework, communitarians explore the ways conceptions of the good are formed, shared, trusted, and enforced (Etzioni, 2015). Etzioni (2015) suggested that communitarianism emerged as a critique and resistance to John Rawls's *A Theory of Justice* (1971), which situates the individual as having inviolable rights, which means individual rights are never accountable to society as a whole. Individuals have rights in which society can never change, adapt, remove, or challenge. The main argument against Rawls's theory is that it is extreme. Having such a liberal conception of individual rights fails to acknowledge that the individual is embedded into something much bigger than the self—society. Benhabib advocates a communitarian sentiment.

According to Benhabib (1992), there are two strands of communitarian thinking: first, the integrationist and second, the participationist. Integrationists want to reconstitute a community with an integrated vision of fundamental values and principles while participationists see community as emerging from the community engaging together—fully participating in community life. Benhabib (1992) advocates for a communitarian view that is participationist, one that privileges values of autonomy, pluralism, reflexivity, and tolerance. The difference between the two is the integrationist perspective does not allow for each individual in participation with creating the integrative vision. Benhabib (1992) states that it is only through each individual in participation with others that an "interactive universalism" can be created (p. 11). This makes sense because the question that guides Benhabib's (1992) inquiry is "How should we think about ethical life?" Benhabib (1992) comes from a feminist perspective because she is concerned with how one situates reason and the moral self within the contexts of gender and community. Her attention to community as a fully participative spatial experience provides a horizon of significance from which we can explore metaphors related to community.

For this chapter, I chose four metaphors that provide examples of how philosophy of communication inquiry navigates understandings of community. As offered in previous chapters, these selected metaphors are just that, a selection of metaphors taken from many other metaphors that could have been chosen for discussion. I selected these particular metaphors, **witness**, **dialogic civility**, **professional civility**, and **self in community**, because they resonate with my own particular interests and they are each grounded within an ethical framework. Too often, discussions about, by, or for the community do not hold explicit reference to ethics. Each of these metaphors are imbued with explicit ethical commitments—selection of these metaphors enable ethicality in meaning making. This is explicitly present in the first metaphor of tenacious hope.

Witness

Community depends on the notion of witness, the act of witnessing, bearing witness. Hannah Arendt was well aware that communities could not move forward in constructive ways without human testament (Arnett, 2013a). What is it that makes human testament possible? It takes courage and conviction of people to tell their stories and share their observations and experiences with others. Witnessing is an ethic; it is the fulfilling of one's responsibility

(Arnett, 2017). It has been argued that the use of the terms *witness* and *testimony* are widespread and being used with different connotative implications (Ben-Pazi, 2015). The question that drove Emmanuel Levinas's interest in witness and witnessing was attached to the possibility of responsibility attached to the act; he asked, "What does it mean to be a witness?" and "What is the ethical responsibility of the act of witnessing?" To be a witness, for Levinas, meant to know the other and to bear a responsibility toward otherness (Ben-Pazi, 2015). The strength of a community relies on how the community members bear witness for one another and for taking responsibility for the act of witnessing.

This kind of witnessing, in a philosophical sense, is not the same as one serving as a witness in a formal court setting where one provides testimony of some kind of knowledge. While this is important for participants in a community to do, it is different from conceptualizing what witnessing means philosophically and what it means to witness otherness. Both are important to community. On the one hand, testifying and bearing witness in court has a different *telos* than the notion of bearing witness to otherness. In court, one's obligation is to tell the truth about something that one has knowledge of—it is a witnessing, but it is driven by formal structures in the court system. Bearing witness to otherness is part of one's social ontology; it is a basic human condition for existence. In philosophy of communication inquiry, witness and witnessing are an integral part of existence (Ben-Pazi, 2015). The moment one witnesses something particular is the moment at which one assumes the responsibility to bear witness. In many cases, the one who is called into bearing witness is an "unintentional witness," which means there was no intentionality to be a witness, but because of circumstances they are called to the responsibility of witnessing (Ben-Pazi, 2015). This might mean that some people resist being a witness when the responsibility arises, but from Levinas's perspective, there is no escaping the responsibility of bearing witness.

Bearing witness involves making a choice, to witness or not to witness. This means that to bear witness (or not) is an encountering of the limits of the person (Ben-Pazi, 2015). The existence of witnessing in general sets up a relationship between the I and the Other, and depending on one's choice, this relationship can include acts of cruelty, which means one might choose to not be a witness; one might stay neutral, or remain a voyeur. This is the temptation of witnessing; one must make a choice and once the decision is made, one either chooses a move toward the infinite (to witness) or away from the infinite (not to witness).

From a philosophy of communication inquiry perspective, bearing witness can be considered a category of belonging, participation, and taking responsibility (Ben-Pazi, 2015). Martin Heidegger (1996) found witnessing as an act of revelation of *Dasein*, of Being. This means that Dasein can be understood as "testifying to existence through its own authentic existence" (Ben-Pazi, 2015, p. 236). Bearing witness is an exposure of existence—a revelation. This exposure to existence wards against meaninglessness; for Heidegger, bearing witness aligns with authenticity of existence. Authenticity mitigates meaninglessness. This means that bearing witness for the Other announces Dasein's existence, which in itself provides meaningfulness in existence.

Bearing witness acknowledges existence through spoken word or image. In a practical sense, bearing witness to events and people occurs in media all of the time, but there is some criticism that this kind of witnessing is not enough and that in media, bearing witness "must do more moral work than mere observation or recognition" (Hill, 2018, p. 28). Bearing witness is more than seeing something and sharing it—it requires a moral response for one to take action upon their responsibility to the Other. The more technologies invite bearing witness, the more the practice of witnessing is debated and problematized (Givoni, 2014). In contemporary contexts, the "era of the witness" has reframed witnessing and testimony as gestures that instigate the possibility of subjective transformation, not to just provide and produce empirical truths (Givoni, 2014). However, there continues to be criticism of the practice of witnessing as being lax in reflexive witnessing. This establishes an argument that witnessing should not only hold an ethical responsibility to the Other but that it be a reflexive endeavor for the one doing the witnessing (Givoni, 2014).

Dialogic Civility

Dialogic civility is a metaphor that announces the significance of public respect in interpersonal interactions that include all kinds of communicative behavior (Arnett & Arneson, 1999). As a metaphor, it is also agreed on by a large number of communicative agents in such a way that it creates a communicative backdrop for interpersonal communication and relationships (Arnett & Arneson, 1999). Dialogic civility provides a narrative backdrop that guides interpersonal communication at a time of narrative contention and confusion. Dialogic civility provides a metaphorical horizon of significance that includes conceptual commonplaces to fully understand how it is important to how we come to meaning and to human relationships. These conceptual commonplaces include practice, praxis, metaphor, narrative, metanarrative, metanarrative decline, and interpersonal communication. Exploring these commonplaces will assist with unfolding dialogical civility as a pragmatic opportunity for making deeper connections with others and for being the bedrock of community and its communicative center.

Dialogic civility is grounded in historicality, which counters the therapeutic model of communication where one privileges the self at the expense of the Other. Historicality situates the historical moment as significant to interpretation and developing healthy communicative understandings. Communication between persons is an ever-changing process that cannot be divorced from one's communicative understanding of the historical moment of interpretation (Arnett & Arneson, 1999). Implications of the metaphor, dialogic civility, include a foregrounding of the interconnectivity between how we communicate interpersonally and those commonsense questions that govern particular historical moments. For example, how we communicate with and what we communicate to Others should be connected to genuine human problems and those questions tied to the particular historical moment in a commonsense way (Arnett & Arneson, 1999). This requires an authenticity on the part of the communicants and an overall care for the Other that allows one to set aside their own egoic desires.

The challenge is to not miss the historical moment; in missing the historical moment, one's communication becomes anachronistic, inauthentic, and unhelpful (Arnett & Arneson, 1999). Meeting the historical moment is what allows meaning to unfold. Having a living dialogue between one and the Other means that one listens to the demands of the historical moment and communicates with currency. Dialogic civility does not just mean that one is civil and respectful in language usage and communicative affect; dialogic civility also aims for building meaning and for communicative exchanges to be meaningful. One example of this can be situated in an exchange between teacher and student and the use of this book for class. At the end of each chapter in this book there is a section entitled "Connections, Currency, Meaning" that is designed to open class discussion for practical and pragmatic application of chapter contents. These sections are focused around public moral argument from a philosophy of communication inquiry perspective.

At the writing of this book, the world is in a global pandemic from the COVID-19 virus and race relations are at the brink of breaking in the United States after a horrific incident where a Minnesota police officer killed a Black man, in public, while someone took a video of the incident that involved the police officer pressing his knee to the neck of the man who was lying on the ground next to a police car. The video showed the man, George Floyd, begging to breathe and telling the officer he could not breathe. The White officer did not listen to Floyd, who was arrested for a nonviolent crime and in police custody. At times, the White officer seemed to smile for the camera. The recording also caught the moment when Floyd stopped breathing, and even though Floyd was no longer breathing or moving, the officer maintained pressure on Floyd's neck long after his life expired. Using this book to engage the conversation about the pandemic or about race relations in the United States in meaningful ways can assist with developing deeper understandings of philosophy of communication inquiry and its relevance to individual lives and the life of communities.

In a few years, the historical moment will be different because we know historical moments are ever changing. If these examples are not changed, updated, or refreshed, the meaningfulness of this book will decline and not be relevant in constructive ways. The questions that govern public discourse change as the world changes, and the world changes every day. It is only a matter of time before anything that is written becomes anachronistic. To truly find understanding and meaning in community, one must listen to the historical moment and meet it where it is. The process of listening to the historical moment in order to meet it where it is requires the ability to discern those commonsense questions that guide public discourse and public action (Arnett & Arneson, 1999). Any narrative that fails to be relevant to the contemporary moment and those emergent questions within it is simply a failed tradition—a tradition that is no longer necessary or relevant. In the context of the case of George Floyd, the tradition of policing endorsed and used by the White police officer who killed Floyd is a dead tradition because policing has been changing and moving toward social justice, equity, and inclusion for many years now, except not at the same pace and not in the same geographical locations. Questions governing this particular historical moment are tied deeply to how we invite all voices into public discourse and how we privilege those voices previously marginalized; the Floyd event opened the door for true dialogue in public moral argument and no doubt will lead to transformation across policing. Missing the questions of this historical moment would mean that there is no chance for change or trans-formation of a dead tradition; but the questions were not missed and each day since, there has been public dialogue, protests, and active sociopolitical conversations. Policy change is on the horizon. We have witnessed this kind of transformation before in the 20th century, for example when in 1955 Rosa Parks would not give up her seat on a bus for a White person, and in 1957 when the Little Rock Nine (nine Black high school students) were not allowed to enter a White high school during the beginning of desegregating the public school system. It simply takes time to listen, engage, and do. However, the key to dialogic civility is in meeting the historical moment, listening to it, engaging in relevant and respectful dialogue, and making inclusive decisions based on what is relevant in that particular time.

Dialogic civility emphasizes **praxis** over **practice**. Practice refers to communication engaged in an unreflective manner and is a routine kind of action that does acknowledge fluid particularities that often accompany interpersonal communication (Arnett & Arneson, 1999). Praxis is informed communication that is a coinformed by theory and action (Arnett & Arneson, 1999). Understanding dialogic civility metaphorically allows for nuances and interpretive connotation to shape one's understanding and engagement with others. Understanding the narrative backdrop of dialogic civility is helpful in seeing stories and how they interplay together, which cultivates an integrated vision of one's environments. Understanding that there can be metanarratives, which are implicit yet uniformly agreed-on virtue structures in community that guide community engagement and structures is essential as one uniquely participates in community. On the other hand, one must also recognize metanarrative decline when it occurs—this occurs when the previously held commitment to a metanarrative ends, disrupts, or otherwise falls. All of these commonplaces for understanding come together and shape interpersonal communication in community (Arnett & Arneson, 1999). These coordinates are necessary for effective, respectful, and community growth through healthy interpersonal communication. This is how a community makes meaning together; this also means that meaning is co-constructed, coendorsed, and conavigated.

Recognizing the importance of dialogic civility in community is key for building healthy, meaning-laden communities. Dialogic civility is imbued with hermeneutic humility but the community is not the only place where hermeneutic humility should be apparent in communicative structures. An associated metaphor, professional civility, is another kind of civility that is essential in organizations and in all professionalisms and professions.

Professional Civility

Professional civility is a metaphorical counterpart to dialogic civility. Civility itself is the root of both professional and dialogic civility. P.M. Forni (2002, 2008) developed civility as a mode of engagement for the 20th and 21st centuries. Reminding his readers of a time past where respect and honor were woven into interpersonal and public discourse, Forni's life work culminated in his devotion to the Johns Hopkins Civility Project, which for now is somewhat in pause since his passing in 2018. Professional civility is a metaphorical couplet crafted by Janie Harden Fritz to counter the challenges her research identified in organizational communication. Fritz (2013) identified certain communicative practices responsible for contributing to problematic relationships in organizations that negatively affect a significant number of work relationships in organizations. Work relationships and how people work together necessarily impact community building, sustaining, and thriving. Some of these problematic communicative practices include social undermining, interpersonal harassment, and bullying (Fritz, 2013). Organizations are key components of our communities and the communicative practices people engage within organizations are easily transferrable to community engagement. Additionally, what happens within organizations, good or bad, necessarily impacts the larger community in both impersonal and interpersonal ways. For this reason, I included professional civility as a metaphor for community.

Fritz (2013) suggests that there is a crisis of incivility in workplaces across the United States and that this carries significant implications to organizational members including employee turnover and employee productivity. If employee turnover is not tempered, consequences can negatively impact poverty, unemployment, and community engagement and activities. If employee productivity is not adequate or stable, there is risk to organizational sustainability. If organizations have to move or relocate or worse, if they close due to lack of productivity, there can be far and wide consequences to the financial health of the community as well as public morale and negative attention to industrial growth and development in the community. Fritz (2013) states that people in organizations spend a lot of time with other people during their workday, so it pays to give attention to healthy and supportive communicative practices to ward off rudeness and incivility. People, the organization, and the community, if we see it as the host, are better off when civility is the guiding metaphor for human engagement. Fritz is interested in the question, "How do we situate civility within a theoretical framework for ethical communication in the workplace with special attention to the professions?" Fritz identifies civility as a communicative virtue and situates its importance in organizations.

Especially in the United States, we spend a lot of time in organizations (Fritz, 2013). Behaving civilly with others at work is "an integral part of a flourishing human existence that defines the good of, and for, human life" (Fritz, 2013, p. 3). Fritz (2013) also suggests civility contributes to the well-being of others within whom one encounters. Civility protects and promotes the other in ways that no other behavior can do—civility "protects and promotes respect for human beings and supports the various social contexts within which human lives find meaning and significance" (Fritz, 2013). While Fritz situates professional civility in the professions (she defines the original professions as theology, law, medicine, and education), professional civility can be a guiding asset for any kind of public engagement because it protects and promotes good within a specific community context. Professions engage in organizational structures; organizations are types of communities themselves.

Within any human community (an organization, a profession, an industry, a government) civility is a marker for any professional identity (Fritz, 2013). Civility is not only a virtue that is tied to professional identity, but it is also tied to the goods of the particular profession or the community. Fritz (2013) situates the roots of the crisis of incivility in the workplace is actually steeped deeply in the trends of the social world and society at large. It is already in our communities, and remembering the goods of civility as a communicative virtue can remedy the challenges that incivility has authored in our communities. Incivility has attacked the goods of persons and the goods of productivity. To recuperate these experiences, civil discourse, respect, and initiatives of human dignity at the micro and macro levels can work to mitigate the bad and open new spaces for the communicative good.

When considering civility in organizations and professions, it is helpful to recognize that members of these entities must behave properly and respectfully—all of their verbal and nonverbal communication shapes how they engage civilly (Fritz, 2013). The good of their productivity benefits the community and society at large. The good of the place must also be established through civility because all human engagement happens *somewhere*. Place matters because place builds a reputation and affects whomever it engages through any means. The place where organizations work is wall papered with all kinds of human interactions, so place matters as much as productivity matters. People bring their emotions and energies to the place to work—keeping the place healthy is necessary or individuals can shift into negative communication patterns such as incivility.

All of the work that is done in organizations is done for other people who are members of the human community. The people doing the work in organizations are also working with other people. How they engage with one another matters, and we have seen how this can unfold in a negative way in the many cases of workplace violence. The human matters, and each human in an organization or professional setting is also part of the broader human community as well as the local human community; how one is communicated with matters to everything about the person. Being civil with others at work will make a difference in the world at very basic levels. Protecting production, place, persons, and professions is all part of professional civility; it is a commitment to the larger human communicative story.

Civility itself has been associated with having good manners, being polite, and knowing personal and public etiquette (Fritz, 2013). It is really all about behavior and how we behave in a variety of circumstances. Some norms of civility are universal; others are particular to people, places, and things. However, civility is also very much a part of the human collective social imagination, and this is connected to engagement in the public sphere (Fritz, 2013). Fritz (2013) explains civility is a moral call to action in the public sphere, and this can occur from within an organization or within a broader context of community. Lastly, tradition is a central metaphor connected to professional civility (Fritz, 2013). Tradition is tied to tradition of practice in the professions as well as traditions related to narrative in the professions. It is through the traditions of professions and their practice that we can identify professional ideals and what is valued as the goods of the professions. Dialogic civility and professional civility are counterparts—there are very few, if any, human beings who do not engage in both private/personal and public contexts or settings. Every human being is a member of some kind of community, especially if we understand community to be a community that "begins in a common situation, involves real caring for one another despite differences, and is manifest in genuine dialogue" (Cissna & Anderson, 1994, p. 26). Community is tied to active human affairs and professional civility is the ground from which person-to-person communication should occur. The last metaphor for this chapter emerged from Calvin Schrag's book *The Self After Postmodernity* (1997) and reading this book will provide a snapshot of the significance of metaphor in philosophy of communication inquiry.

Self in Community

The self in community is a metaphorical phrase included in Schrag's thinking about the self and its relation to the world. Schrag (1997) begins by stating that the self is curiously diversified. He states that to know the self, one must render an account of one's self (as we discussed in Chapter 12 pertaining to the philosopher Judith Butler), tell a story of the self in context, and provide discernment of perceptual profiles between self and other. This means, to really know oneself, one must know oneself in community. The stories that one tells announces the self as an interconnected actor who is a receiver of action and who performs action in community.

For Schrag (1997), a community is a place where there are conversations; he suggests the self must be attuned to those conversations and in fact become part of them. Community means being with others. Community is a narratival space of discourse; there are two couplet metaphors that are situated with the self in community, narratival neighborhoods and conversational horizons. In making sense out of our surroundings and experiences, narratival neighborhoods acknowledge an other in making meaning since we gather data, consider experience, have communicative engagement, and make communicative observations in order to make sense out of our experiences. Meaning making through philosophy of communication inquiry is inextricably tied to the other—we cannot make meaning without our community partners (Schrag, 2010). In narratival neighborhoods, we have ongoing conversations that provide opportunities to question the exchanges and entwine oneself to reflections and reminiscences of conversational engagement (Schrag, 2010). All of this conjures meaning; this means meaning emerges through a dialogic process that happens either in community or as a consequence of community engagement. Narratival neighborhoods are historical and temporal dwelling spaces against a backdrop of conversational horizons (Arnett & Holba, 2012). Narratival neighborhoods demand recognition that others came before us, there are others around us, and we live in a socially framed community and world. Human history is created from this narratival living space that has been shaped through the lives of other people both seen and those unseen (Arnett & Holba, 2012). Narratival neighborhoods are comprised of communicative experiences, communicative reminiscing and reflecting, and a commitment to clear meaning making that is also fluid and evolving. Within narratival neighborhoods, conversational horizons of meaning are discoverable; once discovered, meaning can adapt and assist in responding to the historical moment (Arnett & Holba, 2012). This movement keeps community healthy, current, and attentive to the historical moment.

Conversational horizons are "multiple profiles of communicative performances" set against the "backdrop of differentiated world horizons" (Schrag, 2010, p. 63). The horizon accommodates and illuminates differentiated spheres of interest as it attunes itself to the changing stories and narratives that bind together, even if only loosely. Community is imbued with these conversational horizons and the self becomes entwined in a dynamic fashion within them, learning, changing, and evolving the conversations through the engagement. Schrag (2010) suggests horizons of meaning are comprised of the temporal textuality of these neighborhoods to conversations, reminiscences, and reflections; these kinds of punctuations suggest that there is no communicative meaning in a historical event and that the hermeneutics of everyday life enable temporal sense making (Arnett & Holba, 2012). With narratival neighborhoods set against the backdrop of conversational horizons, communities evolve and grow responsive to the external conditions guiding and shaping the historical moment.

Schrag (2010) states that we do philosophy with others; we cannot help it because our stories, narratives, and horizons are interrelated, interconnected, and interdependent on one another. There is no meaning that happens individually without some kind of interaction either through conversation, reflection (on what is said or read), reminiscence, or some otherwise communicative experience. As social beings, we evolve through our interactivity with others situated within a communicative environment of past, present, and future intertextuality that is attentive to the historical moment and open to transcend what is said and what is done.

Connections, Currency, and Meaning

The metaphors in this chapter, witness, dialogic civility, professional civility, and self in community, represent the sentiment that community can be envisioned as a gestalt of the interconnectivity and interdependence of persons. This interdependence relies on communicative competence imbued with moral reasoning and moral accountability. After considering metaphors in these last three chapters, metaphors of self, Other, and community, the fabric of philosophy of communication inquiry demonstrates an attunement to a strong sense of moral and ethical discernment that recognizes the folding and unfolding of human communicative engagement. This reveals dynamic relational implications in both public and private spheres. Philosophy of communication inquiry attends to the questions shaping and guiding historical moments and reflects on the "nature and function of human communication" (Arneson, 2007, p. 8). Metaphors assist philosophy of communication inquiry with creating temporal dwellings designed to enable innovative ways of understanding hermeneutically what is disclosed to us—they assist with navigating the temporal nature of existence in meaningful ways.

Connections: The metaphors in this chapter are interconnected in several ways. There is interdependence between self, Other, and community through the following claims:

1. Interdependence requires communicative action and agency.

2. Interdependence depends on "goods" that are shared or common.

3. Interdependence requires communicative competence that is attentive to the historical moment.

4. Interdependence involves having awareness of questions that shape the historical moment and assist with hermeneutic understanding.

The idea that in philosophy of communication inquiry there is not one interpretation of given phenomena is helpful in keeping meaning open with the ability to evolve as space and time change. It is dangerous to think that one has the one or only answer; this is something that occurs all of the time in academia, in media, in government, and in most other domains of engagement. However, it is the consequence of seeing the world though a black-and-white lens that limits possibilities in understanding, interpretation, and in what we think we know.

Currency: In this last chapter, it is most important to understand that currency, or the notion that one is attuned to the nuances and sentiments of or within the given historical moment, is one of the most important aspects that contribute to how we make and find meaning in our lives. It makes no sense to form opinions and judgments about something if one does not understand the current moment in time. This is a hermeneutical error that happens quite often when we judge the past from a contemporary mind-set. When we do this, we stand above history and judge, which always creates misunderstandings and conflicts. An example of this today involves the defacing and tearing down of statues that represent some part of the American past. The "anti-statue movement" (Olsen, 2020), according to a column in the *Washington Post*, has become absurd. In the history of the world, tearing down statues happens during revolutions as a sign of victory, revenge, signaling freedom from oppression. However, today, it has gotten out of hand, which risks meaning the removal of the statue meaningless. In New York City, the defacing of a statue of George Washington at the steps of the Federal Hall National Monument in June 2020 seems absurd. While Washington did own slaves, which was common during that time in our country's history, he was also a general in the Revolutionary War and the first acknowledged president of the America, which means he "founded a nation dedicated to the idea whose incompatibility with slavery made its eradication inevitable" (Olsen, 2020). Without George Washington, we cannot know how the United States would be today. Instead of defacing and vandalizing his statue, we should ask ourselves, "Is there another way to make a constructive change that does not diminish his contribution to building the country?" Engaging in dialogic civility might provide different outcomes and include more people in the discussion to reach a new way forward.

The absurdity of this kind of protest is an example of standing above history to judge it. Olsen (2020) states:

> Modern Western civilization and its revolutionary ideals, however, have allowed for the peaceful, pan-racial democracies protesters say they want. The West's ideals of universal freedom and human equality permit it to reform itself peacefully and extend the reality of freedom to fit the reality of human diversity. *We take a multiethnic, free state for granted, but no such thing had ever existed before modern times.* That is the achievement that statues to people such as Washington and Grant honor, an achievement that makes today's protesters possible. (Olsen, 2020)

This is a hermeneutical error that erases history, and once history is erased, we no longer can learn from it. How can we learn from it if the particular text of the history, in this case, the statue, is no longer present or interpretable? In community, dialogic civility could lead the transformation, and maybe the statue would still be removed, but the decision to do it would be for a different reason and there could even be something more appropriate to replace it. When we stand above history instead of in it, we make these kinds of hermeneutical errors that can have broad and wide negative implications.

The Emancipation Memorial from Lincoln Park in Capital Hill also received scrutiny, and while Lincoln is attributed with ending slavery during his presidency, the statue to some is interpreted as bias since Lincoln is standing over a Black man kneeling at his feet, though others interpret the Black man beginning to rise (Miller, 2020). In looking at the statue, meaning can be ambiguous. Instead of defacing the statue or tearing it down, legislators have initiated the process to remove the statue and replace it with something else. Given this is a dialogic process, no doubt the statue will be redesigned in a more constructive and clearer way representing the end of slavery in this country. This kind of change engages dialogic processes while still honoring the country—no country is perfect, but democracy allows for ongoing changes to make a more perfect union.

Meaning: Community makes meaning through engagement of all of its constituents. There has to be free and equal opportunity for contributing to meaning making. Of course, the individual chooses when and how to participate in meaning making directly but is always involved in meaning making whether directly indirectly. It is the nature of human beings to have meaning in their lives. Meaning making always involves a hermeneutical process—this is the aim of philosophy of communication inquiry, to assist one in finding meaning. Being guided by history, being attentive to questions that shape and guide historical moments, understanding the role of tradition and approaches in looking at phenomena, and realizing there is always more than one way to find meaning, and that there is more than one meaning, which requires remaining open to interpretive possibilities, is an instructive map on one's journey to find meaning in the world.

Conclusion

This chapter explored metaphors for community in philosophy of communication inquiry. Since human beings are social people with a distinctive social ontology, metaphors for self and Other are not sufficient to explore the human process of making meaning—community matters. In many ways, we rely on the Other for how we make sense of ourselves in the world in which we live. The metaphors in this chapter, witness, dialogic civility, professional civility, and self in community, provide a way of making meaning that recognizes the interrelationality of self and Other. Community is the environment that provides the structure for this interrelationaity to grow and continue to provide openings for self and Other. How we philosophize about community has to recognize both the self and Other in a collective and reciprocal relationship. In all of our attempts to find meaning around us, we must remember that to do philosophy of communication inquiry, attending to the guiding themes of this book, tradition, approach, question, and metaphor, all play a role in how that meaning emerges. It is with this in mind that I invite you to consider how you might expand your thinking through philosophy of communication inquiry.

PART IV

Connections, Currency, Meaning

P art IV explored the importance of the use of metaphors in the praxis of philosophy of communication inquiry. It first discussed metaphors as a figure of speech in literary circles as well as understanding metaphors as a philosophical concept. In philosophy of communication inquiry, metaphors are used both ways, especially in the practice of engaging in public moral debates, but also, and most often, the use of metaphor as a philosophical concept is explicated in a philosophy. The last three chapters in this section provided examples of the use of metaphor in philosophy of communication inquiry, organized by metaphors for self, Other, and community.

Connections

The use of metaphors as a philosophical concept embodies the expression of multiperspectival understanding through lived experience. Metaphors engage our thinking at varying depths and assist in how we make sense of experiences. Metaphors allow for making connections in implicit and explicit ways and can open understanding and meaning to new ways of seeing phenomena. Different philosophers will understand and use metaphors differently, perhaps making connections between different perspectives, all of which informs, shapes, and reshapes how we engage in public moral argument. This section emphasizes how one thinks like a philosopher of communication engaged in the praxis of philosophy of communication inquiry through the use of metaphors as philosophical concepts.

Currency

Currency underscores the importance of metaphors and their ability to open meaning. Metaphors have to be relevant to the human experience and they also must be understood within their particular historical moment. If metaphors are not understood within their current historical moment, they lose power and can become anachronistic. If we look at a contemporary case of public moral argument and identify and evaluate metaphors and evidence from all sides of the debate, we begin to engage in the praxis of philosophy of communication inquiry. For enriching classroom discussion, brainstorm as one large group or several smaller groups and identify pressing issues relevant to you today. You can use the issues you found during your brainstorm from Part I, Part II, or Part III "Connections, Currency, Meaning" or you might have other or new issues that emerged due to your research and discussions. Remember as I stated earlier about public moral argument, there are three criteria that make an issue appropriate for public moral argument:

1. There must be an argument (remember, an argument is a claim, a stated reason, and evidence to back up the claim).

2. The argument must occur in a public setting where it can touch others.

3. The issue has to be an explicitly moral issue.

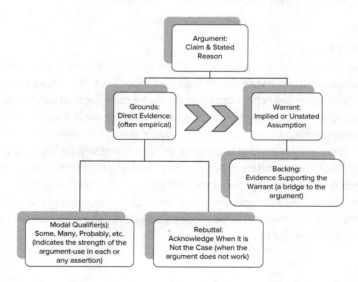

FIGURE IV.1   Schematic for Stephen Toulmin's argument model.

Use some time during class or for homework to explore information and gather evidence to engage in a public moral debate in the classroom, or make the stakes higher and hold a public moral argument forum in a public setting on campus. Remember, you have to have an argument, you have to touch the public in some way, and the issue must be an explicitly moral issue. Here are the two initial examples from the previous sections in Part I, Part II, and Part III, but I encourage you to find your own issues with the most currency.

1. Issue: Police brutality

   Argument: Policing reform is necessary to save Black people's lives because too many Black men are being unjustifiably killed by police.

2. Issue: Abortion and women's reproductive rights

   Argument: *Roe v. Wade* should be overturned because abortion is committing murder since fetuses are living beings.

As you begin gathering evidence and perspectives from different voices, try to determine the metaphors that guide the discussion and argument. Ask yourself, "How are they working in the narrative to open understanding and meaning? How do the metaphors shape the question or questions that are being pursued in the public discourse or debate?" Anything can be a metaphor, but the key is to be able to articulate the meaning it provides dimensionally as well as how it opens to meaning and multiple interpretations. Some metaphors are dense and jargon laden while others are more easily opened and understood. Once you can identify the metaphor and how it is being used to open meaning or direct one's attention to something else, ask yourself, how does this metaphor open and inform your own understanding of the philosophical concept or thought? How does the metaphor guide your own participation in the public moral issue and argument?

Meaning

Metaphors are important to at least be aware of when we engage in public argument because it is through the use of metaphor that we can reach multiple audiences, expand meaning, and see things in new ways. In the doing of philosophy of communication inquiry, metaphors are just a part of the discourse as they coinform understanding and meaning along with tradition, history, approaches, and questions. Metaphors open meaning in ways that give us insight into the varied arguments that are important to the public forum.

Metaphors shape and guide inquiry. They unfold meaning in ways that sometimes surprise us. They have the potential to reach large audiences, and they can translate dense topics to something approachable and meaningful to a variety of people. Metaphors help to shape the meaning as it is unfolding. So, as you are gathering your information and selecting potential evidence, you need recognize there are metaphorical concepts that play a role in guiding understanding and meaning; understanding things metaphorically can assist with effectively pursuing hot topics and in developing arguments for public settings where there will be a range of audience members and argument participants. Good luck with thinking through your research by allowing metaphors to unfold and be integrated into your argument; allow the metaphor to partner with identifying the question(s), be situated within a historical moment, and then allow these aspects to be informed by an approach(es), while recognizing the tradition within which the argument and perspectives are situated. This process allows one to provide a robust experience in the praxis of philosophy of communication inquiry.

Figure Credit

Fig. IV.1: Adapted from Stephen E. Toulmin, *The Uses of Argument.* Copyright © 1958 by Cambridge University Press.

GLOSSARY

Acknowledgment – A communicative behavior that provides attention to others and that creates a dwelling space for others in our lives. There is positive acknowledgment and negative acknowledgment. Positive acknowledgment recognizes something specific about an individual that usually makes one feel good, though can make someone feel not so good if one does not feel deserving of the acknowledgment. Negative acknowledgment can be hurtful and can cause someone to question their actions and their life. Negative acknowledgment comes in forms of negative communicative behavior such as gossiping, bullying, sarcasm, misrepresenting something, and lies (just a few examples). Negative acknowledgment risks causing a social death. As a metaphor, acknowledgment was developed by Professor Michael J. Hyde of Wake Forest University, who suggests offering positive or constructive acknowledgment is a moral thing to do for or toward the other.

Answerability – This refers to the idea that one is responsible for one's own actions, recognizing that any action changes the world in some way. The second way to understand answerability is to accept there is an obligation on the part of the one performing an ethical act to make the act intelligible for the other, which sets up the possibility for a communicative exchange.

Approaches – Refers to how a philosopher of communication engages phenomena. Some people refer to this as a method or methodology, but this term is typically used in the context of a strict scientific method. In philosophy of communication inquiry, approaches refer to mind-set; a mind-set is concerned with how someone thinks about the phenomena and how one comes to understand it.

Communicological approach – The study of human discourse situated as a human science. Advanced by Professor Emeritus Richard Lanigan from Southern Illinois University who advocates for a human science platform in understanding human communication, which brings attention to the performance and practice of intrapersonal, interpersonal, group, and cultural levels of communication.

Communicative competence – In Jürgen Habermas's theory of communicative action, this refers to communicants being equipped with the appropriate skills to engage in communicative settings appropriately; to provide appropriate, relevant, and most fitting responses to any given communicative setting and exchange. There are three elements of communicative competence: a truth claim, the listener must understand and accept the speaker's intention, and the speaker adapts to the hearer's world view (even if it is not the speaker's world view).

Communicative praxis – This is a metaphor from Calvin O. Schrag's philosophy of communication that points to a communicative space of understanding between and among people; it is a space that is temporal and contextual. Communicative praxis is comprised of the following metaphorical map: distanciation, idealization, recollection, understanding, explanation, comprehension, self-implicature, decentered subject, dialogical consciousness, and new humanism.

Communicative rationality – In Jürgen Habermas's theory of communicative ction, communicative rationality refers to the ideal that a speaker is able to meet the illocutionary goal establishing the conditions for communicative competence preparing one's understanding about or of something with at least one other communicant. The illocutionary goal should be action oriented. Communicative rationality is met when the discussion is unrestrained, all participants have a right to speak, a set of norms for equal participation should be established before speaking, and all participants need to overcome their individual subjective perspective (this means being open to allow your own perspective change or be altered in some way).

Communicology – According to the Communicological Institute, it is the science of communication.

Communitarianism – A system of social organization that is based on smaller communities that self-govern and privilege individual ties to family while recognizing that individual identities are constituted through the individual's relationship to the community. There are two kinds of communitarian approaches, the integrationist and the participant.

Conversational horizons – A multiplicity of profiles engaging in communicative performance set against a backdrop of varied and differentiated world horizons. The horizons accommodate and illuminate differentiated spheres of interests attuning to the changing and evolving stories that bind people together. (See Calvin O. Schrag's work)

Critical approach – Refers to a social theory approach to human communication that is explanatory, normative, practical, and self-reflective. Critical approaches seek to emancipate all human beings from oppressive structures and processes that limit human engagement and participation in the lifeworld.

Dark times – A metaphor used by philosophers to denote deep concern for a particular time period. Bertolt Brecht's poem "To Posterity" introduced the couplet and Hannah Arendt employed it in her work, *Men in Dark Times* (1955). Dark times is a metaphor that refers to disorder, hunger, massacres, and other kinds of injustices; it denotes despair, outrage, and wrong living.

Derivative "I" – Emerges from a place of response; the "I" finds identity in response to the Other. Derivative "I" is a byproduct or outcome of the Other. (See the work of Ronald C. Arnett)

Dialogic civility – A metaphor that announces the significance of public respect in interpersonal interactions. As a metaphor, it foregrounds the interconnectivity between how we communicate interpersonally and those commonsense questions that emerge in given historical moments. It reflects civil and relevant communicative engagement. (See the work of Ronald C. Arnett and Pat Arneson)

Dialogical – Referring to dialogue, describes a process of human communication where meaning is co-constructed between communicants. An approach to philosophy of communication inquiry that situates ethics within human communication.

Dialogical consciousness – From Calvin O. Schrag's theory of communicative praxis, dialogical consciousness is the textured interplay of presence and absence, reminiscence and forgetfulness, and disclosure and hiddenness. The backdrop of these interplays and entwinements include temporality, embodiment, and multiplicity.

Dialogism – This is Mikhail Bakhtin's theory of dialogue; dialogism recognizes the value of the multiplicity of voices and perspective in dialogue and discourse.

Distanciation – In Calvin O. Schrag's theory of communicative praxis, distanciation refers to entering a conversation through distance and openness. This allows for signative meaning to emerge.

Embodiment – This refers to an embodied thought due to the decentering of the locus of interiority. Thoughts move to a tangible form.

Empathy – In Edith Stein's interpersonal philosophy, empathy is the primary quality necessary for human relationships. Empathy begins with a sensory appearance that has both sympathetic and reflective sentiment. As an inner intuition, there are psychic and spiritual aspects to empathy, which Stein referred to as a phenomenological bridge between persons. There are two types of empathy according to Stein, reiterated empathy (when one realizes the self is one point of orientation among many others—it is not about the self) and comprehended empathy (when one turns back to an earlier historical moment in spiritual reflection—meaning expands).

Empiricism – A way of knowing based on observation and experience.

Emplotment – A concept in Paul Ricoeur's narrative theory, emplotment refers to a sequence of characters and events that come alive through their stories that are attentive to the moment and that call us out and require a response.

Enlarged Mentality – This is a term coming from Hannah Arendt's theory of judgment that borrows terms developed by Immanuel Kant that refers to the ability to think representatively—to think for oneself and to be able to make judgments about things in an impartial way. It reflects having a broad understanding and the ability to see things objectively and not tethered to external influences.

Ethical – An approach to philosophy of communication inquiry that is perspective laden, which allows for the inclusion of diverse perspectives without one perspective being dominant over other perspectives.

Existential homelessness – A metaphor that represents a loss of trust in existence and being situated in a negative dwelling space that lacks nourishment and care for the other. (See the work of Ronald C. Arnett)

Existential rootedness – From the work of Ozum Üçok-Sayrak, existential rootedness refers to an orientation that is immersed in a communication ethic as it recognizes the embeddedness of human agents in their surroundings—it is an orientation that illuminates an exposedness and struggle in the world with others.

Existential vacuum – This refers to having a total sense of meaninglessness in one's life.

Hermeneutic humility – A metaphor grounded in phenomenological humility, which allows for multiple interpretations through multiple approaches to understanding phenomena. (See the work of Schrag and Ramsey)

Hermeneutics – The study of interpretation.

Heteroglossia – In Mikhail Bakhtin's theory of dialogism, heteroglossia refers to multiple, coexistent linguistic structures or codes that open to possibilities of meaning.

Historical consciousness – This refers to understanding the temporality of historical experiences and how the past, present, and future are thought to be connected.

Historicity – An element of the hermeneutical experience, historicity is a dynamic experience of understanding that how we interpret the past is complex and changes over time, allowing for meaning to emerge and reemerge, asking one to accept that there is no fixed meaning in the word. Historicity frames how a question is understood differently across different historical periods.

Horizons – A term developed by Hans Georg Gadamer that refers to a range of vision that one has from a particular vantage point. It is comprised from multiple influences and has varied nuances. Read more about this in Gadamer's addressing philosophical hermeneutics.

Hospitality – A metaphor reflecting an invitation to the Other; a counterpart to welcome or welcoming the Other. Hospitality opens to the infinity of the Other and requires a responsible response to the Other. (See the work of Emmanuel Levinas and Jacques Derrida)

Humanism – This refers to a cultural and intellectual movement of the Renaissance period that emphasized secular concerns as a result of the rediscovery and study of literature, art, and civilization of ancient Greece and Rome.

Idealization – In Calvin O. Schrag's theory of communicative praxis, idealization assists the shift from expressive meaning to signative meaning through a play of idealities that are situated within the history of discourse and action. Idealization understands the idealities of personal ideals, the typification of social action, established institutional goals, and individual and collective norms.

Integrationist – One kind of communitarian thinking that seeks to reconstitute a community with an integrated vision of fundamental values and principles.

Interpellation – In Judith Butler's subject formation, the process of interpellation occurs after performativity—a kind of linguistic interaction referring to an action that calls out the other, demanding a response.

Kairos – This is the Greek word for time, referring to timeliness or a time outside of chronological time.

Kronos – This is the Greek word for chronological time or measured time.

Logocentrism – Refers to privileging words and language to reflect reality.

Logotherapy – This refers to a process in which a therapist tries to make the patient aware of their responsibleness, leaving it to the patient to understand to what and to whom they are responsible.

Metaphors – A figure of speech, that is, a word or phrase, used in a nonliteral or ambiguous sense for the purpose of creating a vivid effect or to provoke some kind of comparison. Metaphors can work in a figurative way that is indiscernible in discovery and descriptions of truths. As a philosophical concept, metaphor serves as a function of discourse that can be seen as a discursive linguistic act that takes it beyond the figure of speech understanding. In this way, metaphor is a double reference that provides connotative value and meaning. As a symbolic language, metaphor becomes a phenomenological disclosure of being.

Metaphysics of presence – Using presence to determine truth and reality while not acknowledging what is absent or hidden.

Methodolatry – This refers to idolizing one approach while ignoring or discrediting another approach to knowing and interpreting.

Moderate Enlightenment – Refers to an enlightenment movement (opposed to the Radical Enlightenment) that is grounded in utilitarian ideals and it is the enlightenment movement that most students learn about in history education.

Modernity's amnesia – This is a metaphor that refers to the forgetfulness of the "conditions for existence" and dwelling places that nurture the human condition. Modernity's amnesia was articulated by Ronald C. Arnett and later used by Ozum Üçok-Sayrak.

Moral blindness – This refers to the inability for a human being to be sensitive to another being's suffering.

Multiplicity – This refers to the existence of and the possibility of encountering an ensemble of phenomena in an ongoing fashion.

Narratival interpretation – This involves interpretation through a holistic understanding and analytical explanation. This term emerged from Calvin O. Schrag and Ramsey Eric Ramsey's couplet, hermeneutic humility.

Narratival neighborhoods – Refers to narratival spaces of discourse; gathering spaces (face-to-face or virtual) where there are ongoing conversations that provide opportunities to question the exchanges and entwine oneself to reflections and reminiscences of conversational engagement. (See the work of Calvin O. Schrag)

Narrative – An approach to philosophy of communication inquiry that acknowledges narratives provide a backdrop of stories that illuminate relationships within a given historical moment. Multiple ideas and stories come together within a historical horizon and within these contexts questions emerge that assist in guiding understanding and meaning making.

Narrative fidelity – In Walter Fisher's narrative rationality, this refers to a narrative that is truthful or faithful to what one already knows or understands. The narrative cannot be based on lies or deception.

Narrative probability or coherence – In Walter Fisher's narrative rationality, this refers to whether a narrative makes sense; is the narrative holding up in a logical way?

Narrative rationality – This is comprised of narrative fidelity and narrative probability or coherence. (See the work of Walter Fisher)

Other – Capitalized, refers to the personalized other.

other – Uncapitalized, refers to the general usage of the other, such as another.

Parody – This refers to an imitation of something using exaggeration for comic relief.

Participationist – An approach to communitarianism that sees the community as emerging from community engaging together, fully participating in community life.

Performativity – In Judith Butler's framework for subject formation, performativity refers to the enactment (constitution) of the self through engagement with other and with context.

Phenomenology – The study of phenomena; a way to inquire about the human experience by asking questions about what and how things present themselves.

Philosophical leisure – A metaphor that refers to giving sustained attention to the thing itself; engaging in an activity for the sake of the activity itself and not for any other predetermined outcome. Josef Pieper describes it as a philosophical act. (See the work of Annette M. Holba)

Phonocentrism – The act of privileging speech over writing.

Phronesis – A Greek word reflecting having practical wisdom. Aristotle developed this concept related to ethics and politics and Habermas relies upon it in his Theory of Communicative Action. Many other philosophers also advance the notion of phronesis.

Polyphony – In Mikhail Bakhtin's theory of dialogism, polyphony refers to the simultaneous multiplicity of voices and perspectives in a text.

Practice – In the context of dialogic civility, it refers to communication engaged in an unreflective manner and a routine kind of action. Practice does not acknowledge fluid particularities that accompany interpersonal communication.

Praxis – In the context of dialogic civility, it refers to informed communication that is coinformed by theory and action.

Problematization – A concept in Foucault's philosophy that advocates the questioning of what is taken for granted; it is a push to re-examine what is accepted as the norm or what is deemed acceptable.

Professional civility – This is a metaphorical couplet describing constructive and civil communicative practices as a communicative virtue that protect the good of the organization and the professional individual. (See the work of Janie Harden Fritz)

Psychoanalytical approach – This refers to a way of examining human communicative behavior that focuses on the unconscious mind and how it drives actions, experiences, and thoughts.

Public moral argument – This refers to the setting that includes three elements: an argument, a place or space where any number of people come together to engage ideas and argument, and that is around a moral issue.

Radical Enlightenment – An Enlightenment movement guided by the ideals of civic humanism and led by radical thinkers who opposed the moderate ideals of utilitarian ways of thinking. The radical enlightenment thought was overshadowed by the moderate enlightenment. Read more about this in the work of philosophers/historians including Arran Gare, Johann Gottfried Herder, and Johnathan Irvine Israel.

Rationalism – A way of knowing through reason and rational arguments.

Recollection – In Calvin O. Schrag's theory of communicative praxis, recollection refers to an operative role of reminiscence that assists with moving toward signative meaning instead of recalling things as independent, disjointed, disconnected, or isolable things.

Recuperative praxis – This refers to the idea that philosophical leisure can recuperate the human condition through theory-informed action of leisure. (See the work of Annette M. Holba)

Questions – In philosophy of communication inquiry, questions guide the inquiry and allow the querent to see multiple layers of embedded context that assist with practical understanding.

Satire – This refers to the use of irony, humor, exaggeration, ridicule, or mockery to criticize people, situations, or structures often in the context of politics, business, and entertainment.

Self in Community – This is a metaphoric phrase that Calvin Schrag uses to reflect his thinking about the self in relation to the world. See the work of Calvin Schrag (1997) *The self after postmodernity.*

Semiotics – Often referred to as the study of signs and symbols that focuses on the process of how they work to make meaning.

Signative meaning – This refers to meaning gained through the interplay of speech and language within history; it is a couplet used by Calvin O. Schrag in his theory of communicative praxis.

Signification – This refers to the act of coming to meaning through representation—the process of using something to signal something else. Further reading of the works of Saussure, Pierce, Eco, Derrida and others known in semiotics can provide a variety of ways of thinking about this process.

Skepticism – A way of knowing that begins with the assumption that knowledge should be doubted, questioned, and tested before accepting it. There are different kinds of skepticism or different ways of being skeptical.

Subject formation – In Judith Butler's theory of identity, subject formation occurs through performativity and interpellation. Subject formation refers to how the subject is constituted.

Superaddressee – In Mikhail Bakhtin's theory of dialogism, the superaddressee is considered an "indefinite, unconcretized other" that can influence communicative outcomes. It has been described as a transcendent listener and a metalinguistic aspect of dialogue.

Temporality – This refers to a new understanding that time is not fixed—it changes and is in flux.

Textuality – This refers to textual interplay that implies a weightiness, an ethos, and a spatial importance that is attentive to multiple dimensional contexts and events.

Traditionalism – A way of knowing that acknowledges that knowledge comes from an interplay of the context of people, relationships, and stories in a transactional environment.

Traditions – A perspective that is informed by prejudices and preferences; it is necessary to be aware of one's prejudices and preferences and understand their role in how one makes meaning and how one communicates with the others. In this awareness of prejudices and preferences, questioning and reflecting on them is necessary for learning and engaging within a diverse world.

Transversal comprehension – This refers to managing conflicts of interpretation by intercalculating and inserting something into the interspaces in order to mitigate interpretational meaning.

Unity of contraries – In Martin Buber's dialogic philosophy, unity of contraries refers to contrary terms presented together, demonstrating the tensions between extremes. Recognizing the unity of contraries also illuminates the notion that there is no absolute knowledge; there is only a continuum within and between extremes.

Web of metaphorical significance – From Arnett and Arneson's (1999) *Dialogic Civility*, this refers to multiple individual metaphors that connect to a historical moment and guiding narrative, together painting a philosophical picture of dialogic civility.

Welcome – This is a metaphor that invites the Other into a relationship of some kind. (See the work of Emmanuel Levinas and Jacques Derrida)

Witness – Witness and witnessing in philosophy of communication often refer to the moment one witnesses something particular at which time one assumes responsibility to bear witness, which sets up a relationship between the self and the Other.

PHILOSOPHY OF COMMUNICATION RESOURCES

The following is a gathering of philosophy of communication resources. It is not intended to be a complete or exhaustive list of readings. For a fuller listing by philosopher, see the bibliographies in Arnett and Holba (2012).

The sources gathered for this book and offered here include some of the early publications on philosophy of communication and some of the recent publications that I have come across. As the conversation continues, philosophy of communication resources will expand with new scholarship (for longer lists, vertically) and expand by bringing in new sources that have been reinterpreted and reconsidered in the context of philosophy of communication (for a wider listing of text already in existence, horizontally).

Books and Book Chapters

Allen, B. (2010). *Difference matters: Communicating social identity*. Waveland.

Anderson, R., & Cissna, K. N. (1997). *The Martin Buber–Carl Rogers dialogue: A new transcript with commentary*. State University of New York Press.

Arendt, H. (1958). *The human condition*. University of Chicago Press.

Arendt, H. (1978). *The life of the mind* (M. McCarthy, Ed.). Harcourt Brace.

Aristotle. (1998). *The Nicomachean ethics* (W. D. Ross, Trans., J. L. Ackrill, & J. O. Urmson, Eds.). Oxford University Press.

Aristotle. (2007). *On rhetoric: A theory of civic discourse* (2nd ed.) (G. Kennedy, Trans.). Oxford University Press.

Arneson, P. (Ed.). (2007). *Exploring communication ethics: Interviews with influential scholars in the field*. Peter Lang.

Arneson, P. (Ed.). (2007). *Perspectives on philosophy of communication*. Purdue University Press.

Arnett, R. C. (1994). Existential homelessness: A contemporary case for dialogue. In R. Anderson, K. Cissna, & R. C. Arnett (Eds.), *The reach of dialogue: Confirmation, voice, and community* (pp. 229–245). Hampton Press.

Arnett, R. C. (2007). Hannah Arendt: Dialectical communicative labor. In P. Arneson (Ed.), *Perspectives on philosophy of communication* (pp. 67–88). Purdue University Press.

Arnett, R. C. (2008). Rhetoric and ethics. In W. Donsbach (Ed.), *International encyclopedia of communication* (pp. 4242–4246). Wiley/International Communication Association.

Arnett, R. C. (2009). Emmanuel Levinas: Priority of the other. In C. G. Christians & J. C. Merrill (Eds.), *Ethical communication: Moral stances in human dialogue* (pp. 200–206). University of Missouri Press.

Arnett, R. C. (2013). *Communication ethics in dark times: Hannah Arendt's rhetoric of warning and hope.* Southern Illinois University Press.

Arnett, R. C. (2017). *Levinas's rhetorical demand: The unending obligation of communication ethics.* Southern Illinois University Press.

Arnett, R. C., & Arneson, P. (1999). *Dialogic civility in a cynical age: Community, hope, and interpersonal relationships.* State University of New York Press.

Arnett, R. C., & Arneson, P. (2016). *Philosophy of communication ethics: Alterity and the Other.* Fairleigh Dickenson University Press.

Arnett, R. C., Fritz, J. H., & Bell, L. M. (2008). *Communication ethics literacy: Dialogue and difference.* SAGE.

Arnett, R. C., & Holba, A. M. (2012). *An overture to philosophy of communication: The carrier of meaning.* Peter Lang.

Arnett, R. C., Holba, A. M., & Mancino, S. (2018). *An encyclopedia of communication Ethics: Goods in contention.* Peter Lang.

Benhabib, S. (1992). *Situating the self: Gender, community and postmodernism in contemporary ethics.* Routledge.

Benhabib, S. (2003). *The reluctant modernism of Hannah Arendt* (2nd ed.). Rowman & Littlefield.

Bracci, S. L., & Christians, C. G. (Ed.) (2002). *Moral engagement in public Life: Theorists for contemporary ethics.* Peter Lang.

Buber, M. (1965/1966). *The knowledge of man: A philosophy of the interhuman.* Harper & Row.

Buber, M. (1972). *Between man and man.* Macmillan.

Butler, J. (1987). *Subjects of desire: Hegelian reflections in twentieth-century France.* Columbia University Press.

Butler, J. (2005). *Giving an account of oneself.* Fordham University Press.

Butler, J. (2006). *Gender trouble: Feminism and the subversion of identity.* Routledge.

Casmir, F. L. (Ed.). (1997). *Ethics in intercultural and international communication.* Erlbaum.

Chang, B. G., & Butchart, G. C. (Eds.) (2012). *Philosophy of communication.* MIT Press.

Christians, C. G., & Traber, M. (Eds.). (1997). *Communication ethics and universal values.* SAGE.

Cook, M., & Holba, A. (2008). *Philosophies of communication: Implications for everyday experience.* Peter Lang.

Cooren, F. (2010). *Action and agency in dialogue: Passion, incarnation and ventriloquism.* John Benjamins.

Gadamer, H.-G. (1960/1980). *Dialogue and dialectic: Eight hermeneutical studies on Plato* (P. C. Smith, Trans.). Yale University Press.

Gadamer, H.-G. (1960/1986). *Truth and method.* Crossroads.

Grant, C. B. (2010). *Beyond universal pragmatics: Studies in the philosophy of communication.* Peter Lang.

Holba, A. (2007). *Philosophical leisure: Recuperative praxis for human communication.* Marquette University Press.

Holba, A. M. (2012). *Transformative leisure: A philosophy of communication.* Marquette University Press.

Hyde, M. J. (1982). *Communication philosophy and the technological age.* University of Alabama Press.

Hyde, M. J. (2001). *The call of conscience: Heidegger and Levinas, rhetoric and the euthanasia debate.* University of South Carolina Press.

Hyde, M. J. (2004). *The ethos of rhetoric.* University of South Carolina Press.

Hyde, M. J. (2006). *The life-giving gift of acknowledgment.* Purdue University Press.

Hyde, M. J. (2010). *Perfection: Coming to terms with being human.* Baylor University Press.

Hyde, M. J. (2018). *The interruption that we are: The health of the lived body, narrative, and public moral argument.* University of South Carolina Press.

Jaska, J. A., & Pritchard, M. S. (1994). *Communication ethics methods of analysis.* Wadsworth.

Jensen, V. R. (1997). *Ethical issues in the communication process.* Erlbaum.

Johannesen, R. L. (2002). *Ethics in human communication.* Waveland.

Kelly, J. C. (1981). *A philosophy of communication: Explorations for a systematic model.* Center for the Study of Communication and Culture.

Klyukanov, I. E. (2010). *A communication universe: Manifestations of meaning, stagings of significance.* Rowman & Littlefield.

Langsdorf, L. (2002). In defense of poiesis: The performance of self in communicative praxis. In M. B. Matustík & W. L. McBride (Eds.), *Calvin O. Schrag and the task of philosophy after postmodernity* (pp. 281–296). Northwestern University Press.

Langsdorf, L., & Smith, A. (1995). *Recovering pragmatism's voice: The classical tradition, Rorty, and the philosophy of communication*. State University of New York Press.

Lanigan, R. L. (1972). *Speaking and semiology: Maurice Merleau-Ponty's phenomenological theory of existential communication*. Mouton.

Lanigan, R. L. (1988). *Phenomenology of communication: Merleau Ponty's thematics in communicology and semiology*. Duquesne University Press.

Lanigan, R. L. (1992). *The human science of communicology: A phenomenology of discourse in Foucault and Merleau-Ponty*. Duquesne University Press.

Makau, J. M., & Arnett, R. C. (Eds.). (1997). *Communication ethics in an age of diversity*. University of Illinois Press.

Pearce, W. B. (1989). *Communication and the human condition*. Southern Illinois University Press.

Phillips, D. E. (1981). *Karl Barth's philosophy of communication*. Verlag.

Radford, G. P. (2004). *On the philosophy of communication*. Wadsworth.

Ramsey, R. E. (1998). *The long path to nearness: A contribution to a corporeal philosophy of communication and the groundwork for an ethics of relief*. Prometheus.

Ramsey, R. E., & Miller, D. J. (2003). *Experiences between philosophy and communication: Engaging the philosophical contributions of Calvin O. Schrag*. State University of New York Press.

Rorty, R. (1979). *Philosophy and the mirror of nature*. Princeton University Press.

Rorty, R. (1982). *Consequences of Pragmatism*. University of Minnesota Press.

Schrag, C. O. (1997). *The self after postmodernity*. Yale University Press.

Schrag, C. O. (2003). *Communicative praxis and the space of subjectivity*. Purdue University Press.

Schrag, C. O. (2010). *Doing philosophy with others: Conversations, reminiscences, and reflections*. Purdue University Press.

Stewart, J. R. (1995). *Language as articulate contact: Toward a post-semiotic philosophy of communication*. State University of New York Press.

Voudoures, K. I., & Poulakos, J. (2002). *Greek philosophy of communication*. Ionia.

Journal Articles

Anton, C. (1999). Beyond the constitutive-representational dichotomy: The phenomenological notion of intentionality. *Communication Theory, 9*(1), 26–57.

Arnett, R. C. (1981). Toward a phenomenological dialogue. *The Western Journal of Speech Communication, 45*(3), 201–212.

Arnett, R. C. (1990). The practical philosophy of communication ethics and free speech as the foundation for speech communication. *Communication Quarterly, 38*(3), 208–217.

Arnett, R. C. (2001). Dialogic civility as pragmatic ethical praxis: An interpersonal metaphor for the public domain. *Communication Theory, 11*(3), 315–338.

Arnett, R. C. (2010). Defining philosophy of communication: Difference and identity. *Qualitative Research Reports in Communication, 11*(1), 1–6.

Arnett, R. C. (2011). Civic rhetoric—Meeting the communal interplay of the provincial and the cosmopolitan: Barack Obama's Notre Dame speech, May 17, 2009. *Rhetoric & Public Affairs, 14*(4), 631–671.

Arnett, R. C., Arneson, P., & Holba, A. (2008). Bridges not walls: The communicative enactment of dialogic storytelling. *Review of Communication, 8*(3), 217–234.

Arnett, R. C., Bell, L. M., & Fritz, J. M. H. (2010). Dialogic learning as first principle in communication ethics. *Atlantic Journal of Communication, 18*(3), 111–126.

Arnett, R. C., Fritz, J. M. H., & Holba, A. M. (2007). The rhetorical turn to otherness: Otherwise than humanism. *Cosmos and History: The Journal of Natural and Social Philosophy, 3*(1), 115–133.

Arnett, R. C., & Nakagawa, G. (1983). The assumptive roots of empathic listening: A critique. *Communication Education, 32*(4), 368–378.

Arthos, J. (2000). Who are we and who am I? Gadamer's communal ontology as palimpsest. *Communication Studies, 51*(1), 15–34.

Arthos, J. (2002). Chapman's Coatesville Address: A hermeneutic reading. *Quarterly Journal of Speech, 88*(2), 193–208.

Arthos, J. (2007). A hermeneutic interpretation of civic humanism and liberal education. *Philosophy & Rhetoric, 40*(2), 189–200.

Arthos, J. (2008). Gadamer's rhetorical imaginary. *Rhetoric Society Quarterly, 38*(2), 171–197.

Aune, J. A. (2007). "Only connect": Between morality and ethics in Habermas' communication theory. *Communication Theory, 17*(4), 340–347.

Barnlud, D. C. (1962). Toward a meaning-centered philosophy of communication. *Journal of Communication, 12*(4), 197–211.

Bemis, J. L., & Phillips, G. M. (1964). A phenomenological approach to communication theory. *Communication Theory, 13*(4), 262–269.

Berger, C. R., & Douglas, W. (1981). Studies in interpersonal epistemology: III. Anticipated interaction, self-monitoring, and observational context selection. *Communication Monographs, 48*(3), 183–196.

Bergman, M. (2009). Experience, purpose, and the value of vagueness: On C. S. Peirce's contribution to the philosophy of communication. *Communication Theory, 19*(3), 248–277.

Bergo, B. (2005). What is Levinas doing? Phenomenology and the rhetoric of an ethical unconscious. *Philosophy & Rhetoric, 38*(2), 122–144.

Bertelsen, D. A. (1993). Sophistry, epistemology, and the media context. *Philosophy & Rhetoric, 26*(4), 296–301.

Bettina, B. (2005). What is Levinas doing? Phenomenology and the rhetoric of an ethical un-conscious. *Philosophy & Rhetoric, 38*(2), 122–144.

Bialostosky, D. (2006). Architectonics, rhetoric, and poetics in the Bakhtin school's early phenomenological and sociological texts. *Rhetoric Society Quarterly, 36*(4), 355–377.

Bineham, J. L. (1994). Displacing Descartes: Philosophical hermeneutics and rhetorical studies. *Philosophy & Rhetoric, 27*(4), 300–312.

Bivins, T. H., & Newton, J. H. (2003). The real, the virtual, and the moral: Ethics at the intersection of consciousness. *Journal of Mass Media Ethics, 18*(3–4), 213–229.

Brock, B. L. (1985). Epistemology and ontology in Kenneth Burke's Dramatism. *Communication Quarterly, 33*(2), 94–104.

Brock, B. L., Burke, K., Burgess, P. G., & Simons, H. W. (1985). Dramatism as ontology or epistemology: A symposium. *Communication Quarterly, 33*(1) 17–33.

Brummett, B. (1990). A eulogy for epistemic rhetoric. *Quarterly Journal of Speech, 76*(1), 69–72.

Butchart, G. C. (2006). On ethics and documentary: A real and actual truth. *Communication Theory, 16*(4), 427–452.

Butler, J. (2002). Is kinship already heterosexual? Differences: A *Journal of Feminist Cultural Studies, 13*(1), 14–44.

Butler, J. (2005). On never having learned how to live. *Radical Philosophy, 16*(3), 27–34.

Butler, J. (2011). Hannah Arendt's death sentences. *Comparative Literature Studies, 48*(3), 280–295.

Butler, J. (2012). Precarious life, vulnerability, and the ethics of cohabitation. *Journal of Speculative Philosophy, 26*(2), 134–151.

Caraher, B. G. (1981). Metaphor as contradiction: A grammar and epistemology of poetic metaphor. *Philosophy & Rhetoric, 14*(2), 69–88.

Catt, I. E. (1986). Rhetoric and narcissism: A critique of ideological selfism. *The Western Journal of Speech Communication, 50,* 242–253.

Catt, I. E. (2014). The two sciences of communication in philosophical contexts. *The Review of Communication, 14,* 201–228.

Chaudhary, Z. R. (2010). The labor of mimesis. *Social Semiotics, 20*(4), 357–365.

Chen, K. H. (1987). Beyond truth and method: On misreading Gadamer's praxical hermeneutics. *Quarterly Journal of Speech, 73*(2), 183–199.

Deetz, S. (1973). Words without things: Toward a social phenomenology of language. *Quarterly Journal of Speech, 59*(1), 40–51.

Deetz, S. (1978). Conceptualizing human understanding: Gadamer's hermeneutics and American communication studies. *Communication Quarterly, 26*(2), 12–23.

Descombes, V. (2007). A philosophy of the first-person singular. *Communication Theory, 17*(1), 4–15.

Desilet, G. (1991). Heidegger and Derrida: The conflict between hermeneutics and deconstruction in the context of rhetorical and communication theory. *Quarterly Journal of Speech, 77*(2), 152–175.

Dresner, E. (2006). Davidson's philosophy of communication. *Communication Theory, 16*(2), 155–172.

Eicher-Catt, D. (2010). What E-prime "is not": A semiotic phenomenological reading. *ETC: A Review of General Semantics, 67*(1), 17–34.

Eicher-Catt, D., & Catt, I. E. (2013). Pierce and Cassirer, "life" and "spirit": A communicology of religion. *Journal of Communication and Religion, 36*(2), 77–217.

Fausti, R. P., & Luker, A. H. (1965). A phenomenological approach to discussion. *The Speech Teacher, 14*(1), 19–23.

Felts, A. A. (1978). Hermeneutic phenomenology: A critique of Leonard Hawes' conception. *Communication Quarterly, 26*(4), 58–64.

Fish, S. L. (1976). A phenomenological examination of femininity. *Journal of Applied Communication Research, 4*(2), 43–53.

Fish, S. L., & Dorris, J. M. (1975). Phenomenology and communication research. *Journal of Applied Communication Research, 3*(1), 9–26.

Franke, W. (2000). Metaphor and the making of sense: The contemporary metaphor renaissance. *Philosophy & Rhetoric, 33*(2), 137–153.

Gadamer, H. G. (1990). Hearing—seeing—reading. (R. C. Norton, Trans.). *Language & Communication, 10*(1), 87–92.

Gehrke, P. J. (2002). Turning Kant against the priority of autonomy: Communication ethics and the duty to community. *Philosophy and Rhetoric, 35*(1), 1–21.

Gehrke, P. J. (2007). Historical study as ethical and political action. *Quarterly Journal of Speech, 93*(3), 355–357.

Gehrke, P. J. (2010). Being for the Other-to-the-Other: Justice and communication in Levinasian ethics. *Review of Communication, 10*(1), 5–19.

Gross, A. (2010). Rhetoric, narrative, and the lifeworld: The construction of collective identity. *Philosophy & Rhetoric, 43*(2), 118–138.

Hatch, J. B. (2006). The hope of reconciliation: Continuing the conversation. *Rhetoric & Public Affairs, 9*(2), 259–277.

Hatch, J. B. (2009). Dialogic rhetoric in letters across the divide: A dance of (good) faith toward racial reconciliation. *Rhetoric & Public Affairs, 12*(4), 485–532.

Hsiang-Ann, L. (2006). Toward an epistemology of participatory communication: A feminist perspective. *Howard Journal of Communications, 17*(2), 101–118.

Hyde, M. J. (1980). The experience of anxiety: A phenomenological investigation. *Quarterly Journal of Speech, 66*(2), 140–154.

Johnson, R. R. (2010). The ubiquity paradox: Further thinking on the concept of user centeredness. *Technical Communication Quarterly, 19*(4), 335–351.

Jovanovic, S., & Wood, R.V. (2004). Speaking from the Bedrock of ethics. *Philosophy & Rhetoric, 37*(4), 317–334.

Katz, S. B. (1995). The epistemology of the Kabbalah: Toward a Jewish philosophy of rhetoric. *Rhetoric Society Quarterly, 25,* 107–122.

Kelley, V. (2002). "Good speech": An interpretive essay investigating an African philosophy of communication. *Western Journal of Black Studies, 26*(1), 44–54.

Klyukanov, I. E. (2012). Communication – that which befalls us. *Empedocles: European Journal for the Philosophy of Communication, 4*(1), 15–27.

Klyukanov, I. E., & Sinekopova, G. V. (2016). Beyond the binary: Toward the paraconsistencies of Russian communication codes. *International Journal of Communication, 10,* 2258–2274.

Lanigan, R. L. (1982). Semiotic phenomenology: A theory of human communication praxis. *Journal of Applied Communication Research, 10*(1), 62–73.

Lillywhite, H. (1952). Toward a philosophy of communication. *Journal of Communication, 2*(1), 29–32.

Lipari, L. (2004). Listening for the other: Ethical implications of the Buber-Levinas encounter. *Communication Theory, 14*(2), 122–141.

Lipari, L. (2009). Listening otherwise: The voice of ethics. *The International Journal of Listening, 23*(1), 44–59.

Lipari, L. (2010). Listening, thinking, being. *Communication Theory, 20*(3), 348–362.

Macsoud, S. J. (1971). Phenomenology, experience, and interpretation. *Philosophy & Rhetoric, 4*(3), 139–149.

Martinez-Ramos, D. (2009). On rational madness: Love and reason in Socrates and Lacan. *Communication Review, 12*(2), 162–173.

Maxcy, D. J. (1994). Meaning in nature: Rhetoric, phenomenology, and the question of environmental value. *Philosophy & Rhetoric, 27*(4), 330–346.

Pinchevski, A. (2005). Displacing incommunicability: Autism as an epistemological boundary. *Communication & Critical/Cultural Studies, 2*(2), 163–184.

Pullman, G. L. (1994). Reconsidering sophistic rhetoric in light of skeptical epistemology. *Rhetoric Review, 13*(1), 50–68.

Rodríguez, J. I., & Cai, D. A. (1994). When your epistemology gets in the way: A response to Sprague. *Communication Education, 43*(4), 263–272.

Roy, A., & Starosta, W. J. (2001). Hans-Georg Gadamer, language, and intercultural communication. *Language & Intercultural Communication, 1*(1), 6–20.

Ryan, K. J., & Natalle, E. J. (2001). Fusing horizons: Standpoint hermeneutics and invitational rhetoric. *Rhetoric Society Quarterly, 31*(2), 69–90.

Schrag, C. O. (1985). Rhetoric resituated at the end of philosophy. *Quarterly Journal of Speech, 71*(2), 164–174.

Scult, A. (1999). Aristotle's rhetoric as ontology: A Heideggerian reading. *Philosophy & Rhetoric, 32*(2), 146–159.

Sikka, T. (2011). Technology, communication, and society: From Heidegger and Habermas to Feenberg. *Review of Communication*, 11(2), 93–106.

Smith, D. L. (2003). Intensifying phronesis: Heidegger, Aristotle, and rhetorical culture. *Philosophy & Rhetoric*, 36(1), 77–102.

Stern, B. B. (1984). A philosophy of communications for the marketing manager: Three "T's" in an MBA course. *Business Communication Quarterly*, 47(1), 28–30.

Stewart, J. (1983). Interpretive listening: An alternative to empathy. *Communication Education*, 32(4), 379–391.

Stewart, J. (1986). Speech and human being: A complement to semiotics. *Quarterly Journal of Speech*, 72(1), 55–73.

Sutton, J. (1986). The death of rhetoric and its rebirth in philosophy, *Rhetorica*, 4(3), 203–226.

Tell, D. (2004). Burke's encounter with ransom: Rhetoric and epistemology in "four master tropes." *Rhetoric Society Quarterly*, 34(4), 33–54.

Thomas, D. (1994). Reflections on a Nietzschean turn in rhetorical theory: Rhetoric without epistemology? *Quarterly Journal of Speech*, 80(1), 71–76.

Thorne, S. L. (2005). Epistemology, politics, and ethics in sociocultural theory. *Modern Language Journal*, 89(3), 393–409.

Wood, J. T. (1998). Ethics, justice, and the "private sphere." *Women's Studies in Communication*, 21(2), 127–149.

Zeytinoglu, C. (2011). Appositional (communication) ethics: Listening to Heidegger and Levinas in chorus. *Review of Communication*, 11(4), 272–285.

Zickmund, S. (2007). Deliberation, phronesis, and authenticity: Heidegger's early conception of rhetoric. *Philosophy & Rhetoric*, 40(4), 406–415.

REFERENCES

Almasy, S. Yan, H., & Maxouris, C. (2020, May 26). *As COVID-19 cases rise in 17 states, Americans still divided on whether masks should be mandated.* CNN. https://www.cnn.com/2020/05/26/health/us-coronavirus-tuesday/index.html

Appleby, J. O., Hunt, L. A., & Jacob, M. C. (2011). *Telling the truth about history.* Norton.

Arendt, H. (1958). *The human condition.* University of Chicago Press.

Arendt, H. (1998). *The human condition.* (2nd ed.) University of Chicago Press.

Arendt, H. (1993). *Men in dark times.* Harvest Books.

Arendt, H. (2005). *The promise of politics.* Schocken.

Aristotle. (1984). *The rhetoric and poetics of Aristotle.* Modern Library.

Aristotle. (2001). Politics. In R. McKeon (Ed.), *The basic works of Aristotle* (pp. 1114–1316). Modern Library.

Arneson, P. (2007). Introduction. In P. Arneson (Ed.), *Perspectives on philosophy of communication* (pp. 1–20). Purdue University Press.

Arneson, P. (2018). Martha C. Nussbaum: Story-laden care. In R. C. Arnett, A. M. Holba, & S. Mancino (Eds.), *An encyclopedia of communication ethics: Goods in contention* (pp. 360–364). Peter Lang.

Arnett, R. C. (1986). *Communication and community: Implications of Martin Buber's dialogue.* Southern Illinois University Press.

Arnett, R. C. (1994). Existential homelessness: A contemporary case for dialogue. In R. Anderson, K. N. Cissna, & R. C. Arnett (Eds.). *Reach of dialogue: Confirmation, voice, community* (pp. 229–248). Hampton Press.

Arnett, R. C. (2007). Interpretive inquiry as qualitative communication research. *Qualitative Research Reports in Communication, 8*(1), 29–35.

Arnett, R. C. (2012). *An overture to philosophy of communication: The carrier of meaning.* Peter Lang.

Arnett, R. C. (2013a). *Communication ethics in dark times: Hannah Arendt's rhetoric of warning and hope.* Southern Illinois University Press.

Arnett, R. C. (2013b). The responsive "I": Levinas's derivative argument. *Argumentation and Advocacy, 40*(1), 39–50.

Arnett, R. C. (2016). Philosophy of communication: Qualitative research, questions in action. *Qualitative Research Reports in Communication, 17*(1), 1–6.

Arnett, R. C. (2017). *Levinas's rhetorical demand: The unending obligation of communication ethics.* Southern Illinois University Press.

Arnett, R. C. (2018). David Hume: Power of sensations. In R. C. Arnett, A. M. Holba, & S. Mancino (Eds.), *Encyclopedia of communication ethics: Goods in contention* (pp. 233–237). Peter Lang.

Arnett, R. C., & Arneson, P. (1999). *Dialogic civility in a cynical age: Community, hope, and interpersonal relationships.* State University of New York Press.

Arnett, R. C., Fritz, J. M. H., & Holba, A. M. (2007). The rhetorical turn to Otherness: Otherwise than human. *Cosmos and History: The Journal of Natural and Social History, 3*(1), 115–133.

Arnett, R. C., Fritz, J. M. H., & Holba, A. M. (2008). Bridges not walls: The communicative act of storytelling. *The Review of Communication, 8*(3), 217–234.

Arnett, R. C., & Holba, A. M. (2012). *An overture to philosophy of communication: The carrier of meaning.* Peter Lang.

Arnett, R. C., Holba, A. M., & Mancino, S. (2018). *An encyclopedia of communication ethics: Goods in contention.* Peter Lang.

Aquinas, T. (2018). *Summa theologica.* Coyote Canyon Press.

Audi, R. (Ed.). (1999). *The Cambridge dictionary of philosophy.* Beacon.

Augustine. (2014). *On Christian doctrine.* Beloved Publishing.

Bakhtin, M. M. (1981). *The dialogic imagination: Four essays.* University of Texas Press.

Bakhtin, M. M. (1986). *Speech genres and other late essays.* University of Texas Press.

Bakhtin, M. M. (1993). *Toward a philosophy of the act.* University of Texas Press.

Barthes, R. (1972). *Mythologies.* Hill and Wang.

Barthes, R. (1977). The death of the author. In *Image-music-text* (pp. 142–148). Hill and Wang.

Baseheart, M. C. (1997). *Person in the world: Introduction to the philosophy of Edith Stein.* Kluwer.

Bauman, Z., & Donskis, L. (2013). *Moral blindness: The loss of sensitivity in liquid modernity.* Polity.

Bellah, R. N., Madsen, R. Sullivan, W. M., Swidler, A., & Tipton, S. M. (1985). *Habits of the heart: Individualism and commitment in American life.* University of California Press.

Benhabib, S. (1992). *Situating the self: Gender, community, and postmodernism in contemporary ethics.* Routledge.

Ben-Pazi, H. (2015). Ethical dwelling and the glory of bearing witness. *Levinas Studies, 10,* 221–228.

Bergo, B. (2007). Ethical selfhood: Emmanuel Levinas's contribution to a philosophy of communication. In P. Arneson (Ed.). *Perspectives on philosophy of communication* (pp. 113–136). Purdue University Press.

Bianchi, C., & Vasallo, C. (2015). Introduction: Eco's interpretive semiotics: Interpretation, encyclopedia, translation. *Semiotica, 206*, 5–11.

Bitzer, L. (1968). The rhetorical situation. *Philosophy & Rhetoric, 1*(1), 1–14.

Bonquin, L. (2020, May 25). Coronavirus: Americans ignore social distancing to celebrate Memorial Day, COVID-19 deaths close to 100,000. *Latin Times.* https://www.latintimes.com/coronavirus-americans-ignore-social-distancing-celebrate-memorial-day-covid-19-deaths-458772

Buber, M. (1965). *Between man and man*. Macmillan.

Buber, M. (1966). *The knowledge of man: A philosophy of the interhuman.* Harper & Row.

Bugliosi, V., & Gentry, C. (1974). *Helter skelter: The true story of the Manson murders.* Norton.

Burns, A. (2018). Dealing with fake news in the journalism classroom. *Communication: Journalism Education Today, 51*(3), 11–20.

Burke, K. (1966). *Language as symbolic action: Essays on life, literature, and method.* University of California Press.

Burke, K. (1969). A grammar of rhetoric. University of California Press.

Burke, K. (1984). *Permanence and change: An anatomy of purpose.* University of California Press.

Butler, J. (1990). *Gender trouble: Feminism and the subversion of identity.* Routledge.

Butler, J. (2005). *Giving an account of oneself.* Fordham University Press.

Chandler, D. (2002). *Semiotics: The basics* (2nd. Ed.). Routledge.

Chandler, D. (2007). *Semiotics: The basics.* Routledge.

Charles, S., & Lipovesky, G. (2006). *Hypermodern times.* Polity.

Chastain, M. (2018). Edith Stein: Empathy and knowing. In R. C. Arnett, A. M. Holba, & S. Mancino (Eds.), *An encyclopedia of communication ethics: Goods in contention* (pp. 478–482). Peter Lang.

Cicero. (1942). *On the orator.* Loeb Classical Library.

Cicero. (1968). *On invention.* Loeb Classical Library.

Cissna, K. N., & Anderson, R. (1994). Communication and the ground of dialogue. In R. Anderson, K. N. Cissna, & R. C. Arnett (Eds.). *The reach of dialogue: Confirmation, voice, and community* (pp. 9–30). Hampton Press.

Cissna, K. N., & Anderson, R. (2018). Martin Buber: Dialogic ethics. In R. C. Arnett, A. M. Holba, S. Mancino. *An encyclopedia of communication ethics: Goods in contention.* pp. 75–79. Peter Lang.

Cobley, P., & Jansz, L. (1993). *Introducing semiotics.* Totem.

Cobley, P., & Jansz, L. (2012). *Introducing semiotics: A graphic guide.* Icon Books.

Cooren, F. (2018a). Jacques Derrida: Hospitality that haunts. In R. C. Arnett, A.M. Holba, & S. Mancino (Eds.), *An encyclopedia of communication ethics: Goods in contention* (pp. 116–120). Peter Lang.

Cooren, F. (2018b). Materializing communication: Making the case for a relational ontology. *Journal of Communication, 68*, 278–288.

Coulthard, G. S. (2014). *Red skin, white masks: Rejecting the colonial politics of recognition.* University of Minnesota Press.

Critchley, S., & Schroeder, W. R. (1998). (Eds.). *A companion to continental philosophy.* Blackwell.

Crow, M. M., & Dabars, W. B. (2015). *Designing the new American university.* Johns Hopkins University Press.

Dezenhall, E. (2003). *Nail 'em!: Controlling high profile attacks on celebrities and businesses.* Prometheus.

Derrida, J. (1973). Différance. In *Speech and phenomena, and other essays on Husserl's theory of signs* (pp. 129–160). Northwestern University Press.

Derrida, J. (1978). *Writing and difference.* University of Chicago Press.

Derrida, J. (1997). *Of grammatology.* Johns Hopkins University.

Derrida, J. (1998). *Resistances of Psychoanalysis.* P. Kamuf, P-A. Brault, M. Naas (Trans.). Stanford University Press.

Derrida, J. (1999). A word of welcome. In J. Derrida *Adieu to Emmanuel Levinas.* P-A. Brault & M. Naas (Trans.). pp. 15–152. Stanford University Press.

Eagleton, T. (2004). *After theory.* Basic Books.

Eco, U. (1976). *A theory of semiotics.* Indiana University Press.

Eco, U. (1979). *The role of the reader.* Indiana University Press.

Eco, U. (1990). *The limits of interpretation.* Indiana University Press.

Eco, U. (1992). *Interpretation and Overinterpretation.* Cambridge University Press.

Eicher-Catt, D. (2005). The myth of servant-leadership: A feminist perspective. *Women & Language, 28*(1), 17–25.

Eicher-Catt, D. (2010). What E-Prime is not: A semiotic phenomenological reading. *ETC: A Review of General Semantics, 67*(1), 17–34.

Etzioni. A. (2015). Communitarianism. In M. T. Gibbons (Ed.), *The encyclopedia of political thought.* Wiley.

Evans, G. R. (2001). *The medieval theologians: An introduction to theology in the medieval period.* Wiley.

Fawkes, J. (2018). Seyla Benhabib: Communicating with a concrete other. In R. C. Arnett, A. M. Holba, & S. Mancino. *An encyclopedia of communication ethics: Goods in contention.* pp. 50–54. Peter Lang.

Finnegan, C. A., & Kang, J. (2004). "Sighting" the public: Iconoclasm and public sphere theory. *Quarterly Journal of Speech, 90*(4), 377–402.

Fish, W. (2010). *Philosophy of perception: A contemporary introduction.* Routledge.

Fisher, W. R. (1989). *Human communication as narration: Toward a philosophy of reason, value, and action*. University of South Carolina Press.

Forni, P. M. (2002). *Choosing civility: The twenty-five rules of considerate conduct*. St. Martin's Press.

Forni, P. M. (2008). *The civility solution: What to do when people are rude*. St. Martin's Press.

Foss, S. K., & Griffin, C. L. (1995). A proposal for an invitational rhetoric. *Communication Monographs, 62*(1), 2–18.

Foucault, M. (1988). *Madness and civilization: A history of insanity in the age of reason*. Vintage Publications.

Foucault, M. (1994). The order of things: An archaeology of the human sciences. Vintage Publications.

Frankl, V. E. (1984). *Man's search for meaning*. Pocket Books.

Fritz, J. H. M. (2013). *Professional civility: Communicative virtue at work*. Peter Lang.

Fritz, J. M. H. (2018). Charles Taylor: Communication ethics and *Sources of the Self*. In R. C. Arnett, A.M. Holba, & S. Mancino (Eds.). *An encyclopedia of communication ethics: Goods in contention* (pp. 483–487). Peter Lang.

Gadamer, H. G. (2002). *Truth and method*. Continuum.

Gare, A. (2006). Reviving the radical enlightenment: Process philosophy and the struggle for democracy [Keynote address]. *Sixth International Whitehead Conference*, Salzburg, Austria.

Gehrke, P. J. (2002). Turning Kant against the priority of autonomy: Communication ethics and the duty to the community. *Philosophy and Rhetoric. 35*(1), 1–21.

Gehrke, P. J. (2010). Being for the Other-to-the-Other: Justice and communication in Levinasian ethics. *The Review of Communication, 10*(1), 5–19.

Gehrke, P. (2018). Jurgen Habermas: Discourse ethics. In R. C. Arnett, A. M. Holba, & S. Mancino (Eds.), *An encyclopedia of communication ethics: Goods in contention* (pp. 197–201). Peter Lang.

Givoni, M. (2014). The ethics of witnessing and the politics of the governed. *Theory, Culture & Society, 31*(1), 123–142.

Goodnight, T. (2007). The engagement of communication: Jurgen Habermas on discourse, critical reason, and controversy. In P. Arneson (Ed.), *Perspectives on philosophy of communication* (pp. 91–110). Purdue University Press.

Habermas, J. (1984). *The theory of communicative action: Reason and the rationalization of society*, Vol. 1. (T. McCarthy, Trans). Beacon.

Habermas, J. (1987). *The theory of communicative action: Lifeworld and system: A critique of functionalist reason*, Vol. 2. (T. McCarthy, Trans). Beacon.

Hadot, P. (1995). *Philosophy as a way of life*. Blackwell.

Hadot, P. (2002). *What is ancient philosophy?* Harvard University Press.

Hanh, T. N. (2014). *No mud, no lotus: The art of transforming suffering*. Parallax.

Harden, J. M. H. (2018). Alasdair MacIntyre: Communication ethics—tradition(s), narrative(s), virtue(s). In R. C. Arnett, A. M. Holba, & S. Mancino (Eds.), *Encyclopedia of communication ethics: Goods in contention* (pp. 299–303). Peter Lang.

Hart, T. (2007). Reciprocal revelation: Toward a pedagogy of interiority. *Journal of Cognitive Affective Learning*, 3(2), 1–10.

Hauser, G. A. (1999). *Vernacular voices: The rhetoric of publics and public spheres.* University of South Carolina Press.

Heidegger, M. (1962). *Being and time.* (J. Macquarrie & E. Robinson, Trans.). HarperCollins. (Original work published 1953)

Heidegger, M. (1968). *What is called thinking?* Harper Perennial.

Heidegger, M. (1996). *Being and time.* (J. Stambaugh, Trans.). State University of New York Press. (Original work published 1953)

Hendricks, V. (2007). *Mainstream and formal epistemology.* Cambridge University Press.

Herder, J. G. (2001/2002). On the change of taste. In M. Forster (Ed.) *Herder: Philosophical writings* (pp. 247–256). Cambridge University Press.

Herrick, J. A. (2001). *The history and theory of rhetoric: An introduction.* (2nd ed.). Pearson.

Herrick, J. A. (2005). *The history and theory of rhetoric: An introduction.* (4th ed.). Routledge.

Herrick, J. A. (2017). *The history and theory of rhetoric: An introduction.* (6th ed.). Routledge.

Hicks, S. (2011). *Skepticism and socialism from Rousseau to Foucault.* Ockham's Razor.

Hill, D. W. (2018). Bearing witness, moral responsibility and distant suffering. *Theory, Culture & Society*, 36(1), 27–45.

Holba, A. (2014). Wisdom traditions and the inner landscape: Becoming more human through contemplative practice. *Journal of Communication Ethics, Religion, and Culture*, 49(1), 9–29.

Holba, A. M. (2007). *Philosophical leisure: Recuperative praxis for human communication.* Marquette University Press.

Holba, A. M. (2008). Revisiting Martin Buber's I-it: A rhetorical strategy. *Human Communication*, 11(4), 495–510.

Holba, A. M. (2010). The question of philosophical leisure: A philosophy of communication. In M. Haney & D. Kline (Eds.). *The value of time and leisure in a world of work* (pp. 39–55). Lexington.

Holba, A. M. (2013). *Transformative leisure: A philosophy of communication.* Marquette University Press.

Hoopes, J. (1991). *Peirce on signs: Writings on semiotic by Charles Sanders Peirce.* University of North Carolina Press.

Hornblower, S., & Spawforth, A. (2003). *The Oxford classical dictionary.* (3rd ed.). Oxford University Press.

Hume, D. (2008). *An enquiry concerning human understanding.* Oxford University Press. (Original work published 1748)

Hutcheon, L. (2002). *The politics of postmodernism.* Routledge.

Hyde, M. J. (2006). *The life-giving gift of acknowledgment.* Purdue University Press.

Hyde, M. J. (2018). *The interruption that we are: The health of the lived body, narrative, and public moral argument.* University of South Carolina Press.

International Communicology Institute. (n.d.). *Definition communicology.* http://communicology.org/content/%E2%8C%98-definition-communicology

Isocrates. (2000). Nicocles. In D. C. Mirhady & Y. L. Too (Trans.). *Isocrates I.* pp. 169–181. University of Texas Press.

Jardine, A. (2020). At the risk of thinking: An intellectual biography of Julia Kristeva. Bloomsbury Academic.

Johnstone, C. L. (2009). *Listening to the logos: Speech and the coming of wisdom in ancient Greece.* University of South Carolina Press.

Kant, I. (1965). *Critique of pure reason.* (N. K. Smith, Trans.). Bedford St. Martin. (Original work published 1781)

Kant, I. (1987). *Critique of judgment.* (W. S. Pluhar, Trans.). Hackett Publishing. (Original work published in 1790)

Kant, I. (2002). *Critique of practical reason.* (W. S. Pluhar, Trans.). Hackett Publishing. (Original work published 1788)

Kant, I. (2004). *Prolegomena to any future metaphysics.* (G. Hatfield, Trans). Cambridge University Press. (Original work published 1783)

Kearney, R., & Rainwater, M. (1996). *The continental philosophy reader.* Routledge.

Kimball, B. A. (2010). *The liberal arts tradition: A documentary history.* University Press of America.

King, M. L. K., Jr. (1963). *Why we can't wait.* Beacon Press.

Kirby, A. (2006). The death of postmodernism and beyond. *Philosophy Now, 58,* 34–37.

Klyukanov, I. (2010). *A communication universe: Manifestations of meaning, stagings of significance.* Rowman & Littlefield.

Klyukanov, I. (2012). Communication—that which befalls us. *Empedocles: European Journal for the Philosophy of Communication, 4*(1), 15–27.

Klyukanov, I. E. & Sinekopova, G. V. (2018). Mikhail Bakhtin: Mutual outsideness. In R. C. Arnett, A. M. Holba, S. Mancino. *An encyclopedia of communication ethics: Goods in contention.* pp. 40–44. Peter Lang.

Koskinen, C. A-L., & Lindström, U. A. (2013). Listening to the Otherness of the Other: Envisioning listening based on a hermeneutical reading of Levinas. *The International Journal of Listening, 27,* 146–157.

Kristeller, P. O. (1979). *Renaissance thought and its sources.* Columbia University Press.

Kristeva, J. (1984). Revolution in poetic language. Columbia University Press.

Krüger, L. (1984). Why do we study the history of philosophy? In R. Rorty, J. B. Schneewind, & Q. Skinner, (Eds.), *Philosophy in history: Essays in the historiography of philosophy.* (pp. 77–102). Cambridge University Press.

Kuehn, M. (2001). *Kant: A biography.* Cambridge University Press.

Lacan, J. (1949). The mirror stage as formative of the function of the I as revealed in psychoanalytic experience [Keynote address]. 16th International Congress of Psychoanalysis, Zürich, Switzerland.

Lacan, J. (1991). *The seminar, book II: The ego in Freud's theory and in the technique of psychoanalysis.* Norton.

Lanigan, R. L. (1988). *Phenomenology of communication: Merleau-Ponty's thematics in communicology and semiology.* Duquesne University Press.

Lanigan, R. L. (1992). *The human science of communicology: A phenomenology of discourse in Foucault and Merleau-Ponty.* Duquesne University Press.

Lasch, C. (1984). *The minimal self: Psychic survival in troubled times.* Norton.

Lasch. C. (1991). *The culture of narcissism: American life in an age of diminishing expectations.* Norton.

Levinas, E. (1969). *Totality and infinity: An essay on exteriority.* Duquesne University Press.

Levinas, E. (2000). *Entre nous: Thinking-of-the-other.* Columbia University Press.

Lipari, L. (2018). Judith Butler: Giving an account of oneself. In R. C. Arnett, A. M. Holba, & S. Mancino (Eds.), *An encyclopedia of communication ethics: Goods in contention* (pp. 86–90). Peter Lang.

Lyotard, J. F. (1984). *The postmodern condition: A report on knowledge.* University of Minnesota Press.

Maciejewski, J. J. (2018). Thomas Aquinas: Communication as virtue. In Ronald C. Arnett, Annette M. Holba, & Susan Mancino (Eds.)., *An Encyclopedia of communication ethics: Goods in contention* (pp. 16–20). Peter Lang.

MacIntyre, A. (2007). *After virtue: A study in moral theory.* Notre Dame University Press.

Mark, J. J. (2017). The origin and history of the BCE/CE dating system. *Ancient History Encyclopedia.* (Spring 2019). https://www.ancient.eu/article/1041/

McAllister, L. L. (1996). *Hypatia's daughters: 1,500 years of women philosophers.* Indiana University Press.

McGaughey, D. R. (1988). Ricoeur's metaphor and narrative theories as a foundation for a theory of symbol. *Religious Studies, 24*(4), 415–437.

McKerrow, R. (2018). Michel Foucault: Truth telling. In R. C. Arnett, A. M. Holba, &S. Mancino (Eds.), *An encyclopedia of communication ethics: Goods in contention* (pp. 167–171). Peter Lang.

Merleau-Ponty, M. (1967/2013). *Phenomenology of perception*. Routledge.

Merleau-Ponty, M. (1975). *Primacy of perception*. Northwestern University Press.

Midgley, W. (2011). Look who's listening: Using the superaddressee for understanding connections in dialogue. In L. Abawi & J. Conway (Eds.), *Creating connections in teaching and learning* (pp. 153–164). Information Age.

Miller, M. (2020, June 23). *Norton puts emancipation statue in Lincoln Park under scrutiny for removal*. WTOP News. https://wtop.com/dc/2020/06/norton-puts-emancipation-statue-in-lincoln-park-under-scrutiny-for-removal/

Morson, G. S. & C. Emerson. (1990). *Mikhail Bakhtin: Creation of a prosaics*. Stanford University Press.

Mullins, K. J. (2008, March 16). Did the Manson family kill anybody else? *Digital Journal*. http://www.digitaljournal.com/article/251727

Murray, J. W. (2002). The paradox of Emmanuel Levinas: Knowledge of the absolute Other. *Qualitative Research Reports in Communication*, 3(2), 39–46.

Nancy, J-L. (1997). *The sense of the world*. University of Minnesota Press.

Nietzsche, F. (1999). On truth and lying in a non-moral sense. In R. Geuss (Ed.) & R. Speirs (Trans.), *The birth of tragedy and other writings* (pp. 139–153). Cambridge University Press.

Nietzsche, F. (2006). *Thus spoke Zarathustra*. Cambridge University Press.

Nietzsche, F. (2018). *Thus spoke Zarathustra*. Logos.

Nietzsche, F. (2010). On truth and lie [falsity] in their extra-moral sense. (T. Carman, Trans.). *On truth and untruth: Selected writings* (pp. 15–50). HarperCollins.

Nussbaum, M. C. (2010). *From disgust to humanity: Sexual orientation and constitutional law*. Oxford University Press.

Nussbaum, M. C. (2011). *Creating capabilities: The human development approach*. Belknap Press.

Olsen, H. (2020, June 22). The anti-statue movement has taken a turn into absurdity. *Washington Post*. https://www.washingtonpost.com/opinions/2020/06/22/anti-statue-movement-has-taken-turn-into-absurdity/

Palmer, R. (1969). *Hermeneutics: Interpretation theory in Schleiermacher, Dilthy, Heidegger, and Gadamer.* Northwestern University Press.

Perelman, C., & Olbrechts-Tyteca, L. (1969). *The new rhetoric: A treatise on argumentation*. University of Notre Dame Press.

Perumalil, A. (2009). The history of women in philosophy. Global Vision Publishing.

Pieper, J. (1998). *Leisure: The basis of culture*. St. Augustine's Press.

Pieper, J. (2001). Scholasticism: Personalities and problems of Medieval philosophy. St. Augustine's Press. (original work published 1960)

Piercey, R. (2009). *The uses of the past from Heidegger to Rorty: Doing philosophy historically.* Cambridge University Press.

Pinchevski, A. (2018). Emmanuel Levinas: The Other. In R.C. Arnett, A. M. Holba, & S. Mancino (Eds.), *An encyclopedia of communication ethics: Goods in contention* (pp. 278–282). Peter Lang.

Plato. (1987). *The Gorgias.* (D. J. Zeyl Trans.). Hackett.

Plato. (1997). *Apology.* (J. J. Helm Trans.). Bolchazy-Carducci.

Plato. (2017). *The apology.* (B. Jowett Trans.). Create Space.

Preston, A. (2007). *Analytic philosophy: The history of an illusion.* Continuum.

Ramsey, R. E. (1998). *The long path to nearness: A contribution to a corporeal philosophy of communication and the groundwork for an ethics of relief.* Humanity.

Ramsey, C. O., & Miller, D. J. (1993). Communication studies and philosophy: Convergence without coincidence. In I. Angus & L. Langsdorf (Eds.), *The critical turn: Rhetoric and philosophy in postmodern discourse* (pp. 281–296). Southern Illinois University Press.

Ramsey, R. E., & Miller, D. J. (2003). *Experiences between philosophy and communication: Engaging the philosophical contributions of Calvin O. Schrag.* State University of New York Press.

Randall, J. H. (1976). *The making of the modern mind.* Columbia University Press.

Reagan, C. E. (1996). *Paul Ricoeur: His life and his work.* University of Chicago Press.

Ricoeur, P. (1974). Metaphor and the main problem of hermeneutics. *New Literary History, 6*(1), 95–110.

Ricoeur, P. (1977). *The rule of metaphor: The creation of meaning in language.* University of Toronto Press.

Ricoeur, P. (1984). *Time and narrative* (Vol. 1). University of Chicago Press.

Ricoeur, P. (1988). *Time and narrative,* (Vol. 2). University of Chicago Press.

Ricoeur, P. (1990). *Time and narrative,* (Vol. 3). University of Chicago Press.

Robinson, D. (2001). *Nietzsche and postmodernism.* Icon Books.

Roe v. Wade, 410 U.S. 113 (1973).

Rorty, R. (1979). *Philosophy and the mirror of nature.* Princeton University Press.

Salih, S. (2002). *Judith Butler.* Routledge.

Salih, S. (2004). The Judith Butler reader. Blackwell.

Schrag, C. O. (1997). *Self after post modernity.* Yale University Press.

Schrag, C. O. (2003). *Communicative praxis and the space of subjectivity.* Purdue University Press.

Schrag, C. O. (2010). *Doing philosophy with others: Conversations, reminiscences, and reflections.* Indiana University Press.

Schrag, C. O., & Ramsey, R. E. (1994). Method and phenomenological research: Humility and commitment in interpretation. *Human Studies, 17*(1), 131–137.

Sedgwick, M. (2009). *Against the modern world: Traditionalism and the secret intellectual history of the twentieth century.* Oxford University Press.

Sennett, R. (1992). *The fall of public man.* Norton.

Sim, S. (2011). *The Routledge companion to postmodernism.* Routledge.

Simpson, D. P. (1968). *Cassell's Latin dictionary.* Wiley.

Singer, P. (2017). *Ethics in the real world: 82 brief essays on things that matter.* Princeton University Press.

Sokolowski, R. (2000). *Introduction to phenomenology.* Cambridge University Press.

Spector, J. J. (1973). *The aesthetics of Freud: A study of psychoanalysis and art.* Praeger.

Stein, E. (1989). *The collected works of Edith Stein: On the problem of empathy,* Vol. 3. ICS Publications.

Strathern, P. (2000). Foucault in 90 minutes. Ivan R. Dee Publisher.

Svenaeus, F. (2017). Edith Stein's phenomenology of sensual and emotional empathy. *Phenomenology and the Cognitive Sciences, 17,* 741–760.

Taylor, C. (1984). Philosophy and its history. In R. Rorty, L. B. Schneewind, & Q. Skinner (Eds.), *Philosophy in history* (pp. 17–30). Cambridge University Press.

Taylor, C. (1989). *Sources of the self: The making of modern identity.* Harvard University Press.

Taylor, C. O. (1991). *The ethics of authenticity.* Harvard University Press.

Taylor, C. (2007). *A secular age.* Harvard University Press.

Toulmin, S. E. (1958). *The uses of argument.* Cambridge University Press.

Üçok-Sayrak, O. (2019). *Aesthetic ecology of communication ethics: Existential rootedness.* Fairleigh Dickenson University Press.

Van Doren, C. (1991). *A history of knowledge: Past, present, and future.* Ballantine.

Van Steenburgh, E. W. (1965). Metaphor. *The Journal of Philosophy, 62*(22), 678–688.

Walton, T. (1978). *The Walton experience: The incredible account of one man's abduction by a UFO.* Berkley.

Warnke, G. (1987). *Gadamer: Hermeneutics, tradition, and reason.* Stanford University Press.

Weil, S. (1952). *The need for roots: Prelude to a declaration of duties towards mankind.* Routledge & Kegan Paul.

Weil, S. (1973). *Waiting for God.* Harper & Row.

Weitz, M. (1966). *20th century philosophy: The analytic tradition.* The Free Press.

White House. (2020). *Proposed state or regional gating criteria.* https://www.whitehouse.gov/openingamerica/#criteria

Wiener, L., & Ramsey, R. E. (1995). *Leaving us to wonder: An essay on the questions science can't ask.* State University of New York Press.

Winter, R. (2002). *Still bored in a culture of entertainment: Rediscovering passion and wonder.* InterVarsity Press.

Young, J. (2020, March 29). *Cardi B speaks out on Minnesota looting amid George Floyd's death: "It is what it is."* Fox News. https://www.foxnews.com/entertainment/cardi-b-minnesota-looting-george-floyd-death

INDEX

A

abortions, 57–58, 62–63, 157, 281
absence/presence, 103–104
acknowledgment, 249, 255–258
Adolf Eichmann trial, 186
age of digital interactive media, 6
analytic tradition, 31–32
Anaximander, 30
Anaximenes, 30
ancient or classical period, 53–54
    "after the death of Jesus Christ,", 53
    "before Christ,", 53
    Christian European influence, 53
answerability, 143
anti-statue movement, 276–277
appearances, 101–103
approaches, 10–11
    communicological, 11–12
    critical, 11–12, 47–49
    diagnostic, 48
    dialogical, 11
    ethical, 11
    narrative, 11, 47
    psychoanalytical, 11
    synthetic, 48
Aquinas, Thomas, 180–181
Arendt, Hannah, 37, 170, 185, 265
Aristotelian philosophy and logic, 34
    modes of proof, 73–74
    Politics, 179
    rationality, 138–139
    rhetoric, 39–40, 74–75
    The Rhetoric, 72, 94
Arnett and Arneson, 21
Arnett, Ronald C., 8, 13, 15, 45–46, 48, 91, 147, 240, 264
Art Communicology, 7
attention, 103
Audi, Robert, 81

B

backing, 17
Bakhtin, Mikhail, 80, 133, 142–144
Barthes, Roland, 100
bearing witness, 266–267
being-toward-death, 50
belief empiricism, 71–72
Belletristic movement, 41
Benhabib, Seyla, 133, 144–146, 264
bitterness, 71
Black Lives Matter movement, 208
Brigadoon village, 106–107
Buber, Martin, 21, 80, 133, 140–142
    Between Man and Man, 142
    I-it and I-thou moments of dialogic exchange, 141
    kinds of communicative expressions, 141
Burke, Kenneth, 171, 217–218
Burns, Alison, 86
Butler, Judith, 133, 149–151

C

causation, 181
Christian faith tradition, 104
Christianity, 186
Christ's resurrection and return, 104
chronological time period, 53
classical philosophical traditions, 27–30
Clinical Communicology, 7
cointending, 106–107
commemorative thinking and repetition, 84
common factor principle, 105
communicative center, 263
communicative competence, 122–123
communicative dwellings, 45
communicative engagement, 123
communicative praxis, 15, 49–50, 83–84, 87, 169, 196–202